Principles of Insurance

Principles of Insurance

(As Per the Syllabus of M.G. University, Kottayam, for B.Com., IInd Semester)

P. K. Gupta

M.Com. (Finance), Ph.D., FICWA, FCS, CFA, LII

Anil Kumar Meena

B.Sc. (H), MBA (Finance)
Insurance Consultant

First Edition : 2010

Himalaya Publishing House

MUMBAI • NEW DELHI • NAGPUR • BENGALURU • HYDERABAD • CHENNAI • PUNE • LUCKNOW • AHMEDABAD • ERNAKULAM • BHUBANESWAR • INDORE

First Edition: 2010

Published by : Mrs. Meena Pandey
for **HIMALAYA PUBLISHING HOUSE PVT. LTD.,**
"Ramdoot", Dr. Bhalerao Marg, Girgaon, **Mumbai - 400 004.**
Phones: 2386 01 70/2386 38 63, Fax: 022-2387 71 78
Email: himpub@vsnl.com
Website: www.himpub.com

Branch Offices:

New Delhi : "Pooja Apartments", 4-B, Murari Lal Street, Ansari Road, Darya Ganj, **New Delhi - 110 002.** Phone: 23270392, 23278631 Fax: 011-23256286

Nagpur : Kundanlal Chandak Industrial Estate, Ghat Road, **Nagpur - 440 018.** Phone: 2738731, 3296733 Telefax : 0712-2721215

Bengaluru : No. 16/1 (Old 12/1), 1st Floor, Next to Hotel Highlands, Madhava Nagar, Race Course Road, **Bengaluru - 560 001.** Phone : 22281541, 22385461, Telefax: 080-22286611

Hyderabad : No. 3-4-184, Lingampally, Besides Raghavendra Swamy Matham, Kachiguda, **Hyderabad - 500 027.** Phone: 040-65501745, Mob.: 09848130433

Chennai : No. 85/50, Bazullah Road, T. Nagar, **Chennai - 600 017.** Phone: 044-28144004/28144005

Pune : First Floor, "Laksha" Apartment, No. 527, Mehunpura, Shaniwarpeth, (Near Prabhat Theatre), **Pune - 411 030.** Phone: 020 - 24496323/24496333

Lucknow : C-43, Sector - C, Ali Gunj, **Lucknow - 226 024.** Phone: 0522-2339329

Ahmedabad : 114, "SHAIL", 1st Floor, Opp. Madhu Sudan House, C.G.Road, Navrang Pura, **Ahmedabad – 380 009.** Phone: 079-26560126, Mobiles: 09327324149,09314679413

Ernakulam : 39/104 A, Lakshmi Apartment, Karikkamuri Cross Rd., Ernakulam, **Cochin – 622011**, Kerala. Phone: 0484-2378012, 2378016, Mob- 09344199799

Bhubaneswar : 5 Station Square, **Bhubaneswar (Orissa) - 751 001.** Mobile - 9861046007, E-mail:- orissa@himpub.com

Indore : Kesardeep Avenue Extension, 73, Narayan Bagh. Flat No. 302, IIIrd Floor, Near Humpty Dumpty School, Narayan Bagh, **Indore (M.P.)** Mob-09301386468

DTP by : HPH, Editorial Office, Bhandup **(Anupama)**

Printed by : Bengaluru

PREFACE

Insurance is not a new area of academic study or profession. With the increasing dynamism of risk and the growth of professional risk management, the insurance device has become more and more popular these days. The recent liberalisation of the economy has resulted into the availability of large number of alternative products/ financial services. This has paved the way for the potential and unconventional entrants to penetrate the financial market through innovative higher product profile and portfolios, resulting into a sudden spurt in the demand of insurance professionals. The study of insurance as an academic discipline *in new form* is an obvious outcome. More and more academic institutions all over the countries are offering highly specialised insurance programmes to cater to this demand.

Recently, the universities in India and abroad have introduced insurance as a specialised study both at graduate and postgraduate level. This has accentuated the dire demand for the literature on insurance in the Indian context. It is expected that the book shall be useful to the students and as well as the trainers. We expect and would be highly obliged, if we receive comments and criticism from the readers. This would further help me in improving the book.

Organisation of the Book

The book has been organised into five modules:

Module 1 introduces the concept of risk management to the readers. Chapter 1 conceptualises the risk definitions, classes of risk and the methods of handling risk and the role and importance of insurance contracts. It attempts to provide an overall view of the risk management and control systems. Chapter 2 discusses the various principles underlying insurance contracts. Chapter 3 discusses the IRDA Act, of 1999 and the regulations framed thereunder.

Module 2 discusses the various facets of life insurance. Chapter 4 contains the basics of life insurance. Chapter 5 explains the product development processes. Chapter 5-8 deals with the life insurance business, the practical aspects of selection and treatment of risk, pricing, claims, the players and products and life insurance agency business.

Module 3 and 4 discuses the dominant, standard non-life insurance categories, viz., and fire and marine. Chapter 9 discusses the various marine insurance products, maritime frauds and claim settlements. Chapter 10 talks about the fire insurance contracts, various fire policies, pricing and claim settlement procedures.

Module 5 deals with various non-traditional urban insurances including the burglary and personal accident insurance and also reinsurances. Chapter 11,12 and 13 respectively discuss the reinsurance business, health business and motor and miscellaneous insurances respectively.

We again hope that the book shall definitely be useful to the readers and provide an in-depth insight into the various facets of insurance business in India.

New Delhi , January 2010 **P.K.Gupta and Anil Kumar Meena**

PREFACE

SYLLABUS

Module 1: Introduction — Definition — Role and Importance — Insurance Contract — Principles of Insurance — Insurance and Assurance — Types of Insurance: Life and General — Introduction to IRDA Act.

Module 2: Life Insurance — Features — Classification of Policies — Surrender Value — Introduction to Actuarial Science — Bonus — Policy Conditions — Application and Acceptance — Prospectus — Proposal Forms and Other Related Documents — Age Proof — Special Reports — Assignments — Nominations — Loans — Surrenders — Foreclosure.

Module 3: Policy — Maturity Claims — Survival Benefit — Payments — Death Claims — Waiver of Evidence of Title — Early Claims — Claim Concession — Presumption of Death — Accident and Disability Benefits — Settlement Options.

Module 4: Marine Insurance — Nature — Insurance Policies — Policy Conditions — Clauses — Marine Losses — Payments of Claims.

Module 5: Fire Insurance — Nature and Use — Contracts — Kinds of Policies — Policy Conditions — Classes — Payments of Claims Insurance —Insurance — Health Insurance — Motor Insurance — Burglary and Personal Accident Insurance in India — Urban Non-traditional Insurance.

Contents

Module I

Chapter - 1:	Introduction to Insurance	3 – 22
Chapter - 2:	Principles of Insurance	23 – 40
Chapter - 3:	Basic Insurance Law	41 – 104

Module II

Chapter - 4:	Introduction to Life Insurance	107 – 139
Chapter - 5:	Product Development	140 – 158
Chapter - 6:	Life Insurance — Risk	159 – 193
Chapter - 7:	Assignment of Life Policies	194 – 208

Module III

Chapter - 8:	Life Insurance Claims	211 – 228

Module IV

Chapter - 9:	Maritime Losses and Claims Insurance	231 – 256

Module V

Chapter - 10:	Fire Insurance	259 – 281
Chapter - 11:	Reinsurance	282 – 309
Chapter - 12:	Health Insurance	310 – 334
Chapter - 13:	Motor Miscellaneous Insurance	335 – 370

Module I

CHAPTER 1

INTRODUCTION TO INSURANCE

Learning Objectives

After reading this chapter,you will be able to understand:

- Concept of Risk
- Risk and Uncertainty
- Types of Risk
- Classification of Pure Risk
- Methods of Handling Risk
- Definition of Insurance
- Cost and Benefits of Insurance
- Elements of an Insurable Risk
- Insurance Contracts
- Insurance *vs.* Wager
- Insurance *vs.* Gambling

1.1 The Concept of Risk

People express risk in different ways. To some, it is the chance or possibility of loss, to others, its may be uncertain situations or deviations or what statisticians call dispersions from the expectations. Different authors on the subject have defined risk differently. However, in most of the terminology the term risk includes exposure to adverse situations. The indeterminateness of outcome is one of the basic criteria to define a risk situation. Also, when the outcome is indeterminate, there is a possibility that some of them may be adverse and therefore need special emphasis. Let us have a look at the popular definitions of risk.

According to the Dictionary, risk refers to the possibility that something unpleasant or dangerous might happen.

"Risk is a condition in which there is a possibility of an adverse deviation from a desired outcome that is expected or hoped for."

"At its most general level, risk is used to describe any situation where there is uncertainty about what outcome will occur. Life is obviously risky."

- The degree of risk refers to the likelihood of occurrence of an event. It is a measure of accuracy with which the outcome of a chance event can be predicted.

In most of the risky situations, two elements are commonly found:

1. The outcome is uncertain,i.e.,there is a possibility that one or other(s) may occur. Therefore, logically, there are at least two possible outcomes for a given situation.
2. Out of the possible outcomes, one is unfavourable or not liked by the individual or the analyst.

1.2 Risk vs. Uncertainty

Uncertainty is often confused with the risk. Uncertainty refers to a situation where the outcome is not certain or unknown. Uncertainty refers to a state of mind characterised by doubt, based on the lack of knowledge about what will or what will not happen in the future.

Uncertainty can be perceived as opposite of certainty where you are assure of outcome or what will happen. Accordingly, some weights or probabilities can be assigned into risky situations but uncertainty, the psychological reaction to the absence of knowledge lacks this privilege.

Decision under uncertain situations is very difficult for the decision-maker. It all depends upon the skill, the judgement and of course luck.

Uncertainty being a perceptual phenomenon implies different degrees to different person. Assume a situation where an individual has to appear for the first in the newly introduced insurance examination.

(a) an individual student undergone a training in insurance.

(b) an individual with training or experience in insurance.

A's perception towards uncertainty (of performance in examination) is different from that of B. Nonetheless, in both situations, the outcome that is the questions which will be asked in the examination are different.

1.2.1 Loss and Chance of Loss

A risk refers to a situation where there is the possibility of a loss. What is a loss?

Loss has been defined in many ways. *Loss in accounting sense means that portion of the expired cost for which no compensating value has been received.*

Loss refers to the Act or instance of losing the detriment ora disadvantage resulting from losing.

Loss means being without something previously possessed.

The chance of loss refers to a fraction or the relative frequency of loss. The chance of loss in insurance sense is the probability of loss.

For example, assume there are 10,000 factories in the insurance pool which may be affected due to earthquake and on the basis of past experience, 5 have been affected, then the probability of loss is 0.0005.

The whole game of insurance business is based on the probability of loss. If the insurer estimates correctly, he wins else loses or is forced to close the business.

From the insurer's perspective, it is the probability of loss that essentiates the need for insurances. The probabilities of losses may be *ex-post* or *ex-ante*. In practice, the *ex-ante* probabilities are widely used for undertaking risk in insurance business.

The chance or probabilities of loss estimation requires accounting for causes of losses popularly characterised as *perils* and *hazards*.

1.2.2 Perils

A peril refers to the cause of loss or the contingency that may cause a loss. In literary sense, it means the serious and immediate danger. Perils refer to the immediate causes of loss. Perils may be general or specific, e.g., fire may affect assets like building, automobile, machinery, equipment and also, humans. Collusion may cause damage to the automobile resulting in a financial loss.

1.2.3 Hazards

Hazards are the conditions that increase the severity of loss or the conditions affecting perils. These are the conditions that create or increase the severity of losses. Economic slow down is a peril that may cause a loss to the business, but it is also a hazard that may cause a heart attack or mental shock to the proprietor of the business. Hazards can be classified as follows:

(1) *Physical Hazards* — Property Conditions — consists of those physical properties that increase the chance of loss from the various perils. E.g., stocking crackers in a packed commercial complex increases the peril of fire.

(2) *Intangible Hazards* — Attitudes and Culture — Intangible hazards are more or less psychological in nature. These can be further classified as follows:

(a) *Moral Hazard*— Fraud — These refer to the increase in the possibility or severity of loss emanating from the intention to deceive or cheat. For example — putting fire to a factory running in losses. With an intention to make benefit out of exaggerated claims, deliberately indulging into automobile collusion or damaging it or tendency on part of the doctor to go for unnecessary checks when they are not required, since the loss will be reimbursed by the insurance company.

(b) *Morale Hazard*— Indifference — It is the attitude of indifference to take care of the property on the premise that the loss will be indemnified by the insurance company. So, it is the carelessness or indifference to a loss because of the existence of insurance contract. For example — smoking in an oil refinery, careless driving etc.

(c) *Societal Hazards*— Legal and Cultural — these refer to the increase in the frequency and severity of loss arising from legal doctrines or societal customs and structure. For example, the construction or the possibility of demolition of buildings in unauthorized colonies.

1.3 Types of Risks

Financial and Non-Financial Risks

Financial risk involves the simultaneous existence of three important elements in a risky situation — (*a*) that someone is adversely affected by the happening of an event, (*b*) the assets or income is likely to be exposed to a financial loss from the occurrence of the event and (*c*) the peril can cause the loss. When the possibility of a financial loss does not exist, the situation can be referred to as *non-financial* in nature. Financial risks are more *particular* in nature.

Individual and Group Risks

A risk is said to be a *group* risk or *fundamental* risk if it affects the economy or its participants on a macro basis. These are impersonal in origin and consequence. They affect most of the social segments or the entire population. These risk factors may be socio-economic or political or natural calamities, e.g., earthquakes, floods, wars, unemployment or situations like 11th September attack on U.S. etc.

Individual/particular risks are confined to individual identities or small groups. Thefts, robbery, fire etc. are risks that are particular in nature. Some of these are insurable. The methods of handling fundamental and particular risks differ by their very nature, e.g., Social insurance programmes may be undertaken by the government to handle fundamental risks. Similarly, fire insurance policy may be bought by an individual to prevent against the adverse consequences of fire.

Static and Dynamic Risks

Dynamic risks are those resulting from the changes in the economy or the environment. These risk factors mainly refer to the macro economic variables like inflation, income and output levels, and technology changes. Dynamic risks emanate from the economic environment and therefore, these are difficult to anticipate and quantify. Contrary to this, static risks are more or less predictable and are not affected by the economic conditions. The possibility of loss in a business or unemployment after undergoing a professional qualification, loss due to act of others etc. are static and accordingly suitable for insurance.

Quantifiable and Non-quantifiable Risks

The risk which can be measured like financial risks are known to be quantifiable while the situations which may result in repercussions like tension or loss of peace are called as non-quantifiable.

Pure and Speculative Risks

Pure risk situations are those where there is a possibility of loss or no loss. There is no gain to the individual or the organisation. For example, a car can meet with an accident or it may not meet with an accident. If an insurance policy is bought for the purpose, then if accident does not occur, there is no gain to the insured. Contrarily, if the accident occurs, the insurance company will indemnify the loss.

Speculative risks are those where there is possibility of gain as well as loss. The element of gain is inherent or structured in such a situation. For example — if you invest in a stock market, you may either gain or lose on stocks.

The distinguishing characteristics of the pure and speculative risks are:

(*a*) Pure risks are generally insurable while the speculative ones are not.

(*b*) The conceptual framework of the risk pooling can be applied to pure risks, while in most of the cases of speculative risks where it is not possible. However, there may be some situation where the law of mathematical expectation might be useful.

(*c*) Speculative risk carry some inherent advantages to the economy or the society at large while pure risks like uninsured catastrophes may be highly damaging.

1.4 Classifying Pure Risks

Since pure risks are generally *insurable*, the discussion on risk is skewed towards pure risks only. On the presumption that insurable pure risks being *static* can be classified as follows:

Personal Risks

These are the risks that directly affect the individual's capability to earn income. Personal risks can be classified into the following types:

(a) Premature death: death of the bread earner with unfulfilled or unprovided financial obligations.

(b) ***Old age:*** it refers to the risk of not having sufficient income at the age of retirement or the age becoming so that there is a possibility that the individual may not be able to earn the livelihood.

(c) ***Sickness or disability:*** the risk of poor heath or disability of a person to earn the means of survival. E.g. the possibility of damage of limbs of a driver due to an accident.

(d) ***Unemployment:*** the risk of unemployment due to socio-economic factors resulting in financial insecurity.

Property Risks

These are the risks to the persons in possession of the property being damaged or lost. The immovable like land and building being damaged due to flood, earthquake or fire — the movables like appliances and personal assets being destroyed due to fire or stolen. The losses may be direct or indirect/consequential. A direct loss implies the visible financial loss to the property due to mishappenings. Whereas, the indirect ones are the losses arising from the occurrence of an incident resulting in direct/physical damages or loss. The loss to crops due to flood is a direct loss — the destruction of the growing power is a consequential one.

Liability Risks

These are the risks arising out of the intentional or unintentional injury to the persons or damages to their properties through negligence or carelessness. Liability risks generally arise from the law. E.g. liability of the employer under the workmen's compensation law or other labour laws in India.

In addition to the above categories, risks may also arise *due to the failure of others.* For example, the financial loss arising from the non-performance or standard performance in a contract — in engineering/construction contracts.

1.5 Methods of Handling Risk

Although the various techniques of risk management have been discussed at length in the following chapter, the following discussion will give you a brief idea of how the risk can be handled:

1. *Avoidance* — avoid the risk or the circumstances which may lead to losses. For example — not to visit border areas at the time of war tensions. Avoid manufacturing and marketing a product of which patent/copyright is doubtful.
2. *Loss Control*
   - Loss Prevention — Reduce Loss Frequency — for example not to smoke in a factory producing inflammable products, getting training before driving etc.
   - Loss Reduction — Lower Loss Severity — deployment of fire fighting equipment, first aid boxes etc.

3. *Retention* — to retain in full or part of the risk. A risk is said to be actively retained if the individual is fully aware of the risk and its implications and prefers to retain it. On the contrary, it is said to be passive, if the individual is ignorant of the risk or there is carelessness on part of the exposed.
4. *Transfer* — to transfer the risk to another individual or organisation either by:
    - *Contractual Agreements* — insurance, derivatives, diversification strategies etc.
    - *Corporatising* — converting the sole proprietor/partnership business into a company from an organisation. It is well-known that in case of a proprietor firm, the proprietor is individually liable in an unlimited sense and in case of partnership firm, the partners are jointly and severally liable which is also in the nature of unlimited liability. However, in case of companies the liability of the shareholders is generally limited to the extent of capital contributed by them.
    - *Insurance* — It is one of the cheapest mode generally used by individuals for risk management. Individual use life and non-life coverages for personal, property and liability risks.

1.6 Definition of Insurance

The term "insurance" can be defined in both financial and legal terms. The financial definition focuses on an arrangement that redistributes the cost of unexpected losses. That is, the collection of a small premium payment from all exposed and distributed to those suffering loss. The legal definition focuses on a contractual arrangement whereby one party agrees to compensate another party for losses. The financial definition provides for the funding of the losses whereas the legal definition provides for the legally enforceable contract that spells out the legal rights, duties and obligations of all the parties to the contract. Let us have a look at these definitions.

In Financial Sense

Insurance is a social device in which a group of individuals (insureds) transfer risk to another party (insurer) in order to combine loss experience, which permits statistical prediction of losses and provides for payment of losses from funds contributed (premiums) by all members who transferred risk.

In Legal Sense

A contract of insurance is a contract by which one party in consideration of the price paid to him proportionate to the risk provides security to the other party that he shall not suffer loss, damage or prejudice by the happening of certain specified events. Insurance is meant to protect the insured against uncertain events which may cause disadvantage to him. Life insurance however is a distinctive type of insurance where there is certainty of the payment of a specified amount either on the death of the insured or on the maturity of the policy whichever is earlier.

1.7 Costs and Benefits of Insurance

The purpose of insurance mode of risk transfer is to provide economic protection against the losses that may be incurred but to chance events such as — *(a)* death, *(b)* disability, *(c)* economic losses. One party (the insurer) for a set amount of money, (premium) agrees to pay the other party (insured or beneficiary), a sum of money (benefit) upon the occurrence of an event which may or may not occur. Insurance provides economic protection against losses that may be incurred due to chance events that may or may not occur during the effective time of the contract called a policy. The insurance of business organisations is essential in the sense that adverse events, if not guarded, may affect — the business itself, the business owner or owner's personal property and may also threaten the continued operation of the business and threaten the owner's financial well-being.

Insurance Device

The fundamental characteristics of insurance are:

(a) It involves transfer of risk from the individual to the group, and

(b) There is a sharing (pooling) of losses on some equitable basis such that fortuitous losses will be indemnified (paid).

More specifically, the cost and benefits of insurance are:

Benefits

- Reimbursement for losses
- Reduction in tension and fear
- Avenue for investment — life insurance investment officer attractive return.
- Prevention Insurance to Society
- Cost of Business operations — Social wastage of resources
- Fraudulent and exaggerated claims — Malacious and undesirable transfer of wealth.

1.8 Elements of an Insurable Risk

For pure risk to be insurable, it should posess the following characteristics.

• Large Numbers of Exposure Units

The theory of insurance is based on law of large numbers. Therefore the prime necessity for a rise to be insurable is that there must be a sufficiently large number of homogenous exposure in order that losses are reasonable predictable. Also, the probabilistic estimates used by the insurance company, by logic, assume large number of units in a distribution and insurance products are priced accordingly.

• Define and Measurable (Calculable) Loss

The losses are fairly predictable and can be measured in money terms. Loss of peace of mind, tension etc. or loss of life cannot be indemnified.

• Determinable Probability Distribution

The probability distribution of the happening of adverse event is determinable. This condition is necessary to establish the free premium accorcing to the theory of equivalence. If there is not determinable distribution, there is no question of issuing a cover by an insurance company.

• Random (Fortuitous) Loss

The adverse event may or may not occur in future and once which the insurance company has not control. Naturally, if the event is non-random or the loss has occurred in the past, there is no question of insurance. Also, it is important to note that randomness is ensured by underwriters who guard against adverse selection — the tendency of the poorer than average insured to seek or continue insurance coverage.

• Non-catastrophic Loss

The losses should be non-catastrophic. Not all the units in a homogenous group will be subject to an adverse event. Recall that if all the units meet losses, the company will be ruined only few out of a large group will be exposed.

• Premium should be Economically Feasible

Since, the insurance pool is structured to be sufficiently large, the price charged by the insurer for buying the risk is generally low. It should be sufficient to cause the rich for the insurer as well as viable for the insured.

1.9 Insurance Contract

Insurance contracts are agreements between insurance companies and insured for the purpose of transferring from insured to the insurer a part of the risk of loss arising out of contingent event. Therefore all the provisions of Indian Contract Act, 1872, in general are applicable to insurance contracts. Under Section 10 of the Indian Contract Act, following conditions are necessary to form a valid contract:

(*a*) Agreement between two parties

(*b*) Lawful object

(*c*) Capacity to contract

(*d*) Consideration

(*e*) Possibility of performance etc.

Offer and Acceptance

The offer for entering into insurance contract generally come from the insured (proposer). The insurance company may also propose to make the contract. In order to constitute a valid acceptance, offer and its acceptance must fulfil the requirements as prescribed by the Indian Contract Act, 1872. Whether the offer is made by the insurer or insured, the moot point is acceptance.

Any act that precedes it is an offer or a counter-offer. All that precede the offer or counter-offer is an invitation to offer. In insurance, the publication of prospectus, the canvassing of the agents are invitations to offer. When the proposer proposes to enter the contract it is an offer and if there is any alteration in the offer that would be a counter-offer. If this alteration or change (counter-offer) is accepted by the proposer, it would be an acceptance. In absence of counter-offer, the acceptance of offer will be an acceptance by the insurer. At the moment, the notice of acceptance is given to other party, it would be a valid acceptance.

On acceptance of the proposal by the insurer, a valid and binding contract comes into existence. If the insurer indicates a higher premium than the normal as per proposal or conditions of acceptance are different from the standards ones, such indication tantamounts to a counter-offer which the proposer may or may not accept. It is necessary that in order to make a binding contract of insurance, the parties must agree upon every material term affecting the agreement.

In case of Life insurance a valid and binding contract comes into existence upon payment of first premium. When a proposal form duly filled in by the proposer is accepted by the insurer, the acceptance communicated to the proposer is in reality a counter-offer indicating that the proposal will be accepted on payment of the premium and communication of the assent of the proposer to special terms, if any. Unless the proposer assents to or complies with the terms of insurer no contract would come into existence.

Every contract of insurance must be in writing and must comply with the provisions of the Indian Stamp Act. An oral or informal contract gives the insured a right to call for a stamped policy, even after the loss insured against has occurred in view of the Indian Stamp Act, 1899.

An issuance of a policy may some time takes time after acceptance of risk in view of underwriting and administrative procedures. The issuers may issue a cover note for a stipulated period which is also a valid evidence of contract.

Legal Object

For a valid contract, the object of the agreement should be lawful and must not be prohibited by any law. Any subject matter of contract that is (*i*) not forbidden by law, or (*ii*) is not immoral, or (*iii*) opposed to public policy, or (*iv*) which does not defeat the provisions of any law, is lawful. The subject matter of insurance in the proposal form and also the consideration should be legal. If there is any contract to defraud the insurer rather than based on round principles of indemnity, the contract is void.

Mistake and Misrepresentation

A contract of insurance is a contract uberrimae fidei, *i.e.*, is based on the principle of utmost good faith. If utmost good faith is not observed by either party insurer or insured the contract may be avoided by the other.

Capacity to Contract

The rules laid down under the Indian Contract Act, 1872, defining the contractual capacity of the parties apply generally to insurance contracts in the same manner as they apply to other types of contracts.

Every person is competent to contract (*a*) who is of the age of majority according to the law, (*b*) who is of sound mind, and (*c*) who is not disqualified from contracting by any law to which he is subject.

The capacity of an insurer to enter into contracts of insurance depends upon its constitution.

A minor is, therefore, incompetent to contract, and a contract with a minor is a nullity; but under certain circumstances, an insurer may issue a policy on the life of a minor. Under the system of deferred assurance policies, the insurance contract is with a parent or legal guardian, who is competent to contract.

Consideration

For insurance contracts, consideration is in the form of premium to be paid by the insured and a promise to pay, compensate or indemnify in accordance with the terms and conditions incorporated in the policy, on the part of the insurer. A premium is the price for the risk undertaken by the insurers. It is the consideration receivable by the insurers from the insured in exchange for their undertaking to pay the sum insured in case the event insured against takes place.

Amount of premium is not the criteria, but a contract without payment of premium is void.

Free Consent

Parties entering into the contract should enter into the contract by their free and genuine consent. The consent shall be free with it is not caused by : (1) coercion, (2) undue influence, (3) fraud, or (4) misrepresentation, or (5) mistake. When there is no free consent except fraud the contract becomes voidable at the option of the party whose consent was so obtained. In case of fraud, the contract would be void. The proposal for free consent, must sign a declaration to this effect, the person explaining the subject-matter of the proposal to the proposer must also accordingly make a written declaration on the proposal.

The proposer must full disclose all material information and sign a declaration in the proposal. Also, the insurer must full disclose the product details to the proposer.

1.9.1 Functions of an Insurance Contract

The formulation of every contract depends upon the parties and subject-matter of contract. The insurance contract performs the following functions:

(1) to define the risk that is to be transferred

(2) to state the conditions under which the contract applies and

(3) to explain the procedure for settling losses.

1.9.2 Nature of Contract

An insurance contract as four principle attributes:

(*a*) *Entirety*—all the terms and conditions are to be found in the policy document. If the terms and conditions are oral or not stated explicitly they are difficult for parties to prove.

(*b*) *Personal*—the contact follows the person, the insured, rather than property.

(*c*) *Unilateral* — After the insured pays the premiums the performance is obligatory on one party, *i.e.,* the insurer.

(*d*) *Aleatory*—performance is conditioned upon an event that may or may not happen.

1.9.3 Elements of Insurance Contract

The four basic elements to every insurance contract are:

(*a*) Application: An application is required for every contract of insurance. In the application, which is an offer to enter into a contract, the prospective insured sets forth the facts and figures required by the insurance carrier's underwriting department. The application may be brief and oral, or of any length and in written form. In life insurance, the application itself becomes a part of the contract.

(*b*) Binders: A binder is a memorandum specifying some of the details of the property or liability policy to be issued by the company. It is memorandum of insurance issued pending delivery of the formal policy. The binder may be oral or written and may be given either by an agent or a company. A broker, not being an agent of an insurance company, cannot issue binders. The binder is usually a temporary document and ordinarily would remain in force no more than ten days. For example, in automobile insurance a car buyer wants immediate coverage. By binding the insurance company to the risk, the agent need not wait for the insurance to become effective.

Binders are not used in life insurance. Given the long-term nature of the contract and the insurer's inability to cancel a life insurance policy, the life insurer requires an opportunity to examine the application (and possible the applicant) before being bound to a lifetime contract. However, in place of binders the life insurance agent can provide the applicant with a receipt (assuming the first premium installment is paid) that will provide varying insurance benefits depending on the nature of the receipt.

(c) **Policy Forms:** Policy forms are formal written contract of insurance that sets forth all of the terms of the agreement. The policy had two parts:

Heading: It is the declaration page and identifies the risk by specifying the name of the issued, the address location of the risk, period covered by the policy, description of the subject being insured, the amount of insurance the amount of the premium, and any warranties of representations made by the insured.

Body: It is the contract itself containing the various clauses pertaining to agreements exclusion and condition.

Back: It specifies the rights of the insured and the duties of the insurer. The condition, and stipulations define the rights and duties of the parties aside from injury agreement.

Standardization of policy forms is an ongoing process, and most insurance contracts have uniform language for the greater part of their terms. Such standardisation makes possible economies of operation, statistical uniformity, and better communication between the insured, his agent, and the insurance company. Where language has been standardised, determination of the meaning of the words and phrases by the courts reduces the chance a misunderstanding.

Endorsement: An endorsement is a form that is used to modify the policy contract. Endorsements may extend or restrict coverage, permit transfers of interest in property, transfer coverage, transfer coverage from one place to another, increases or decreases limits of coverage, provide for assignment of policies or changes in beneficiary designations, provide for changes in settlement options elected, or in any other legal manner permit amendments to the contract. Endorsements are usually done by party forms or by embossing through rubber stamps of the desired alteration.

1.9.4 Maxims Applicable to Insurance Contracts

The following maxims are elemental to insurance contracts and their interpretation.

(*a*) *Uberrimae fidei*— Utmost good faith.

(*b*) *Spes successions*— hope of succession — direct and not hope of insurable interest.

(*c*) *Causa proxima*— the proximate and immediate cause of loss is important.

(*d*) *Pari Delicto*— parties to be equally blamed — in case of illegal policies, the premium cannot be recovered/returned.

(*e*) *Salus Populist supermen*— by the regard for pubic interest and welfare is the highest in law.

(*f*) *Rao ipsa loquitor* — the thing speaks for itself for example in case of accidents, the circumstances of the case and not more occurrence of the events has to be seen.

1.10 Insurance Versus Gasmbling

If gambling events were insurable, the gambler would be put in the enviable position of being unable to lose because if it is head, he wins else if fails, he collects the money from insurance company. Since, the insurance premium must include the charge for the losses and the expenses of operating the insurance pool, the resulting premium must be more than the mathematically fair value of the potential loss. Moreover, the gambler presumably enjoys the risk of gambling and therefore would be unlikely to pay the premium needed for transferring the risk being enjoyed. Law prohibits the use of insurance for gambling purposes because fraud and murder would increase thus making a social device prohibitively expensive and therefore making the system fail. In summary, the gambling can be distinguished from an insurance contract in the following ways:

(a) Gambling creates risk while insurance transfers an existing risk.

(b) Gambling deals with speculative risk—there might be gains or losses, while Insurance deals with pure risk.

1.11 Insurance Versus Wager

Insurance contracts are often confused with wagering contracts. The main points of difference between the two are:

(a) Insurance contracts are legal ones; enforceable at court of law while wagering contracts are void contracts.

(b) Parties to an insurance contract are identifiable at the inception of the contract but in wagers, the parties to suffer losses are identified after the occurrence of the event.

(c) Insurance contracts are contracts of indemnity; wagers are winning or lose contracts.

(d) At the inception of the insurance contracts the parties have to disclose fully all material facts, however wager does not requires such disclosure.

(e) Insurance contracts have social objective, *viz.*, to provide a cover against the ill effects of unforeseen events. However, wagers create additional risk and have harmful effects on society.

However, insurance contracts are conditional contracts in the sense that the performance of the contract depends upon the happening of the contracted event.

1.12 Summary

Risk is any situation where there is uncertainty about what outcome will occur. Uncertainty is often confused with the risk. Uncertainty refers to a situation where the outcome is not certain whereas a risk refers to a situation where there is the possibility of a loss. The cause of loss is referred as a peril. Hazard is the condition that increases the severity of loss or the conditions affecting perils. Risk is classified in different ways. Pure risks are generally insurable. The various techniques of risk management are Avoidance, Loss Prevention, Loss Reduction, Risk Retention, Transfer, and Insurance. Insurance is the last step of risk management. The term insurance can be defined as a contract between the insurer and the insured. The purpose of insurance is to provide economic protection against the losses. Following conditions are necessary to form a valid insurance contract: Agreement between two parties, Lawful object, Capacity to contract, Consideration, and Possibility of performance. The basic elements to every insurance contract are Application, Binders, and Policy Forms. Insurance contracts are entirely different from gambling and a wagering contract.

1.13 Test Yourself

1. Define risk. What are the different types of risk?
2. What do you mean by Hazard? Briefly explain the different types of Hazards.
3. Explain various risk management techniques.
4. "Insurance is the last step of risk management" Comment.
5. What are the major characteristics of an insurable risk?
6. What are the necessary conditions to form a valid insurance contract?
7. Distinguish between the following:
   (a) Risk and Uncertainty
   (b) Peril and Hazard
   (c) Loss Prevention and Loss Reduction
   (d) Insurance and Wager Contract
   (e) Pure and Speculative Risk
8. Define insurance. How does it differ from Gambling?
9. What are the basic elements of an insurance contract?
10. Briefly explain the different functions of an insurance contract.
11. Discuss the important benefits of insurance.

Choose the Correct answer from the choice given:

1. The Concept of Risk can be defined in
   (a) Single way (b) Double way
   (c) Different way (d) None of these

2. According to the Dictionary, risk refers to the possibility that
   (a) Something unpleasant (b) Dangerous might happen
   (c) a and b (d) Neither a nor b
3. A peril refers to the cause of
   (a) Loss (b) Gain
   (c) Loss or gain (d) Neither gain nor loss
4. Dynamic risks are those resulting from the changes in the
   (a) Social (b) Economic
   (c) Financial (d) None of these
5. The risk which can be measured like financial risks are known to be
   (a) Quantifiable (b) Unquantifiale
   (c) Non-Quantifiable (d) None of these
6. Pure risk situations are those where there is a possibility of
   (a) Loss (b) Gain
   (c) Both a and b (d) Neither a nor b
7. Personal risk may be
   (a) Premature death (b) Old age
   (c) Sickness or disability (d) Unemployment
   (e) All of these
8. Methods of handling risk
   (a) Avoidance (b) Loss control
   (c) Retention (d) Transfer
   (e) All of these
9. Benefit of insurance may be
   (a) Reimbursement for losses (b) Reduction in tension and fear
   (c) Avenue for investment (d) All of these
10. Which conditions is/are necessary to form a valid contract
    (a) Agreement between two parties (b) Lawful object
    (c) Capacity to contract (d) Consideration
    (e) All of these

11. The insurance contract performs the following function/s
    (a) To define the risk that is to be transferred
    (b) To state the conditions under which the contract applies and
    (c) To explain the procedure for settling losses.
    (d) All of the above

State whether the following statements are 'True' or 'False'.

1. Risk refers to the possibility that something unpleasant or dangerous might happen.
2. Risk is a condition in which there is no possibility of an adverse deviation from a desired outcome that is expected or hoped for.
3. Uncertainty being a perceptual phenomenon implies same degrees to different person.
4. Uncertainty can be perceived as opposite of certainty.
5. The whole game of insurance business is based on the probability of loss.
6. The probabilities of losses may be *ex-post* or *ex-ante.*
7. A peril refers to the cause of gain.
8. Hazards are the conditions that decrease the severity of loss or the conditions affecting perils.
9. A risk is said to be a *group* risk or *fundamental* risk if it affects the economy or its participants on a macro basis.
10. Social insurance programmes may be undertaken by the people to handle fundamental risks.
11. Dynamic risks are those resulting from the changes in the atmosphere.
12. Risk factors mainly refer to the micro economic variables like inflation, income and output levels, and technology changes.
13. Pure risks are generally insurable while the speculative ones are not.
14. The conceptual framework of the risk pooling can be applied to pure risks, while in most of the cases of speculative risks where it is not possible.
15. Unemployment is a personal risk.
16. Liability risks generally arise from the people.
17. Risk can be avoid.
18. Insurance, derivatives, diversification strategies are contractual agreement.
19. The term "insurance" can be defined in both financial and legal terms.
20. The financial definition focuses on an arrangement that redistributes the cost of expected losses.

21. The financial definition provides for the funding of the gains.
22. The purpose of insurance mode of risk transfer is to provide economic protection against the gains.
23. The theory of insurance is based on law of small numbers.
24. The losses are fairly predictable and can be measured in money terms.
25. The adverse event may or may occur in future.
26. The probability distribution of the happening of adverse event is undeterminable.
27. The losses should be catastrophic.
28. The offer for entering into insurance contract generally come from the uninsured.
29. On acceptance of the proposal by the insurer, a valid and binding contract comes into existence.
30. In case of Life insurance, a valid and binding contract comes into existence upon payment of last premium.
31. For a valid contract, the object of the agreement should be unlawful and must be prohibited by any law.
32. The rules laid down under the Indian Contract Act, 1862,
33. Parties entering into the contract should enter into the contract by their free and genuine consent.
34. The formulation of every contract depends upon the people and subject matter of contract.
35. Gambling creates risk while insurance transfers an existing risk.
36. Wagering is a contract.
37. Insurance contracts are legal ones; enforceable at court of law while wagering contracts are void contracts.
38. Insurance contracts are contracts of indemnity; wagers are winning or lose Contracts.
39. Insurance contracts have economic objective, *viz.*, to provide a cover against the ill effects of unforeseen events.

Fill in the blanks.

1. Uncertainty is often confused with the ....
2. Uncertainty refers to a situation where the outcome is not certain or ....
3. A risk refers to a situation where there is the possibility of a ....
4. Loss refers to the ....
5. The chance of loss refers to a fraction or ....

6. A peril refers to the cause of loss or .... that may cause a loss.
7. Perils refer to the immediate causes of ....
8. Perils may be general or ....
9. Hazards are the conditions that increase the severity of loss or the conditions affecting ....
10. *Financial risk* involves the simultaneous existence of three important elements in a .... situation.
11. A Risk is said to be a .... or fundamental risk.
12. Risk factor may be a socio-economic or political or ....
13. Dynamic risks are those resulting from the changes in the economy or the ....
14. The risk which can be measured like financial risks are known to be ....
15. The situations which may result in repercussions like tension or loss of peace are called as ....
16. Pure risk situations are those where there is a possibility of loss or ....
17. Speculative risks are those where there is possibility of gain as well as ....
18. The element of gain is inherent or structured in such a ....
19. Pure risks are generally insurable while the .... ones are not.
20. Since pure risks are generally ....
21. The term "insurance" can be defined in both financial and .... terms.
22. Insurance is a social device in which a group of individuals (insureds) transfer ....
23. A contract of .... is a contract by which one party in consideration of the price paid to him .... to the risk provides security to the other party that he shall not suffer ....
24. The purpose of insurance mode of risk transfer is to provide .... protection against the losses.
25. Insurance contracts are .... between insurance companies and insured.
26. The insurance company may also propose to make the ....
27. Any act that precedes it is an offer or a ....
28. In case of Life insurance, a valid and binding contract comes into existence upon payment of ....
29. A premium is the price for the risk undertaken by the ....

30. Parties entering into the contract should enter into the contract by their free and Genuine ....

31. Gambling creates risk while insurance transfers an existing ....

32. Gambling deals with .... Risk.

33. Insurance deals with .... risk.

34. Insurance contracts are often confused with .... Contract.

35. Insurance contracts are .... ones; enforceable at court of law while wagering contracts are .... contracts.

36. Risk is any situation where there is ....

CHAPTER 2

PRINCIPLES OF INSURANCE

Learning Objectives

After reading this chapter, you will be able to understand:

- Pooling in Insurance
- Dual Application of Law of Large Number
- Functions of Insurance
- Importance of Insurance
- Kinds of Insurance
- Principles of Insurance

2.1 Pooling in Insurance

Pooling or sharing of losses is the heart of insurance. Pooling is the spreading of losses incurred by a few people over an entire group so that in the process, average loss is substituted for actual loss. Pooling involves the grouping of a large number of exposure units so that the law of large numbers can operate to provide a substantially accurate prediction of future losses. There should be a large number of similar but not necessarily identical exposure units that are subject to the some perils. Thus, pooling implies *(a)* the sharing of losses by the entire group *(b)* prediction of future losses with some accuracy based on the law of large number.

There are two forms of pooling. One form of pooling is known as *'bulk buying'* which enables a group of individuals or businesses to collectively purchase insurance. The group collectively obtains the services from an insurer. Another of pooling is *self-insurance.* In case of self-insurance, individuals or businesses come together to provide their own insurance through the establishment of mutual funds. Members contribute to the this fund, which is used to pay for any compensation pay-outs.

2.2 Dual Application of Law of Large Numbers

The effects of pooling arrangements are derived from law of large numbers. By the law of large numbers, an insurer can predict future loss experience with of great accuracy. In making predictions on the basis of historical data, the insurance company assumes that things will happen in the future as they have happened in the past. But it may not be true. It is likely that the probability estimates the probability of loss is constantly changing. The insurer estimates the probability of expected loss by taking a sample. He expects the actual loss a large sample will improve the estimates of the probability of loss. As the number is increased, more accuracy can be expected. The requirements of a large number has dual application:

(i) To estimate the underlying probability accurately, the insurance company must have a sufficiently large sample, the more accurate will be the estimate of the probability.

(ii) Once the estimate of the probability has been made, it must be applied to sufficiently large number of exposure units to permit the underlying probability to work itself out.

In this sense, to the insurance company, the law of large number means that the larger the number of cases examined in the sampling process, the better the chance of that actual expedience will approximate a good estimate of the probability.

2.3 Function of Insurance

Insurance is simply defined as contractual agreement whereby one party agrees to compensate another party for losses. The party agreeing to pay for the losses is called the insurer. The party whose loss causes the insurer to make a claim payment is called the insured. The payment the insurer receives from the insured is called premium. The insurance contract is called insurance policy. Insurance performs a variety of functions which are advantageous to the common people, directly or indirectly. As such, functions of insurance can be divided into three categories.

(a) Primary Functions.

(b) Secondary Functions

(c) Other Functions.

(a) **Primary Functions:** The main primary functions are as follows:

(i) **It provides certainty:** Insurance provides certainty at payments of the uncertain losses. There are different types of uncertainty in a risk. There are uncertainty of happening of the loss, time of loss, and amount of loss, etc. The insured converts all his uncertainties into certainties by paying premium to the insurer. Insurance is a mean for compensating the losses caused by the uncertainty events.

(ii) **Insurance shares risks (Pooling of risk):** Polling or the sharing of losses is the heart of insurance. Pooling is the spreading of losses incurred by the few over the entire group. Risk is uncertain and the losses arising from the risk is also uncertain. When the risk takes place, the loss is shared by all persons by means of insurance.

(iii) **Insurance provides protection:** Another function of insurance is to provide financial security to the persons against the risks to uncertain events. Under the insurance contract the insurance company guarantees the insured person to compensate the losses whenever it occurs. Hence, the insurance provides the feeling of security against any uncertain events.

(b) **Secondary Functions:** The following are the secondary functions.

(i) **It provides capital:** It provides capital for productivity in various forms. The amount received on account of premiums by various insurance companies is made available for the industrial development of the country in various financing forms such as, by providing of share capital, providing long-term loans to companies and term loans and loans to the government to invest in the country's public sector industries.

(ii) **It improves efficiency:** Insurance by reducing the worries and miseries of losses increases the efficiency of an individual or a business. The carefree person can devote his body and soul together for better achievement. Business firms relieved of the various risks involved in uncertainties, become able to give due attention to other factors which effect the total efficiency of the organization such as, labour force materials management, marketing, etc.

(iii) **It helps economic progress:** The insurance by protecting the society from huge losses of damage, destruction and death, provides an initiative to work hard for the betterment of the masses. As a result, economic progress is immensely provided by the masses. The property, the valuable assets, the man, the machine and the society cannot loss much at the disaster.

(iv) **It prevents losses:** Insurance company not only secures the losses but also advises the adoption of various methods and techniques which help in reducing the risks or losses. In India, Loss Prevention Association has been established with the objective to suggest the publicise various techniques which help in reducing the losses and accidents caused by uncertain events.

(c) **Other Functions:**

(i) **Expands the foreign trade:** Insurance provides security to the international traders, shippers and banking and financial institutions which are the main functionaries to foreign trade. Thus, insurance promotes foreign trade and helps in earning and securing valuable foreign exchange. Marine and fire insurance play a vital role in this regard by providing much needed protection against the perils of sea.

(ii) **It judges the worth of the insurable:** Before insuring the assets or property of any individual/organization, the insurer, generally, conduct an investigation of the asset as a whole with a view to judge the current worth of the asset or property.

(iii) **It encourages savings:** Nowadays, Insurance is considered to be a better alternative technique of making savings. Under the contract of insurance, the insured has to pay a definite premium compulsorily. Such forced savings curbs the unnecessary expenses of the individuals.

(iv) **It creates self-confidence:** Insurance, by providing a feeling of security among the insureds, also creates self-confidence in them. Because, insurance not only provides protection against the risk, but also provides capital to the insured which becomes a sources of financial stability and strength.

(v) **It provides social security:** Insurance is defined as a social device. It provides an instrumental force to fight against evils of poverty, unemployment, disease, old age, fateful accidents and other calamities of nature. Insurance has helped in a greater way by establishing or devising various types of insurance in our country. Insurance also educates the society regarding the adoption of techniques for minimizing the happening of controllable uncertain events.

(vi) **Credit Facilities:** Individuals/businessmen are in the position to raise loans and get credits facilities from various financial institutions and banks by pledging their insurance policies. In case the insured become unable to return the !oan or credit, then the financial institutions can recover their amount out of the policy's surrender value.

2.4 Importance of Insurance

The insurance has the following characteristics which are, generally, observed in care of life, marine, fire and general insurances.

- **Contract:** Insurance is a contract by which one party in a consideration called premium, takes over a particular risk of the other party and promises to pay to the insured or his nominee a certain sum or ascertainable sum of money on the happening or occurrence of an uncertain event.
- **Device of sharing risk:** Insurance is a device of sharing risk which may occur to individual or his family or corporates. Insurance shares the risk of large number of exposure units which is a large group of roughly similar, but not necessarily identical and are subject to the same peril or group of perils.
- **Co-operative device:** Insurance is a device of cooperation of large number of persons who agree to share the financial loss arising due to a particular risk which is insured. Such a group of persons may be brought together voluntarily or through publicity or through solicitasion of the agents. An insurer by himself will not be able to compensate all the losses. By insuring a large number of persons, the insurer will be able to pay the amount of loss.

- **Protection of financial risks:** Insurance covers only such risks which can be measured in monetary terms. Insurance compensates only financial losses.
- **Good faith:** The contract of insurance requires absolute and utmost good faith on the part of both parties to the contract. Generally, this condition applies particularly to the insured who is in possession of all material facts required to be explained in the contract of insurance. A material fact is a fact which would influence the mind of a underwriter in deciding whether to accept a risk for insurance.
- **Contract of indemnity:** All contracts of insurance are contracts of indemnity. The basic object of the insurance is to shift the loss of the person to the insurance company. The insurance company pays only the cash loss so caused and nothing else because this is based on the principle of indemnity which means compensation upto the limit of actual loss or value of policy whichever is lower.
- **Certainty and contingency:** Life insurance contract is a contract of certainty because the death or expiry of the term of policy will certainly occur; so the payment is certain. Whereas in other insurance contacts, the contingency is the fire, theft, earthquake, accident or etc. which may or may not occur. If the contingency occurs payment is made otherwise no amount is paid to the insured.
- **Insurance is not gambling:** The contract of insurance is not gambling because he insured is assured to get his loss indemnified only in the event of occurrence of such uncertain event as stipulated in the contract of insurance, whereas the gambling may either result into profit or loss.
- **Insurance can-not be named as charity:** Premium payable under an insurance is the cost of risk so covered. Hence, it cannot be treated as charity. Charity lacks the elements of contract of indemnity and compensation of loss to the person whosoever makes it.

2.5 Kinds of Insurance

The commonly known categories of various insurance covers are —

Non-life Insurance

Property

Personal and business property insurance that covers risks against fire, marine, theft and burglary. The types of insurance under this category are:

- Home Insurance/Domestic Cover
- Business insurance
- Commercial Insurance

Liability

This protects the insured against injury or damage claims made by a third party. The types of insurance under this category are:

- Motor insurance
- Workmen Compensation
- Liability Insurance
- Aviation Insurance
- Project and Engineering Insurance

Health

In case of an illness or injury suffered by the insured or his/her dependents, health insurance covers their medical expenses incurred. The types of insurance under this category are:

- Hospital Insurance
- Medical Cover

Life Insurance

Life Insurance products can be broadly divided into various categories, which include money back, pension, endowment and specialised plans. The popular life products are:

- Money Back
- Pension
- Women, Girl Child and Couple
- Endowment
- Whole Life
- Child Insurance.

2.6 Principles of Insurance

- Principle of Indemnity

The principle of indemnity implies that *on the happening of an event insured against, the Insured will be placed by the insurer in the same pecuniary (monetary) position that he/she occupied immediately before the event. Indemnity means that the insured person is placed, financially, in the same position, as he was before the loss.*

The non-life insurance covers, viz., Property and Liability are basically contracts of indemnity. However, the indemnity must not be construed as an instrument to profit. The indemnity goes along with two checks:

(*a*) to prevent the insured from benefiting under the contract

(*b*) to reduce the impact of moral hazards

The exceptions to the application of indemnity are found in Personal Accident Policies, Agreed Value policies in Marine Insurance and valuables and reinstatement policies like in Engineering policies. These are also contracts of indemnity but by a special application of the principle, the measure of indemnity is decided at the time of entering into the contract itself in the event of a claim the insured must:

- prove that he/she has sustained a monetary loss
- prove the extent and value of his/her loss
- prove the extent and value of his/her loss
- transfer any rights which he/she may have for recovery from another source to the Insurer, if he/she has been fully indemnified.

Example

In a valued (marine) policy, if there is damage/loss to the cargo, the claim is limited to the value expressed in the policy cover irrespective of the actual value of the cargo lost or damaged. The settlement of the loss will be subject to (*a*) Sum insured, (*b*) Average and (*c*) Excess/Deductible.

It is important to note that the contract of life insurance is not as such insurance, but it is in the nature of assurance. This is logical in the sense that life can not be indemnified, instead if a person dies, then under the contract of life insurance the sum assured will be paid by the insured.

• Utmost Good Faith

Under the contract of insurance, the insured is duty bound to disclose all material facts relating to the risk to be covered.

Utmost good faith is a positive duty voluntarily to disclose, accurately and fully, all facts material to the risk being proposed, whether requested or not.

A material fact is a fact, which would influence the mind of a prudent underwriter in deciding whether to accept a risk for insurance and on what terms. Both the parties to a contract are expected to observe good faith. However, the good faith assumes utmost importance when Material Facts are concerned and therefore utmost good faith should be observed on matters relating to Material facts. Examples of material facts in various classes of insurance are:

(1) *Motor*: Details of any young drivers

(2) *Household*: Details of any commercial use of private dwelling house

(3) *Commercial:* Previous losses/hazards

(4) *Life:* Details of Heart Diseases

Duty of disclosure applies to both the *Proposer* and the *Insurer*. Duty of disclosure operates at: inception — until the date cover is confirmed by the Insurers renewal — up to the renewal date mid term alterations — until the Insurers confirm cover in respect of the alterations.

Breach of utmost good faith is essentially a violation of *"Consensus ad idem"*, a pre-requisite for a valid contract. The breach may relate to (*a*) misrepresentation or (*b*) non-representation. Intentional misrepresentation may be termed as fraudulent and the intentional non-disclosure may be termed as concealment of facts. When misrepresentation or non-representation is unintentional, it may be termed as breach of general duty. The utmost good faith is vital from an insurer's perspective. It is important for the insurer to decide about:

(*a*) Acceptance or rejection of a proposal

(*b*) Pricing of the insurance cover

(*c*) Contribution to indemnity

(*d*) Powers of subrogation under the contract

(*e*) Imposition of conditions and warranties

• Subrogation

Subrogation in general, means the legal right of one person, having indemnified the other in a contractual obligation to do so, to stand in the place of another and avail of all the rights and remedies of the another, whether enforced or not.

It entitles the Insurer who has granted an indemnity to receive after payment of a loss the advantage of every right of the Insured. Subrogation condition is a corollary to the Principle of Indemnity. A loss may occur accidentally or by the action or negligence of third party (not workmen). The property owners have a right to proceed against the offending third party to recover the loss/damage and also under their insurance policy but not under both. If the insured opts to recover the loss under the insurance policy which is faster and does not involve litigation, he will surrender his rights against the third parties in favour of the insurers signing a 'Letter of subrogation' on an appropriate stamp paper.

An exception to this are life insurance policies wherein insured/beneficiaries can claim under an insurance policy and also proceed against the offending third party.

The insurer must exercise the right of recovery in the name of the Insured (prevents the Insured from obtaining more than one indemnity).

Example

The Insurer of an importer of electrical goods receives a claim in respect of a faulty toaster. The Insurer pays the claim but takes over the insured's rights to claim back against the manufacturer. The insurance company can proceed with this claim in the Insured's name.

Subrogation rights only apply where there is a legal liability under the policy *i.e.*, where policy cover existed and the claims are paid. However, the policy conditions customarily provide for such subrogation rights before the claim payment. However, recovery from third parties can be made only if claim is paid.

• Insurable Interest

The Insured must have an insurable interest in the subject matter of insurance, *i.e.*, he/she must benefit by its safety or be prejudiced by its loss.

It is the legal right to insure arising out of financial relationship recognised under law, between the insured and the subject matter of insurance.

Insurance contracts without insurable interests have no sanction of the law as they amount to speculation The owner of a property has absolute insurance interest When a person insures a property, what is insured therein, is his interest in that property. By this principle, insurance interest exists to other parties like lessor, lessee, financiers, etc., but their interest is limited to the extent of their financial commitment only. The insurable interest must exist both at the time of the proposal and at the time of claims. However, in the case of marine insurance contracts, which are assignable without the consent of the insurers, insurable interest must exist at the time of loss only (Marine insurance contracts are governed by Marine Insurance Act of 1963). Insurable Interest may be created either by :

Obligation to Insure

(*a*) By Statute

(*b*) By Contract

(*c*) By Custom

Option to Insure

(*a*) Owners

(*b*) Mortgagors

(*c*) Lessors

(*d*) Trustees

(*e*) Tenants

Example

Everybody would have an insurable interest in their own personal possessions, *e.g.*, car, watch. An employee would have no insurable interest in their desk at work but the employer has. A husband has insurable interest in his wife.

• Proximate Cause

It is defined as the active efficient cause that sets into motion a train of events, which bring about a result, without the intervention of any force started and working actively from a new and independent source. Therefore there must be an efficient cause, which brings about a loss with no other intervening cause, which breaks the chain of events. A loss could be due to a cause of causes. In the chain reaction, it is the dominant cause, which would be the proximate cause to be considered for the purpose of a claim. It is always the duty of the insured to prove that the loss arose out of the insured peril, which is proximate.

Example

Firemen remove undamaged stock from a burning building to avoid its involvement in the fire. It is stacked in the open yard and subsequently damaged by rain. Was the proximate cause of the damage the fire or the rain? If the rain damage occurred before the Insured had an opportunity to protect it then the proximate cause of the damage would be the fire. However, if the stock were left unprotected for an unreasonably long period, the rain would be a new and independent cause of damage.

If there are more than one cause operating together and one of the cause is excepted peril, the claim shall not be payable under the policy. However, if the results of the operation of an insured peril can be separated from the excluded peril, the claim shall be payable in respect of insured peril.

Example

During the war period, a bomb was dropped on a factory, which caused fire to the factory. The proximate cause of loss in this case is enemy action and not fire.

• Contribution

Contribution condition is a corollary to the Principle of indemnity. If an insured obtains more than one policy covering the same risk, he cannot recover the same loss from more than one source so that more than 'Indemnity' does not benefit him. Although the Insured may affect more than one policy to cover the same property or interest, he/she cannot recover in total more than a full indemnity. Contribution condition checks that each policy pays only a rateable portion under each separate policy. Application of contribution principle can arise only when the policies :

- Cover the same peril
- Cover the same subject matter
- Are effected by or on behalf of the same Insured

Example

An insured loses his/her watch on holidays. He/she has holiday insurance and All Risks Cover on his/her household policy. The cost of the claim should be shared under both policies

Example

If an insured has taken three policies from insurers X, Y and Z for Rs. 5,00,000, Rs. 5,00,000 and Rs. 2,00,000 respectively, an the loss to the property due to the operation of the insured peril is Rs. 1,20,000, then the ratio of contribution will be 5: 5: 2. Hence, the claim payable by X, Y and Z will be Rs. 50,000, Rs. 50,000 and Rs. 20,000 respectively.

In the same example if the value of the property at the t me of loss was Rs. 15,00,000 then the indemnity in respect of X, Y and Z shall be reduced proportionately by the factor {Sum Insured/Actual Value}. Such cases shall be deemed to be cases of under insurance and the under cover shall be construed tc *self insured* by the insured. Hence, the losses shall be borne by the parties X, Y, Z and insured as Rs. 16,667, Rs. 16,667, Rs. 6,667 and Rs. 10,000 respectively.

- Arbitration

When liability under the policy is admitted but the quantum is disputed, the insured cannot rush to a Court of law without first referring the dispute to Arbitration as per 'Indian Arbitration and Reconciliation Act — 1996'. In keeping with the provisions of the Act, the insured may appoint an arbitrator to be followed by appointment of another arbitrator by the insurers They can also appoint a single arbitrator, to represent both of them. If the two separate arbitrators cannot reach an agreement, both the arbitrators can appoint a third arbitrator called umpire. The award of the Arbitrators is binding on both the parties to the dispute and cannot be challenged unless a point of law is involved. The jurisdiction of Arbitration proceedings is w thin Indian territory. However, when foreign funding is involved, the financiers who are also joined in the policy as co-insured, may insist upon conducting the Arbitration proceedings in their own country. In such a case, the insurers may agree to modify the arbitration condition suitably.

2.7 Summary

Basic concept of insurance is sharing of losses of a few by a group of people.There should be a large number of exposure units who face similar risk. The effects of pooling arrangements are derived from law of large numbers. Insurance is thus a device of cooperation of large number of persons who agree to share the financial loss arising due to a particular risk which is insured Insurance performs a variety of functions which are advantageous to the common people, directly or indirectly. It provides certainty and protection. Insurance plays major role in developing our nation's economy. It encourages savings and provides social security. Insurance also provides credit facilities to Individuals as well as businessmen. Insurance is generally classified as Life and Non-life. Life Insurance products can be broadly divided into various categories such as whole life, endowment, term, money back and etc.

There are certain principles which are applicable to insurance. The principle of indemnity implies that on the happening of an event insured against, the Insured will be placed by the insurer in the same pecuniary (monetary) position that he/she occupied immediately before the event. Principle of Utmost Good Faith states that the insured is duty bound to disclose all material facts relating to the risk to be covered. Principle of Subrogation entitles the Insurer who has granted an indemnity to receive after payment of a loss the advantage of every right of the Insured. The Insured must have an insurable interest in the subject matter of insurance. Principle of Proximate Cause states that there must be an efficient cause, which brings about a loss with no other intervening cause, which breaks the chain of events. Under the Principle of Contribution, if an insured obtains more than one policy covering the same risk, he cannot recover the same loss from more than one source. This principle is not applicable to life insurance.

2.8 Test Yourself

1. Define pooling of insurance. What are the different forms of pooling?
2. Explain the law of large number. What are the applications of law of large number?
3. How does insurance play a major role in developing our nation's economy?
4. "Pooling is the spreading of losses incurred by the few over the entire group" comment.
5. What are the important characteristics of insurance?
6. "Insurance is an important source of savings and investment." Explain how.
7. How does insurance improve efficiency of (i) an individual and (ii) a business firm?
8. Briefly explain the classification of insurance.
9. Define Principle of Indemnity. State whether this principle is applicable to life insurance. Justify your answer.
10. Mr. X has taken fire insurance policy with ABC Insurance Company and DEF Insurance Company, covering the same property for a sum insured Rs. 8 lakhs and Rs. 16 lakhs respectively. There was a fire loss and the loss is Rs. 12 lakhs. How will each insurance company settle the claim?
11. Illustrate the importance of the principle of Utmost Good Faith with suitable example.
12. Define Insurable Interest. Under which circumstances one person can have insurable interest on others life?

13. Describe the Proximate cause in the following situations:

(i) During an earthquake, a school building caught fire and was totally destroyed. (Earthquake/fire)

(ii) A motorcycle driven at a high speed slipped due to rainwater on the road and damaged. (Speed/Rain Water)

(iii) A commercial vehicle carrying highly inflammables goods was hit by a truck and got fire. (Accident/Fire)

(iv) An explosion blasts a dam; water enters the village and damages the crops. (Explosion/Water)

(v) During violence in a rally organized by a political party, some articles of furniture were stolen. (Theft/Violence)

Choose the Correct answer from the choice given:

1. The pooling implies

(a) The sharing of losses by the entire group

(b) Prediction of future losses with some accuracy based on the law of large number

(c) Both of these

(d) None of these

2. Function of insurance is/are

(a) Primary Functions

(b) Secondary Functions

(c) Other Functions

(d) All of the above

3. Primary function provide

(a) Provides certainty

(b) Insurance shares risks

(c) Insurance provides protection

(d) All of the above

4. Secondary function/s is/are of

(a) Provides capital

(b) Improves efficiency

(c) Helps economic progress

(d) Prevents losses

(e) All of the above

5. Other function/s is are of
   (a) Expands the foreign trade
   (b) It judges the worth of the insurable
   (c) Encourages servings and Credit facilities
   (d) Creates self-confidence and provide social security
   (e) All of the above
6. Kinds of insurance is/are
   (a) Life insurance
   (b) Non-life insurance
   (c) Health insurance
   (d) Liability insurance
   (e) All are types of insurance
7. Health Insurance provides
   (a) Hospital insurance
   (b) Medical cover
   (c) Both of them
   (d) None of these
8. The indemnity goes along with following checks
   (a) To prevent the insured from benefiting under the contract
   (b) To reduce the impact of moral hazards
   (c) Both of them
   (d) None of them
9. Obligation to Insure is/are
   (a) By Statute
   (b) By Contract
   (c) By Custom
   (d) All of these
   (e) None of these
10. Option to Insure is/are
   (a) Owners and Trustees
   (b) Mortgagors and Tenants

(c) Lessors

(d) None of these

(e) All of these

11. Application of contribution principle can arise only when the policies

(a) Cover the same peril

(b) Cover the same subject matter

(c) Are effected by or on behalf of the same Insur

(e) All of these

(f) Any one

State whether the following statements are 'True' or 'False'.

1. Pooling or sharing of losses is the heart of insurance .
2. There are three forms of pooling.
3. One form of pooling is known as self insurance or Bulk-buying.
4. The effects of pooling arrangements are derived from law of few numbers.
5. The insurer estimates the probability of expected loss by taking a sample.
6. He expects the actual loss a few sample will improve the estimates of the probability of gain.
7. The insurance company must have a sufficiently large sample, the more accurate will be the estimate of the probability.
8. Functions of insurance can be divided into three categories.
9. Private function of insurance provides certainty.
10. Secondary function of Insurance provides capital and economic progress.
11. Other function expands the foreign trade.
12. The insurance has the following characteristics which are, generally, observed in case of life, marine, fire and general insurances.
13. Insurance is a device of sharing risk which may occur to individual or his family or corporates.
14. Insurance is a device of cooperation of few number of persons who agree to share the financial loss arising due to a particular risk which is insured.
15. By insuring a few number of persons, the insurer will be able to pay the amount of loss.
16. Insurance compensates only economic losses.
17. Insurance covers only such risks which can be measured in monetary terms.

18. The contract of insurance requires absolute and utmost good faith on the part of same parties to the contract.
19. Life insurance contract is a contract of uncertainty because the death or expiry of the term of policy will certainly occur.
20. The contract of insurance is gambling.
21. Contract of insurance is wagering.
22. Insurable interest is not defined in any written law.
23. In the case of life insurance, insurable interest should exist at the time of claim.
24. Health insurance covers their personal expenses incurred.
25. The principle of indemnity implies that on the happening of an event insured against.
26. The non-life insurance covers, *viz.,* health and liability are basically contracts of indemnity.
27. To prevent the insured from benefiting under the Agreement.
28. Under the contract of insurance, the insured is duty bound to disclose all material facts relating to the life to be covered.
29. Duty of disclosure applies to both the *Proposer* and the *Insurer.*
30. It entitles the insurer who has granted an indemnity to receive after payment of a loss the advantage of every right of the policyholder.
31. Subrogation condition is a corollary to the principle of indemnity.
32. The insurer must exercise the right of recovery in the name of the nominee.
33. The Insured must have an insurable contract in the subject matter of insurance.
34. It is the legal right to insure arising out of financial relationship recognized under law, between the insured and the subject matter of insurance.
35. Firemen remove damaged stock from a burning building to avoid its involvement in the fire.
36. If there are more than one cause operating together and one of the cause is excepted peril, the claim shall not be payable under the policy.
37. Contribution condition is a corollary to the Principle of indemnity.

Fill in the blanks.

1. There are......... forms of pooling.
2. One form of pooling is known as ....
3. An insurer can predict future .... experience with of great accuracy.

4. To estimate the underlying probability accurately, the .... company must have a sufficiently large sample, the more accurate will be the estimate of the ....
5. Insurance is simply defined as contractual ....
6. The party agreeing to pay for the losses is called the ....
7. The payment the insurer receives from the insured is called ....
8. Insurance is simply defined as contractual .... whereby one party agrees to compensate another party for ....
9. The insurer estimates the probability of expected loss by taking a ....
10. Insurance provides .... at payments of the .... looses.
11. Insurance is a mean for compensating the .... caused by the .... Events.
12. ....is considered to be a better alternative technique of making savings.
13. ....not only provides protection against the risk, but also provides capital to the insured which becomes a sources of ....and ....
14. Insurance is defined as a .... Device.
15. The insurance has the following characteristics which are, generally, observed in ...., ... , ..., and ....
16. Insurance is a contract by which one party in a .... called premium. Insurance is a device of sharing .... which may occur to .... or to his or ....
17. The insurer will be able to pay the amount of ....
18. Insurance covers only such risks which can be measured in .... terms.
19. The contract of insurance requires .... and .... on the part of both parties to the ....
20. All contracts of insurance are contracts of ....
21. The contract of insurance is not ....
22. .... payable under an insurance is the cost of risk so covered.
23. The commonly known categories of various insurance covers are .... and ....
24. Personal and business property insurance that covers risks against ...., ..., ..., and ....
25. This protects the insured against injury or damage claims made by a ....

26. In case of an illness or injury suffered by the insured or his/her dependents, ... covers their .... incurred.

27. Life Insurance products can be broadly divided into .... categories.

28. The popular life products are....................., ...

29. The non-life insurance covers, *viz.,* .... and ....are basically contracts of ....

30. The indemnity goes along with .... checks.

31. The exceptions to the application of indemnity are found in .... policies.

32. It is important to note that the contract of life insurance is not as such .... but it is in the nature of ....

33. Under the contract of ...., the insured is duty bound to disclose all material facts relating to the............. to be covered.

34. ....in general, means the legal right of one person, having .... the other in a contractual obligation to do so, to stand in the place of another and avail of all the rights and remedies of the another, whether enforced or not.

35. A loss may occur .... or by the ....or .... of third party.

36. The insurer must exercise the .... of recovery in the name of the ....

37. .... rights only apply where there is a legal liability under the policy.

38. The Insured must have an .... in the subject matter of ....

39. Firemen remove .... stock from a burning building to avoid its involvements in the ....

40. The award of the Arbitrators is .... binding on both the to the dispute and cannot be challenged unless a point of low ....

41. The insurers may agree to modify the .... condition suitably.

CHAPTER 3

BASIC INSURANCE LAW

Learning Objectives

After reading this chapter, you will be able to understand:

- Constitution, Powers and Regulations of IRDA under the IRDA Act, 1999.

IRDA Act, 1999 and Regulations

The Insurance Regulatory and Development Authority Act 1999 provides for the establishment of an Authority to protect the interests of holders of insurance policies, to regulate, promote and ensure orderly growth of the nsurance industry and for matters connected therewith or incidental thereto and further to amend the Insurance Act, 1938, the Life Insurance Corporation Act, 1956 and the General Insurance Business (Nationalisation) Act, 1972.

The Statement of Objects and Reasons of the Act provides that the insurance industry requires a high degree of regulation. The Insurance Act, 1938 provided for the institution of the Controller of Insurance to act as a strong and powerful supervisory and regulatory authority with powers to direct, advise, caution, prohibit, investigate, inspect, prosecute, search, seize, amalgamate, authorise, register and liquidate insurance companies. However, after the nationalisation of Life Insurance in 1956 and the General Insurance in 1972, the role of Controller of Insurance diminished in significance over a period of time.

3.1 Constitution of the Authority

Section 2(b) of the IRDA Act, 1999 defines the Authority as the Insurance Regulatory and Development Authority established under Section 3 of the Act. The Section 3 lays down the procedure for establishing the Authority. It is established by a notification by the Central Government in the *Official Gazettee*. The date of operation of the Authority is also notified by the Central Government by a notification. The other important characteristics of the Authority are as follows:

- It is a body corporate with perpetual succession and common seal.
- It has the powers to acquire, hold and dispose the property in its name. The property may be a movable or immovable.
- It has the powers to enter into contract in its name.
- It can sue the parties and it can be sued by the parties.
- The Central Government by notification decides the principal place of office of the Authority and the Authority has the powers to open branches or other offices as required by it.
- It consists of a Chairperson, not more than five wholetime members, and not more than four part-time members. (S. 4).
- All the members are appointed by the Central Government by a notification.
- The Chairperson and members are appointed from the person of ability, integrity having the standing and experience or knowledge in life insurance or general insurance, actuarial science, finance, economics, law, accountancy, administration or any other discipline which is useful for the Authority, and preferably, the Chairperson and one of the whole time members should be experienced persons or have the knowledge in the life insurance or the general insurance or actuarial science. (S. 4).
- The term of the office of the Chairperson and the wholetime members of five years and the part-time members will hold office for a period not more than the five years from the date of joining the office.
- The Chairperson will be in the office till the attains the age of sixty five years and the whole time member will be in the office till he attains the age of sixty two years (S. 5).
- The Chairperson or the whole time member or part-time member can relinquish the office by giving a notice of three months to the Central Government.
- The Central Government can remove the Chairperson, wholetime member or the part-time member for the reasons of they become insolvent, physically or mentally incapable of performing duties, convicted for the moral turpitude, has acquired the financial or other interest in the insurance business, or the position of the member or the Chairperson is detrimental to the interest of the insurance or public or the policyholders. (S. 6)
- The Central Government, before removing a person from the office, has to give opportunity to the member to explain the reasons and after hearing him, if not satisfied can remove a member from service giving causes of removal.
- Any defect found in the process of appointment or any irregularity of procedures or appointment of members cannot vitiate the appointment of the

member. The existence of vacancy in the body of the Authority does not affect the proceedings of the meeting of the Authority.

- The Chairperson or the members should not take any employment at least for a period of two years after they leave their positions. Under special circumstances, they can hold any office with the previous approval of the Central Government (S. 8).
- The salaries, allowance and other remunerations will be paid to the Chairperson and members as per the provisions laid down by the Central Government. The allowances and other service conditions will be prescribed by a notification.

3.2 Duties, Powers and Functions of the Authority

Duties

- The primary duty of the IRDA is to regulate, promote and ensure orderly growth and conduct of the insurance business and reinsurance business (S.14).
- It has to maintain proper accounts and other relevant records, prepare annual statements of accounts in such form as may be prescribed by the Central Government in consultation with the CAG.
- It has to comply with the directions of the Central Government and CAG will arrange the audit of the accounts and rectify any defects pointed by the audit conducted by it.
- The Authority has to submit the audited balance sheet and other financial statements to the Central Government and the Government will lay the reports before the houses of the Parliament.
- The Authority has to submit all the financial statements to the Central Government within nine months from the completion of the relevant financial year.
- It has the duty to scrutinise all existing and new insurance products, rates charged, terms and conditions offered and act in best interest of consumers.
- The authority is duty bound to follow the directions issued by the Central Government and report the outcome of the directions.
- Authority has the general duty to protect the interest of policyholders in matters concerning assignment, nomination, settlement of insurance claim, surrenders etc., and other terms and conditions of contract of insurance.

Powers

- The Authority has the general supervisory power of insurance industry and it has the administrative powers.

- Powers to appoint the staff and officers required to conduct the business of the Authority smoothly.
- Authority can even delegate some general or special powers by an order in writing to the Chairperson or the Members of the Authority along with conditions if it feels it as necessary.
- Power to constitute committees of the members and delegate the powers to the committee.
- Power to hold and acquire movable or immovable property.
- Power to issue a certificate of registration, renew, modify, withdraw, suspend or cancel such registration to the insurer.
- Power to prepare a code of conduct to the agents, surveyors and loss assessors and other intermediaries associated with insurance business.
- Power to levy fees and other charges for carrying out the purposes of this Act.
- Power to call information from insurers inspect accounts and other documents, conduct enquiries and investigate, including the audit of the insurers, intermediaries' and other organizations connected with the insurance business.
- It has the power to regulate the margin of solvency and investment of funds by insurance companies.
- Power to exercise the powers sanctioned by other insurance laws of the country or by other notifications issued by the Central Government from time to time.
- It has the powers to make regulations with the consultancy of Insurance Advisory Committee in the field of finalizing the service conditions of the members regarding the meeting and transactions to be carried out by the Advisory committee in promoting the insurance business.

Functions

- Promoting and regulating the professional organizations connected with the insurance and reinsurance business.
- Promoting efficiency in the conduct of insurance business in India.
- To act as adjudicator in the settlement of disputes between the insurers, intermediaries of the insurers.
- To act as supervisory authority and regulate the functioning of Tariff Advisory Committee and various insurance companies.
- To control and regulate the rates, advantages, terms and conditions that may be offered by insurers in respect of general insurances, which are not controlled by the Tariff Advisory Committee (Non-Tariff Products).
- To formulate the regulations concerning insurance in rural and social sectors.

Other Provisions

The Central Government has the powers under the Act to direct the Authority and grant funds under the head with sanction of the Parliament. The fund so constituted is called the Insurance Regulatory and Development Fund. This fund can be used to meet the expenses of the salaries, allowances and other remuneration of the members, officers and other employees of the Authority and to meet all other expenses required to discharge the duties and functions of the Authority. Registration fees, application fees from insurers and other intermediaries are also credited to the fund. A credit is also received u/S 7 of the Insurance Act, 1938.

The Central Government under the Act has the power to g ve directions to the Authority on the questions of policy of insurance business. If the Central Government finds that the Authority is not able to discharge the functions or perform the duties prescribed under the provisions of this Act or the Authority has defaulted in complying with the directions of the Central Government or the provisions of the Act, the financial position of the Authority is under deterrent conditions and if the Central Government feels that the Authority is working against the interest of public, can supercede the Authority and exercise its powers. This it may do by giving a notice with reasons and the authority may continue to act accordingly for a period not exceeding six months. Authority has to submit report of action taken to the Parliament. The Central Government has the power to make following rules in relation to the authority :

1. The format of annual statement of accounts of the authority form and manner of submission of returns and statements and particulars are to be furnished.
2. Rules concerning the fixation of remunerations and service conditions of the staff, officers, members of the Authority.
3. To fix the allowances payable to part-time members of the Authority.
4. Any matter as may be required for by Insurance Advisory Committee.

The Act empowers the IRDA to appoint a committee by notification, to provide the advice on various insurance matters to the Authority called as Insurance Advisory Committee (IAC). This committee is established by a notification by the Authority. IAC contains not more than 25 members excluding *ex-officio* members to represent the various interests of commerce, industry, transport, agriculture, consumer forums, surveyors, agents, intermediaries, organizations engaged in safety and loss prevention, research bodies and employees association of insurance companies and intermediaries. The chairperson and the members of the authority are the *ex-officio* members the Insurance Advisory Committee. The objects of the automatically IAC shall be to advise the Authority on matters relating to the framing the regulations in relation to service conditions of the staff, conducting the transactions of various meetings and deciding the powers to be delegated etc., and any other matters required by the Authority.

The Regulatory Authority is under a duty to submit all the rules framed by it for the approval of Parliament. The provisions of other insurance laws are also applicable for the Authority, which are not in contradiction with the policy of public interest.

IRDA is also generally subject to various insurance and other laws in the best interest of the public.

IRDA Regulations

Various regulations have been framed by IRDA since its inception. These relate to licencing of insurers, regulation of intermediaries, reporting requirements, business practices, etc.

Regulations Framed under Insurance Regulatory and Development Authority Act, 1999 and the Insurance (Amendment) Act, 2002

1. Insurance Regulatory and Development Authority (Actuarial Report and Abstract) Regulations, 2000.
2. Insurance Regulatory and Development Authority (Obligation of Insure of Rural or Social Sectors) Regulation, 2000.
3. Insurance Regulatory and Development Authority (Insurance Advertisements and Disclosure) Regulations, 2000.
4. Insurance Regulatory and Development Authority (Licensing of Insurance Agents) Regulations, 2000.
5. Insurance Regulatory and Development Authority (General Insurance — Reinsurance) Regulations, 2000.
6. Insurance Regulatory and Development Authority (Appointed Actuary) Regulations, 2000.
7. Insurance Regulatory and Development Authority (Assets, Liabilities and Solvency Margin of Insurers) Regulations, 2000.
8. Insurance Regulatory and Development Authority (Meetings) Regulations, 2000.
9. Insurance Regulatory and Development Authority (Registration of Indian Insurance Companies) Regulations, 2000.
10. Insurance Advisory Committee (Meetings) Regulations, 2000.
11. Insurance Regulatory and Development Authority (Investment) Regulations, 2000.
12. Insurance Regulatory and Development Authority (Preparation of Financial Statements and Auditor's Report of Insurance Companies) Regulations, 2002.
13. Insurance Regulatory and Development Authority (Licensing, Professional Requirements and Code of Conduct) Regulations, 2000.
14. Insurance Regulatory and Development Authority (Conditions of Service of Officers and Other Employees) Regulations, 2000.

15. Insurance Regulatory and Development Authority (Life Insurance — Reinsurance) Regulations, 2000.

16. Insurance Regulatory and Development Authority (Investment) (Amendment) Regulations, 2001.

17. Insurance Regulatory and Development Authority (Third Party Administrators — Health Services) Regulations, 2001.

18. Insurance Regulatory and Development Authority (Re-insurance Advisory Committee) Regulations, 2001.

19. Insurance Regulatory and Development Authority (Protection of Policy Holders' Interest) Regulations, 2002.

20. Insurance Regulatory and Development Authority (Investment) (Amendment) Regulations, 2002.

21. Insurance Regulatory and Development Authority (Assets, Liabilities and Solvency Margin of Insurers) (Amendment) Regulations, 2002.

22. Insurance Regulatory and Development Authority (Licensing of Corporate Agents) Regulations, 2002.

23. Insurance Regulatory and Development Authority (Licensing of Insurance Agents) (Amendment) Regulations, 2002.

24. Insurance Regulatory and Development Authority (Insurance Bookers) Regulations, 2002.

25. Insurance Regulatory and Development Authority (Manner of Payment of Premium) Regulations, 2002.

26. Insurance Regulatory and Development Authority (Obligations of Insurers to Rural or Social Sectors) (Amendment) Regulations, 2002.

27. Insurance Regulatory and Development Authority (Protection of Policyholders Interest) (Amendment) Regulations, 2002.

Schedules to the IRDA Act

Amendments to the Insurance ACT, 1938
(4 of 1938)

1. In the Act, except in clause (5B) of Section 2 and Section 2B, for "Controller" wherever it occurs, substitute "Authority" and such consequential changes as the rules of grammar may require shall also be made.

2. In Sections 27, 27A, 27B, 31, 32A, 40A, 48B, 64F, 64G, 64-I, 64J, 64L, 64R, 64UC, 64UM, 113 and 115, for "Central Government" wherever they occur, substitute "Authority".

3. Section 2, :

(*a*) after clause (1), insert the following :

'(IA) "Authority" means the Insurance Regulatory and Development Authority established under sub-section (1) of Section 3 of the Insurance Regulatory and Development Authority Act, 1999;';

(*b*) for clause (5B), substitute the following:

'(5B) "Controller of Insurance" means the officer appointed by the Central Government under section 2B to exercise all the powers, discharge the functions and perform the duties of the Authority under this Act or the Life Insurance Corporation Act, 1956 (31 of 1956) or the General Insurance Business (Nationalisation) Act, 1972 (57 of 1972) or the Insurance Regulatory and Development Authority Act, 1999;

(*c*) After clause (7), insert the following:

'(7A) "Indian insurance company" means any insurer being a company :

(*a*) which is formed and registered under the Companies Act, 1956 (1 of 1956);

(*b*) in which the aggregate holdings of equity shares by a foreign company, either by itself or through its subsidiary companies or its nominees, do not exceed twenty-six per cent paid-up equity capital of such Indian insurance company;

(*c*) whose sole purpose is to carry on life insurance business or general insurance business or re-insurance business.

Explanation: For the purposes of this clause, the expression "foreign company" shall have the meaning assigned to it under clause (23A) of Section 2 of the Income-tax Act, 1961 (43 of 1961).';

(*d*) in clause (14), for "Section 114", substitute "this Act".

4. After Section 2, insert the following:

"2A. Interpretation of certain words and expressions : Words and expressions used and not defined in the Life Insurance Corporation Act, 1956 (31 of 1965), the General Insurance Business (Nationalisation) Act, 1972 (57 of 1972) and the Insurance Regulatory and Development Authority Act, 1999 shall have the meanings respectively assigned to them in those Acts."

5. Section 2B, for sub-section (1), substitute the following:

"(1) If at any time, the Authority is superseded under sub-section (1) of section 19 of the Insurance Regulatory and Development Authority Act, 1999, the Central Government may, by notification in the *Official Gazette*, appoint a person to be the Controller of Insurance till such time the Authority is reconstituted under sub-section (3) of Section 19 of that Act."

6. Section 2C, in sub-section (1), after the second proviso, insert the following:'*Provided* also that no insurer other than an Indian insurance company shall begin to carry on any class of insurance business in India under this Act on or after the commencement of the Insurance Regulatory and Development Authority Act, 1999."

7. Section 3,

(*a*)In sub-section (1), after the first proviso, insert the following:

"*Provided* further that a person or insurer, as the case may be, carrying on any class of insurance business in India, on or before the commencement of the Insurance Regulatory and Development Authority Act, 1999, for which no registration certificate was necessary prior to such commencement, may continue to do so for a period of three months from such commencement or, if he had made an application for such registration within the said period of three months, till the disposal of such application:

Provided also that any certificate of registration, obtained immediately before the commencement of the Insurance Regulatory and Development Authority Act, 1999, shall be deemed to have been obtained from the Authority in accordance with the provisions of this Act."

(*b*) in sub-section (2):

(*i*) in the opening portion, for "Every application for registration shall be accompanied by-", substitute the following:

"Every application for registration shall be made in such manner as may be determined by the regulations made by the Authority and shall be accompanied by-";

(*ii*) in clause (d), for "working capital," substitute "paid-up equity capital or working capital;"

(*iii*) in clause (f), in the proviso, omit "and" occurring and the end;

(*iv*) for clause (g), substitute the following:

"(*g*) the receipt showing payment of fee as may be determined by the regulations which shall not exceed fifty thousand rupees for each class of business as may be specified by the regulations made by the Authority;

(*h*) such other documents as may be specified by the regulations made by the Authority."

(*c*) after sub-section (2A), insert:

"(2AA). The Authority shall give preference to register the applicant and grant him a certificate of registration if such applicant agrees, in the form and manner as may be specified by the regulations made by the Authority, to carry on the life insurance business or general insurance business for providing health cover to individuals or group of individuals."

(*d*) in sub-section (4),:

(*i*) in clause (f), for "of any rule or order made thereunder, or", substitute the following:

"of any rule or any regulation or order made or, any direction issued thereunder, or";

(*ii*) in clause (h), insert "or" at the end;

(*iii*) after clause (h), insert the following :

"(*i*) if the insurer makes a default in complying with any direction issued or order made, as the case may be, by the Authority under the Insurance Regulatory and Development Authority Act, 1999, or

"(*j*) if the insurer makes a default in complying with, or acts in contravention of, any requirement of the Companies Act, 1956 (1 of 1956) or the Life Insurance Corporation Act, 1956 (31 of 1956) or the General Insurance Business (Nationalisation) Act, 1972 (57 of 1972) or the Foreign Exchange Regulation Act, 1973 (46 of 1973)."

(*e*) in sub-section (5C), :

(*i*) for "clause (h)", substitute "clause(h) or clause (i) or clause (j)"

(*ii*) for "any requirement of this Act or of any rule or order made thereunder", substitute the following :

"any requirement of this Act or the Insurance Regulatory and Development Authority Act, 1999 or of any rule or any regulation, or any order made thereunder or any direction issued under those Acts";

(*f*) after sub-section (5D), insert the following :

"(5E) The Authority may, by order, suspend or cancel any registration in such manner as may be determined by the regulations made by it :

Provided that no order under this sub-section shall be made unless the person concerned has been given a reasonable opportunity of being heard."

(*g*) for sub-section (7), substitute the following :

"(7). The Authority may, on payment of such fee, not exceeding five thousand rupees, as may be determined by the regulations, issue a duplicate certificate of registration to replace a certificate lost, destroyed or mutilated, or in any other case where the Authority is of the opinion that the issue of duplicate certificate is necessary."

8. Section 3A, :

(*a*) in sub-section (1), for "the 31st day of December, 1941.", substitute the following:

"the 31st day of March, after the commencement of the Insurance Regulatory and Development Authority Act, 1999."

(*b*) in sub-section (2), :

(*i*) for "prescribed fee", substitute "fee as determined by the regulations made by the Authority";

(*ii*) for clause (i), substitute the following :

"(i) exceed one-fourth of one per cent of such premium income or rupees five crores, whichever is less,";

(*iii*) for clause (ii), substitute the following :

"(ii) be less, in any case, than fifty thousand rupees for each class of insurance business:";

(*c*) in sub-section (3), for "prescribed fee", substitute "fee as determined by the regulations made by the Authority";

(*d*) in sub-section (4), for "prescribed fee", substitute "fee as determined by the regulations made by the Authority, and". For Section 6, substitute the following:

"6.. Requirement as to capital: No insurer carrying on the business of life insurance, general insurance or re-insurance in India on or after the commencement of the Insurance Regulatory and Development Authority Act, 1999, shall be registered unless he has, :

(*i*) a paid-up equity capital of rupees one hundred crores, in case of a person carrying on the business of life insurance or general insurance; or

(*ii*) a paid-up equity capital of rupees two hundred crores, in case of a person carrying on exclusively the business as a re-insurer:

Provided that in determining the paid-up equity capital specified under clause (i) or clause (ii), the deposit to be made under Section 7 and any preliminary expenses incurred in the formation and registration of the company shall be excluded:

Provided further that an insurer carrying on business of life insurance, general insurance or re-insurance in India before the commencement of the Insurance Regulatory and Development Authority Act, 1999 and who is required to be registered under this Act, shall have a paid-up equity capital in accordance with clause (i) and clause (ii), as the case may be, within six months of the commencement of that Act."

10. Section 6A,:

(*a*) in sub-section (4), in clause (b),:

(*i*) in sub-clause (i), omit "and" occurring at the end;

(*ii*) in sub-clause (ii), for "sanction of the Central Government has been obtained to the transfer.", substitute "approval of the Authority has been obtained to the transfer;"

(*iii*) after sub-clause (ii), insert the following:

'(iii) where, the nominal value of the shares intended to be transferred by any individual, firm, group, constituents of a group, or body corporate under the same management, jointly or severally exceeds one per cent of the paid-up equity capital of the insurer, unless the previous approval of the Authority has been obtained for the transfer.

Explanation: For the purposes of this sub-clause, the expressions "group" and "same management" shall have the same meanings respectively assigned to them in the Monopolies and Restrictive Trade Practices Act, 1969 (54 of 1969).

(*b*) in sub-section (11),

(*i*) for "Explanation 1.", substitute "Explanation";

(*ii*) omit Explanation 2.

11. After Section 6A, insert the following :

"6AA. Manner of divesting excess shareholding by promoter in certain cases. (1) No promoter shall at any time hold more than twenty-six per cent or such other percentage as may be prescribed, of the paid-up equity capital in an Indian insurance company.

Provided that in a case where an Indian insurance company begins the business of life insurance, general insurance or re-insurance in which the promoters hold more than twenty-six per cent of the paid-up equity capital or such other excess percentage as may be prescribed, the promoters shall divest in a phased manner the share capital in excess of the twenty-six per cent of the paid-up equity capital or such excess paid-up equity capital as may be prescribed, after a period of ten years from the date of the commencement of the said business by such Indian insurance company or within such period as may be prescribed by the Central Government.

Explanation: For the removal of doubts, it is hereby declared that nothing contained in the proviso shall apply to the promoters being foreign company, referred to in sub-clause (b) of clause (7A) of Section 2.

(2) The manner and procedure for divesting the excess share capital under sub-section (1) shall be specified by the regulations made by the Authority."

12. Section 7,:

(*a*) in sub-section (1),-

(*i*) omit "not being an insurer specified in sub-clause (c) of clause (9) of Section 2";

(*ii*) for clauses (a) and (b), substitute the following :

"(*a*) in the case of life insurance business, a sum equivalent to one per cent of his total gross premium written in India in any financial year commencing after the 31st day of March, 2000, not exceeding rupees ten crores;

(*b*) in the case of general insurance business, a sum equivalent to three per cent of his total gross premium written in India, in any financial year commencing after the 31st day of March, 2000, not exceeding rupees ten crores;

(*c*) in the case of re-insurance business, a sum of rupees twenty crores;";

(*d*) omit sub-sections (1A), (1B), (1C), (1D) and (1E).

13. Section 11, :

(*a*) in sub-section (1), for "calendar year", substitute "financial year";

(*b*) after sub-section (1), insert the following :

"(1A) Notwithstanding anything contained in sub-section (1), every insurer, on or after the commencement of the Insurance Regulatory and Development Authority Act, 1999, in respect of insurance business transacted by him and in respect of his shareholders' funds, shall at the expiration of each financial year, prepare with reference to that year, a balance-sheet, a profit and loss account, a separate account of receipts and payments, a revenue account in accordance with the regulations made by the Authority.

(1B) Every insurer shall keep separate accounts relating to funds of shareholders and policy-holders."

14. Section 13, :

(*a*) in sub-section (1), :

(*i*) for "once at least in every three years", substitute 'every year";

(*ii*) in the first proviso, for "not later than four years" substitute "not later than two years";

iii) after the second proviso, insert the following :

"*Provided* also that for an insurer carrying on life insurance business in India immediately before the commencement of the Insurance Regulatory and Development Authority Act, 1999, the last date as at which the first investigation after such commencement should be caused by an actuary, shall be the 31st day of March, 2001";

(*iv*) after the third proviso, insert the following :

"*Provided* also that every insurer on or after the commencement of the Insurance Regulatory and Development Authority Act, 1999, shall cause an abstract of the report of actuary to be made in the manner specified by the regulations made by the Authority.";

(*b*) in sub-section (4), after the proviso, insert the following :

"*Provided* further that the statement referred to in sub-section (4) shall be appended in the form and in the manner specified by the regulations made by the Authority."

15. After Section 27B, insert the following :

"27C. *Prohibition of investment of funds outside India :* No insurer shall directly or indirectly invest outside India the funds of the policy-holders.

27D. *Manner and conditions of investment :*

(1) Without prejudice to anything contained in Sections 27, 27A and 27B, the Authority may, in the interests of the policy-holders, specify by the regulations

made by it, the time, manner and other conditions of investment of assets to be held by an insurer for the purposes of this Act.

(2) The Authority may give specific directions for the time, manner and other conditions subject to which the funds of policy holders shall be invested in the infrastructure and social sector as may be specified by regulations made by the Authority and such regulations shall apply uniformly to all the insurers carrying on the business of life insurance, general insurance, or re-insurance in India on or after the commencement of the Insurance Regulatory and Development Authority Act, 1999.

(3) The Authority may, after taking into account the nature of business and to protect the interests of the policy-holders, issue to an insurer the directions relating to the time, manner and other conditions of investment of assets to be held by him :

Provided that no direction under this sub-section shall be issued unless the insurer concerned has been given a reasonable opportunity of being heard."

16. Section 28A, in sub-section (1), for "31st day of December", substitute "31st day of March".

17. Section 28B, in sub-section (1), for "31st day of December", substitute "31st day of March".

18. Section 31B, :

(a) in sub-section (1), for "Central Government" at both the places where they occur, substitute "Authority";

(*b*) in sub-section (2), for "a statement in the prescribed from", substitute "a statement, in the form specified by the regulations made by the Authority";

(*c*) after sub-section (3), insert the following :

"(4) Every direction under this section shall be issued by an order made by the Authority:

Provided that no order under this section shall be made unless the person concerned has been given an opportunity of being heard."

19. After Section 32A, insert the following :

"32B. Insurance business in rural or social sector : Every insurer shall, after the commencement of the Insurance Regulatory and Development Authority Act, 1999, undertake such percentages of life insurance business and general insurance business in the rural or social sector, as may be specified, in the *Official Gazette* by the Authority, in this behalf.

32C. Obligations of insurer in respect of rural or unorganised sector and backward classes. : Every insurer shall, after the commencement of the Insurance Regulatory and Development Authority Act, 1999 discharge the obligations specified under Section 32B to provided life insurance or general insurance policies to the persons residing in the rural sector, workers in the unorganised or informal sector or for economically vulnerable or backward classes of the society and other categories of persons as may be specified by regulations made by the Authority and such insurance policies shall include insurance for crops."

20. For Section 33, substitute the following :

Investigation : 33. Power of investigation and inspection by Authority : (1) The Authority may, at any time, by order in writing, direct any person (hereafter in this section referred to as "Investigating Authority") specified in the order to investigate the affairs of any insurer and to report to the Authority on any investigation made by such Investigating Authority :

Provided that the Investigating Authority may, wherever necessary, employ any auditor or actuary or both for the purpose of assisting him in any investigation under this section.

(2) Notwithstanding anything to the contrary contained in Section 235 of the time, and shall, on being directed to do so by the Authority, cause an inspection to be made by one or more of his officers of any insurer and his books and account and the Investigating Authority shall supply to the insurer a copy of this report on such inspection.

(3) It shall be the duty of every manager, managing director or other officer of the insurer to produce before the Investigating Authority directed to make the investigation under sub-section (1), or inspection under sub-section (2), all such books of account, registers and other documents in his custody or power and to furnish him with any statement and information relating to the affairs of the insurer as the said Investigating Authority may require of him within such time as the said Investigating Authority may specify.

(4) Any Investigating Authority, directed to make an investigation under sub-section (1), or inspection under sub-section (2), may examine on oath, any manager, managing director or other officer of the insurer in relation to his business and may administer oaths accordingly.

(5) The Investigating Authority shall, if he has been directed by the Authority to cause an inspection to be made, and may, in any other case, report to the Authority on any inspection made under this section.

(6) On receipt of any report under sub-section (1) or sub-section (5), the Authority may, after giving such opportunity to the insurer to make a representation in connection with the report as, in the opinion of the Authority, seems reasonable, by order in writing :

(*a*) require the insurer, to take such action in respect of any matter arising out of the report as the Authority may think fit; or

(*b*) cancel the registration of the insurer; or

(*c*) direct any person to apply to the court for the winding up of the insurer,

if a company, whether the registration of the insurer has been cancelled under clause (b) or not.

(7) The Authority may, after giving reasonable notice to the insurer, publish the report submitted by the Investigating Authority under sub-section (5) or such portion thereof as may appear to it, to be necessary.

(8) The Authority may by the regulations made by it specify the minimum information to be maintained by insurers in their books, the manner in which such information shall be maintained, the checks and other verifications to be adopted by insurers in that connection and all other matters incidental thereto as are, in its opinion, necessary to enable the Investigating Authority to discharge satisfactorily his functions under this section.

Explanation : For the purposes of this section, the expression "insurer" shall include in the case of an insurer incorporated in India :

(*a*) all its subsidiaries formed for the purpose of carrying on the business of insurance exclusively outside India; and

(*b*) all its branches whether situated in India or outside India.

(9) No order made under this section other than an order made under clause (b) of sub-section (6) shall be capable of being called in question in any court.

(10) All expenses of, and incidental to, any investigation made under this section shall be defrayed by the insurer, shall have priority over that debts due from the insurer and shall be recoverable as an arrear of land revenue.'

21. Section 33A, omit "Central Government or the" :

22. Section 34H, :

(*a*) in sub-section (1), :

(*i*) for "Controller", substitute "Chairperson of the Authority";

(*ii*) for "an Assistant Controller of Insurance", substitute "an officer authorised by the Authority";

(*b*) in sub-sections (5) and (7) for "Controller" wherever it occurs, substitute "Chairperson of the Authority".

23. Section 35 :

(*a*) in sub-section (1), for "sanctioned by the Controller", substitute "approved by the Authority";

(*b*) in sub-section (3), :

(*i*) in the first paragraph, for "to sanction any such scheme substitute "to approve any such scheme";

(*ii*) in the second paragraph for "the amalgamation or transfer if sanctioned", substitute "the amalgamation or transfer if approved".

24. Section 36,

(*a*) in sub-section (1) for "may sanction the arrangement", substitute "may approve the arrangement";

(*b*) in sub-section (2), :

(*i*) for "the insurers concerned in the amalgamation, the Controller may sanction", substitute "the insurers concerned in the amalgamation, the Authority may approve";

(*ii*) for "contracts as sanctioned by the Controller", substitute "contracts as approved by the Authority".

25. Section 37, in clause (c) for "scheme sanctioned", substitute "scheme approved".

26. In Section 40A, in sub-section (3), for the portion beginning with the words "an amount exceeding" and ending with the words "ten per cent of the premium payable on the policy", substitute "an amount not exceeding fifteen per cent of the premium payable on the policy where the policy relates to fire or marine insurance or miscellaneous insurance."

27. Section 42, :

(*a*) for sub-section (1), substitute the following :

"(1) The Authority or an officer authorised by it in this behalf shall, in the manner determined by the regulations made by it and on payment of the fee determined by the regulations, which shall not be more than two hundred and fifty rupees, issue to any person making an application in the manner determined by the regulations, a licence to act as an insurance agent for the purpose of soliciting or procuring insurance business.

(*i*) in the case of an individual, he does not suffer from any of the disqualifications mentioned in sub-section (4); and

(*ii*) in the case of a company or firm, any of its directors or partners does not suffer from any of the said disqualifications.

Provided further that any licence issued immediately before the commencement of the Insurance Regulatory and Development Authority Act, 1999 shall be deemed to have been issued in accordance with the regulations which provide for such licence."

(*b*) for sub-section (3) substitute the following :

"(3) A licence issued under this section, after the date of the commencement of the Insurance Regulatory and Development Authority Act, 1999, shall remain in force for a period of three years only from the date of issue, but shall, if the applicant, being an individual does not, or being a company or firm, any of its directors or partners does not, suffer from any of the disqualifications mentioned in clauses (b), (c), (d), (e) and (f) of sub-section (4) and the application for renewal of licence reaches the issuing authority at least thirty days before the date in which the licence ceases to remain in force, be renewed for a period of three years at any one time on payment of the fee determined by the regulations made by the Authority, which shall not be more than rupees two hundred and fifty, and additional fee of an amount determined by the regulations not exceeding rupees one hundred by way of penalty, if the application for renewal of the licence does not reach the issued authority at least thirty days before the date on which the licence ceases to remain in force";

(*c*) in sub-section (3A), for the proviso, substitute the following:

"*Provided* that the Authority may, if satisfied that undue hardship would be caused otherwise, accept any application in contravention of this sub-section of payment by the applicant of a penalty of seven hundred and fifty rupees";

(*d*) in sub-section (4), after clause (*d*) insert the following:

"(*e*) that he does not possess the requisite qualifications and practical training for a period not exceeding twelve months, as may be specified by the regulations made by the Authority in this behalf;

(*f*) that he has not passed such examination as may be specified by the regulations made by the Authority in this behalf:

Provided that a person who had been issued a licence under sub-section (1) of this section or sub-section (1) of Section 64UM shall not be required to possess the requisite qualifications, practical training and pass such examination as required by clauses (*e*) and (*f*);

(*g*) that he violates the code of conduct as may be specified by the regulations made by the Authority.";

(*e*) for sub-section (6), substitute the following :

"(6) The Authority may issue a duplicate licence to replace a licence lost, destroyed or mutilated, on payment of such fee not exceeding rupees fifty as may be determined by the regulations";

(*f*) in sub-section (7),

(*i*) for "fifty rupees", substitute "five hundred rupees";

(*ii*) for "one hundred rupees", substitute "one thousand rupees";

(*g*) in sub-section (8), for "fifty rupees", substitute "five thousand rupees".

28. Section 42A, in sub-section (1), :

(*a*) for "Controller or an officer authorised by him" substitute" Authority or an officer authorised by it";

(*b*) for "an application to him", substitute "an application to it".

29. After Section 42C, insert the following:

"42D. Issue of licence to intermediary or insurance intermediary.

(1) The Authority or an officer authorised by it in this behalf shall, in the manner determined by the regulations made by the Authority and on payment of the fees determined by the regulations made by the Authority, issue to any

person making an application in the manner determinec by the regulations, and not suffering from any of the disqualifications herein mentioned, a licence to act as an intermediary or an insurance intermediary under this Act :

Provided that,:

(*a*) in the case of an individual, he does not suffer from any of the disqualifications mentioned in sub-section (4) of Section 42, or

(*b*) in the case of a company or firm, any of its directors or partners does not suffer from any of the said disqualifications.

(2) A licence issued under this section shall entitle the holder thereof to act as an intermediary or insurance intermediary.

(3) A licence issued under this section shall remain in force for a period of three years only from the date of issue, but shall, if the applicant being an individual does not, or being a company or firm any of its directors cr partners does not suffer from any of the disqualifications mentioned in clauses (b), (c), (d), (e) and (f) of sub-section (4) of Section 42, and the application for renewal of licence reaches the issuing authority at least thirty days before the date on which the licence ceases to remain in force, be renewed for a period of three years at any one time on payment of the fee, determined by the regulations made by the Authority and additional fee for an amount determined by the regulations, not exceeding one hundred rupees by way of penalty, if the application for renewal of the licence does not reach the issuing authority at least thirty days before the date on which the licence ceases to remain in force.

(4) no application for the renewal of a licence under this section shall be entertained if the application does not reach the issuing authority before the licence ceases to remain in force:

Provided that the Authority may, if satisfied that undue hardship would be caused otherwise, accept any application in contravention of this sub-section on payment by the applicant of a penalty of seven hundred and fifty rupees.

(5) The disqualifications above referred to shall be the following :

(*a*) that the person is a minor;

(*b*) that he is found to be of unsound mind by a court of competent jurisdiction;

(*c*) that he has been found guilty of criminal misappropriation or criminal breach of trust or cheating or forgery or an abetment of or attempt to commit any such office by a court of competent jur sdiction:

Provided that, where at least five years have elapsed s nce the completion of the sentence imposed on any person in respect of any such offence, the Authority shall ordinarily declare in respect of such person that his conviction shall cease to operate as a disqualification under this clause;

(*d*) that in the course of any judicial proceedings relating to any policy of insurance of the winding up of an insurance company or in the course of an investigation of the affairs of an insurer it has been found that he has been guilty of or has knowingly participated in or connived at any fraud dishonestly or misrepresentation against an insurer or an insured;

(*e*) that he does not possess the requisite qualifications and practical training for a period not exceeding twelve months, as may be specified by the regulations made by the Authority in this behalf;

(*f*) that he has not passed such examinations as may be specified by the regulations made by the Authority in this behalf;

(*g*) that he violates the code of conduct as may be specified by the regulations made by the Authority.

(6) If it be found that an intermediary or an insurance intermediary suffers from any of the foregoing disqualifications, without prejudice to any other penalty to which he may be liable, the Authority shall, and if the intermediary or an insurance intermediary has knowingly contravened any provision of this Act may cancel the licence issued to the intermediary or insurance intermediary under this section.

(7) The Authority may issue a duplicate licence to replace a licence lost, destroyed or mutilated, on payment of such fee, as may be determined by the regulations made by the Authority.

(8) Any person who acts as an intermediary or an insurance intermediary without holding a licence issued under this section to act as such, shall be punishable with fine, and any insurer or any person who appoints as an intermediary or an insurance intermediary or any person not licensed to act as such or transacts any insurance business in India through any such person, shall be punishable with fine.

(9) Where the person contravening sub-section (8) is a company or a firm, then, without prejudice to any other proceedings which may be taken against the company or firm, every director, manager, secretary or other officer of the company, and every partner of the firm who is knowingly a party to such contravention shall be punishable with fine.".

30.Section 64UA, in sub-section (1), in sub-clause(a), for "Controller or Insurance", substitute "Chairperson of the Authority".

31. Section 64UB:

(*a*) for sub-section (1), substitute the following:

"(1) The Authority may, by notification in the *Official Gazette*, make regulations to carry out the purposes of this Part";

(*b*) in sub-section (2), for "rules", substitute "regulations";

(*c*) in sub-section (3) for "Central Government" at both the places where it occur, substitute "Authority";

(*d*) in sub-section (5), for "Controller of Insurance", substitute "Chairperson of the Authority".

32. Section 64UC in sub-section (1), in proviso, for "the controller may, with the previous approval of the Central Government", substitute "the Authority may."

33. Section 64UD, after sub-section (1), insert the following:

"*Provided* that the Chairperson of the Authority shall become the Chairman of the Advisory Committee with effect from the commencement of the Insurance Regulatory and Development Authority Act, 1999 and function as such, and any Chairman of the Tariff Committee holding office immediately before such commencement shall cease to be the Chairman."

34. Section 64UJ, in sub-section (5), for "Central Govemment", wherever it occurs, substitute "Authority".

35. Section 64UM:

(*a*) in sub-section (1),:

(*i*) in paragraph (B), after "the Insurance (Amendment) Act, 1968", insert "but before the commencement of the Insurance Regulatory and Development Authority Act, 1999";

(*ii*) after paragraph (B), insert the following:

"(BA) Every person who intends to act as a surveyor or loss assessor after the expiry of a period of one year from the commencement of the Insurance Regulatory and Development Authority Act, 1999, shall make an application to the Authority within such time, in such manner and on payment of such fee as may be determined by the regulations made by the Authority:

Provided that any licence issued immediately before the commencement of the Insurance Regulatory and Development Authority Act, 1999 shall be deemed to have been issued in accordance with the regulations providing for such licence";

(*iii*) in paragraph (C), for "as may be prescribed", substitute "as may be determined by the regulations";

(*iv*) in paragraph (D), in clause (*i*):

(A) for item (*a*), substitute the following:

"(*a*) has been in practice as a surveyor or loss assessor on the date of commencement of the Insurance Regulatory and Development Authority Act, 1999, or";

(B) in item (*f*), for "prescribed ", substitute, "specified by the regulations made by the Authority";

(*b*) after sub-section (1), insert:

"(1A) Every surveyor and loss assessor shall comply with the code of conduct in respect of their duties, responsibilities and other professional requirements as may be specified by the regulations made by the Authority."

36. Section 64V:

(*a*) in sub-section (1),:

(*i*) in clause (i), after sub-clause (g), insert the following:

"(h) such other asset or assets as may be specified by the regulations made in this behalf";

(*ii*) in clause (ii):

(A) in sub-clause (b), in items (i) and (ii), for "40 per cent", substitute "50 per cent";

(B) after sub-clause (f), insert the following:

"(g) such other liability which may be made in this behalf to be included for the purpose of clause (ii)";

(*b*) for sub-section (2), substitute the following:

"(2) Every insurer shall furnish to the Authority with his returns under section 15 or section 16, as the case may be, a statement certified by an auditor approved by the Authority in respect of general insurance business, or an actuary approved by the Authority in respect of life insurance business, as the case may be, of his assets and liabilities assessed in the manner required by this section as on the 31st day of March of the preceding year.

(3) Every insurer shall value his assets and liabilities in the manner required by this section and in accordance with the regulations which may be made by the Authority in this behalf."

37. Section 64VA:

(*a*) in sub-section (1), for "at all times", substitute "at all times before the commencement of the Insurance Regulatory and Development Authority Act, 1999";

(*b*) after sub-section (1), insert the following:

'(1A) Every insurer shall, at all times, on or after the commencement of the Insurance Regulatory and Development Authority Act, 1999, maintain an excess of the value of his assets over the amount of his liabilities of not less than the amount arrived at as follows (hereinafter referred to in this section as the "required solvency margin"), namely:

(*i*) in the case of an insurer carrying on life insurance business, the required solvency margin shall be the higher of the following amounts:

(*a*) fifty crores of rupees (one hundred crores of rupees in case of re-insurers); or (*b*) the aggregate sums of the results arrived at in items (I) and (II) stated below:

(I) the aggregate of the results arrived at by applying the calculation described in item (A) below (Step - I) and the calculation described in item (B) below (Step II):

(A) for Step I:

(A.1) there shall be taken, a sum equal to a percentage determined by the regulations not exceeding five per cent of the mathematical reserves for direct business and re-insurance acceptances without any deduction for re-insurance cessions.

(A.2) the amount of mathematical reserves at the end of the preceding financial year after the deduction of re-insurance cessions shall be expressed as a percentage of the amount of those mathematical reserves before any such deduction; and

(A.3) the sum mentioned in item (A.1) above shall be multiplied:

(A.3.1) where the percentage arrived at under item (A.2) above is greater than eighty-five per cent (or in the case of a re-insurer carrying on exclusive re-insurance business, fifty per cent), by that greater percentage; and

(A.3.2) in any other case, by eighty-five per cent (or in the case of re-insurer carrying on exclusive re-insurance business, by fifty per cent);

(B) for Step II:

(B.1) there shall be taken, a sum equal to a percentage determined by the regulations made by the Authority not exceeding one per cent of the sum at risk for the policies on which the sum at risk is not a negative figure, and

(B.2) the amount of sum at risk at the end of the preceding financial year for policies on which the sum at risk is not a negative figure after the deduction of re-insurance cession shall be expressed as a percentage of the amount of that sum at risk before any such deduction, and

(B.3) the sum arrived at under item (B.1) above shall be multiplied:

(B.3.1) where the percentage arrived at under item (B.3.2) above is greater than fifty per cent, by that greater percentage; and

(B.3.2) in any other case, by fifty per cent,

(*i*) a percentage determined by the regulations made by the Authority of the value of assets determined in accordance with the provisions of section 64V;

(*ii*) in the case of an insurer carrying on general insurance business, the required solvency margin, shall be the highest of the following amounts:

(*a*) fifty crores of rupees (one hundred crores of rupees in case of re-insurer); or

(*b*) a sum equivalent to twenty per cent of net premium income; or

(*c*) a sum equivalent to thirty per cent of net incurred claims,

Subject to credit for re-insurance in computing net premiums and net incurred claims being actual but a percentage, determined by the regulations not exceeding fifty per cent:

Provided that if in respect of any insurer, the Authority is satisfied that either by reason of an unfavourable claim experience or because of sharp increase in the volume of the business, or for any other reason, compliance with the provisions of this sub-section would cause undue hardship to the insurer, the Authority may direct, for such period and subject to such conditions, such solvency margin not being less than the lower of the amount mentioned in sub-clause (i) or sub-clause (ii) above, as the case may be.

Explanation: For the purposes of this sub-section, the expressions :

(*i*) "mathematical reserves" means the provision made by an insurer to cover liabilities (excluding liabilities which have fallen due and liabilities arising from the deposit back arrangement in relation to any policy whereby an amount is deposited by re-insurer with the cedant) arising under or in connection with policies or contracts for life insurance business. Mathematical reserves also include specific provision for adverse deviations of the bases, such as mortality and morbidity rates, interest rates, and expense rates, and any explicit provisions made, in the valuation of liabilities, in accordance with the regulations made by the Authority for this purpose;

(*ii*) "net incurred claims" means the average of the net incurred claims during the specified period of not exceeding three preceding financial years;

(*iii*) "sum at risk" in relation to a life insurance policy, means a sum which is :

(*a*) in any case in which an amount is payable inconsequence of death other than a case falling within sub-clause (b) below, the amount payable on death, and

(*b*) in any case in which the benefit under the policy in question consist of the making, in consequence of death, of the payments of annuity, payment of sum by instalments or any other kind of periodic payments, the present value of that benefit, less in either case the mathematical reserves in respect of the relevant policies."

(*c*) after sub-section (2), insert the following :

"(2A) If, at any time an insurer does not maintain the required solvency margin in accordance with the provisions of this section, he shall, in accordance with the provisions of this section, he shall, in accordance with the directions issued by the Authority, submit a financial plan, indicating a plan of action to correct the deficiency to the Authority within a specified period not exceeding three months.

(2B) An insurer who has submitted a plan under sub-section (2A) to the Authority shall propose modifications to the plan if the Authority considers it inadequate, and shall give effect to any plan accepted by the Authority as adequate.

(2C) An insurer who does not comply with the provisions of sub-section (2A) shall be deemed to be insolvent and may be wound up by the Court";

(*d*) after sub-section (6); insert the following :

"(7) Every insurer shall furnish to the Authority his returns under section 15 or section 16, as the case may be, in case of life insurance business a statement certified by an actuary approved by the authority, and in case of general insurance business a statement certified by an auditor approved by the Authority, of the required solvency margin maintained by the insurer in the manner required by sub-section (1A)."

38. Section 70 in sub-section (1), for "the Controller a certificate of registration", substitute "the Authority, before the date of commencement of the Insurance Regulatory and Development Authority Act, 1999, a certificate of registration."

39. Section 95, in sub-section (1), for "In this Part -", substitute "In this part, before the date of commencement of the Insurance Regulatory and Development Act, 1999, ".

40. Section 101A :

(*a*) in sub-section (1), for "the Central Government" substitute "the Authority, with the previous approval of the Central Government";

(*b*) in sub-section (2), for "the Central Government" substitute "the Authority."

41. Section 101B :

(*a*) in sub-section (1), for "the Central Government", substitute "the Authority with the previous approval of the Central Government";

(*b*) in sub-section (2), for "prescribed", substitute determined by the regulations made by the Authority".

42. For Sections 102 to 105, substitute the following :

"102. *Penalty for default in complying with, or act in contravention of, this Act:* If any person who is required under this Act, or rules or regulations made thereunder:

(*a*) to furnish any document, statement, account, return or report to the Authority, fails to furnish the same; or

(*b*) to comply with the directions, fails to comply with such directions;

(*c*) to maintain solvency margin, fails to maintain such solvency margin;

(*d*) to comply with the directions on the insurance treaties, fails to comply with such directions on the insurance treaties,

He shall be liable to a penalty not exceeding five lakh rupees for each such failure and punishable with fine.

103. *Penalty for carrying on insurance business in contravention of Section 3,7. and 98:* If a person makes a statement, or furnishes any document, statement, account, return or report which is false and which he either knows or believes to be false or does not believe to be true,

(*a*) he shall be liable to a penalty not exceeding five lakh rupees for each such failure; and

(*b*) he shall be punishable with imprisonment which may extend to three years or with fine for each such failure.

104. *Penalty for false statement in document:* If a person fails to comply with the provisions of section 27 or section 27A or section 27B or section 27C or section 27D, he shall be liable to a penalty not exceeding five lakh rupees for each such failure.

105. *Wrongfully obtaining or withholding property:* If any director, managing director, manager or other officer or employees of an insurer wrongfully obtains possession of any property or wrongfully applies to any purpose of the Act, he shall be liable to a penalty not exceeding two lakh rupees for each such failure.

105A. *Offences by companies:* (1) Where any offence under this Act has been committed by a company, every person who, at the time the offence was committed, was in charge of, and was responsible to, the company for the conduct of the business of the company as well as the company shall be deemed to be guilty of the offence and shall be liable to be proceeded against and punished accordingly;

Provided that nothing contained in this sub-section shall render any such person liable to any punishment, if he proves that the offence was committed without his knowledge or that he had exercised all due diligence to prevent the commission of such offence.

(2) Notwithstanding anything contained in sub-section (1), where any offence under this Act has been committed by a company and it is proved that the offence has been committed with the consent or connivance of, or is attributable to any neglect on the part of, any director, manager, secretary or other officer of the company, such director, manager, secretary or other officer shall be deemed to be guilty of that offence and shall be liable to be proceeded against and punished accordingly.

Explanation : For the purposes of this section, :

(*a*) "company" means any body corporate, and includes :

(*i*) a firm; and

(*ii*) an association of persons or a body of individuals whether incorporated or not; and

(*b*) "director", in relation to :

(*i*) a firm, means a partner in the firm;

(*ii*) an association of persons or a body of individuals, means any member controlling the affairs thereof.

105B. Penalty for failure to comply with Section 32B.: If an insurer fails to comply with the provisions of Section 32B, he shall be liable to a penalty not exceeding five lakh rupees for each such failure and shall be punishable with imprisonment which may extend to three years or with fine for each such failure.

105C. Penalty for failure to comply with Section 32C.: If an insurer fails to comply with the provisions of section 32C, he shall be liable to a penalty not exceeding twenty-five lakh rupees for each such failure and in the case of subsequent and continuing failure, the registration granted to such insurer under Section 3 shall be cancelled by the Authority."

43. In sections 110A, 110B and 110C, for "Controller" wherever it occurs, substitute "Chairperson of the Authority".

44. Section 110G, for "Controller" at both the places where it occurs, substitute "Chairperson of the Authority".

45. Section 110H, in sub-section (1), for "under sections", substitute "under Section 27D,".

46. Section 114, in sub-section (2), :

(*a*) after clause (a), insert the following :

"(*aa*) such other percentage of paid-up equity capital in excess twenty-six per cent of the paid-up equity capital and the period within which such excess paid-up equity capital shall be divested under sub-section (1) of Section 6AA.";

(*b*) omit clauses (g) and (ll),

47. After section 114, insert the following :

"114A. *Power of Authority to make regulations :* (1) The Authority may, by notification in the *Official Gazette*, make regulations consistent with this Act and the rules made thereunder, to carry out the purposes of this Act.

(2) In particular, and without prejudice to the generality of the foregoing power, such regulation may provide for all or any of the following matters, namely :

(*a*) the matters including fee relating to the registration of insurers under Section 3;

(*b*) the manner of suspension or cancellation of registration under sub-section (5E) of Section 3;

(*c*) such fee, not exceeding five thousand rupees, as may be determined by the regulations for issue of a duplicate certificate of registration under sub-section (7) of Section 3;

(*d*) the matters relating to the renewal of registration and fee therefore under Section 3A;

(*e*) the manner and procedure for divesting excess share capital under sub-section (2) of Section 6AA;

(*f*) the preparation of balance-sheet, profit and loss account and a separate account of receipts and payments and revenue account under sub-section (1A) of Section 11;

(*g*) the manner in which an abstract of the report of the actuary to be specified under the fourth proviso to sub-section (1) of Section 13;

(*h*) the form and manner in which the statement referred to in sub-section(4) of Section 13 shall be appended;

(*i*) the time, manner and other conditions of investment of assets held by an insurer under sub-sections (1), (1A) and (2) of Section 27D;

(*j*) the minimum information to be maintained by insurer in their books, the manner in which such information should be maintained, the checks and other verifications to be adopted by insurers in that connection and all other matters incidental thereto under sub-section (8) of Section 33;

(*k*) the manner for making an application, the manner and the fee for issue of a licence to act as an insurance agent under sub-section (1) of Section 42;

(*l*) the fee and the additional fee to be determined for renewal of licence of insurance agent under sub-section (3) of Section 42;

(*m*) the requisite qualifications and practical training to act as an insurance agent under clause (e) of sub-section (4) of Section 42;

(*n*) the passing of examination to act as an insurance agent under clause (f) of sub-section (4) of Section 42;

(*o*) the code of conduct under clause (g) of sub-section (4) of Section 42;

(*p*) the fee not exceeding rupees fifty for issue of duplicate licence under sub-section (6) of Section 42;

(*q*) the manner and the fees for issue of a licence to an intermediary or an insurance intermediary under sub-section (1) of Section 42D;

(*r*) the fee and the additional fee to be determined for renewal of licence of intermediaries or insurance intermediaries under sub-section (3) of Section 42D;

(*s*) the requisite qualifications and practical training of intermediaries or insurance intermediaries under clause (e) of sub-section (5) of Section 42D;

(*t*) the examination to be passed to acts as an intermediary or insurance intermediary under clause (f) of sub-section (5) of Section 42D;

(*u*) the code of conduct under clause (g) of sub-section (5) of Section 42D;

(*v*) the fee for issue of duplicate licence under sub-section (7) of Section 42D;

(*w*) such matters as specified under sub-section (2) of Section 64UB relating to the Tariff Advisory Committee;

(*x*) the matters relating to licensing of surveyors and loss assessors, their duties, responsibilities and other professional requirements under Section 64UM;

(*y*) such other asset or assets as may be specified under clause (h) of sub-section (1) of section 64V for the purposes of ascertaining sufficiency of assets under Section 64VA;

(*z*) the valuation of assets and liabilities under sub-section (3) of Section 64V;

(*za*) the matters specified under sub-section (1A) of Section 64VA relating to sufficiency of assets;

(*zb*) the matters relating to re-insurance under sections 101A and 101B;

(*zc*) the matters relating to redressal of grievances of policy-holders to protect their interest and to regulate, promote and ensure orderly growth of insurance industry; and

(*zd*) any other matter which is to be, or may be, specified by the regulation made by the Authority or in respect of which provision is to be made or may be made by the regulations.

(3) Every regulation made under this Act shall be laid, as soon as may be after it is made, before each House of Parliament, while it is in session, for a total period of thirty days which may be comprised in one session or in two or more successive sessions, and if, before the expiry of the session immediately following the session or the successive sessions aforesaid, both Houses agree in making any modification in the regulation or both Houses agree that the regulation should not be made, the regulation shall thereafter have effect only in such modified form or be of no effect, as the case may be, so, however, that any such modification or annulment shall be without prejudice to the validity of anything previously done under that regulation."

48. Section 116 A, for "Central Government", at both places where they occur, substitute "Central Government, before the date of commencement of the Insurance Regulatory and Development Authority Act, 1999,".

The Second Schedule
(See Section 31)

Amedments to the Life Insurance Corporation Act 1956 (31 of 1956)

1. In the Act, for "Controller" wherever it occurs, substitute "Authority".

2. After Section 30, insert the following :

"30A. *Exclusive privilege of Corporation to cease :* Notwithstanding anything contained in this Act, the exclusive privilege of carrying on life insurance business in India by the Corporation shall cease on and from commencement of the Insurance Regulatory and Development Authority Act, 1999 and the Corporation shall, thereafter, carry on life insurance business in India in accordance with the provisions of the Insurance Act, 1938 (4 of 1938).".

The Third Schedule
(See Section 32)

Amedment to the General Insurance Business (Nationalisation) ACT, 1972 (57 of 1972)

After Section 24, insert the following :

"24A. *Exclusive privilege of Corporation and acquiring companies to cease.* Notwithstanding anything contained in this Act, the exclusive privilege of the Corporation and the acquiring companies of carrying on general insurance business in India shall cease on an from the commencement of the Insurance Regulatory and Development Authority Act, 1999 and the Corporation and the acquiring companies shall, thereafter, carry on general insurance business in India in accordance with the provisions of the Insurance Act, 1938 (4 of 1938)."

Insurance Regulatory and Development Authority (Appointed Actuary) Regulations, 2000

These regulations deals with the appointment of actuaries. Every insurance company has to appoint an actuary titled as 'appointed actuary'. For this purpose the insurance company has to make an application to IRDA. The qualifications of actuary are defined in the regulations. The appointed actuary has the following powers:

(a) access to all information or documents in possession, or under control, of the insurer if such access is necessary for the proper and effective performance of the functions and duties of the appointed actuary;

(b) to seek any information for conducting his duties from any officer or employee of the insurer;

(c) to attend all meetings of the management including the directors of the insurer;

(d) to speak and discuss on any matter, at such meeting that relates to the actuarial advice given to the directors, that may affect the solvency of the insurer, that may affect the ability of the insurer to meet the reasonable expectations of policyholders; or on which actuarial advice is necessary;

(e) to attend any meeting of the shareholders or the policyholders of the insurer; or any other meeting of members of the insurer at which the insurer's annual accounts or financial statements are to be considered or at which any matter in connection with the appointed actuary's duties is discussed.

The following are the duties of appointed actuary:-

(a) rendering actuarial advice to the management of the insurer, in particular in the areas of product design and pricing, insurance contract wording, investments and reinsurance;

(b) ensuring the solvency of the insurer at all times;

(c) complying with the provisions of the section 64V of the Act in regard to certification of the assets and liabilities and maintenance of required solvency margin that have been valued in the manner required under the said section;

(d) drawing the attention of management of the insurer, to any matter on which he or she thinks that action is required to be taken by the insurer to avoid any contravention of the Act or prejudice to the interests of policyholders;

(e) complying with the Authority's directions from time to time in relation to certification of reports, the bases of premium and their fairness, declaration of bonuses maintenance of records for actuarial valuation of liabilities and assets of the insurer, accuracy of mathematical reserves, observance of actuarial principles and protecting the interest of the policyholders.

An appointed actuary shall enjoy absolute privilege to make any statement, oral or written, for the purpose of the performance of his functions as appointed actuary.

Insurance Regulatory and Development Authority (Actuarial Report and Abstract) Regulations, 2000

These regulations deal with the manner and contents of Actuarial Report and Abstracts to be submitted to IRDA. Some of the important terms are defined as under:

(a) "Authority" means the Insurance Regulatory and Development Authority established under sub-section (1) of Section 3 of the Insurance Regulatory and Development Authority Act, 1999 (41 of 1999);

(b) "extra premium' means a charge for any risk not provided for in the minimum contract premium;

(c) "group business" means those insurance contracts which are group policies as mentioned under sub-section (2) of Section 4 of the Act;

(d) "guarantees" means the terms in regard to benefits or premiums or charges, which may not be altered during the currency of the policy;

(e) "individual business" means individual insurance contracts issued on single/joint lives;

(f) "inter valuation period" means, as respects any valuation, the period to the valuation date of that valuation from the valuation date of the preceding valuation in connection with which an abstract was prepared under the Act or under the enactments repealed by the Act, or, in a case where no such valuation has been made in respect of the class of business in question, from the date on which the insurer began to carry on that class of business;

(g) "maturity date" means a fixed date on which benefit may become payable either absolutely or contingently;

(h) "non-par policies" or "policies without participation in profits" means policies which are not entitled for any share in surplus (profits) during the term of the policy;

(i) "office yearly premium" means regular premium (excluding extra premiums which are required to be shown separately) payable by the policyholder to secure the basic benefits under the policy in a policy year ;

(j) "options" means the rights available to a policyholder under a policy;

(k) "par policies" or "policies with participation in profits" means polices which are not non-par policies as defined under clause (i);

(l) "policies with deferred participation in profits" means polices entitled for participation in profits after a certain period from the date of commencement of the policy,

(m) "premium term" means the period during which premiums are payable;

(n) "riders" or "rider benefits" means add-on benefits, which are in addition to basic benefits under a policy;

(o) "valuation date" means as respects any valuation the date as at which the valuation is made;

The actuarial report and abstract must be prepared in accordance with the format specified by regulation 4 of such regulations and the report must be sent within nine months from the end of the relevant period.

The Abstract and Statement must be appended the following:

(a) a certificate signed by the principal officer that full and accurate particulars of every policy under which there is a liability, either actual or contingent, has been furnished to the appointed actuary for the investigation; and

(b) a certificate signed by the appointed actuary with his remarks to the effect that the data furnished by the principal officer has been included in conducting the valuation of liabilities for the purpose of investigation, reasonable steps have been taken to ensure the accuracy and completeness of the data and compliance have been made for IRDA Act, 1999, guidance notes issued by the Actuarial Society of India with the concurrence of the Authority and that mathematical reserves are adequate to meet the insurer's future commitments under the contracts, and the policyholders' reasonable expectations.

Abstracts and statements shall be prepared separately in respect of (a) Linked Business; (b) Non-Linked Business; and (c) Health Insurance Business. Also, the statements must be annexed to the abstract in the prescribed formats respectively.

The abstract include description of valuation date, new products, foreign operations, valuation methods, valuation bases and provisions made. The other information required to appended includes:-

(i) Returns on Assets as specified under Regulation 5;

(ii) Distribution of surplus as specified under Regulation 6;

(iii) Principles adopted in distribution of surplus as specified under Regulation 7;

(iv) Negative Reserves and Guaranteed Surrender Value Deficiency Reserves as specified under Regulation 9;

(v) Miscellaneous, if any.

Insurance Regulatory and Development Authority (Insurance Advertisements and Disclosure) Regulations, 2000

These regulations deal with insurance advertisement and disclosure. An "insurance advertisement" means and includes any communication directly or indirectly related to a policy and intended to result in the eventual sale or solicitation of a policy from the members of the public, and shall include all forms of printed and published materials or any material using the print and or electronic medium for public communication and any other communication with a prospect or a policyholder that urges him to purchase, renew, increase, retain, or modify a policy of insurance.

The "intermediary or insurance intermediary includes insurance brokers, reinsurance brokers, insurance consultants, surveyors and loss assessors, or any other person representing or assisting an insurer in one or more of the prescribed activities.

The "unfair or misleading advertisement" will mean and include any advertisement:

(i) that fails to clearly identify the product as insurance;

(ii) makes claims beyond the ability of the policy to deliver or beyond the reasonable expectation of performance;

(iii) describes benefits that do not match the policy provisions;

(iv) uses words or phrases in a way which hides or minimizes the costs of the hazard insured against or the risks inherent in the policy;

(v) omits to disclose or discloses insufficiently, important exclusions, limitations and conditions of the contract;

(vi) gives information in a misleading way;

(vii) illustrates future benefits on assumptions which are not realistic nor realisable in the light of the insurer's current performance;

(viii) where the benefits are not guaranteed, does not explicitly say so as prominently as the benefits are stated or says so in a manner or form that it could remain unnoticed;

(ix) implies a group or other relationship like sponsorship, affliation or approval, that does not exist;

(x) makes unfair or incomplete comparisons with products which are not comparable or disparages competitors.

(xi) A "prospect" means any party that enters or proposes to enter into an insurance contract directly, or through an insurance intermediary.

Every insurer or intermediary or insurance agent must have a compliance officer who is responsible to oversee the advertising programme and exercise control over it and maintain register of advertisement contracts.

All advertisements must be filed on the prescribed manner to the authority. Any change in an advertisement is considered a new advertisement.

The insurer in writing prior to its issue must approve every advertisement by an insurance agent that affects an insurer. Only properly licensed intermediaries can advertise or solicit insurance through advertisements. Every insurer or intermediary's web site or portal shall include disclosure statements, which outline the site's specific policies *vis-à-vis* the privacy of personal information for the protection of both their own businesses and the consumers they serve and display their registration/ license numbers on their web sites.

Every advertisement for insurance must state clearly and unequivocally that *insurance is the subject matter of the solicitation*; and state the full registered name of the insurer/ intermediary/ insurance agent.

A third party cannot conduct the advertisement programme of the insurer in any manner unless approved in certain cases. The IRDA has full authority to act upon complaints received or on its own. The insurers are required to adhere to follow standards of professional conduct as prescribed by the Advertisement Standards Council of India (ASCI) and discharge its functions in the interest of the policyholders.

Also, every proposal for an insurance product shall carry the following stipulation, as prescribed in Section 41 of the Insurance Act, 1938 (4 of 1938):— "No person shall allow or offer to allow, either directly or indirectly, as an inducement to any person to take out or renew or continue an insurance in respect of any kind of risk relating to lives or property in India, any rebate of the whole or part of the commission payable or any rebate of the premium shown on the policy, nor shall any person taking out or renewing or continuing a policy accept any rebate, except such rebate as may be allowed in accordance with the published prospectus or tables of the insurer." Non-compliance is punishable with fine of Rs. 500/-.

Insurance Regulatory and Development Authority (Meetings) Regulations, 2000

These regulations provide for the matters relating to meetings of the Authority for transaction of business and procedure to be followed. The meeting of IRDA must be held not less than six times in a year, to transact its business. These also deal with serving of notices of meetings, appointment of chairman, and quorum.

The quorum for transaction of business at a meeting of the Authority shall be a minimum of one-third of the appointed members present. Where at any time the total strength of the Authority is less than four, the total number of members, being not less than two, shall constitute the quorum during such time.

The manner of adjournment of meetings, leave of absence and emergent meeting are specified in the regulations. The person responsible must duly record the minutes of meeting. Also, no member, other than the Chairperson or a person specifically authorised by him, shall give information to the Press or any other public media on matters relating to the working of the Authority and decisions taken at meetings.

Insurance Regulatory and Development Authority (Registration of Indian Insurance Companies) Regulations, 2000

Every insurer must be registered with IRDA. The important definitions under the regulations are:-

"general annuity business" means the business of effecting contracts to pay annuities on human life but does not include contracts under pension business;

"health insurance business" or "health cover means the effecting of contracts which provide sickness benefits or medical, surgical or hospital expense benefits, whether in-patient or out patient, on an indemnity, reimbursement, service, prepaid, hospital or other plans basis, including assured benefits and long term care;

"*Indian promoter*" means and includes—-

(i) a company formed under the Companies Act, 1956 (1 of 1956), which is not a subsidiary as defined in Section 4 of that Act;

(ii) a banking company as defined in subsection (4A) of Section 2 of the Act but does not include a foreign bank or branch thereof functioning in India;

(iii) a Public financial institution as defined in Section 4A of the Companies Act, 1956 (1 of 1956);

(iv) a co-operative society registered under any relevant law for the time being in force;

(v) a person, who is an Indian citizen or a combination of persons who are Indian citizens;

"infrastructure facility" means —

(i) a road, highway, bridge, airport, port, Railways including BOLT, road transport system, a water supply project, irrigation project, industrial parks, water treatment system, solid waste management system, sanitation and sewerage system;

(ii) generation or distribution or transmission of power;

(iii) telecommunication;

(iv) project for housing;

(v) any other public facility of a similar nature as may be notified by the Authority in this behalf in the *Official Gazette*;

"linked business' means life insurance contracts or health insurance contracts under which benefits are wholly or partly to be determined by reference to the value of underlying assets or any approved index;

"non-linked business" means life insurance contracts or health insurance contracts which are not linked business;

"pension business' includes business of effecting contracts to manage investments of pension funds or superannuation schemes or contracts to pay annuities that may be approved by the Authority in this behalf;

The regulations prescribe for the manner of registration and application. The paid capital requirements for life and non-life business are Rs. 100 crores and for re-insurance business is Rs. 20 crores. In case of foreign participation, the manner of calculation of 26% capital is specified. The registration is subject to submissions and thorough scrutiny by the authority. The insurers existing at that time have to obtain the certificate within 3 months. The registration number to be used for all purposes including advertisements. In case the IRDA find that any insurer has violated the terms and conditions of the certificate, the registration shall be cancelled.

Insurance Regulatory and Development Authority (Preparation of Financial Statements and Auditor's Report of Insurance Companies) Regulations, 2002

These regulations deal with the method and format of preparation of Financial Statements and Auditor's Report of Insurance Companies. An insurer carrying on life insurance business, after the commencement of these Regulations, has to comply with the requirements of Schedule A of the regulations and an insurer carrying on general insurance business, after the commencement of these Regulations, shall comply with the requirements of Schedule B. The report of the auditors on the financial statements of every insurer and reinsurer shall be in conformity with the requirements of Schedule C, or as near as thereto, as the circumstances permit. The Authority may, from time to time, issue separate guidelines in the matter of appointment, continuance or removal of auditors of an insurer or reinsurer, as the case may be, and such guidelines may include prescriptions regarding qualifications and experience of auditors, their rotation, period of appointment, etc.

The schedules provide for accountings standards to be followed, classification of assets and liabilities, income statements and position statements, contents of management report etc. separately for life and non-life insurers.

Insurance Regulatory and Development Authority Protection of Policyholders' Interests) Regulations, 2002

In order to protect the interests of the policyholders, these regulations provide for various disclosures at point of sale and after sale of the insurance products. These disclosures are in respect of product terms and conditions including scope of cover, riders, certificate of information disclosure to the prospective customer etc. The intermediaries have to observe the code of conduct as prescribed and the proposal forms should contain the information as prescribed by the regulations. It clearly states out the matters to be stated in life insurance policy and matters to be stated in general insurance policy.

The life insurance policy must clearly state the primary documents, which are normally required to be submitted by a claimant in support of a claim, and the claims shall be processed without delays. The disputes must be settled in accordance with prudent practices and the policy contract.

The regulations also provide for various matters of policy servicing by insurers and disclosure of material information to the policyholders.

The Insurance Advisory Committee (Meetings) Regulations, 2000

These regulations deal with the conduct of meetings of Insurance Advisory Committee constituted by IRDA under Section 25 of the IRDA Act, 1999. There must at least be three meetings of the committee every year. The Designated Officer shall normally circulate the notice and agenda for the meeting seven days in advance to the members personally upon acknowledgement or dispatched by registered post or courier service or transmitted through any other secure and reliable modern means of communication. The quorum for transaction of business at a meeting of the Advisory Committee or sub-committee shall be a minimum of one-third of the total strength and any fraction that might arise while calculating the one-third total strength is disregarded.

If at any such meeting, quorum is not present, the Chairperson or the presiding member, as the case may be, shall after waiting for thirty minutes from the scheduled commencement time of the meeting, adjourn the meeting for such hour on the same day or some other day as he may think fit. Where at the adjourned meeting also the required quorum is not present, the members present shall constitute the quorum and proceed with the transaction of business.

All members are required to attend all the meetings of the Advisory Committee or sub-committee or obtain a valid leave of absence. If any member ceases to attend consecutively three meetings of the Advisory Committee without just and sufficient cause, the Authority may consider exclusion of his name from the Advisory Committee and fill in the resultant vacancy, as it may consider necessary.

The minutes of the proceedings at the meetings must be recorded in the prescribed manner, which shall contain the names of members present at the meeting and a fair and correct summary of the decisions arrived at the meeting.

The regulations prohibit the members, other than the Chairperson or a person specifically authorised by him shall give information to the Press or to any other public media on matters relating to the decisions taken at the meetings of the Advisory Committee or sub-committees.

Insurance Regulatory and Development Authority (Obligations of Insurers to Rural Social Sectors) Regulations, 2000 and amendments in 2002

These regulations imposes responsibility on insurers to insure rural and social sectors. The *"Rural sector" shall mean any place as per the latest census which meets the following criteria—*

(i) a population of less than five thousand;

(ii) a density of population of less than four hundred per square kilometer; and

(iii) more than ***twenty five*** per cent of the male working population is engaged in agricultural pursuits.

"Social sector" includes unorganised sector, informal sector, economically vulnerable or backward classes and other categories of persons, both in rural and urban areas;

"Unorganised sector" includes self-employed workers such as agricultural labourers, bidi workers, brick kiln workers, carpenters, cobblers, construction workers, fishermen, hamals, handicraft artisans, handloom and khadi workers, lady tailors, leather and tannery workers, papad makers, powerloom workers, physically handicapped self-employed persons, primary milk producers, rickshaw pullers, safai karmacharis, salt growers, seri culture workers, sugarcane cutters, tendu leaf collectors, toddy tappers, vegetable vendors, washerwomen, working women in hills, or such other categories of persons;

(a) "economically vulnerable or backward classes" means persons who live below the poverty line;

(b) "other categories of persons" includes persons with disability as defined in the Persons with Disabilities (Equal Opportunities, Protection of Rights, and Full Participation) Act, 1995 and who may not be gainfully employed; and also includes guardians who need insurance to protect spastic persons or persons with disability;

Every insurer, who begins to carry on insurance business after the commencement of the Insurance Regulatory and Development Authority Act, 1999 (41 of 1999), shall, for the purposes of sections 32B and 32C of the Act, ensure that he undertakes the following obligations, during the first five financial years, pertaining to the persons in—

(a) **rural sector,**

(i) in respect of *a life insurer,* —

(I) ***seven*** per cent in the first financial year;

(II) ***nine*** per cent in the second financial year;

(III) Twelve per cent in the third financial year;

(IV) Fourteen per cent in the fourth financial year;

(V) Sixteen per cent in the fifth year;

of total policies written direct in that year;

(i) in respect of *a general insurer,*—

(ii) two per cent in the first financial year;

(iii) three per cent in the second financial year;

(iv) five per cent thereafter,

of total gross premium income written direct in that year.

(b) **social sector**, in respect of all insurers, —

(I) five thousand lives in the first financial year;

(II) seven thousand five hundred lives in the second financial year;

(III) ten thousand lives in the third financial year;

(IV) fifteen thousand lives in the fourth financial year;

(V) twenty thousand lives in the fifth year;

Provided that in the first financial year, where the period of operation is less than twelve months, proportionate percentage or number of lives, as the case may be, shall be undertaken and provided further that, in case of a general insurer, the obligations specified shall include insurance for crops and provided further that the Authority may normally, once in every five years, prescribe or revise the obligations as specified in Regulation 3.

Insurance Regulatory and Development Authority (Licensing of Insurance Agents) Regulations, 2000

These guidelines deal with the appointment and licensing of agents by insurance companies. The agents are of two categories:-

(I) "Composite insurance agent" means an insurance agent who holds a license to act as an insurance agent for a life insurer and a general insurer.

(II) "Corporate Agent" means a person other than an individual as defined in above category.

As per the guidelines, every person desiring to obtain or renew a license to act as an insurance agent or a composite insurance agent shall make an application in prescribed manner and fulfil the eligibility requirements which include qualifications, practical training (100 hours) and passing the examination prescribed.

The guidelines provide for the duties of insurance agents – that every insurance agent shall:-

(i) identify himself and the insurance company of whom he is an insurance agent;

(ii) disclose his licence to the prospect on demand;

(iii) disseminate the requisite information in respect of insurance products offered for sale by his insurer and take into account the needs of the prospect while recommending a specific insurance plan;

(iv) disclose the scales of commission in respect of the insurance product offered for sale, if asked by the prospect;

(v) indicate the premium to be charged by the insurer for the insurance product offered for sale;

(vi) explain to the prospect the nature of information required in the proposal form by the insurer, and also the importance of disclosure of material information in the purchase of an insurance contract;

(vii) bring to the notice of the insurer any adverse habits or income inconsistency of the prospect, in the form of a report (called "Insurance Agent's Confidential Report") along with every proposal submitted to the insurer, and any material fact that may adversely affect the underwriting decision of the insurer as regards acceptance of the proposal, by making all reasonable enquiries about the prospect;

(viii) inform promptly the prospect about the acceptance or rejection of the proposal by the insurer;

(ix) obtain the requisite documents at the time of filing the proposal form with the insurer; and other documents subsequently asked for by the insurer for completion of the proposal;

(x) render necessary assistance to the policyholders or claimants or beneficiaries in complying with the requirements for settlement of claims by the insurer;

(xi) advise every individual policyholder to effect nomination or assignment or change of address or exercise of options, as the case may be, and offer necessary assistance in this behalf, wherever necessary;

The guidelines prohibit insurance agents from the practices like :-

(a) soliciting or procuring insurance business without holding a valid licence;

(b) inducing the prospect to omit any material information in the proposal form;

(c) inducing the prospect to submit wrong information in the proposal form or documents submitted to the insurer for acceptance of the proposal;

(d) behaving in a discourteous manner with the prospect;

(e) interfering with any proposal introduced by any other insurance agent;

(f) offering different rates, advantages, terms and conditions other than those offered by his insurer;

(g) demanding or receive a share of proceeds from the beneficiary under an insurance contract;

(h) forcing a policyholder to terminate the existing policy and to effect a new proposal from him within three years from the date of such termination;

(i) having, in case of a corporate agent, a portfolio of insurance business under which the premium is in excess of fifty percent of total premium procured, in any year, from one person (who is not an individual) or one organisation or one group of organisations;

An agent cannot apply for fresh licence to act as an insurance agent, if his licence was earlier cancelled by the designated person, and a period of five years has not elapsed from the date of such cancellation. He cannot also become or remain a director of any insurance company;

The insurance agents is to ensure the remittance of premiums by policyholders within stipulated time. The licence of the agent can be cancelled any time if he indulges in malpractices.

Insurance Regulatory and Development Authority (Assets, Liabilities, and Solvency Margin of Insurers) Regulations, 2000

These guidelines provide for the valuation of Assets and Liabilities and maintenance of the solvency margin by insurers. Every insurer has to prepare a statement of the value of assets and liabilities in form prescribed respectively for life and general insurance companies. Also every insurer shall prepare a statement of solvency margin in accordance with schedules to the regulations for life and general insurance insurers.

Also an insurer doing business outside India has to submit a statement in prescribed form in respect of the statements or returns or any such particulars made to a public authority of that country and IRDA may prescribe setting of special reserves for this purpose.

Schedule I to the regulations defined 'non-mandated investments' means those investments that are neither approved securities nor approved investments. In respect of valuing the assets, the following assets should be placed with value zero:-

(a) Agent's balances and outstanding premiums in India, to the extent they are not realised within a period of thirty days;

(b) Agents' balances and outstanding premiums outside India, to the extent they are not realisable ;

(c) Sundry debts, to the extent they are not realisable;

(d) Advances of an unrealisable character;

(e) Furniture, fixtures, dead stock and stationery;

(f) Deferred expenses;

(g) Profit and loss appropriation account balance and any fictitious assets other than pre-paid expenses;

(h) Reinsurer's balances outstanding for more than three months;

(i) Preliminary expenses in the formation of the company;

(2) The value of computer equipment including software shall be computed as under:—

(i) seventy five per cent of its cost in the year of purchase;

(ii) fifty per cent of its cost in the second year;

(iii) twenty-five per cent of its cost in the third year; and

(iv) zero per cent thereafter.

All other assets of an insurer have to be valued in accordance with the Insurance Regulatory and Development Authority (Preparation of Financial Statements and Auditor's Report of Insurance Companies) Regulations, 2000.

IRDA (General Insurance - Reinsurance) Regulations, 2000

These regulations deal with the conduct of general insurance business by non-life insurers. For the purpose of such regulations certain terms are defined as follows:

'cession' means the unit of insurance passed to a reinsurer by the insurer which issued a policy to the original insured and, accordingly, a cession may be the whole or a portion of single risks, defined policies or defined divisions of business, as agreed in the reinsurance contract;

'facultative' means the reinsurance of a part or all of a single policy in which cession is negotiated separately and that the reinsurer and the insurer have the option of accepting or declining each individual submission;

'Indian re-insurer' means an insurer who carries on exclusively reinsurance business and is approved in this behalf by the Central Government;

'pool' means any joint underwriting operation of insurance or reinsurance in which the participants assume a predetermined and fixed interest in all business written;

'retrocession' means the transaction whereby a reinsurer cedes to another insurer or reinsurer all or part of the reinsurance it has previously assumed;

'retention' means the amount which an insurer assumes for his own account. In proportionate contracts, the retention may be a percentage of the policy limit. In excess of loss contracts, the retention is an amount of loss;

'treaty' means a reinsurance arrangement between the insurer and the reinsurer, usually for one year or longer, which stipulates the technical particulars and financial terms applicable to the reinsurance of some class or classes of business;

The regulations lay emphasis on the objectives of maximising retention within the country, developing adequate capacity, securing the best possible protection for the reinsurance costs incurred and simplifying the administration of business.

Every insurance company is require to commence the reinsurance programme from the beginning of every financial year and every insurer shall submit to a report 45 days before the commencement of the financial year.

The insurer is also required to submit details of reinsurance treaties. The insurers can place their reinsurance business outside India if over a period of the past five years counting from the year preceding for which the business has to be placed, enjoyed a rating of at least BBB (with Standard & Poor) or equivalent rating of any other international rating agency. Placements with other reinsurer shall require the approval of the Authority. The Indian reinsurer has to organise domestic pools for reinsurance surpluses in fire, marine hull and other classes in consultation with all insurers on the basis, limits and terms which are fair to all insurers and assist in maintaining the retention of business within India.

Surplus over and above the domestic reinsurance arrangements class wise can be placed by the insurer independently with any of the approved reinsurer(s) subject to a limit of 10% of the total reinsurance premium ceded outside India being placed with any one reinsurer. Every insurer must offer an opportunity to other Indian insurers including the Indian reinsurer to participate in its facultative and treaty surpluses before placement of such cessions outside India. The Indian reinsurer shall retrocede at least 50% of the obligatory cessions received by it to the ceding insurers after protecting the portfolio by suitable excess of loss covers. Such retrocession shall be at original terms plus an over-riding commission to the Indian reinsurer not exceeding 2.5%. The retrocession to each ceding insurer shall be in proportion to its cessions to the Indian reinsurer.

Every insurer shall be required to submit to the Authority statistics relating to its reinsurance transactions in such forms as the Authority may specify, together with its annual accounts.

Every insurer wanting to write inward reinsurance business shall have a well-defined underwriting policy for underwriting inward reinsurance business. The insurer shall ensure that decisions on acceptance of reinsurance business are made by persons with necessary knowledge and experience. The insurer shall file with the Authority a note on its underwriting policy stating the classes of business, geographical scope, underwriting limits and profit objective. The insurer shall also file any changes to the note as and when a change in underwriting policy is made.

Outstanding Loss Provisioning

Every insurer shall make outstanding claims provisions for every reinsurance arrangement accepted on the basis of loss information advices received from Brokers/ Cedants and where such advices are not received, on an actuarial estimation basis.

In addition, every insurer shall make an appropriate provision for incurred but not reported (IBNR) claims on its reinsurance accepted portfolio on actuarial estimation basis.

Insurance Regulatory and Development Authority (Investment) Regulations, 2000

These regulations deal with investments by insurance companies. The life insurer without prejudice to Section 27 or Section 27A of the IRDA Act must invest and at all times keep invested his controlled fund in the following manner:

S.No	Type of Investment	Percentage
(i)	Government Securities	25%
(ii)	Government Securities or other approved securities (including (I) above, not less than	50%
(iii)	Approved Investments as specified in **Schedule I**	
(a)	Infrastructure and Social Sector Explanation: For the purpose of this requirement, Infrastructure and Social Sector shall have the meaning as given in regulation 2(h) of Insurance Regulatory and Development Authority (Registration of Indian Insurance Companies) Regulations, 2000 and as defined in the Insurance Regulatory and Development Authority (Obligations of Insurers to Rural and Social Sector) Regulations, 2000 respectively	Not less than 15%
(b)	Others to be governed by Exposure/Prudential Norms specified in Regulation 5	Not exceeding 20%
(iv)	Other than in Approved Investments to be governed by Exposure/Prudential Norms specified in Regulation 5	Not exceeding 15%

Pension and General Annuity Business: Every insurer shall invest and at all times keep invested assets of Pension Business, General Annuity Business and Group Business in the following manner:

S.No	Type of Investment	Percentage
(i)	Government securities, being not less than	20%
(ii)	Government Securities or other approved securities inclusive of (i) above, being not less than	40%
(iii)	Balance to be invested in Approved Investments as specified in **Schedule I** and to be governed by Exposure/Prudential Norms specified in Regulation 5	Not exceeding 60%

No unapproved investments can be made and all investments shall be made in graded securities and the grading shall not be less than of 'very strong' rating by a reputed and independent rating agency (e.g., AA of Standard and Poor). Every insurer shall invest assets in securities which are actively traded in any Stock Exchange in India and which are attributable to segregated funds, in respect of linked business.

In respect of non-life insurers, without prejudice to Section 27 or Section 27B of the Act, every insurer carrying on the business of general insurance shall invest and at all times keep invested his total assets in the following manner:-

S.No	Type of Investment	Percentage
(i)	Central Government Securities **being not less than**	20%
(ii)	State Government securities and other Guaranteed securities including (i) above **being not less than**	30%
(iii)	Housing and Loans to State Government for Housing and Fire Fighting equipment, **being not less than** 5%	
(iv)	Investments in Approved Investments as specified in **Schedule II**	
(a)	Infrastructure and Social Sector Explanation: For the purpose of this requirement, Infrastructure and Social Sector shall have the meaning as given in regulation 2 (h) of Insurance Regulatory and Development Authority (Registration of Indian Insurance Companies) Regulations, 2000 and as defined in the Insurance Regulatory and Development Authority (Obligations of Insurers to Rural and Social Sector) Regulations, 2000 respectively	Not exceeding 10%
(b)	Others to be governed by Exposure/ Prudential Norms specified in Regulation 5	Not less than 30%
(v)	Other than in Approved Investments to be governed by Exposure/Prudential Norms specified in Regulation 5	Not exceeding 25%

All investments shall be made in graded securities and the grading shall not be less than of 'very strong' rating by a reputed and independent rating agency (e.g., AA of Standard and Poor). Every reinsurer carrying on reinsurance business in India shall invest and at all times keep invested his total assets in the manner specified.

The exposure norms are as follows:

Type of Investment	Limit for Investee Company	Limit for the entire group to which the investee company belongs	Limit for the industry sector to which the investee company belongs
(a) Equity/Preference Shares/Convertible portion of Debentures at face value.	(i) **As on any date** Not exceeding 20% of the total capital employed*.	(i) **As on any date** Not exceeding 15% of the total capital employed* of the group companies	Not exceeding 15% of the total capital employed* in all such companies.
(b) Debentures — (face value) including private placed NCD and Non-convertible portion of Convertible Debentures.			
(c) Short/Medium/Long Term Loans and any other direct financial assistance.	(ii) **During the year** Not exceeding 5% of estimated annual accretion of funds.	(ii) **During the year** Not exceeding 10% of estimated annual accretion of funds	

* Total capital employed means total of equity shares, preference shares, debentures, long/ medium/short term loans (excluding public deposits), free reserves but excluding revaluation reserves of the invitee company as shown in its last audited balance sheet.

Exposure Norms for Investment in Public Financial Institutions	
Equity Share and Preference Shares (at their face value).	Not exceeding 15% in general of the paid up equity/ preference capital of the institution or the existing holding % level, if higher.
Investment in Equity Capital, Bonds, Debentures, Term Loans.	Not exceeding 10% of the capital employed by an institution as per the last audited Balance Sheet.
Total Investment *vis-a-vis* Net Worth of the Company.	Not exceeding 60% of Net worth of the institution.
Total Investment in a Financial Year.	7.5% of annual accretions.
Total Investments in all the Financial Institutions.	Annual aggregate financial assistance to all Development Financial Institutions put together in a single year shall not exceed 20% of the estimated annual accretions for the year.

Prudential norms for various instruments are also specified by the regulations. Insurers are required to file returns with the IRDA in the manner prescribed. IRDA has power to Call for additional information if required and the insurer has duty to report extraordinary events affecting the investment portfolio.

Every insurer has to constitute an Investment Committee which shall consist of a minimum of two non-executive directors of the Insurer, the Principal Officer, Chiefs of Finance and Investment divisions, and wherever appointed actuary is present, the Appointed Actuary. The decisions taken by the Investment Committee shall be properly recorded and be open to inspection by the officers of the Authority. The valuation of Assets and Accounting of Investments shall be as per the Insurance Regulatory and Development Authority (Preparation of Financial Statements and Auditor's Report of Insurance Companies) Regulations, 2000.

Insurance Surveyors and Loss Assessors (Licensing, Professional Requirements and Code of Conduct) Regulations, 2000

These guidelines provide that every person intending to act as a surveyor and loss assessor in respect of general insurance business has to obtain a licence from IRDA subject to fulfilment of qualifications, training and other requirements. In case of Corporate Surveyors and Loss Assessors, the directors or partners have to fulfil such requirements. The fee structure for various categories of surveyor and loss assessor is prescribed. The licence can be cancelled in violation of the norms specified. The IRDA has power to constitute a committee called "Surveyors and Loss Assessors Committee" for assisting the Authority on the matters and affairs relating to Insurance Surveyors and Loss Assessors. This committee consist of one officer from the IRDA, two representatives of the Surveyors and Loss Assessors, a representative of insurers and a representative of the policyholders. The functions of the committee include specifying eligibility requirements for surveyor and loss assessors, development of ethical code etc.

Exposure Norms for Investment in Public Financial Institutions	
Equity Share and Preference Shares (at their face value).	Not exceeding 15% in general of the paid up equity/ preference capital of the institution or the existing holding % level, if higher.
Investment in Equity Capital, Bonds, an Debentures, Term Loans.	Not exceeding 10% of the capital employed by institution as per the last audited Balance Sheet.
Total Investment *vis-a-vis* Net Worth of the Company.	Not exceeding 60% of Net worth of the institution.
Total Investment in a Financial Year.	7.5% of annual accretions.
Total Investments in all the Financial Institutions.	Annual aggregate financial assistance to all Development Financial Institutions put together in a single year shall not exceed 20% of the estimated annual accretions for the year.

Prudential norms for various instruments are also specified by the regulations. Insurers are required to file returns with the IRDA in the manner prescribed. IRDA has power to Call for additional information if required and the insurer has duty to report extraordinary events affecting the investment portfolio.

Every insurer has to constitute an Investment Committee which shall consist of a minimum of two non-executive directors of the Insurer, the Principal Officer, Chiefs of Finance and Investment divisions, and wherever appointed actuary is present, the Appointed Actuary. The decisions taken by the Investment Committee shall be properly recorded and be open to inspection by the officers of the Authority. The valuation of Assets and Accounting of Investments shall be as per the Insurance Regulatory and Development Authority (Preparation of Financial Statements and Auditor's Report of Insurance Companies) Regulations, 2000.

Insurance Surveyors and Loss Assessors (Licensing, Professional Requirements and Code of Conduct) Regulations, 2000

These guidelines provide that every person intending to act as a surveyor and loss assessor in respect of general insurance business has to obtain a licence from IRDA subject to fulfilment of qualifications, training and other requirements. In case of Corporate Surveyors and Loss Assessors, the directors or partners have to fulfil such requirements. The fee structure for various categories of surveyor and loss assessor is prescribed. The licence can be cancelled in violation of the norms specified. The IRDA has power to constitute a committee called "Surveyors and Loss Assessors Committee" for assisting the Authority on the matters and affairs relating to Insurance Surveyors and Loss Assessors. This committee consist of one officer from the IRDA, two representatives of the Surveyors and Loss Assessors, a representative of insurers and a representative of the policyholders. The functions of the committee include specifying eligibility requirements for surveyor and loss assessors, development of ethical code etc.

The surveyor and loss assessor has to act in accordance with the professional code of conduct, impartial in his duties and also advising the insurer and the insured about loss minimisation, loss control, security and safety measures, wherever appropriate, to avoid further losses. The surveyors and loss assessors are divided into three categories, *viz.*, Category A, Category B and Category C. IRDA maintain the register of surveyors and loss assessors. Every licensed surveyor and loss assessors are required to submit statements and returns in prescribed form to the authority who can order inspection in respect of conduct of business by surveyor and loss assessors.

IRDA (Life Insurance – Reinsurance) Regulations, 2000

Every life insurer has to develop a programme of reinsurance in respect of lives covered by him, which shall be duly certified by the Appointed Actuary with appropriate details. IRDA has power to amend the reinsurance programme of the life insurer. The reinsurer, chosen by the insurer shall enjoy a credit rating of a minimum of BBB of Standard and Poor or equivalent rating of any international rating agency. Provided that placement of business by the insurer with any other reinsurer shall be with the prior approval of the Authority. No reinsurance shall be done on original premium basis unless the Authority approves such programme. No life insurer shall have reinsurance treaty arrangement with its promoter company or its associate/group company, except on terms, which are commercially competitive in the market and with the prior approval of the Authority, which shall be final and binding. Every insurer shall submit to the Authority statistics relating to its reinsurance transactions in such forms as it may specify, together with its annual accounts. Every insurer who wants to write inward reinsurance business shall adopt a well-defined underwriting policy for underwriting inward reinsurance business. The insurer is required to submit the report on such business in the prescribed manner.

The IRDA (Third Party Administrators - Health Services) Regulations, 2001

These regulations deal with Third Part Administrators in context of health business. The “Health Services” means all the services to be rendered by a TPA under an agreement with an insurance company in connection with “health insurance business” or ‘health cover’ as defined in regulation 2(f) of the IRDA (Registraiion of Indian Insurance Companies) Regulations, 2000, but does not include the business of an insurance company or the soliciting, directly or through an insurance intermediary including an insurance agent of insurance business.

“TPA” means a Third Party Administrator who, for the time being, is licensed by the Authority, and is engaged, for a fee or remuneration, by whatever name called as may be specified in the agreement with an insurance company, for the provision of health services. The regulations provide that companies registered under the Companies Act, 1956 with a minimum paid up capital of Rs. 1 crore (Rupees One crore only) can be appointed as TPA. At no point of time of its functioning the TPA shall have a working capital of less than Rs. 1 crore and at least one of the directors of the TPA shall be a qualified medical doctor registered with the Medical Council of India. The aggregate holdings of equity shares by a foreign company shall not at any time exceed 26% of the paid up equity capital of a third party administrator. Any transfer of shares exceeding 5% of the paid up share capital shall be intimated by the TPA to the Authority within 15 days of the transfer indicating the names and particulars of the transferor and transferee.

All TPA have to obtain a license from the Authority to function as a TPA for rendering health services. The regulations provide for payment of fees on application by TPA and procedure for grant of license. More than one TPA may be engaged by an insurance company and, similarly, a TPA can serve more than one insurance company.

Every TPA has to appoint, with due intimation to the Authority, from among its directors or senior employees, a Chief Administrative Officer (CAO) or Chief Executive Officer (CEO) who shall be responsible for the proper day-to-day administration of the activities of the TPA. The qualifications are also prescribed for CAO/CEO. The licence is valid for 3 years and is renewed subsequently. The licence granted to a TPA may after due notice be revoked or cancelled by the Authority for reasons provided therein which include breach of terms of issue, professional misconduct and malpractices. The code of conduct of TPA provide the that CAO/CEO shall:-

(a) establish its or his or their identity to the public and the insured/policyholder and that of the insurance company with which it has entered into an agreement;

(b) disclose its licence to the insured/policyholder/prospect;

(c) disclose the details of the services it is authorised to render in respect of health insurance products under an agreement with an insurance company;

(d) bring to the notice of the insurance company with whom it has an agreement, any adverse report or inconsistencies or any material fact that is relevant for the insurance company's business;

(e) obtain all the requisite documents pertaining to the examination of an insurance claim arising out of insurance contract concluded by the insurance company with the insured/policyholder;

(f) render necessary assistance specified under the agreement and advice to policyholders or claimants or beneficiaries in complying with the requirements for settlement of claims with the insurance company;

(g) conduct itself /himself in a courteous and professional manner;

(h) refrain from acting in a manner, which may influence directly or indirectly insured/policyholder of a particular insurance company to shift the insurance portfolio from the existing insurance company to another insurance company;

(i) refrain from trading on information and the records of its business;

(j) maintain the confidentiality of the data collected by it in the course of its agreement;

(k) refrain from resorting to advertisements of its business or the services carried out by it on behalf of a particular insurance company, without the prior written approval by the insurance company;

(l) refrain from inducing an insured/policyholder to omit any material information, or submit wrong information;

(m) refrain from demanding or receiving a share of the proceeds or indemnity from the claimant under an insurance contract;

(n) follow the guidelines/directions that may be issued down by the Authority from time to time.

TPA must maintain all the records and documents of transactions in the manner prescribed, confidentially, and in accordance with accepted professional standards of record keeping and for a period of not less than 3 years. These shall also be available to the insurer on demand. IRDA has power to constitute Committees consisting of members drawn from various sources including the TPAs, insurance companies, Authority, or any other persons as may be decided by the Authority to look into the proper and efficient performance of the TPAs. Every TPA has to furnish to the insurance company and the Authority an annual report and any other return, as may be, required by the Authority on its activities.

Insurance Regulatory and Development Authority (Insurance Brokers) Regulations, 2002

As per the regulations, a "composite broker" means an insurance broker who for the time-being licensed by the Authority to act as such, for a remuneration, arranges insurance for his clients with insurance companies and/or reinsurance for his client(s) and "direct broker" means an insurance broker who for the time-being licensed by the Authority to act as such, for a remuneration carries out the functions as specified under regulation 3 either in the field of life insurance or general insurance or both on behalf of his clients.

The functions of a direct broker include risk assessment, risk advisory services, advising appropriate covers, assisting in claims settlement etc. Reinsurance brokers has to familiarize himself with the client's business and risk retention philosophy, selecting and negotiating reinsurance deals on behalf of the client, collect premiums, assist in the negotiation and settlement of claims and maintain the records. A composite broker shall carry out any one or more of the functions in the said categories.

IRDA grants licence to brokers subject to fulfillment of eligibility requirements, payment of fees and observance of code of conduct.

Any applicant seeking to become an insurance broker under these regulations should satisfy the following conditions:

(i) it shall have a minimum amount of capital as mentioned below:

Category	Minimum amount (Rupees)
(a) Direct broker	fifty lakhs
(b) Reinsurance broker	two hundred lakhs
(c) Composite broker	two hundred and fifty lakhs

(ii) the capital in the case of a company limited by shares and a co-operative society shall be in the form of equity shares;

(iii) the capital in the case of other applicants shall be brought in cash;

(iv) the applicant shall exclusively carry on the business of an insurance broker as licensed under these regulations.

No part of the capital of an applicant shall be held by a non-Indian interest beyond 26% at any time. The licence can be cancelled if the code of conduct is breached.

No insurance broker shall be paid or contract to be paid by way of remuneration (including royalty or licence fees or administration charges or such other compensation), an amount exceeding:

(A) on direct general insurance business %

(i) on tariff products:

(a) 10 per cent of the premium on that part of the business which is compulsory under any statute or any law in force;

(b) 12½ per cent of the premium on others.

(ii) on non-tariff products:

17½ per cent of the premium on direct business.

(B) on direct life insurance business %

(i) individual insurance

(a) 30 per cent of first year's premium

(b) 5 per cent of each renewal premium

(ii) annuity

(a) immediate annuity or a deferred annuity in consideration of a single premium, or where only one premium is payable on the policy:

2 per cent of premium

(b) deferred annuity in consideration of more than one premium:

(i) 7½ per cent of first year's premium

(ii) 2 per cent of each renewal premium

(iii) group insurance and pension schemes:

(a) one year renewable group term insurance, gratuity, superannuation, group savings linked insurance —

7½ per cent of risk premium

Note: Under group insurance schemes there will be no remuneration for the savings component.

(b) single premium -

2 per cent of risk premium

(c) annual contributions, at new business procurement stage -

5 per cent of non risk premium with a ceiling of Rupees three lakhs per scheme.

(d) single premium new business procurement stage -

0.5 per cent with a ceiling of Rupees five lakhs per scheme.

(e) remuneration for subsequent servicing -

(i) one year renewable group term assurance -

2 per cent of risk premium with a ceiling of rupees 50, 000/- per scheme.

(C) on reinsurance business%

(i) as per market practices prevalent from time to time.

The business of the insurance broker shall be carried in such a manner that, not more than 50 per cent of the premium (quantum, receipts, etc., as the case may be) in the first year of business, 40 percent of the premium in the second year of business, and 30 per cent of the premium from the third year of business onwards shall emanate from any one client.

Every insurance broker shall before the commencement of his business, deposit and keep deposited with any scheduled bank a sum equivalent to 20% of the initial capital in fixed deposit, which shall not be released to him unless the prior permission of the Authority is obtained . Provided that the Authority may impose a separate limit of deposit, in any case not exceeding Rupees one hundred lakhs, for a person covered by regulation 2(1)(j)(v). Every insurance broker shall furnish to the Authority as and when called upon to do so a statement certified by the Bank in which such fixed deposit is kept.

The brokers shall act as trustee of the insurance money collected on behalf of the client. Every insurance broker shall take out and maintain and continue to maintain a professional indemnity insurance cover throughout the validity of the period of the licence granted to him by the Authority

Limit of indemnity for any one claim and in the aggregate for the year in the case of insurance brokers shall be as follows:

Category of insurance broker	Limit of indemnity
(a) Direct broker	three times remuneration received at the end of every financial year subject to a minimum limit of rupees fifty lakhs.
(b) Reinsurance broker	three times remuneration received at the end of every financial year subject to a minimum limit of rupees two crores and fifty lakhs.
(c) Composite broker	three times remuneration received at the end of every financial year subject to a minimum limit of rupees five crores.

The brokers have to maintain records on the prescribed manner which can be inspected by IRDA through a designated inspector.

Insurance Regulatory and Development Authority (Licensing of Corporate Agents) Regulations, 2002

Corporate Agents have to obtain license from IRDA, which shall be granted subject to fulfilment of eligibility requirements and code of conduct and payment of requisite fees. These are similar to the one discussed for the agents above.

Insurance Regulatory and Development Authority (Manner of Receipt of Premium) Regulations, 2002

As per the regulations, the he premium to be paid by any person proposing to take an insurance policy or by the policyholder to an insurer may be made in any one or more of the following manner(s), namely:-

(a) Cash;

(b) Any recognized banking negotiable instrument such as cheques, including demand drafts, pay orders, banker's cheques drawn on any scheduled bank in India;

(c) Postal money orders;

(d) Credit or Debit Cards held in his name;

(e) Bank Guarantee or Cash Deposit;

(f) Internet;

(g) E-transfer;

(h) Direct credits via standing instructions of proposer or the policyholder or the life insured through bank transfers; and

(i) any other method of payment as may be approved by the Authority from time to time.

In all cases of risks covered by the policies issued by an insurer, the attachment of risk to an insurer will be in consonance with the terms of Section 64VB of the Act and except in the cases where the premium has been paid in cash, in all other cases the insurer shall be on risk only after the receipt of the premium by the insurer. Provided that in the case of a policy of general insurance that where the remittance made by the proposer or the policyholder is not realised by the insurer, the policy shall be treated as *void ab-initio.*

Provided further that in the case of a policy of life insurance, the continuance of the risk or otherwise shall depend on the terms and conditions of the policy already entered into.

The insurer may at its option recover the collection charges of the instrument from the proposer.

Insurance Regulatory and Development Authority (Distribution of Surplus) Regulations 2002

These regulations deal with distribution of surplus by insurance companies. The two types of policyholders defined in the regulations are as follows:-

"participating policyholders" means the holders of 'par policies' and policies with deferred partcicpation in profits', which are defined in the INSURANCE REGULATORY AND DEVELOPMENT AUTHORITY (Acturial Report and Abstract Regulations) REGULATIONS, 2000;

"non-participating policyholders" means the holders of 'non-par policies' which is defined in the INSURANCE REGULATORY AND DEVELOPMENT AUTHORITY (Acturial Report and Abstract Regulations) REGULATIONS, 2000;

a life insurer registred under Section 3 of the Insurance Act. 1938 shall be required to maintain separately:

(a) a life fund for participating policyholders and

(b) a life fund for non-particpating policyholders.

The life insurer can distribute the valuation surplus arising out of valuation of assets and liabilities in the following manner:

(a) one hundred per cent, in case of a life fund maintained for non-participating policyholders:

(b) one-ninth of the surplus allocated to policyholders in case of a life fund maintained for participating policygolders

Provided that an insurer shall, however be required to obtain prior approval of the Authority in cases where the said allocation is not one-ninth of the surplus.

Provided further that an insurer shall not allocate or reserve exceeding ter per cetnt of the said acturial surplus to its shareholders.

Insurance Regulatory and Development Authority (Micro-Insurance) Regulations 2005

The important terms defined by the regulations are as under:-

"family means a unit comprising of husband, wife, dependant parents and a maximum of three childern.

Provided that where the number of children is more than three, for construting the composition of family as aforesaid, the first three children shall be included.

Provided further that an insurer may, within the aforesaid parameters laid down for the composition of the family, define 'family' as per the requirements of the individual or group.

"life micro-insurance product" means any term insurance contract with or without return of permium, any endowment insurance contract or health insurance contract, with or without an accident benefit rider, either on individual or group basis as per terms stated in Schedule-II appended to these regulations;

"micro-insurance agent" means- (i) a Non-Government Organisation (NGO); or (ii) a Self Help Group (SHG); or (iii) a Micro-Finance Institution (MFI), who is apponited by an insurer to act as a micro-insurance agent for distribution of micro-insurance products.

"micro-insurance policy" means an insurance policy sold under a plan which has been specifically approved by the Authority as a micro-insurance product;

"micro-insurance product" includes a general micro-insurance product or life insurance product, proposal form and all marketing materials in respect thereof;

"general micro-insurance product" means any health insurance contract, any contract covering the belongings, such as hut, livestock or tools or instruments or any persinal accident contract, either on individual or group basis, as per terms stated in Schedule-I appended to these regulations;

The regulations entitle the life insurers to offer life micro-insurance product as well as general insurance product (subject to tie-up with the general insurer) and conversely general insurer can do.

Insurers can appoint exclusive micro-insurance agents who shall work for only one life insurer and one non-life insurer.

Micro-insurance agents can employ specific persons including the corporate and composite agents subject to conditions and must be abide by the code of conduct.

The regulations specify the manner in which the micro-insurance cover has to be made to the policyholder and prohibit underwriting at the level of micro-insurance agents. The commission structure for the micro-insurance agents is:

(a) For Life Insurance Business"

Single premium policies - Ten per-cent of the single premium

Non single premium policies - Twenty per cent of the premium for all the years of the premium paying term

(b) For Non-Life Insurance Business: Fifteen per cent of the premium.

The micro cover is included in the rural and social obligations of insurers. Schedule I and II of the regulations specify the limits to various types of life and non-life covers.

3.3 Summary

Insurance Act, 1938 is the primary law that governs the insurance business in India. This Act prohibit persons to carry on insurances business until he is a public company, a registered society or a corporate body. An eligible organization can apply for License to guidelines for the policy related issues. Section 40 of the Insurance Act 1938 lays down the guidelines for the appointment of agent. An agent should possess a valid license to solicitate insurance business. Any individual who fulfil the requirements can become an agent. Section 7, 8, and 9 of the Insurance Act, 1938 deals with the deposits which are required to be made by the insurer for obtaining license. Guidelines for appointing staff separate account of all receipts and payments in respect of each class of insurance. The Act also specifies the manual in which arrangement and administration of insurance company shall be carried out and also the procedure for winding up of insurance companies.

3.4 Test Yourself

Choose the Correct answer from the choice given:

1. The Insurance Regulatory and Development Authority Act,

   (a) 1999 (b) 2000

   (c) 2001 (d) 2002

2. The insurance act

   (a) 1936 (b) 1937

   (c) 1938 (d) 1940

3. The Life Insurance Corporation Act

   (a) 1954 (b) 1955

   (c) 1956 (d) 1957

4 The General insurance business act

   (a) 1970 (b) 1971

   (c) 1972 (d) 1975

5. Under which section IRDA act defines the Authority as the Insurance Regulatory and Development Authority established under section 3 of the Act.

   (a) 1 (a) (b) 2 (b)
   (c) 3 (c) (d) 4 (b)

6. The primary duty of the IRDA is to regulate, promote and ensure orderly growth and conduct of the insurance business and reinsurance business comes under which section

   (a) 12 (b) 13
   (c) 14 (d) 15

7. The Central Government has the powers under the Act to direct the Authority and grant funds under the head with sanction of the

   (a) Parliament (b) Central government
   (c) State government (d) All of these

8. A credit is also received u/S 7 of the Insurance Act,

   (a) 1935 (b) 1936
   (c) 1938 (d) 1940

9. Abbreviation of IAC is

   (a) Insurance Advisory Committee
   (b) Insurance Authority Committee
   (c) Insurance Advisor Commission
   (d) Insurance Applicable Commission

10. IRDA stands

    (a) Insurance Regulatory and Development Authority
    (b) Insurance Regulation and Development Authority
    (c) Insurance regulator and Department Authority
    (d) Insurance Reputation and Doctrine Amendment

11. Insurance Regulatory and Development Authority (Licensing of Corporate Agents) Regulation

    (a) 2000 (b) 2001
    (c) 2002 (d) 2003

12. Insurance Regulatory and Development Authority (Obligations of Insurers to Rural or Social Sectors) (Amendment) Regulations,

    (a) 2002 (b) 2003
    (c) 2004 (d) 2005

13. Amendments to the Insurance ACT is
   (a) 1936 (b) 1937
   (c) 1938 (d) 1939

14. The principle of utmost good faith is meant to protect the interests of
   (a) The insurer
   (b) The community of policyholders
   (c) The share holders
   (d) None of the above

15. The principle of utmost faith is important to ensure
   (a) That the premium charged is correct
   (b) That no one gets an undue advantage
   (c) That there is no adverse selection
   (d) All the three factors mentioned above

16. Principle of utmost good faith does not apply to
   (a) Facts of common knowledge
   (b) Facts of law
   (c) Facts which are not material for underwriting
   (d) All the three kinds of facts mentioned above

17. Which of the following risks are insurable
   (a) Speculative (b) Economic
   (c) Sure to happen (d) All of the above

18. Insurable interest is
   (a) Defined in the insurance act
   (b) Defined in the contract act
   (c) Defined by the IRDA
   (d) Not defined in any written law

19. In the case of life insurance, the principle of insurable interest operates
   (a) In the same way as in marine insurance
   (b) In the same way as in fire insurance
   (c) In the same way as in motor insurance
   (d) Differently than in other forms of insurances

20. An insurance contract is valid because
    (a) It is not wagering contract
    (b) It promotes socially desirable causes
    (c) It takes care of the destitute
    (d) It provides governments with large funds
21. Retention of risk may be done conveniently by
    (a) Large corporations (b) Small companies
    (c) Single individuals (d) None of the three
22. In the case of life insurance, the risks
    (a) Can be avoided
    (b) Cannot be avoided
    (c) Are avoidable through medical science
    (d) Are avoidable through proper food habits
23. Which one of the following statement is correct
    (a) It is difficult to accurately value a human life
    (b) It is possible to reasonably estimate the value of a human life
    (c) Both of the statement are correct
    (d) Both of the statements are wrong
24. Which one of the following statements is corrects
    (a) Retention of risk is an alternative to insurance
    (b) Insurable interest exists between partners
    (c) Both the statements are correct
    (d) Both the statements are wrong.

State whether the following statements are 'True' or 'False'.

1. The Insurance Regulatory and Development Authority Act,come in tothe existence in 1999.
2. The Life Insurance Corporation Act, 1966 and the General Insurance Business (Nationalisation) Act, 1982.
3. The Statement of Objects and Reasons of the Act provides that the insurance industry requires a low degree of regulation.
4. Section 2(b) of the IRDA Act, 1999 defines the Authority as the Insurance Regulatory and Development Authority established under Section 3 of the Act.

5. The primary duty of the IRDA is to regulate, promote and ensure orderly growth and conduct of the insurance business and reinsurance business (S.14).
6. Authority has the general duty to protect the interest of person in matters concerning assignment, nomination, settlement of insurance claim, surrenders etc., and other terms and conditions of agreement of insurance.
7. Power to constitute committees of the people and delegate the powers to the people.
8. Power to hold and acquire movable or immovable property.
9. Promoting and regulating the professional organizations connected with the insurance and reinsurance business.
10. The Central Government has the powers under the Act to direct the Authority and grant funds under the head with sanction of the organization.
11. The Central Government under the Act has the power to give directions to the Authority on the questions of policy of insurance business.
12. Various regulations have been framed by IRDA since its inception.
13. Regulations Framed under Insurance Regulatory and Development Authority Act, 1998 and the Insurance (Amendment) Act, 2001.
14. Insurance Regulatory and Development Authority (Re-insurance Advisory Committee) Regulations, 2001.
15. Schedules to the IRDA act Amendments to the Insurance ACT, 1938.
16. "9AA. Manner of divesting excess shareholding by promoter in certain cases.
17. 114A. *Power of Authority to make regulations*
18. Insurance Regulatory and Development Authority (Actuarial Report and Abstract) Regulations, 2001
19. Every insurer or intermediary or insurance agent must have a compliance agreement who is responsible to oversee the advertising programme and exercise control over it and maintain register of advertisement contracts.
20. The insurer in writing prior to its issue must approve every advertisement by an insurance agency that affects a man.
21. The meeting of IRDA must be held not less than four times in a year, to transact its business. These also deal with serving of notices of meetings, appointment of coordinators, and quorum.
22. Every insurer must be registered with RBI.
23. *"non-linked business"* means life insurance contracts or health insurance contracts which are not linked business.
24. The regulations prescribe for the manner of registration and enrollment.

25. The registration is subject to submissions and thorough scrutiny by the authority.

26. These regulations deal with the method and format of preparation of Financial Statements and Auditor's Report of Insurance Companies.

27. The regulations also provide for various matters of policy servicing by insurers and disclosure of material information to the policyholders.

28. These regulations deal with the conduct of meetings of Insurance Advisory Committee constituted by IRDA under Section 24 of the IRDA Act, 1999.

29. There must at least be four meetings of the committee every year.

30. The minutes of the proceedings at the meetings must be recorded in the prescribed manner,

31. The insurance agents is/are to ensure the remittance of premiums by policyholders within stipulated time.

32. These guidelines provide for the valuation of Assets and Liabilities and maintenance of the solvency margin by insurers.

33. every insurer shall prepare a statement of faithful margin in accordance with schedules to the regulations for life and general insurance insurers and claims.

34. Schedule I to the regulations defined 'non-mandated investments' means those investments that are neither approved equity nor approved market.

35. Every insurer has to constitute an Investment Committee which shall consist of a minimum of two non-executive directors of the Insurer.

36. No reinsurance shall be done on original premium basis unless the Authority approves such programme

37. "TPA" means a Third Party Administrator.

38. All TPA have to obtain a license from the Authority to function as a TPA for rendering health services.

39. The qualifications are also prescribed for CAO/CEO. The licence is valid for 3 years and is renewed subsequently.

40. TPA must not maintain all the records and documents of transactions in the manner prescribed, confidentially, and in accordance with accepted professional standards of record keeping and for a period of more than 3 years.

41. Every TPA has to furnish to the insurance company and the Authority an annual report and any other return, as may be, required by the Authority on its activities.

42. RBI grants licence to brokers subject to fulfillment of eligibility requirements, payment of fees and observance of code of conduct.

43. Under group insurance schemes there will be no remuneration for the savings component

44. Every insurance broker shall before the commencement of his business, deposit and keep deposited with any scheduled bank a sum equivalent to 50% of the initial capital in fixed deposit,

45. The brokers shall act as trustee of the insurance money collected on behalf of the client.

46. Insurance Act, 1938 is the primary law that governs the insurance business in India.

Fill in the blanks with an appropriate word.

1. The Insurance Regulatory and Development Authority Act ....
2. The insurance act is ....
3. The Life Insurance Corporation Act, ...
4. The General Insurance Business (Nationalisation) Act, ...
5. The Statement of .... And .... of the Act provides that the ....industry requires a high .... of regulation.
6. Section 2(b) of the IRDA Act, ... defines the Authority as the .... established under Section of the act.
7. The primary duty of the IRDA is to .... , ... and ensure orderly .... , and conduct of the insurance business and ....
8. The Authority has to submit the audited .... And .... statements to the Central Government and the Government will lay there ports before the houses of the Parliament.
9. The Authority has to submit all the .... to the .... within .... from the completion of the relevant .... year.
10. Authority has the general duty to protect the interest of in matters concerning assignment, ..., ... , ... etc., and other terms and conditions of contract of ....
11. The Authority has the general supervisory power of .... industry and it has the ....
12. Powers to appoint the staff and officers required to conduct the business of ....
13. Power to constitute committees of the members and delegate the powers to ....
14. Power to hold and acquire .... and .... property.
15. Power to issue a certificate of registration, renew, modify, withdraw, suspend or cancel such registration to the ....

16. Power to prepare a code of conduct to the .... , ... and .... and other .... with insurance business .
17. Power to exercise the powers sanctioned by other insurance laws of the country or by other notifications issued by the............. from time to time.
18. .... and .... in the conduct of insurance business in India.
19. To act as adjudicator in the settlement of disputes between .... And .... of the insurer.
20. To act as supervisory authority and regulate the functioning of .... and various ....
21. The Central Government has the powers under the Act to direct the .... and grant funds under the head with sanction of the ....
22. Registration fees, application fees from insurers and other .... are also credited to the fund.
23. The Central Government under the Act has the .... to give directions to the .... on the questions of policy of ....
24. IAC stands for ....
25. The Regulatory Authority is under a duty to submit all the rules framed by it for the approval of ....
26. Regulations Framed under Insurance Regulatory and Development Authority Act, ... and the Insurance (Amendment) Act, ...
27. Insurance Regulatory and Development Authority (Re-insurance Advisory Committee) Regulations ....
28. Insurance Regulatory and Development Authority (Protection of Policy Holders' Interest) Regulations, ...
29. Amendments to the Insurance ACT, ...
30. In the Act, except in clause (5B) of .... and .... for Controller.
31. A licence issued under this section shall remain in force for a period of .... only from the date of issue .
32. Amedments to the Life Insurance Corporation Act ....
33. Insurance Regulatory and Development Authority ....
34. The qualifications of actuary are defined in the ....
35. Insurance Regulatory and Development Authority (Actuarial Report and Abstract) Regulations, ...
36. These regulations deal with the manner and contents of Actuarial Report and Abstracts to be submitted to ....
37. .... means the terms in regard to benefits or premiums or charges, which may not be altered during the currency of the policy
38. .... means individual insurance contracts issued on single/joint lives.
39. .... means, as respects any valuation, the period to the valuation date of that valuation.

40. ....means a fixed date on which benefit may become payable either absolutely or contingently.

41. means regular premium (excluding extra premiums which are required to be shown separately) payable by the policyholder to secure the basic benefits under the policy in a policy year.

42. .... means the rights available to a policyholder under a policy.

43. ....orpolicies with participation in profits" means polices which are not non-par policies as defined under clause (i)

44. .... means the period during which premiums are payable.

45. .... or ....means add-on benefits, which are in addition to basic benefits under a policy.

46. .... means as respects any valuation the date as at which the valuation is made.

47. ASCI stands for ....

48. The life insurance policy must clearly state the ....

49. The regulations also provide for various matters of policy servicing by insurers and disclosure of material information to the ....

50. .... or .... means persons who live below the poverty line.

51. ....means the unit of insurance passed to a reinsurer by the insurer which issued a policy to the original insure.

52. .... means the reinsurance of a part or all of a single policy in which cession is negotiated separately and that the.

53. .... means an insurer who carries on exclusively reinsurance business and is approved in this behalf by the Central Government.

54. ....means any joint underwriting operation of insurance or reinsurance in which the participants assume a predetermined and fixed interest in all business.

55. .... means the transaction whereby a reinsurer cedes to another insurer or reinsurer all or part of the reinsurance it has previously assumed.

56. .... means the amount which an insurer assumes for his own account. In proportionate contracts, the retention may be a percentage of the policy limit. In excess of loss contracts .... is an amount of loss.

57. .... can be cancelled in violation of the norms specified.

58. The IRDA has power to constitute a committee called .... and.............. for assisting the Authority on the matters and affairs relating to Insurance Surveyors and ....

59. IRDA has power to amend the reinsurance programme of the ....

60. "TPA" means a...................

61. All TPA have to obtain a license from the Authority to function as a TPA for rendering ....

62. .... includes a general micro-insurance product or life insurance product, proposal form and all marketing materials in respect thereof.

Module II

CHAPTER 4

INTRODUCTION TO LIFE INSURANCE

Learning Objectives

After studying this chapter, one can understand

- The history of life insurance
- Meaning and definition of life insurance
- Characteristics of life insurance
- Features of life insurance contracts
- Nature of insurance
- Advantages of life insurance

4.1 History of Life Insurance

The accurate account of the history of life insurance is difficult to give, but the various references; whatever is available indicates the presence of some protection similar to modern day insurance. In this context Manu and Yajnavalkya are credited with such thoughts in Hindu Scriptures. In Rigveda, the Sanskrit word "Yogakshema" found in Manav Dharma shows a communal insurance. Greek and Syrian writers also mentioned about ancient forms of insurance. In middle ages, insurance protection was granted by Anglo-Saxxon Guilds. The members belonged to one religion. Each paid a fixed amount to a common fund. The fund was expended on feasts, fines, mass (for the death, burials) and brothers in need. For long insurance against death was taken as an act against God. So naturally India could not develop insurance business till very late.

4.1.1 World Life Insurance Scenario

Insurance appeared in England in 16th century. Richard Mortin issued the first policy on William Gybbon's life in the year 1536. Annuities were issued earlier to insurance. The W.Gybbon's policy gave great publicity for life insurance. The private insurers took up the business and gathered in Exchange Alley where the business settled. Later two companies by the names "Hand in Hand Society" and "The Mercers' Company" came into existence in the year 1696 and 1698 respectively. The society of assurance for Widows and Orphans was started by Stansfield in 1699. Amicable Society for a perpetual assurance office got in 1706, a charter for operations by private underwriters. In 1719, the business of life insurance was undertaken in joint stock form. In 1721, Parliament passed an act which allowed promotion of companies to take up business of insurance. So many big companies came into existence in Britain like the Royal Exchange Assurance, London Assurance, British Insurance Company, Symons Assurance of Lives, etc.

In Europe insurance was slow to take roots. In France (Pordonaucede la Marine of 1681) insurance on life was prohibited. In 19th century only France allowed life insurance. The first company was (Compagnie Royald' Assurance surla via 1787). In Germany the first company came up in 1806 but closed due to internal wars. The company Arnoldi in Gotha started in 1829 was successful. In USA insurance was started for insuring policies to Colonists. The first public insurance office was started on Pheladelphia in 1721 (Meher and Oster). The slow growth of insurance in USA was due to wild fluctuations in death rates. But with level premiums it spread fast in New England and Bastojn but not before 19th century.

4.1.2 Life Insurance Scenario in India

The modern concept of insurance came into existence with advent of East India Company in 18th century. Many insurers from UK started to come to insure the English residents. But in 19th century, when Indians were recruited to jobs in various offices, then they started seeking protection with insurance companies. The first (foreign) company which started the insurance business in India was 'Oriental Life Insurance Company' at Calcutta in the year 1818. In 1823, "Bombay Life Assurance Company" started giving insurance policies for two-three year terms. Then "Madras Equitable Life Assurance Society" came into existence in 1829. These companies failed due to improper management of valuation, wrong depreciation of investments and defective ratings. After that so many developments took place. Many European Companies tried to establish insurance business in India but failed to survive due to unethical business practices. The British Parliament passed an Insurance Act in 1870 and then a few organised efforts were made in the Life Insurance Sector in India.

In 1871, some prominent citizens of Bombay started the Bombay Life Assurance Society. In 11874, Oriental Government Security Life Assurance Company Ltd. was established as a proprietary business. A few years later, The Bharat (1896) and 'The Empire of India' (1897) were established. During the nation's independent movement, many enterprises, particularly owned by Indian insurers grew up. Some of these are the Limited India Life; the National in 1906, the Hindustan Co-operative in 1907; The Bombay Life; The Asian Life and the Indian Equitable in 1908. The First World War gave a boost to Indian Life Insurance business.

The first attempt to regulate the Insurance business in India was made in 1912 through the Indian Life Assurance Companies Act. This was later broad-based and the Indian Life Insurance Companies Act came into existence from the year 1928 onwards. This act enabled the government to collect statistical information about both life and non-life insurance business. During the period between first and second world wars, Indian economy was in bad shape and the business was depressed. To meet the shortage of credit, industrialists started their own insurance companies. Few of them are The New India, 1919 and the Jupiter General, 1919. Insurance business was marked for high rebates, excessive commissions, increased operating expenses. Business became diversified but Foreign insurers attracted more business than Indian insurers. In 1938, earlier legislation was consolidated and amended with the objective of protecting the interests of the insuring public. The Insurance Act, 1938 came into existence.

After the Second World War, so many new insurance companies came up. The insurance legislation, the low mortality rate, keen competition was helpful to increase the insurance business. In between 1941 and 1945, 25 new companies were started. But bad features like speculation, inflation and financial irregularities were found. Industrialists started banks and insurance companies and interlocked the investment. The government passed the Act in 1950 to stop interlocking. The government took many constructive steps to increase the life insurance business during the first five year plan. The staff and group life insurance schemes were introduced in 1954. Eventhough no new companies came up, the life insurance business was increased. In 1955, the new business was Rs. 220.9 crores on 7,49,000 policies.

The year 1956 was the major milestone in the history of life insurance business. 245 Indian and foreign insurers and provident societies taken over by the Central Government and then nationalized. Life insurance companies (LIC) of India was formed by an Act of Parliament, *viz.,* LIC Act, 1956, with a capital contribution of Rs.5 crores from the government of India. Since then the LIC had been enjoying a monopoly over the life insurance business in India, till the sector was opened up to private companies in 2000.

4.1.3 Insurance Sector Reforms

In 1993, Malhotra Committee headed by former Finance Secretary and RBI Governor, R. N. Malhotra was formed to evaluate the Indian Insurance Industry and recommend its future direction.

The Committee was set up with an objective of complementing the reforms in the Indian Financial sector. The reforms were aimed at "creating a more efficient and competitive financial system suitable for the requirements of the economy keeping in mind the structural changes currently underway and recognizing that insurance is an important part of the overall financial system where it was necessary to address the need for similar reforms."

Malhotra Committee — Purpose and Recommendations

Purpose

(a) To suggest the structure of the insurance industry, to access its strengths and weaknesses of insurance companies in terms of the objectives of creating an efficient and viable insurance industry, which will have a wide reach of insurance services, a variety of insurance products with a high quality of services to the public and servicing as an effective instrument for mobilization of financial resources for development.

(b) To make recommendations for changing structure of insurance industry, for changing general policy framework, etc.

(c) To take specific suggestions regarding LIC and GIC with a view to improve functioning of LIC and GIC.

(d) To make recommendations on regulation and supervision of the insurance sector in India.

(e) To make recommendations on role and functioning of surveyors, intermediaries like agents, etc. in the insurance sector.

(f) To make recommendations on any other matter which are relevant for development of the insurance industry in India.

Recommendations

In 1994, the committee submitted the report and gave the following recommendations now in the point form:

Structure

- Government stake in the insurance companies to be brought down to 50%
- Government should take over the holdings of GIC and its subsidiaries so that these subsidiaries can act as independent corporations
- All the insurance companies should be given greater freedom to operate.

Competition

- Private Companies with a minimum paid up capital of Rs. 1 billion should be allowed to enter the industry
- No Company should deal in both Life and General Insurance through a single entity
- Foreign Companies may be allowed to enter the industry in collaborations with the domestic companies
- Postal Life Insurance should be allowed to operate in the rural market
- Only one State Level Life Insurance Company should be allowed to operate in each state

- The Insurance Act should be changed
- An Insurance Regulatory body should be set up
- Controller of Insurance (Currently a part from the Finance Ministry) should be made independent

Investments

- Mandatory Investments of LIC Life Fund in government securities to be reduced from 75% to 50%
- GIC and its subsidiaries are not to hold more than 5% in any company (There current holdings to be brought down to this level over a period of time)

Customer Service

- LIC should pay interest on delays in payments beyond 30 days
- Insurance companies must be encouraged to set up unit linked pension plans
- Computerisation of operations and updating of technology to be carried out in the insurance industry.

Overall, the committee strongly felt that in order to improve the customer services and increase the coverage of the insurance industry should be opened up to competition.

But at the same time, the committee felt the need to exercise caution as any failure on the part of new players could ruin the public confidence in the industry.

Hence, it was decided to allow competition in a limited way by stipulating the minimum capital requirement of Rs. 1 billion. This amount is not very high for foreign firms, as it translates to only about US $ 25 million. Further, to date it is unclear whether equity should be payable in one go or should be brought in as installments. Also, the foreign equity participation was to be restricted to only 40%.

The committee strongly felt the need to provide greater autonomy to insurance companies in order to improve their performance and enable them to act as independent companies with economic motives. For this purpose, it had proposed setting up an independent regulatory body.

The industry and analysts find that there is lack of clarity in the following areas:

- Though coverage of rural areas was to be made compulsory, it raises the question as to who would subsidize the rural policies as they would be difficult to service and hence costs will go up.
- There is some confusion with respect to investments. Where should the funds be invested? Currently 70% of the funds with LIC & GIC are invested in Government securities. Would new entrants be allowed to invest in GOI securities?
- The report also does not enumerate exit options available to the new entrants. In the event of failure, there should be an arrangement made whereby the

other companies pool in to bail the customers, who in all probability would be middle class individuals.

It was on the basis of this report, that the then Finance Minister P. Chidambaram proposed the opening up of insurance to the private sector, including multinational companies.

4.1.4 Liberalisation of Insurance Sector

The IRDA Bill was drafted keeping the Malhotra Committee recommendations in view and hence the government has ruled out privatisation of public sector insurance companies, LIC and GIC. The bill did not provide for any dilution of 100 per cent government equity in the two premier companies.

The 71-page IRDA bill sought to give a statutory status to the interim Insurance Regulatory Authority and amend the 1938 Insurance Act, the 1956 Life Insurance Corporation Act and the 1972 General Insurance Business (Nationalization) Act to open up the sector. It provides for a nine-member regulatory body with statutory powers.

The IRDA Bill also fixed minimum capital requirement for life and general insurance at Rs. 100 crore and for reinsurance firms at Rs. 200 crore. The minimum solvency margin for private insurers is Rs. 500 million for life insurance companies, Rs. 500 million or a sum equivalent to 20 per cent of net premium income for general insurance and Rs. 1 billion for reinsurance companies. The Malhotra Committee Report justified the entry of foreign insurance companies by arguing that if it is permitted, it should be done on selective basis preferably through joint venture with Indian partner.

When the bill was first introduced in the Parliament, the reactions were mixed. The Vajpayee government reintroduced the bill with some changes. In 1999, the bill was finally passed and IRDA was formed to regulate and promote insurance business in India.

4.1.5 Life Insurance Players in India

The year 2000 was a defining movement in the history of Indian Insurance Industry. For the first time, the sector was opened up to private companies. Now we find a number of private insurance companies entered into the Indian insurance market. If the FDI is raised from 26% to 49%, the number will be multiplied. Following are the private insurance players in the life insurance sector of insure.

1. Bajaj Allianz Life Insurance Company Limited
2. Birla Sun Life Insurance Co. Ltd.
3. HDFC Standard Life Insurance Co. Ltd.
4. ICICI Prudential Life Insurance Co. Ltd.
5. ING Vysya Life Insurance Co. Ltd.
6. Max New York Life Insurance Co. Ltd.

7. Met Life Insurance Co. Ltd. Pvt. Ltd.
8. Kotak Mahindra Old Mutual Life Insurance Limited
9. SBI Mutual Life Insurance Limited
10. Tata AIG Life Insurance Co. Ltd.
11. Reliance Life Insurance Co. Ltd.
12. Aviva Life Insurance Co. Ltd. Pvt. Ltd.
13. Sahara Life Insurance Co. Ltd.
14. Shriram Life Insurance Co. Ltd.
15. Bharti Life Insurance Co. Ltd.
16. Future General Life Insurance Co. Ltd.
17. IDBI Fortis Life Insurance Company Ltd.
18. Canara HSBC Oriental Bank of Commerce Life Insurance Company Ltd.
19. Aegon Religare Life Insurance Company Ltd.
20. DLF Pramerica Life Insurance Company Ltd.

4.2 Life Insurance

Meaning and Definition

Life Insurance, usually referred to as 'life assurance' insures the insured against the happening of certain event *i.e.* death through the time when it may happen is uncertain. The life insurance contract can be described as 'contingent contracts' because the loss of life cannot be compensated and only a specified sum of money is paid if the insured dies. In addition to this, life insurance is considered a better way of making investment alongwith the benefits of protection against the risks of death.

Section 2 of the Indian Insurance Act, 1938 has defined life insurance as:

"Life Insurance business is the business of effecting contracts upon human life."

A life insurance contract may be defined as 'a contract whereby the insurer, in consideration of a premium paid either in lump sum or in periodic instalments, undertakes to pay an annuity or a certain sum of money, either on the death of the insured or on the expiry of a certain number of years.'

In simple words, it may be defined as 'a contract whereby the insurance company, in consideration of periodical premium, agrees to pay a certain amount either on the death or on the maturity of the policy, whichever is earlier.

J. H. Maggee has defined life insurance in the following words:

The life insurance contract embodies an agreement, in which, broadly stated, the insurer undertakes to pay a stipulated sum upon the death of the insured, or at some designated time to a designated beneficiary.

As such, under life insurance, the sum assured under policy is paid to the insured if policy matures during his life time and to his nominees in case of death. The premium may be paid in lump sum or in monthly, quarterly, half-yearly or yearly instalments.

4.3 Characteristics of Life Insurance

1. Like other contracts of insurance, the life insurance contract is also the outcome of an offer made by the insured and its acceptance by the insurer. Usually, contract of life insurance is made in writing.
2. The insurance company agrees to pay a certain sum of money either on the death of the insured or on the maturity of the policy, whichever is earlier.
3. The insured is under obligation to pay periodically the amount of payment till the death of insured or expiry of the period of policy, whichever is earlier.
4. The contract of life insurance is not a contract of indemnity because the loss caused by the death cannot be calculated in money terms, nor is money any compensation for loss of one's life.
5. Insurable interest must be present in the person insured at the time when the policy is taken in case of life insurance, which may or may not be present at the time of insured's death.
6. Life insurance extends the hand of protection to those who are left supportless and helps financially in case of death of the insured. It is also considered to be the best alternative for making savings.
7. Life insurance covers under scope certain other risks which are connected with the human life in addition to the risk of death. For example, in case of total and permanent disability or the living death, temporary disability and medical expenses, compulsory retirement or the economic death risks, etc., have also been covered under the purview of life insurance these days.
8. It relieves the insured from the sword of democles *i.e.* various risks and uncertainties which may occur before and after the death of the insured.

4.4 Features/Characteristics of Life Insurance Contracts

(i) Nature of General Contract.

(ii) Insurable Interest.

(iii) Utmost Good Faith

(iv) Warranties.

(v) Proximate Cause.

(vi) Assignment and Nomination.

(vii) Return of Premium.

(viii) Other Features

In life insurance contract, the first three features are very important while the rest of them are of complementary nature.

4.4.1 Nature of General Contract

Since the life insurance contract is a sort of contract, it is approved by the Indian Contract Act. According to Section 2(H) and Section 10 of Indian Contract Act, the valid contracts must have the following essentialities:

(i) Agreement (offer and acceptance).

(ii) Competency of the parties.

(iii) Free consent of the parties, *i.e.*, the parties must be *ad-idem*.

(iv) Legal consideration.

(v) Legal objective.

1. Offer and Acceptance

An offer or proposal is an intimation to another of one's intention to do or to abstain from doing anything with a view to obtaining the assent of that other person to such an act or abstinence. When the person to whom the proposal or offer is made signifies his assent to it, the offer is said to be accepted. The offer and acceptance in life insurance is of typical nature. The proposal form is completed by the proposer and along with the proposal form first premium is paid. The same may be accepted at normal rates and terms. The Agents' canvassing or publications of prospectus and of uses of insurance constitute invitation to offer because the public in general and individual in particular are invited to make proposal for insurance. Submission of proposal along with the premium is an offer and the despatch of acceptance letter is the acceptance. The risk will commence as soon as the despatched by the insurer. When proposal is not accompanied with first premium, it acceptance letter is would be an invitation to offer by the prospect and the letter of insurer (generally acceptance letter with modification is sent) asking the proposer to pay the first premium without any alteration is an offer and the payment of first premium by the prospect is acceptance. As soon as premium is despatched, acceptance is made provided there was no alteration in the terms and conditions.

Another case may be when the insurer desires to accept the proposal only on certain modifications. The letter (generally the acceptance letter) sent to the prospect about the desire of change in terms and conditions is an offer if the first premium was not sent along with the proposal. But if the first premium was sent along with the proposal, it would be a counter-offer. If the prospect accepts the terms and conditions and sends the first premium if the premium was not already sent, it would be an acceptance. Thus the acceptance letter sent by the insurer is not always acceptance. It would be acceptance only when the first premium was accompanied with the proposal and the proposal is acceptable on normal rates and terms. In other cases it would be an offer or counter-offer.

2. Competency of the Parties

The essential element of a valid contract is that the parties to it must be legally competent to contract. (1)Every person is competent to contract who is of the age of majority according to the law, (2) who is of sound mind, and (3) who is not disqualified from contracting by any law.

The insurer will be competent to contract if he has got the licence to carry on insurance business. The insurer is working within the Article of Association and Memorandum of Association or the Deeds of Partnership. In India, the Life Insurance Corporation is solely authorized to carry on life insurance business.

Majority

Majority is attained when a person completes the age of 18 years. A minor is not competent to contract. A contract by a minor is void excepting contracts for necessaries. The minor can repudiate the contract at any time during his minority. If the life insurance policy is issued to a minor, the insurer cannot repudiate it but the minor can repudiate it during his minority. At the attainment of majority, he has to exercise the option, within a reasonable time, whether he would continue to carry on the policy or not. Generally, insurer accepts the proposal forms completed by the guardians of the minors. So, the incompetency of contract does not arise.

Person of Sound Mind

Persons of sound mind can enter into a contract. A person is said to be of sound mind for the purpose of making a contract if at the time when he makes it, he is capable of understanding it and of forming a rational judgement as to its effects upon his interests. A person who is usually of unsound mind, but occasionally of sound mind may make a contract when he is of sound mind. A person usually of sound mind, but occasionally of unsound mind, may not make a contract when he is of unsound mind. So, an intoxicated person cannot enter into a contract. The contract may be voidable at his option, but in order to be avoided, it must be repudiated by the insured within a reasonable time of his becoming sober. Similarly, when an originally valid contract has been entered into, it will not be affected by one of the parties becoming lunatic afterwards.

Other Disqualification

A contract with an alien enemy is void. An alien enemy is disqualified from, and is incapable of, entering into contract or enforcing it. When an alien with whom an insurance contract has been entered into becomes an enemy afterwards, the contract is either suspended or terminated as from the declaration of war.

3. Free Consent of the Parties

Both parties must be of same mind at the time of contract. If the two parties do not meet in this respect, there is no perfect agreement between them. It is necessary to call it free consent of parties that the contract is not made (consent is not obtained) through coercion, undue influence, fraud, misrepresentation or mistake. In life insurance, both parties must know the exact nature of the risk to be underwritten. If the consent is not free, the contract is generally voidable at the option of the party whose consent was not freely given. According to Section 13, two persons are said to consent freely when they agree upon the same thing in the same sense.

4. Legal Consideration

The presence of a lawful consideration is essential for a legal contract. The insurer must have some consideration in return of his promise to pay a fixed sum at maturity or death whichever may be the case. The consideration need not be money only. It should be anything valuable or to which value may be assigned. It may be interest, right, dividend, etc. In *Raj Narain vs. Hindustan Co-operative Insurance*, the insurance was accepted and the premium was paid but the policy was not issued by the insurers. The insurer died and could not get the policy amount in allegiance of policy because at the payment of premiums, contract was complete. The first premium is consideration and subsequent premiums are merely conditions to contract.

5. Legal Objective

The contract would be legal only when the object is legal. The object of a legal life insurance contract is to protect oneself or one's family against financial losses at the death of the insured. The contract is, sometimes, to provide for financial emergencies that may occur in old age. In brief, the contract will be lawful only when the objective is legal. The objective will be legal only when there is insurable interest. Without having this interest, the object of the contract would not be legal. It would be wager contract and against public policy.

4.4.2 Insurable Interest

Insurable interest is the pecuniary interest. The insured must have an insurable interest in the life to be insured for a valid contract. Insurable interest arises out of the pecuniary relationship that exists between the policy-holder and the life assured so that the former stands to loose by the death of the latter and/or continues to gain by his survival. If such relationship exists, then the former has insurable interest in the life of the latter. The loss should be monetary or financial. Mere emotion and expectation do not constitute insurable interest in the life of his friend or father merely because he gets valuable advices from them.

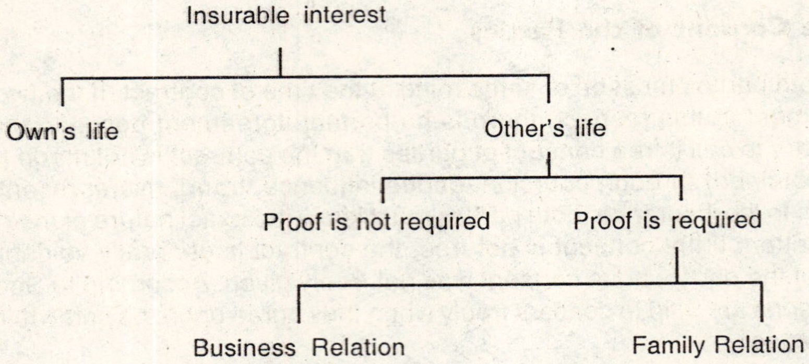

Insurable interest in life insurance may be divided into two categories: (i) insurable interest in own life and (ii) insurable interest in other's life. The latter can be sub-divided into two classes: (a) where proof is not required and (b) where proof is not required. Again this insurable interest (b) can be divided into two classes; (i) insurable interest arising due to business relationship, and (ii) insurable interest in family relation.

Insurable Interest in Own's Life

An individual always has an insurable interest in his own life. Its presence is not required to be proved. Bunyon says, "Every man is presumed to possess an insurable interest in his estate for the loss of his future gains or savings which might be the result of his premature death." According to the definition of insurable interest it is also evident that the person will continue to gain financially while he is surviving and will suffer loss if he is dead because he will be unable to earn or protect the property.

The insurable interest in own life is unlimited because the loss to the insured or his dependents cannot be measured in terms of money and, therefore, no limit can be placed to the amount of insurance that one may take on one's own life. Thus, theoretically, a person can take a policy to any unlimited amount on his own life; but in practice no insurer will issue a policy for an amount larger than amount seems suitable to the circumstances and means of the applicant. Generally, it is mentioned that one cannot purchase policy usually more than ten times of his one year's income. The premium can be paid by third party provided there was no intention to speculation. If there is possibility of wager contract it would be void.

Insurable Interest in Other's Life

Life insurance can be effected on the lives of third parties provided the proposer has insurable interest in the third party. There are two types of insurable interest in other's life. First where proof is not required and second, where proof is required.

A. Proof not Required

There are only two such cases where the presence of insurable interest is legally presumed and therefore need not be proved.

1. **Wife has insurable interest in the life of her husband:** It is presumed and decided by *Reed vs. Royal Exchange* (1795) that wife is presumed to have insurable interest in the life of her husband because husband is legally bound to support his wife. The wife will suffer financially if the husband is dead and will continue to gain if the husband is servicing. Since, the extent of loss or gain cannot be measured in this case; the wife has insurable interest in the husband's life upto an unlimited extent.

2. **Husband has insurable interest in the life of his wife:** The insurable interest is presumed to exist here and no proof is required, insurable interest in the life of her husband because husband is legally. It was decided in *Griffith vs. Fleming* (1909) that the husband has insurable interest in his wife's life because of domestic services performed by the wife. If the wife is dead husband has to employ other person to render the domestic services and certain other financial expenditures will involve at her death which are not calculable. The husband is benefited at the survival of his wife, so it is self-proved that husband has insurable interest in his wife's life. Since, the monetary loss at her death or monetary gain at his survival cannot be measured, there is unlimited insurable interest in the life of wife.

B. Proof is Required

Insurable interest has to be proved in the following cases:

1. ***Business Relationship:*** The policy-holder may have insurable interest in the life of assured due to business and contractual relationship. In this case, the amount of insurable corresponds with the amount of risk involved. Some of such examples are narrated below:

   (a) *A creditor has in the life of his debtor.* The creditor may lose money if the debtor dies before the loan is repaid. The continuance of debtor's life is financially meaningful to the creditor because the latter will get his all money repaid at the former's survival. The maximum amount of loss to a creditor may be the amount of outstanding loan plus interest thereon and the amount of premium paid. So, the maximum amount of insurable interest is limited to the outstanding loan, plus interest amount of premium expected to be paid. The interest is calculated on the estimation of duration of debt to be paid. The maximum amount of interest does not say about the payment of policy amount, it merely, determines the chances of speculation. The full amount of policy is payable irrespective of the payment of loan and interest. Since it is life insurance, the full policy amount is paid.

   (b) *A trustee has insurable interest in respect of the interest of which he is trustee* because at the survival of the other person the trustee is benefited and at the death he will suffer.

   (c) *A surety has insurable interest in the life of his principal.* If the principal (the debtor) is dead, the surety is responsible for payment of outstanding loan and obligated amount. At the survival of principal, he will not suffer this loss. The insurable interest is limited upto the amount of outstanding loan, interest and premium paid.

(d) *A partner has insurable interest in the life of each partner.* At the death of a partner, the partnership will be dissolved and the surviving partner will lose financially. Even if the firm continues at the death of the partner, the firm has to pay deceased partner's share to his dependents. This will involve a huge financial loss to the partnership. Therefore, the firm collectively can purchase insurance policies in the life of each partner of the firm. Since the firm part of money up to the extent of deceased partner goodwill, capital, share of profit and reserve, the firm has insurable interest upto the extent in each partner. Similarly all the partners have insurable interest in life of each partner because they will financially suffer at a death.

(e) *An employer has insurable interest in the life of a key-man.* A key-man is the person whose presence, capital capacity cause profit to the business. If the key-man is dead, the business will reduce profit upto a certain extent. The business suffers reduced profit, expenses involved in appointing and training new persons and the amount to be given to the dependants of key-man at his death. So the business has insurance interest upto such extent in the key-man's life.

(f) *An insurer has in the life assured.* The insurer suffers at the death of life assured and, therefore, he can get reinsurance of the assured persons by him. The insurable interest is limited upto the policy amount.

2. ***Family Relationship:*** The insurable interest may arise due family relationship if pecuniary interest exists between the policy-holders and life assured because mere relationship or ties of blood and of affection does not constitute insurable interest, the proposer must have a reasonable expectation of financial benefit from the continuance of the life of the person to be insured or of financial loss from his death. The interest must be based on value and not on mere sentiments. Similarly, mere moral obligation is not sufficient to warrant existence of insurable interest of the person who is supposed in the life of the person who is supporting. Thus a son can insure his father's life only when he is dependent on him and the father can take insurance policy on his son's life only when he is dependent on his son.

General Rule of Insurance Interest in Life Insurance

1. ***Time of Insurable Interest:*** The insurable interest must exist at the time of proposal. Policy, without insurable interest, will be wager. It is not essential that the insurable interest must be present at the time of claim.

2. ***Services:*** Except the services of wife, services of other relatives will not essentially form insurable interest. There must be financial relationship between the proposer and life assured. In other words, the services performed by the son without dependence of his father, will not constitute insurable

interest of the father, in the life of his son. *Vice-versa* is not essential for forming insurable interest.

3. ***Insurable Interest must be Valuable:*** In business relationship, the value or extent of the insurable must be determined to avoid wager contract of the additional insurance. Insurance is limited only upto the amount of insurable interest.

4. ***Insurable Interest should be Valid:*** Insurable Interest should not be against public policy and it should be recognised by law. Therefore, the consent of life assured is very essential before the policy can be issued.

5. ***The Legal Responsibility may be the Basis of Insurable Interest:*** Since the person will suffer financially upto the extent of responsibility, the proposal has insurable interest to that extent. For instance, a person will be under legal responsibility to the expense at the funeral of his wife and children, he can purchase insurance in their lives upto that extent.

6. ***Insurable Interest must be Definite:*** The insurable interest must be present definitely at the time of proposal. Mere expectation of gain or support will not constitute insurable interest.

7. ***Legal Consequence:*** The insurable interest must be there to form legal and valid insurable contract. Without insurable interest it would be null and void.

4.4.3 Utmost Good Faith

The life insurance requires that the principle of utmost good faith should be preserved by both the parties. The utmost good faith says that the parties, proposer (insured) and insurer must be of the same mind at the time of contract because only then the risk may be correctly ascertained. They must make full and true disclosure of the facts material to the risk.

Material Facts

In life insurance, material facts are age, income, occupation, health, habits, residence, family history and plan of insurance. Material facts are determined not on the basis of opinion, therefore the proposer should disclose not only those matters which the proposer may feel are material but all facts which are material.

Duty of Both Parties

It is not only the proposer but the insurer also who is responsible to disclose all the material facts which are going to influence the decision of the proposer, whether apply or not to apply for insurance. Since the decision is taken mostly on the basis of subject matter, the life to be insured in life insurance, and the material facts relating to the subject matter are known or is expected to be known by the proposer; it is much more responsibility of the proposer to disclose the material facts

Full and True Disclosure

Utmost good faith says that there should be full and true disclosure of all the material facts. Full and True means that there should be no concealment, misrepresentation, half disclosures and fraud of the subject matter to be insured.

Extent of the Duty

The duty of disclosure finishes at the moment when the proposal form has been fully and correctly fulfilled provided there is no such fact which he considers or expected to be considered material and have not been disclosed. The proposer cannot defend on the ground that he had omitted to disclose it by carelessness or by mistake or that he did not regard it material to the contract.

Legal Consequences

In the absence of utmost good faith, the contract will be voidable at the option of the person who suffered loss due to non-disclosure. The international non-disclosure counts fraud and is *void ab initio* and the unintentional non-disclosure is voidable at the option of the party not at fault.

Once the voidable contract has been validated by the party not at fault, the contract cannot be avoided by him later on. For instance, if the insurer has continued to accept the premium when certain non-disclosure, say mis-statement of age, has been disclosed the insurer cannot invalid the contract and cannot refuse to pay the amount of claim. If the party not at default does not exercise its option, the contract will remain valid.

Indisputability of Policy

The doctrine of utmost good faith works as a great hardship for a long period on the plea of mis-statement at the time of proposal. In such cases, it would be very difficult to prove or disprove whether a particular statement made at the time of policy was true. Therefore, to remove this hardship, certain sections in the concerned Act are provided. In India, Section 45 of the Insurance Act 1938 deals with such dispute. It is called indisputable clause, "…. No policy of life insurance, after expiry of two years from the date on which it was effected, be called into question by an insurer on the ground that a statement in the proposal for insurance or in any report of a medical officer or referee or a friend of the insured or in any other document leading to the issue of the policy was inaccurate or false, unless the insurer shows that such statement was on a material matter or suppressed facts which it was material to disclose and that it was fraudulently made by the policy-holder and that the policy-holder knew at the time of making it that the statement was false or that it suppressed facts which it was material to disclose. Provided that nothing in this section shall prevent the insurer from calling for proof of age at any time if he is entitled to do so.

Facts not Required to be Disclosed

The following facts are not required to be disclosed:

(i) Circumstances which are diminishing the risk.

(ii) Facts which are known or reasonably should be known to the insurer in his ordinary course of business.

(iii) Facts which the insurer should infer from the information given.

(iv) Facts which are waived by the insurer.

(v) Facts which are superfluous to disclose by reason of a condition or warranty.

(vi) Facts of public knowledge.

4.4.4 Warranties

Representation

For understanding warranties 'Representations' are to be thoroughly understood because in life insurance those representations which are embodied in the policy and expressly or impliedly forming part of the basis of the contract, are called warranties. Every information given by a proposer for insurance to the insurer during the negotiations is a representation. The representations may be material or non-material.

The material representations are the basis of insurance contract as has been clear in the utmost good faith under material acts. If the proposer's representation is false or untrue, the contract may be voidable at the option of the insurer. The representations made during the negotiations do not form an integral part of the contracts.

Warranties

Warranties are an integral part of the contract, i.e., these are the bases of the contract between the proposer and insurer and if any statement, whether material or non-material, is untrue; the contract shall be null and void and the premium paid by him may be forfeited by the insurer. The policy issued will contain that the proposal and personal statement shall form part of the policy and be the basis of the contract. So that the representation will be warranty as has been disclosed already that the warranties may be (i) informative, and (ii) promissory.

(i) ***Informative Warranties.*** In life insurance, the informative warranties are more important. The proposer is expected to disclose all the material facts to the best of his knowledge and belief.

(ii) ***Promissory Warranties.*** Warranties relating to the future may only be statements about his expectation or intention, for instance, the proper promises that he will not take up any hazardous occupation and will inform the insurer if he will take the hazardous occupation.

Breach of Warranty

If there is breach of warranty, the insurer is not bound to perform his part of the contract unless he chooses to ignore the breach. The effect of a breach of warranty is to render the contract voidable at the option of the other party provided there is no element of fraud. In case of fraudulent representation or promise, the contract will be void *ab initio.*

4.4.5 Proximate Cause

The efficient or effective cause which causes the loss is called proximate cause. It is the real and actual cause of loss. If the cause of loss (peril) is insured, the insurer will pay; otherwise the insurer will not compensate. In life insurance, the doctrine of *Causa Proxima* (PROXIMATE CAUSE) is not applied because the insurer is bound to pay the amount of insurance whatever may be the reason of death. It may be natural or unnatural. So, this principle is not of much practical importance in connection with life assurance, but in the following cases, the proximate causes are observed in the life insurance, too.

(i) ***War-risk.*** Where policy is issued on exclusion of war and aviation risks, the proximate cause of death is important because the insurer waives its liability if death occurred, in this case, while the insured was in field or is engaged in operation of war and aviation. Only premium paid or surrender value whichever is higher is payable and the total policy amount is not payable.

(ii) ***Suicide.*** If suicide occurs within one year of the policy, or there was intention to commit suicide and the payment of the policy would be restricted, only upto the interest of the third party in the policy provided the interest was expressed at least one month before the suicide.

(iii) ***Accident Benefit.*** A problem arises when an insured under an accident policy is killed or suffers an injury which has an immediate cause and also a remote cause. In accident benefit policy, double of the policy amount is paid. So, the cause of death in this policy is of paramount importance.

4.4.6 Assignment and Nomination

The policy in life insurance can be assigned freely for a legal consideration or love and affection. The assignment shall be complete and effectual only on the execution of such endorsement either on the policy itself or by a separate deed. Notice for this purpose must be given to the insurer who will acknowledge the assignment. Once the assignment is completed, it cannot be revoked by the assignor because he ceases to be the owner of the policy unless reassignment is made by the assignee in favour of the assignor. An assignee may be the owner of the policy both on survival of the life assured, or in his death according to the terms of transfer. The life policies are the only policies which can be assigned whether the assignee has an insurable interest or not. Life policies are frequently charged, assigned or otherwise dealt with for they are valuable securities because a fixed sum is certainly paid, in life policies excepting a few say, pure endowment and temporary policies.

Nomination

The holder of a policy of life insurance on his own life may either at the time of affecting policy or at any subsequent time before the policy matures, nominate the person or persons to whom the money secured by the policy shall be paid in the event of his death. A nomination can be cancelled before maturity, but unless notice is given of any such cancellation to the insurer, the insurer will not be liable for any *bonafide* payment to a nominee registered in the records. When the policy matures, or if the nominee dies, the sum shall be paid to the policy-holder or his legal representatives.

4.4.7 Return of Premium

Ordinarily, the premium once paid cannot be refunded. However in the following cases, the premiums paid are returnable.

I. For Reason of Equity

Equity implies a condition that the insurer shall not receive the price of running a risk he runs. Thus, there the contract does not come into effect or it is held to be void ***ab initio***. For example, on account of misrepresentation or breach of warranty, the insured, in the absence of any express condition to the contrary, can claim the return of any part of premiums paid. But if the policy runs for a time and becomes void later on, the insured is not entitled to the return of any part of the premium.

Where the insured is guilty of fraud in obtaining a policy, he will fail in his claim to the sum assured. He cannot also ask for a return of the premium because he will have to allege his own fraud to succeed in his claim and no court will assist such person.

4.4.8 Other Features

Life insurance policies have the following additional features: Life insurance contract is (i) an aleatory contract, (ii) a unilateral contract, (iii) a conditional contract, (iv) a contract of Adhesion, and (v) not a contract of indemnity.

(i) ***Aleatory Contract.*** Aleatory contract means contract depends on chance. In ordinary contract approximately equal value is exchanged by both the parties; but in life insurance contract, the full sum assured may be payable even if all premiums are not paid. Thus, on the chance of death, higher amount is payable. It should be clear, here, that, this does not make the contract of wager because of insurable interest.

(ii) ***Unilateral Contract.*** Life insurance contract is unilateral contract because, here, only the insurer makes an enforceable promise. The proposer had already performed his duty of payment of premiums. If the first premium is paid, the insurer is bound to accept subsequent premium and to pay the amount claim when it arises except on the ground of fraud.

(iii) ***Conditional Contract.*** Life insurance contract is conditional contract because only the insurer shall pay the assured sum only when the contract is continuing by payment of premium. In addition, the insurer's promise to pay the sum assured is also conditional upon the furnishing of satisfactory proof of death and other conditions mentioned in the policy.

(iv) ***Contract of Adhesion.*** Contract of adhesion means that the terms of the contract are not arrived by mutual negotiations between the parties as in the case of ordinary contracts. The proposer is not in a position to bargain about the terms of contract because these terms are already determined. The only course open to the proposer is whether to accept or not a particular policy.

(v) ***Indemnity Contract is not Applied.*** In life insurance, the indemnity contract is not applicable because the value of loss at death cannot be ascertained. It is not possible to ascertain the time upto which the insured would have survived and it is also difficult to ascertain the amount of money to be earned by him during life time. So, the doctrine of subrogation is also not applicable. In life insurance, a fixed sum is paid which may be the sum assured and bonus if the policy is participating one.

According to *J.H. Magee,* "The Life Insurance contract embodies an agreement in which broadly stated, the insurer undertakes to pay a stipulated sum upon the death of insured or at some designated time to a designated beneficiary."

Thus, on the basis of the above definitions it may be concluded that life insurance is a contract by which insurer, in consideration of premium undertakes to pay a certain a sum of money to insured or on the death of the insured to his nominee, whichever is earlier.

4.5 Nature of Insurance

On the basis of present day economic environment, there are few basic needs for which life insurance is needed. The life insurance is concerned with the hazards that stand across the life of every person that is dying prematurely leaving dependent and that of living to old age without visible means of support.

(a) **Family Protection.** To protect the families from the economic hardships after the death of the bread-winner member of the family.

(b) **Investment of Savings.** Savings provide the new source of income when permanent earning stops and Life Assurance provide an immediate source of income for one's family on the death of an insured person prematurely.

(c) **Additional Way of Earnings.** It provides an insured additional earning by way of bonus and interest credited by the Life Insurance Corporation.

(d) **Helpful at the Time of Cessation of Earnings.** Life Assurance is needed because when one ceases to earn money, insurer provides certain sum of money to the insured as per various terms of policies.

So the fundamental principle of life insurance is to save a person from uncertainties like premature death, old age, etc.

4.6 Advantages of Life Insurance

The following are the advantages of Life Insurance:

1. ***Superior Saving Plan.*** This is considered to be the best saving plan in comparison to other plans because it guarantees full protection against risk of death of the saver. In life insurance, on death of the insured, the full sum assured is payable with bonuses wherever applicable the full sum assured is payable. No other saving plan provides this kind of protection.

2. ***Encourage Saving Habits.*** Life Insurance encourages saving habits. Long-term savings can be made in a painless manner because of the easy instalment facility built into the scheme. The insured person can pay premiums through monthly, quarterly, half-yearly or yearly instalments. The salary saving scheme, popularly known as SSS; provides a convenient method of paying premium each month through deduction from one's salary. The employer is authorized by the employee to deduct the insurance premium monthly and remit to the life insurance corporation. The Salary Saving Scheme (SSS) can be introduced in any institution or organisation subject to specified terms and conditions laid down by insurer.

3. ***Suitable for Raising Loans.*** Life Insurance policy can be given as security to raise a loan even for commercial purposes also. The loan can be raised without any delay on safe security of the policy. Even after an initial period payments if the policy holder finds it difficult to continue with the payment of premium, he can surrender the policy for a surrender value amount with the Life Insurance Corporation

4. ***Protection Against Creditors.*** The maturity value of Life Insurance policy can be protected against the claims of the creditors of the life assured by valid assignment of a policy. The policy holder can nominate a person to whom the policy money would be payable in event of his death.

5. ***Tax Relief.*** The Income Tax relief is available for amounts paid by way of premium for life insurance subject to the income tax rates in force. Assesses can avail themselves of provisions in the law for tax relief. In this manner, the assured is required to pay lower premium for his insurance than he would have to pay otherwise.

6. ***Estate Duty.*** Life Insurance ensures the definite sum of money after the death of the insured without resorting to sale of assets at a loss on realization. So it is the best way of making provision for payment of Estate Duty.

7. ***Economic Protection.*** Life Insurance provides economic protection to the family members of the insured in case of his untimely death who might be the sole bread-earner of the family. It reduces the sufferings of the families on happening of a contingent event. It is considered to be the most effective devise for providing family security.

8. ***Investment Element.*** In Life Insurance, the insured is required to pay the premium. The premium is a kind of investment. The premium is returned to the insured along with additional bonus amount after the expiry of the period of contract.

9. ***Helpful to the Government.*** Life Insurance provides long-term funds to the government for different development schemes. This helps the government to develop infrastructure to develop infrastructure and serve the society.

10. ***Money when Needed.*** A suitable insurance plan or a combination of different plans can be taken out as life insurance to meet the specific needs that are likely to arise in future, such as children's education, start-in-life or marriage provision, etc. Alternatively, policy money can be so arranged to be made available at the time of one's retirement from service to be used for any specific purpose, such as for the purchase of plot, house or for other investments. Loans are also granted to the policy holders, subject to certain conditions, for house building or for purchase of flats, etc.

4.7 Difference between Life and Non-life Insurance

Basis of Comparison	Life Insurance	Non-life Insurance
1. Type of Risk	Life insurance is generally to restore the financial consequences of personal risks.	Non-life insurance is to alleviate the losses caused by property risks.
2. Risk`	Classification of risks is much simple under the contract of life insurance.	Classification of risks is bit difficult because it is to be done according to the nature of the subject matter.
3. Tenure	Life insurance policies are effected for a long term, *i.e.*, for 5 yrs, 10 yrs, etc. or even for whole life. Some term assurance policies can rarely have a term of 1, 2, or 3 years.	General insurance policies are generally effected for one year only. After the expiry of this tenure they can be renewed.
4. Object	The object is to secure the future as well as saving and investment.	The object is only to secure the subject matter against losses and damages.
5. Principle of Indemnity	The indemnity principle is not applicable to life insurance, because, determining the value of a human being in monitory terms is absolutely meaningless.	This principle is applicable to general insurance contracts, because the actual amount of loss can be determined in monitory terms so that the insured will not profit from the loss.

6. Insurable Interest	In life insurance, insurable interest must exist at the time of acquiring the policy.	In case of general insurance, insurable insurance must exist at the time of making contract and also at the time of occurrence of loss.
7. Doctrine of Subrogation	Subrogation does not apply to life insurance contracts.	The principle of subrogation is strictly applicable to general insurance contracts.
8. Mitigation of Loss	It can-not be applied to life insurance as only insane man shall like to die for the sake of small amount of money.	The principle of mitigation of loss applies to a contract of non-life insurance.
9. Principle of Contribution	Principle of Contribution is not applied in life insurance, because all insurers are bound to pay the amount on all policies in case of insuring with more than one insurer.	This principle is applicable to general insurance policies because only the actual loss will be indemnified even if one insure with more than one insurer.
10. Determination of Premium	Premium is determined in accordance with the rate of mortality, interest rate and loading of expenses.	In case of general insurance, the premium (tariff) is determined generally based on the past experience of claims settlements.
11. Payment of Premium	Premium can be paid in monthly, quarterly, half-yearly, or yearly installments.	Premium is generally paid in lump sum at the time of taking the policy.
12. Value of Policy	The amount of the policy (sum assured) is payable either on maturity or on the death/ disability of the person. In this case, the assured sum is paid.	In this case, the amount is paid only if the loss occurs. The amount paid is the value of the loss, not the insured amount.
13. Surrender of Policy	Life insurance policies can be surrendered before the maturity of the policy.	There is no option of surrender of a general insurance policy.

4.8 Summary

Insurance appeared in England in 16th century. In India, life insurance business was started in the year 1818 with the establishment of Oriental Life Assurance Company at Calcutta. In 1956 life insurance business was nationalized and LIC of

India was formed. In 1999, the IRDA bill was passed and the sector was opened up for the private players. At present along with the LIC, there are 17 private life insurance companies in India. According to the Indian Insurance Act, 1938, Life insurance business is the business of effecting contracts upon human life.

Life insurance contracts possess the characteristics of any general contract. Major futures of a life insurance contracts are insurable interest, utmost good faith, warranties, proximate cause, assignment and nomination, and return on premium. Principle of indemnity and principle of subrogation are not applicable to life insurance.

Life insurance relieves the insured from the sword of various risks and uncertainties, which may occur before and after the death of the insured. Life insurance is also a major source of savings and investment. It helps the government by providing long-term funds for different development schemes.

4.9 Test Yourself

1. What do you mean by Liberalisation? What are the major impacts of liberalization on Indian life insurance industry?
2. Briefly summarise the history of insurance business in India.
3. What are the major recommendations of Malhotra Committee?
4. Define life insurance. What are the different features of a life insurance contract?
5. Give two situations where a proposal of life insurance can be rejected.
6. Explain the major principles of life insurance.
7. How does insurance, particularly life insurance play a major role in developing our nation's economy?
8. "After the liberalization of Indian financial sector, lot of investment products are available in the market. But life insurance has emerged as a major alternative to all of them in the recent past". Comment.
9. On what conditions one can have insurable interest on other's life?

State whether the following statements are 'True' or 'False'.

1. Insurance appeared in England in 15th century.
2. The modern concept of insurance came into existence with advent of East India Company in 18th century.
3. The first (foreign) company which started the insurance business in India was 'Oriental Life Insurance Company' at Calcutta in the year 1818.
4. In 1824, "Bombay Life Assurance Company" started giving insurance policies for two-three year terms.
5. "Madras Equitable Life Assurance Society" came into existence in 1829.

6. In 1871, some prominent citizens of Bombay started the Bombay Life Assurance Society.
7. The Insurance Act, 1940 came into existence.
8. In between 1941 and 1945, 20 new companies were started .
9. The government passed the Act in 1950 to stop interlocking.
10. The staff and group life insurance schemes were introduce in 1954.
11. The year 1954 was the major milestone in the history of life insurance business.
12. The year 2000 was a defining movement in the history of Indian Insurance industry.
13. 'Life assurance' insures the insured against the happening of certain event, *i.e.,* death through the time when it may happen is uncertain.
14. "Life Insurance business is the business of effecting contracts upon human life".
15. Since the life insurance contract is a sort of contract, it is approved by the Indian Contract Act. According to Section 2(g) and Section 9 of Indian Contract act.
16. Majority is attained when a person completes the age of 18 years. A minor is not competent to contract.
17. Persons of sound mind cannot enter into a contract.
18. A contract with an alien enemy is void.
19. Both parties must be of same mind at the time of contract. If the two parties do not meet in this respect, there is no perfect agreement between them.
20. The presence of a lawful consideration is essential for a legal contract.
21. The contract would be legal only when the object is legal.
22. The objective will be legal only when there is no insurable interest.
23. Insurable interest is the pecuniary interest.
24. The loss should be monetary or financial.
25. An individual always has an insurable interest in other's life.
26. There are three types of insurable interest in other's life.
27. There are only two such cases where the presence of insurable interest is legally presumed and therefore need not be proved.
28. Wife has insurable interest in the life of her husband.
29. Husband has insurable interest in the life of his wife.
30. The policy-holder may have insurable interest in the life of assured due to business and contractual relationship.

31. The creditor may lose money if the debtor dies before the loan is repaid.
32. A surety has insurable interest in the life of his principal.
33. A partner has insurable interest in the life of each partner.
34. An employer has insurable prize in the life of a key-man.
35. The insurable interest must exist at the time of contract.
36. Insurable prize must be valuable.
37. The legal responsibility may be the basis of insurable interest.
38. Insurable Interest must be infinite.
39. The life insurance requires that the principle of utmost good faith should be preserved by both the parties.
40. Utmost good faith says that there should be full and true disclosure of all the material facts.
41. In the absence of utmost good faith, the contract will be voidable at the option of the person who suffered loss due to non-disclosure.
42. Once the voidable contract has been validated by the party not at fault, the contract cannot be avoided by him later on.
43. The doctrine of utmost good faith works as a great hardship for a long period on the plea of mis-statement at the time of proposal.
44. The material representations are the basis of insurance contract as has been clear in the utmost good faith under material acts.
45. Warranties are an integral part of the proposal,
46. In life insurance, the informative warranties are less important.
47. If there is breach of warranty, the insurer is not bound to perform his part of the contract unless he chooses to ignore the breach.
48. The efficient or effective cause which causes the loss is called proximate cause.
49. The policy in life insurance can be assigned freely for a legal consideration or love and affection.
50. A nomination can be cancelled before maturity, but unless notice is given of any such cancellation to the insurer, the insurer will be liable for any *bonafide* payment to a nominee registered in the records.
51. When the policy matures, or if the nominee dies, the sum shall be paid to the policy-holder or his legal representative.
52. On the basis of present day economic environment, there are few basic needs for which life insurance is needed.
53. fundamental principle of life insurance is to save a person from uncertainties like premature death, old age, etc.

Choose the correct answer as given below:

1. Insurance appeared in England in
   (a) 16th century (b) 17th century
   (c) 18th century (d) 19th century
2. The modern concept of insurance came into existence with advent of East India Company in
   (a) 15th century (b) 16th century
   (c) 17th century (d) 18th century
3. The first (foreign) company which started the insurance business in India was
   (a) Oriental Life Insurance Company
   (b) Jeevan Bharti Insurance Company
   (c) Original Life Insurance Company
   (d) British Life Insurance Company
4. Oriental Life Insurance Company was set up in
   (a) Calcutta (b) Mumbai
   (c) Delhi (d) Chennai
5. Bombay Life Assurance Company was set up in
   (a) Bombay (b) Allahabad
   (c) Pune (d) Delhi
6. Bombay Life Assurance Company was set up in
   (a) 1820 (b) 1821
   (c) 1822 (d) 1823
7. Madras Equitable Life Assurance Society came into existence in
   (a) 1827 (b) 1828
   (c) 1829 (d) 1830
8. The British Parliament passed an Insurance Act in
   (a) 1870 (b) 1871
   (c) 1872 (d) 1873
9. Some prominent citizens of Bombay started the Bombay Life Assurance Society in
   (a) 1870 (b) 1871
   (c) 1872 (d) 1873

10. Oriental Government Security Life Assurance Company Ltd. was established as a proprietary in

(a) 1874 (b) 1875

(c) 1876 (d) 1877

11. The First World War gave a boost to Indian business in

(a) Life Insurance Business

(b) Non-life insurance business

(c) For both of them

(d) None of them

12. Which one of the following statement is correct, with reference to life insurance?

(a) The claim payable is subject to the principle of indemnity

(b) The claim payable will depend on the sum assured

(c) The claim payable will depend on the income of the decreased person

(d) The claim payable will depend on the size of the family left behind

13. Which one of the following statements is/are correct with reference to the life insurance?

(a) The claim can be paid only after verification income of the decreased person

(b) The claim amount should not exceed the loss of income to the family

(c) The claim amount payable should be determined by a surveyor

(d) None of the above statement is true

14. An insurance contract is valid because

(a) It is not a wagering contract

(b) It promotes socially desirable causes

(c) It takes care of the destitute

(d) It provides government with large funds

15. Which one of the following statements is/are correct?

(a) A person who has just retired from a lucrative job may not need life insurance.

(b) A person who has spent twenty years in Dubai may not need life insurance.

(c) A person who has just taken up his first job needs life insurance

(d) All the above statements are wrong

16. The major milestone in the history of life insurance business was

(a) 1954 (b) 1955

(c) 1956 (d) 1957

17. Which one of the following statement is correct

(a) The needs of the people are different

(b) The needs of people vary according to the life styles

(c) The needs of people depend on their upbringing

(d) All the above three statements are correct

18. In 1994, the committee submitted the report and gave the some recommendations

(a) Structure (b) Competition

(c) Investment (d) All are correct

(e) None of the above correct

19. Characteristics of life insurance contracts is/are

(a) Nature of General Contract

(b) Insurable interest

(c) Utmost good faith

(d) All are correct

(e) None of the above is correct

20. Nature of general contract is/are

(a) Agreement

(b) Competency of parties

(c) Free consent to the parties

(d) All are correct

(e) None of the above is correct

21. Competency of parties may be

(a) Person of sound mind

(b) Majority

(c) Both of the above are correct

(d) Both of them wrong

22. General Rule of Insurance Interest in Life Insurance is/are

(a) Time of insurable interest

(b) Services

(c) Insurable interest must be valuable

(d) All are correct

(e) All are wrong

23. Warranties may be

(a) Informative warranties

(b) Promissory warranties

(c) Both are correct

(d) Both are wrong

24. Cases of proximity causes is/are

(a) War-risk (b) Suicide

(c) Accident benefit (d) All are correct

(e) All are wrong

25. Additional feature of life insurance is/are

(a) Aleatory contract

(b) Unilateral contract

(c) Conditional contract

(d) All are correct

(e) All are wrong.

26. Nature of insurance may be

(a) Family protection

(b) Investment of Savings

(c) Additional way of earning

(d) All are correct

(e) All are wrong

27. Advantage of life insurance may be
    (a) Superior saving plan
    (b) Encourage saving habits
    (c) Suitable for rising loan
    (d) All are wrong statement
    (e) All are correct

Fill in the blanks with a suitable or appropriate word/s.

1. The modern concept of insurance came into existence with advent of East India Company in ....
2. The first (foreign) company which started the insurance business in India was .... at Calcutta in ....
3. In 1823, ... started giving insurance policies for two-three year terms.
4. "Madras Equitable Life Assurance Society" came into existence in ....
5. The British Parliament passed an Insurance Act in ....
6. The Bharat established in .... and the empire of India established in ....
7. The First World War gave a boost to .... businesses.
8. The New India established in...................... .
9. The Insurance Act .... came into existence .
10. 25 new companies were started between .... and ....
11. The staff and group life insurance schemes were introduced in ....
12. The year .... was the major milestone in the history of life insurance business.
13. Life insurance companies (LIC) of India was formed by an Act of ...., *viz.,* ....
14. Since then the LIC had been enjoying a ....over the life insurance business in India, till the sector was opened up to private companies in ....

15. In 1993, Malhotra Committee headed by former Finance Secretary and RBI Governor, R. N. Malhotra was formed to evaluate the .... and recommend its ....

16. The Committee was set up with an objective of complementing the reform the Indians in...................

17. The year 2000 was a defining movement in the history of ....

18. Life Insurance, usually referred to as .... insures the insured against the happening of certain event .

19. The life insurance contract can be described as ....

20. Majority is attained when a person completes the age of 18 years. A minor is not competent to ....

21. A contract by a minor is .... excepting contracts for necessaries.

22. Persons of sound mind can enter into a ....

23. A contract with an alien enemy is ....

24. Both parties must be of same mind at the time of ....

25. The presence of a lawful consideration is essential for a ....

26. The contract would be legal only when the object is ....

27. The objective will be legal only when there is insurable ....

28. Insurable interest is the .... interest.

29. The loss should be .... or ....

30. An individual always has an insurable interest in his own ....

31. Life insurance can be effected on the lives of third parties provided the proposer has insurable interest in the ....

32. Wife has insurable interest in the life of her ....

33. Husband has insurable interest in the life of his ....

34. A creditor has in the life of his ....

35. The insurable interest must exist at the time of ....

36. Except the services of wife, services of other relatives will not essentially form ....

37. Insurable Interest must be .... as well as ....

38. The efficient or effective cause which causes the loss is called ....

39. The policy in life insurance can be assigned freely for a .... , ... and ....

40. Ordinarily, the premium once paid cannot be ....

41. Equity implies a condition that the .... shall not receive the price of running a risk he runs.

42. Aleatory contract means contract depends on ....

43. Superior Saving Plan is the advantage of ....

CHAPTER 5

PRODCUT DEVELOPMENT

Learning Objectives

After studying this chapter, one can understand:

- Determining the cost of life insurance
- Rate of return on saving companies
- Product development

5.1 Determining the Cost of Life Insurance

The cost of life insurance is a complex subject. In general, Cost can be viewed as the difference between what you pay for a life insurance policy and what you get back. If you pay premiums and get nothing back, the cost of the insurance equals the premiums paid. However, if you pay premiums and later get something back, such as cash values and dividends, your cost will be reduced. Thus, in determining the Cost of life insurance, four major factors must be considered: (1) annual premiums, (2) cash values, (3) dividends, and (4) time value of money. Two widely used cost methods that consider some or all of the preceding factors are the *traditional net cost method* and the *interest-adjusted cost method.* Although the following discussion is based on cash-value life insurance, the same cost methods can be used to deter-mine the Cost of term insurance.

Traditional Net Cost Method

From a historical perspective, life insurers earlier used the traditional net cost method to illustrate the net cost of life insurance. Under this method, the annual premiums for some time period are added together. Total expected dividends to be received during the same period and the cash value at the end of the period are then subtracted from the total premiums to determine the net cost of life insurance. For example, assume that the annual premium for a $10,000 ordinary life insurance policy issued to a female, age 20, is $132.10. Estimated dividends over a 20-year period are $599, and the cash surrender value at the end of the twentieth year is $2294. The average cost per year is minus $12.55 (-$1.26 per $1000).

The traditional net cost method has several defects and is misleading. The most glaring defects are as follows:

- *The time value of money is ignored.* Interest that the policyowner could have earned on the premiums by investing them elsewhere is ignored.
- *The insurance is often shown to be free (to have a negative cost).* This is contrary to common sense, because no life insurer can provide free life insurance to the public and remain in business.
- *The steepness of the dividend scale is ignored.* Some insurers pay small dividends at first and then pay ballooning dividends in later years. The timing and amount of each dividend are ignored.
- *The dividend scale is assumed to remain unchanged.* For most insurers, dividends will change over time.
- *The net cost is based on the assumption that the policy will be surrendered.* The assumption that the policyowner will keep the insurance exactly 20 years (or some other period) and then surrender the policy is questionable.

Exhibit 5.1: Traditional Net Cost Method

Total Premiums for 20 years	$2642
Subtract dividences for 20 years	–593
Net premiums for 20 years	$2043
Subtract the cash value at the end of 20 years	–2294
Insurance cost for 20 years	–$251
Net cost per year (–$251˛20)	–$12.55
Net cost per year (–$12.55˛20)	–$1.26

Interest-Adjusted Cost Method

The interest-adjusted cost method developed by the National Association of Insurance Commissioners is a more accurate measure of life insurance costs. Under this method, the time value of money is taken into consideration by applying an interest factor to each element of cost.

There are two principal types of interest-adjusted cost indexes, the *surrender cost index* and the *net payment cost index.* The surrender cost index is useful if you believe that you may surrender the policy at the end of 10 or 20 years, or some other time period. The net payment cost index is useful if you intend to keep your policy in force, and cash values are of secondary importance to you.

Surrender Cost Index: The surrender cost index *measures the cost of life insurance if you surrender the policy at the end of some time period, such as* 10 or 20 years (see Exhibit 5.2).

The annual premiums are accumulated at 5 per cent interest, which recognizes the fact that the policyowner could have invested the premiums elsewhere. Dividends are also accumulated at 5 per cent interest. Which considers interest earnings on the dividends as well as the amount and timing of each dividend. Using the same policy as before, the accumulated net premiums for 20 years are 53762.

The next step is to subtract the cash value at the end of 20 years from the net premiums, which results in a total insurance cost of $1468. The policyowner pays this amount for the insurance protection for 20 years, after considering the time value of money.

The final step is to convert the total interest-adjusted cost for 20 years into an annual cost. This is done by dividing the total interest-adjusted cost by an *annuity due* factor of 34.719. This factor means that a 51 deposit at the *beginning* of each year at 5 per cent interest will accumulate to $34.719 at the end of 20 years. By dividing the total interest- adjusted cost of $1468 by $34.719, you end up with an annual interest-adjusted cost of $42.28, or $4.23 for each $1000 of insurance. As you can see, the interest-adjusted cost is positive, which means that it costs something to own life insurance when forgone interest is considered. In this case, the average annual cost is $42.28 if the policy is surrendered after 20 years.

Exhibit 5.2: Surrender Cost Index

Total premiums for 20 years, each accumulated at 5%	$4586
Subtract dividends for 20 years, each accumulated at 5%	–824
Net premiums for 20 years	
Subtract the cash value at the end of 20 years	–2294
Insurance cost for 20 years	$1468
Amount to which $1 deposited annually at the beginning each year will accumulate to in 20 years at 5%	$34.719
Interest-adjusted cost per year ($1468¸ 34.719)	$42.28
Cost per $1000 per year ($42.28¸ 10)	$4.23

Net Payment Cost Index: The net payment cost index *measures the relative cost of a policy if death occurs at the end of some specified time period, such as* 10 or 20 *years. It is based on the assumption that you will not surrender the policy.* Therefore, it is the appropriate cost index to use if you intend to keep your life insurance in force.

The net payment cost index is calculated in a manner similar to the surrender cost index except that the cash value is not subtracted (see Exhibit 5.3).

If the policy is kept in force for 20 years, the policy has an annual cost of $108.36 ($10.84 per $1000) after interest is considered.

Exhibit 5.3: Net Payment Cost Index	
Total premiums for 20 years, each accumulated at 5%	$4586
Subtract dividends for 20 years, each accumulated at 5%	–824
Insurance cost for 20 years	$3762
Amount to which $1 deposited annually at the beginning of each year will accumulate to in 20 years at 5%	$34.719
Interest-adjusted cost per year ($3762¸ 34.719)	$108.36
Cost per $1000 per year (4108.36¸ 10)	$10.84

Obtaining Cost Information

If you are solicited to buy life insurance, you can ask the agent to give you interest-adjusted cost data on the policy. Cost data can also be obtained by calling certain price quoting services at their toll-free numbers. In addition, cost data are readily available on the Internet (see Internet Resources). Finally, most policy illustrations include interest-adjusted cost data.

If you use interest-adjusted cost data, keep in mind the following points:

- *Shop for a policy and not an insurer.* Some insurers have excellent low-cost policies at certain ages and amounts, but they are not as competitive when other ages and amounts are considered.
- *Compare only similar plans of insurance.* You should compare policies of the same type with the same benefits. Otherwise, the comparison can be misleading.
- *Ignore small variations in the cost index numbers.* Small cost differences can be offset by other policy features or by services that you can expect to get from an agent or insurer.
- *Cost indexes apply only to a new policy.* The cost data should not be used to determine whether to replace an existing policy with a new one. Other factors should be considered as well
- *The type of policy you buy should not be based solely on a cost index.* You should buy the type of policy that best meets your needs, such as term, whole life, or some combination. Once you have decided on the type of policy, then compare costs.

5.2 Rate of Return on Saving Component

Another important consideration is the rate of return earned on the saving component of a traditional whole life insurance policy. Consumers normally do not know the annual rate return they on the saving component in their policies. A consumer who buys a traditional cash-value policy a low return can lose a considerable amount of

Linton Yield

The Linton yield is one method that can be used to determine the rate of return on the saving portion of a cash-value policy. It was developed by M. Albert Linton, a well-known life insurance actuary. *In essence, the Linton yield is the average annual rate of return on a cash-value policy if it is held for a specified number of years.* It is based on the assumption that a cash-value policy can be viewed as a combination of insurance protection and a savings fund. To determine the average annual rate of return for a given period, *it is* first necessary to determine that part of the annual premium that is deposited in the savings fund. This amount can be determined by subtracting the cost of the insurance protection for that year from the annual premium (less any dividend). The balance of the premium is the amount that can be deposited into the savings fund. Thus, the average annual rate of return is the compound interest rate that is required to make the savings deposits equal the guaranteed cash value in the policy at the end of a specified period.

Calculation of the Linton yield is complex and requires specific information. Unfortunately, current rates of return based on the Linton yield are not readily available to consumers. However, a 1997 Consumer Federation of America study of 109 cash-value policies based on the Linton yield showed that the annual rates of return vary widely. *The study showed that the average annual rates of return for the 109 policies ranged from a minus* 87.9 *per cent for the first year to* 8.2 *per cent for the twentieth year* (see Exhibit 5.4). The study concluded that consumers lose billions of dollars annually by terminating their policies early. The Consumer Federation of America recommends that consumers should not purchase a cash-value policy unless they plan to hold it for at least 20 years.

Annual rates of return based on the Linton yield are usually negative during the early years of the policy. These negative returns reflect the heavy first-year acquisition and administrative expenses when the policy is first sold. An agent receives a commission, and there may be a medical examiner's fee, an inspection report, and other expenses involved in issuing the policy. As a result of these expenses, most cash-value policies have little or no cash value at the end of the first year, and the cash values remain relatively low during the early years. Thus, if you surrender the policy or allow it to lapse during the early years, you will lose a substantial amount of money.

Because current information is not readily available, the Linton yield has limited usefulness as a consumer tool. We must therefore consider other methods. The yearly rate-of-return method discussed next is a simple, but valuable methodology that can enable you to calculate the annual rate of return on the saving component in your policy.

Exhibit 5.4: Average Annual Rates of Return for 109 Cash-Value Policies by Year of Policy

Year	Rate of Return (%)
1	–87.9
2	–54.9
3	–18.9
4	0.0
5	5.6
6	7.3
7	7.7
8	7.7
9	7.6
10	9.8
11	8.0
12	8.0
13	8.0
14	7.9
15	8.1
16	7.8
17	7.8
18	7.8
19	7.8
20	8.2

(***Source:*** Consumer Federation of America, *Rates* of *Return* on *Cash-Value Policies Vary Widely,* Press Release, July 16,1997.)

Yearly Rate-of-Return Method

Professor Joseph M. Belth has developed the yearly rate-of-return method for calculating the saving component of 3 cash-value policy. The yearly rate of return is based on the following formula:

$$i = \frac{(CV + D) + (YPT)(DB - CV)(.001)}{(P + CVP)} - 1$$

where

i = yearly rate of return on the saving component, express as a decimal

CV = cash value at end of policy year

D = annual dividend

YPT = assumed yearly price per $1000 of protection (see benchmark prices in Exhibit 5.5)

DB = death benefit

P = annual premium

CVP = cash value at end of preceding policy year

The first expression in the numerator of the formula is the amount available in the policy at the end of the policy year. The second expression in the numerator is the assumed price of the protection component, which is determined by multiplying the amount of protection by an assumed price per $1000 of protection. Assumed prices per $1000 of protection for various ages are benchmarks derived from certain U.S. population death rates (see Exhibit 19.6). Finally, the expression in the denominator of the formula is the amount available in the policy at the beginning of the policy year.

For example, assume that Mark purchased a $100,000 , participating ordinary life policy at age 35. He is now age 42 and at the beginning of the eighth policy year. He would like to know the yearly rate of return on the saving component for the eighth year of the policy. The annual premium is $1500. The cash value in the policy is $7800 at the end of the seventh policy year and $9200 at the end of the eighth policy year. The eighth-year dividend is $400. Because Mark is' age 42 at the beginning of the eighth policy year, the benchmark price is $4.00 per $1000 (see again Exhibit 5.5).

Exhibit 5.5: Benchmark Prices

Age	Benchmark Price
Under 30	$ 1.50
30-34	$ 2.00
35-39	$ 3.00
40-44	$ 4.00
45-49	$ 6.50
50-54	$ 10.00
55-59	$ 15.00
60-64	$ 25.00
65-69	$ 35.00

70-74	50.00
75-79	50.00
75-79	80.00
80.84	125.00

Note: The benchmark prices were derived from certain U.S. population death rates. The benchmark figure for each five-year age bracket is close to the death rate per $1000 at the highest are in that bracket.

(***Source:*** Adapted from Joseph M.Belth, Life Insurance: A Consumer's Handbook, 2nd ed. (Bloomington, IN: Indiana University Press, 1985), table 9, p. 84 Reprinted by permission of the author.)

Based on the preceding information, the yearly rate of return for the eighth policy year is calculated as follows:

$$i = \frac{(9200 \div 400) + (4)(100{,}000 - 9200)(.001)}{(1500 + 7800)} - 1$$

$$= \frac{(9600) + (4)((90{,}800)(.001)}{(9300)} - 1$$

$$= \frac{9600 \div 363}{9300} - 1$$

$$= \frac{9963}{9300} - 1 = 1.071 - 1 = .071 = 7.1\%$$

The yearly rate of return for the eighth policy year is 7.1 per cent, assuming that the yearly price per $1000 of protection is $4.

The major advantage of Belth's method is simplicity you do not need a computer. The information needed can be obtained by referring to your policy and premium notice, or by contacting your agent or insurer. The same methodology can be used to evaluate an existing life insurance policy. (See the appendix at the end of this chapter.)

5.3 Product Development

Product development in a life insurance company must reflect and integrate many related elements. Products are created to facilitate the achievement of the life insurer's goals, and the product line should reflect the company's character. Its culture, and its long-range strategic plans. Obviously, the insurer's goals should be built around its perception of the needs of its customers. In addition, products must be designed and developed with concern for the needs of the marketing personnel, shareholders, and the public.

Product development is a continuous process. It includes the evolution of an idea, its refinement and ultimately the implementation of a marketable product.

Even then, the process is incomplete until the actual experience in marketing and managing the product has been reviewed and analyzed so that any necessary modifications can be made in a timely manner. This monitoring and analysis may lead to revisions of existing products or to other new products or marketing concepts.

Product development typically is organized by project. Such projects may range from the establishment of a new line of business to the creation of a portfolio of products, or to the design of a sing product to augment an existing product line. When developing and product or group of products, the company must give careful attention to the integration of the ultimate product array, so that it properly and consistently serves the needs of the market in which the insurer operates.

The product development process includes both product design and product implementation. Constraints imposed on development or activities from both inside and inside and outside of the company must be recognized and either eliminated or managed. Product design includes the generation and evaluation of a product idea, the clarification of the idea, and the assessment of its marketability. Product implementation includes the final determination of rates, values, and dividends; the design of policy and application forms; the filing of these forms with regulatory authorities; the creation of supporting marketing materials and administrative systems that facilitate effective distribution and administration of the product; and the actual introduction of the product.

Approximate evaluations of profitability and marketability are made periodically throughout the product development process. A fine-tuning of design and pricing takes place during the implementation phase. The schematic presented in Figure 5.1 provides a visual overview of the concepts involved in the 'product development process.

Only after a life and health insurance company has developed a marketing plan should it consider the products it will develop to meet the needs of its Chosen markets.

In practice, of course, this order define a target market and determine its needs, design products, and then consider how best to market them is often reversed. With established companies, a process of constantly evaluating and upgrading the product portfolio is necessary to respond to a changing external environment and revised company objectives.

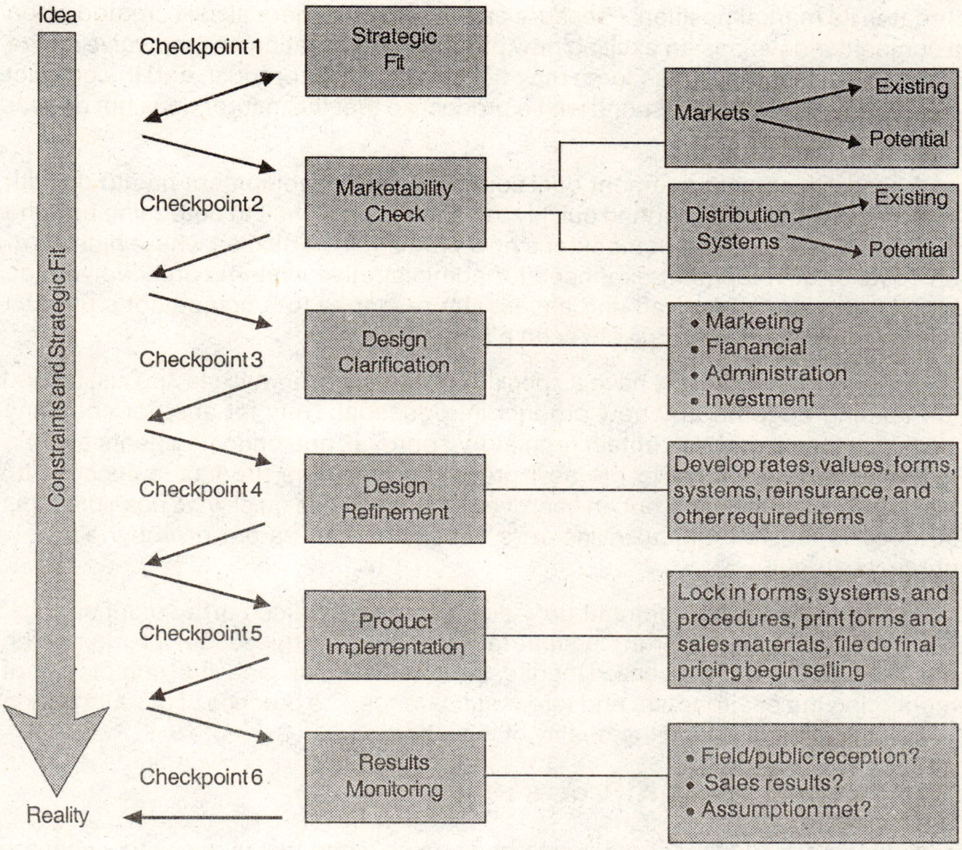

Fig. 5.1: The Product Development Process

Source: Allen D. Booth and Robert D. Shapiro, "The Product Development Program for Insurance Companies," *SOA Part 9L Study Note* (Shaumburg, IL: Society of Actuaries, 1982), p. 3., Reprinted with permission.

Assessing the External Environment

Product development should reflect the changing demographic, social, economic, legal, and competitive environment. Ideally, an insurer's market research function monitors the external environment continuously and forecasts trends, so that the company can develop products to take advantage of new opportunities and to make needed adjustments to its current portfolio.

Competition in life and health insurance comes from both other insurance companies and other financial institutions. Competition from other insurers can have a significant impact on product design. It may relate to competition for agents and brokers to price product features, underwriting, or policyowner service. An insurer must respond to the actions of its major competitors when they develop products that threaten its market position. Pressure on product designers also is created when a competitor develops an exciting new product, thus creating an innovative image for itself. An insurer's sales force may demand a similar product, and the product designers may have to respond with a product so that the insurer does not appear to be falling behind.

One critical management decision in product development has to do with evaluating whether to respond quickly to competition or wait to determine how the market will respond to a competitor's new product. In particular, where high start-up costs or development expenses for administrative systems are involved, an insurer may decide to wait and assess the response to a competitor's product before committing resources to such a product.

Some major insurers have a specific philosophy of always staying just behind the leading edge on any new product introduction. They let another company introduce a new product, obtain regulatory approval, and educate agents and the public about the virtues of the new product. Where the product is successful, these insurers then bring out an improved version of it as quickly as possible. This strategy is feasible because insurers usually cannot patent or copyright new products.

The external environment provides a complex difficult array of influences. Many factors in that environment interact and are synergistic, but all impinge on the product design process. Despite the uncertainties and the complexity of monitoring the environment and forecasting trends, the process of product design is critically dependent on the quality of this effort.

The Product Design Process

Once a marketing strategy has been established that is consistent with the company's corporate objectives and its perception of the external environment, then the broad guidelines are in place for the product design process to begin and decisions about the product portfolio to be made. The insurer's marketing strategy usually will be developed by the senior marketing officers and then approved by senior management. Establishing product design objectives that are consistent with the marketing strategy is a joint effort including not only the marketing department and product design actuaries but also other functional areas such as underwriting, investment, and policyowner service.

Changes in the product mix may be essential if the insurer is to survive. Particular lines of business may have to be eliminated because they are no longer growing and profitable. These decisions are best initiated by staff who have no vested interest (as line personnel might have) in continuing to offer unprofitable existing products. In addition, the design of innovative products usually requires extensive research, which is best performed as a staff function. For these reasons, the product design function usually is a staff function.

The Implementation Process

After the basic product proposal has been approved, the staff must implement the proposal. Implementation includes establishing the administrative procedures and processes necessary to introduce the product to the market. The process includes:

- pricing the final product
- designing the policy contract and application forms
- filing and obtaining legal approval from all appropriate jurisdictions
- developing promotion and training materials
- developing and putting in place all information and other (e.g. underwriting) systems necessary to market and administer the product

Initial product pricing will have begun in the design phase with final determination reserved for the implementation stage. In practice, premium rates cannot be set simply by building in profit along with the other assumptions as to mortality, morbidity, persistency, expenses, and other expected characteristics of the business. Instead, 'premium rates' must be established to balance the various, often conflicting, requirements of management, stockholders (if any), agents, and present and future poliyowners, within the overall constraints resulting from the need to preserve company solvency.

Sophisticated forward planning is a critical element of the premium formulation process. The nature of the business environment demands the ability to react quickly to changes and new opportunities. Actuaries, as managers of the pricing process, must develop detailed forecasts and evaluate anticipated and future scenarios while at the same time work with stochastic values. Although the particular procedural details of premium formulation may vary from company to company and from one line of business to another, the general process includes (1) defining a pricing plan. (2) establishing actuarial assumptions, (3) determining products and prices, and (4) operating and managing results. The process of premium formulation is a continuous and circular process; the experience from one round of pricing is used as the basis for the next round of pricing.

Most companies develop their rates on best-estimate actuarial assumptions, building in a specific profit margin. By developing the premium scale utilizing realistic actuarial assumptions, management of the results is easier. The assumptions underlying asset share and other studies can then function as performance standards for the company.

Price Management

Price management requires systematic comparison of actual with expected results and taking action to rectify any significant deviations from expected results. Thus, a rate increase on an individual health block of business, a revision in a dividend scale, or new rates might be indicated. The projections described previously provide a basis for creating the expected results.

The reason for any significant deviations should be determined. Once the deviations have been defined and appropriate corrective action has been implemented, the process can continue to its next sequence. It is a dynamic circle of planning, product review, and experience analysis. Findings may suggest that existing products or services have entered into the maturity or even decline stages of the product life cycle (discussed next). If needed changes might create undesirable or even unacceptable results (e.g., required premium increase could price the insurer out of particular critical markets), a complete reassessment of the insurer's basic pricing plan may be indicated.

The Product Life Cycle

In marketing theory, the product life cycle is a theoretical construct that attempts to describe the key turning points and stages in the life of an industry product from introduction to decline. Like any generalization, it does not perfectly describe every product's life; however, it does represent a powerful analytical tool that marketers use to set strategy.

The four stages of the product life cycle are introduction, growth, maturity, and decline. These stages are represented in Figure 5.2, a graph that displays the values of hypothetical sales and profits throughout the four stages.

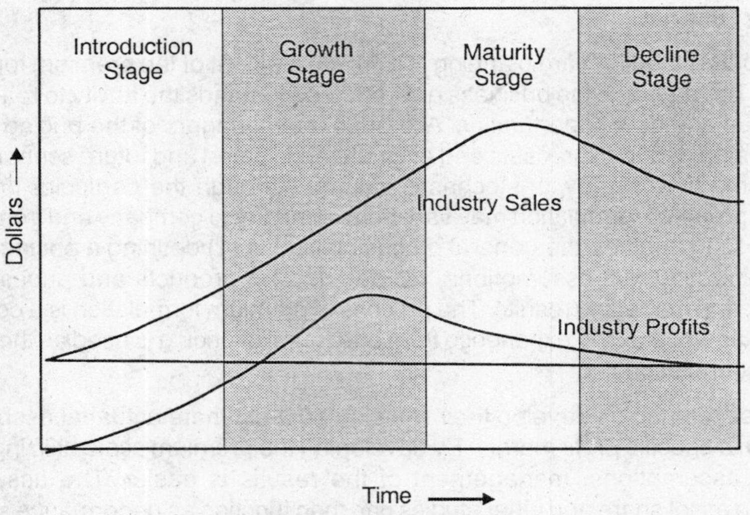

Fig. 5.2: Product Life Cycle

During the introduction stage for a new product, sales are low and profits are negative because of the investment in start-up costs. In this stage, the typical promotion strategy is to convince consumers of the utility and value of the product itself rather than focusing on a particular brand or make. Pricing is not a major concern at this stage, as there are usually few competitors.

As the product moves into the growth stage, sales and profits increase dramatically. Eventually, profit per unit sold declines. This is because new competitors enter the market and offer lower prices or superior products. Promotion focuses on distinguishing the advantages of one brand over another (i.e., product differentiation).

In the maturity stage, sales level off and total profits decline. There are few new entrants because existing competitors keep profit margins low. Some competitors with-draw because of the limited profit potential.

In the decline stage, sales and profits continue to slide. There is a general shakeout of the market. Unprofitable distribution channels are eliminated. Competitors generally sacrifice market share to maintain profit margins.

The product life cycle is a useful concept because it can help predict how the market is likely to work in different phases. For example, a company entering the market during the growth stage would be well advised to build unique, valuable features into its version of the product because consumers will begin to make choices based on individual features once the value of the generic product is well established.

With a couple of key additions, the product life cycle can be adapted as a useful tool for describing the evolution of many life insurance products. One key addition is the regulatory environment for the new product. Another key addition is tax law. Because many products are so dependent on tax efficiencies for their marketability, changes in tax rulings and laws can have a major impact on their development.

5.4 Summary

Product development and determination of cost is the complicated task in life insurance. Cost can be viewed as the difference between what you pay for a life insurance policy and what you get back. In determining the cost of life insurance, four major factors must be considered: annual premiums, cash values, dividends, and time value of money. Traditional net cost method and interest-adjusted cost method are the widely used cost methods. In net cost method, the annual premiums for some time period are added together. Under interest-adjusted cost method, the time value of money is taken into consideration by applying an interest factor to each element of cost. Another important consideration is the rate of return earned on the saving component of a traditional whole life insurance policy.

Product development is a continuous process. The product development process includes both product design and product implementation. Product design includes the generation and evaluation of a product idea, the clarification of the idea, and the assessment of its marketability. Product implementation includes the final determination of rates, values, and dividends; the design of policy and application forms; the filing of these forms with regulatory authorities; the creation of supporting marketing materials and administrative systems that facilitate effective distribution and administration of the product; and the actual introduction of the product. Product life cycle is a theoretical construct that attempts to describe the key turning points and stages in the life of an industry product from introduction to decline. The four stages of the product life cycle are introduction, growth, maturity, and decline.

5.5 Test Yourself

1. Define cost of life insurance. What are four major factors to be considered in determining the Cost of life insurance?
2. Explain Traditional Net Cost Method with suitable illustration.
3. How can one obtain the cost information?
4. Explain how will you calculate the rate of return on saving component?
5. What are the major steps in the process of product development?
6. What are the different stages of product life cycle?

State whether the following statement 'true' or 'false'.

1. The cost of life insurance is a complex subject.
2. In determining the cost of life insurance, three major factors must be considered.
3. Annual premium is a cost of life insurance factor.
4. Cash values is not a cost of life insurance factor.
5. Dividends and time value of money are not the cost factor of life insurance.
6. Life insurers earlier used the traditional net cost method to illustrate the net profit of general insurance.
7. The dividend scale is assumed to remain changed.
8. The net cost is based on the assumption that the policy will be surrendered.
9. The price-adjusted cost method developed by the National Association of Insurance Commissioners is a more accurate measure of life insurance profit.
10. There are two principal types of interest-adjusted cost indexes, the *surrender cost index* and the *net payment cost index.*
11. The annual premiums are accumulated at 50 percent interest, which recognizes the fact that the policy owner could have invested the premiums elsewhere.
12. The final step is to convert the total interest-adjusted cost for 20 years into an annual cost.
13. If you are solicited to buy life insurance, you can ask the agent to give you interest-adjusted cost data on the policy.
14. Shop for a policy and not an insurer.
15. The type of policy you buy should not be based solely on a cost index.
16. Another important consideration is the rate on interest on the saving component of a traditional whole life insurance policy.

17. Annual rates of return based on the Linton yield are usually negative during the early years of the policy.
18. The first expression in the numerator of the formula is the amount available in the policy at the end of the policy year.
19. Introduction of a product is the first stage in product life cycle.
20. Maturity of a product is the first stage in product life cycle.
21. Decline is the second stage of any product in the life of product life cycle.
22. Growth is the second stage of life of any product in the life of product life cycle.
23. During introduction sales are low and profits are negative because of the investment in start-up costs.
24. In the maturity stage, sales level off and total profits decline.
25. As the product moves into the growth stage, sales and profits increase dramatically.
26. In the decline stage, sales and profits continue to slide.
27. The product life cycle is a useful concept because it can help predict how the market is likely to work in different phases.

Choose correct alternative of the following.

1. The cost of life insurance is a

   (a) Complex subject (b) Easy subject

   (c) Both are correct (d) Both of these are wrong

2. In determining the cost of life insurance major factor considered as

   (a) 2 (b) 3

   (c) 4 (d) 5

3. In determining of cost may be

   (a) Annual premiums (b) Cash values

   (c) Dividends (d) Time value of money

   (e) All of the above

4. The annual premiums are accumulated at interest of

   (a) 3 per cent (b) 4 per cent

   (c) 5 per cent (d) 6 per cent

5. The policyowner pays this amount for the insurance protection for

   (a) 20 years (b) 22 years

   (c) 23 years (d) 24 years

6. Generally stages of product development are known as
   (a) 3 stages (b) 4 stages
   (c) 5 stages (d) 6 stages
7. Introduction stage is known as
   (a) First stage (b) Second stage
   (c) Third stage (d) Fourth stage
   (e) None of the above
8. Decline stage is known as
   (a) Second stage (b) Third stage
   (c) Fourth stage (d) Fifth stage
   (e) None of the above
9. Maturity stage is known as
   (a) First stage (b) Second stage
   (c) Third stage (d) Fourth stage
   (e) None of the above
10. Implementation stage comes under the stage
   (a) Growth stage (b) Introduction stage
   (c) Maturity stage (d) Decline stage
   (e) None of the above
11. Maturity stage is known as
   (a) First stage (b) Second stage
   (c) Third stage (d) Fourth stage
   (e) None of the above
12. In the maturity stage, sales level off and total profits
   (a) Decline (b) Rise
   (c) Forward (d) Downward

Fill in the blanks with a suitable or appropriate word/s.

1. The cost of life insurance is a .... subject.
2. In determining the Cost of life insurance, ... major factors must be considered.
3. There are two principal types of interest-adjusted cost indexes, the *surrender cost index* and the .... *cost index*

4. Important consideration is the rate of return earned on the saving component of a traditional whole life ....
5. Annual rates of return based on the ....yield are usually negative during the early years of the ....
6. Product development in a .... must reflect and integrate many related elements.
7. Product development is a .... process.
8. Product development typically is organized by ....
9. The product development process includes both product .... And .... implementation.
10. Approximate evaluations of profitability and marketability are made periodically throughout the .... process.
11. Product development should reflect the changing demographic, social, economic, legal, and ....
12. Competition in comes from both other insurance companies and other .... institutions.
13. Competition from other insurers can have a significant impact on ....
14. Some major insurers have a specific philosophy of always staying just behind the leading edge on any new product ....
15. The external environment provides a complex difficult array of ....
16. Changes in the product mix may be essential if the insurer is to ....
17. Initial product pricing will have begun in the design phase with final determination reserved for the .... stage.
18. Sophisticated forward planning is a critical element of the premium formulation ....
19. The assumptions .... share and other studies can then function as .... standard for the company.
20. .... requires systematic comparison of actual with expected results and taking action to rectify any significant deviations from ....
21. The reason for any significant deviations should be ....
22. It is a dynamic circle of planning, product review, and experience ....
21. The product life cycle is a .... construct that attempts to describe the key turning .... and .... in the life of an industry product from .... to ....
22. The .... stages of the .... life cycle are ...., ... , ... , and ....

23. During the introduction stage for a new............ sales are low and............. are .... because of the investment in the cost-up costs.
24. In the maturity stage, sales level off and total profits ....
25. As the product moves into the growth stage, sales and profits .... dramatically.
26. The product life cycle is a useful concept because it can help predict how the market is likely to work in ....

CHAPTER 6

LIFE INSURANCE - RISK

Learning Objectives

After studying this chapter, one can understand:

- Concept of risk
- Risk and uncertainty
- Need of security
- Hazards
- Personal risk
- Factors affecting risk
- Measurement of risk and mortality
- Risk premium
- Methods of rating
- Classification of risk
- Methods of risk classification
- Treatment of substandard risk
- Methods of calculating economic risk

6.1 The Concept of Risk

People express risk in different ways. To some, it is the chance or possibility of loss, to others, its may be uncertain situations or deviations or what statisticians call dispersions from the expectations. Different authors on the subject have defined risk differently. However, in most of the terminology the term risk includes exposure to adverse situations. The indeterminateness of outcome is one of the basic criteria to define a risk situation. Also, when the outcome is indeterminate, there is a possibility that some of them may be adverse and therefore need special emphasis, Let us have a look at the popular definitions of risk.

According to the Dictionary, risk refers to the possibility that something unpleasant or dangerous might happen.

"Risk is a condition in which there is a possibility of an adverse deviation form a desired outcome that is expected or hoped for."

"At its most general level, risk is used to describe any situation where there is uncertainty about what outcome will occur. Life is obviously risky."

- The degree of risk refers to the likelihood of occurrence of an event. It is a measure of accuracy with which the outcome of a chance event can be predicted.

In most of the risky situations, two elements are commonly found:

1. The outcome is uncertain i.e. there is a possibility that one or other(s) may occur. Therefore, logically, there are at least two possible outcomes for a given situation.
2. Out of the possible outcomes, one is unfavourable or not liked by the individual or the analyst.

6.2 Risk Vs. Uncertainty

Uncertainty is often confused with the risk. Uncertainty refers to a situation where the outcome is not certain or unknown. Uncertainty refers to a state of mind characterized by doubt, based on the lack of knowledge about what will or what will not happen in the future.

Uncertainty can be perceived as opposite of certainty where you are assure of outcome or what will happen. Accordingly, some weights or probabilities can be assigned into risky situations but uncertainty, the psychological reaction to the absence of knowledge lacks this privilege.

Decision under uncertain situations is very difficult for the decision-maker. It all depends upon the skill, the judgement and of course luck

Uncertainty being a perceptual phenomenon implies different degrees to different person. Assume a situation where an individual has to appear for the first in the newly introduced insurance examination.

(a) an individual student undergone a training in insurance.

(b) An individual with training or experience in insurance.

A's perception towards uncertainty (of performance in examination) is different from that of B. Nonetheless, in both situations, the outcome that is the questions which will be asked in the examination are different.

6.3 Need of Security

Human beings have been in search of security right from nomadic days. The history of mankind is a history of the search for security. Man had to face dangers and risks which threatened his very existence. As an individual he would have found it difficult to combat these external dangers. He therefore started living in a group, thereby ensuring group security and cover against possible external dangers. The greatest risk was, of course, that of death, form wild animals, snakes, crocodiles and other crawling creatures and also from natural calamities, such as floods, fires and earthquakes.

As human society developed, commerce and business started flourishing and idea of insurance was promoted in due course. *Insurance is the group effort to reduce the sufferings of an individual as a result of some inevitable calamities.* Death, disability, sickness — are important examples. Loss of property due to external forces also worried the individual human being. The obvious solution was *Insurance.*

> For the provision of protection to life and property, human beings facing the same or similar risks came together and shared in advance the probable future loss that might take place due to specified reasons under specified circumstances, during a specified period. This idea of collective protection was practiced even in ancient society.

In India, the idea of insurance finds expression in the famous word Yogakshema (meaning protecting what has come and using the same for the welfare of the concerned people). References to Yogakshema are found in the Rigveda as well as in various Smritis of different periods.

Kautilya, in his Arthashastra, lays down that the people agree to pay taxes so that they are maintained by those taxes. The king himself should maintain children, aged persons and persons in distress, women without children and the children of helpless persons. It was the duty of the elders to maintain the property of a minor till he attained *majority.* The system of the joint family, which was a natural outcome of Janpad society, practised this concept of sharing individual losses — ensuring co-operation, moral restraint, tolerance and savings. It ensured the division of labour reducing the cost of production, equitable distribution of joint family profits and overall social and economic security.

In the wake of industrialisation, consequent urbanisation and breakup of the *joint* family system, an alternative was sought and that was provided by Insurance. *This search for security is a never-ending process.* With the advent of civilization, the nature of security needed by various human groups is also changing.

Man needs food, shelter and clothing for his survival. For the satisfaction of these needs, he requires money; which comes from his earnings. Earnings are a result of the capacity to earn, which may be extinguished by death or threatened by old age or disability. These may result in the stoppage of income or the reduction in income which is necessary for him and his family's sustenance.

If the breadwinner lives a normal span of life, the financial arrangements which he would have made for himself and his family members would have been fulfilled. However if he happens to die early (premature death), his family would be deprived of the income, which the deceased would have brought-in, had he not died.

The alternative arrangements for such an eventuality can be made with the help of life insurance.

> The greatest risk to which human life is exposed is that of death. Though death is certain, the time when it will strike is uncertain. This uncertainty gives rise to. insurance. Insurance cannot avoid this uncertainty, what Insurance seeks to ensure is the replacement or reimbursement of financial/economic consequences if such an event takes place. Insurance cannot postpone the event. The insured event cannot be brought about earlier.

In that event, there would not be any insurance. For example, a person committing suicide after taking insurance cannot expect the insurance company to pay the policy amount (sum assured) after such an event. In other words, the insured person should not cause the insured event to take place.

Since insurance seeks to deal with the financial consequences of the risk, apart from death, *living too long is also a risk,* because everyday we need money for our sustenance. Apart from natural death and a long life, human beings are exposed to the following risks.

Disability — Natural: This is normally not covered by a life insurance policy. Accidental Disability can however be covered by a life insurance policy as an additional benefit (rider benefit) by paying an additional premium (rider premium) usually at the rate of *Re.1/-* per thousand sum assured per year, over and above the usual premium. Some policies include this amount in the basic premium itself.

Double Accident benefit consists of payment of double the sum assured in the event of a person's death due to accident. Sickness policies are covered by a general insurance policy. However, a life insurance policy may cover some specified sicknesses/illnesses, either by charging an extra premium (rider premium) or by giving it as an additional benefit, by enhancing the basic premium itself.

6.4 Hazards are of Three Types

Hazard is any factor that adds to the risk. Hazard (Peril) in (General Insurance) causes the loss to take place. Thus hazard (peril) is the effect. In popular parlance loss is equated with claim, though it may not be so. Loss may take place, yet a claim may not be payable. Because claim is payable or not payable in accordance with policy conditions. If the cause of the loss, that is the peril, is an uninsured or excluded one, the claim may not be payable, e.g., accidental death or disability taking place as a result of mountaineering etc. Suicide is an excluded peril for a period of one year from the date of F.P.R. It is a permanent exclusion for Double Accident Benefit.

(1) ***Physical Hazard:*** This is specific to age, sex, build (height, weight, chest, abdomen measurements) blood pressure, pulse rate, specific gravity of urine — i.e., personal condition, which will also include defects in vision, hearing, walking etc. any other physical defect, personal history of illnesses, injuries, operations etc. Family history relating to early deaths or long survival of family members, previous insurance history also are of material importance. *Failure to disclose these is a material non-disclosure.*

(2) ***Occupational Hazard:*** If the occupation is hazardous, extra premium has to be charged depending on the extent of hazard involved. Certain occupational risks are not covered by extra premium, but the extra risk involved is excluded by applying exclusion clauses. Sometimes, both the methods may be employed. A few occupational risks are declined, e.g., jockeys, riding boys (horse racing) explorers, steeple Jack.

(3) ***Moral Hazard:*** If insurance is taken without genuine need for the same, moral hazard may be present. Over insurance (without the capacity to pay) also suggests a moral hazard. It involves good faith, personal reputation, character, ethics, speculation, etc. of the proposer. If the behaviour of the proposer is not in conformity with the accepted behavioural norms, moral hazard should be suspected. If a moral hazard is present, the proposal has to be dropped or rejected. Extra mortality resulting from moral hazards cannot be measured. The possibility of non-disclosure of material facts cannot be ruled out. Speculative purpose can be suspected. No amount of premium can be adequate to meet a moral hazard.

The common situations that may give rise to moral hazard are:

(1) Absence of insurable interest.

(2) Insurance not supported by income.

(3) Heavy insurance at advanced age.

(4) Insurance in quick succession.

(5) Insuring at a place other than normal residence.

(6) Suppression of previous insurance history.

(7) Nominating a stranger.

(8) Assignment without natural love and affection and without or with inadequate consideration.

(9) Address c/o Agent. In fact address c/o someone else should be enquired into.

6.5 Personal Risk

Risk is defined as uncertainty concerning the occurrence of a losses. For example, the risk of being killed in an auto accident is present became uncertainty is present.

Personal risks are risks that directly affect an individual. They involve the possibility of the complete loss or reduction of earned income. There are four major personal risks.

(a) ***Risk of Premature Death:*** Premature death is defined ad the defined of the household head with unfulfilled financiai obligations. If the surviving family members receive an insufficient amount of replacement income from other sources or have insufficient financial assets to replace the lost income, they may be financially insecure. Premature death can cause financial problems only if the deceased has dependents to support or does with unsatisfied financial obligations. Thus, the death of a child aged 5 is not premature in the economic sense.

(b) ***Risk of Insufficient Income During Retirement:*** It refers to the risk of not having sufficient income at the age of retirement or the age becoming so that there is a possibility that the individual may not be able to earn the likelihood. When one retires, he loose his earned income. Unless he had sufficient financial assets from which to draw or has access to other sources. Of retirement income such as social security or a private pension, he will be exposed to financial insecurity during retirement.

(c) ***Risk on Poor Health:*** It refers to the risk of poor health or disability of a person to earn the means of survival. For example, losing the legs due to accident, heart surgery which will cost lakhs, etc. Unless the person has adequate health insurance, private savings or other sources of income to meet these losses, he will be financially insecure. The loss of earned income is another major cause of financial insecurity, if the disability is severe. In case of long-term disability, things will become worst and some one must take care of the disabled person. The loss of earned income can be financially very painful.

(d) ***Risk of Unemployment:*** The risk of unemployment is another major threat to financial security. Unemployment can result from business cycle down swings, technological and structural changes inn he economy, seasonal factors and etc. Employers are increasingly hiring temporary or part-time workers to reduce labour costs. Being temporary employers, workers lose their employee benefits. Unless there is adequate replacement income or past savings an which to draw, the workers (unemployed, part-time, temporary) will be financially insecure. IF the duration of unemployment is extended over a long period, past savings and unemployment benefits may be exhausted.

Personal Risk Management

Personal risk management refers to the identification of pure risk faced by an individual or family and to the selection of the most appropriate technique for treating such risks. Personal risk management considers other methods for handling risk in addition to insurance. A personal risk management program involves four steps:

(i) Identifying Potential Losses
(ii) Evaluating Potential Losses
(iii) Selecting the appropriate technique for handling losses
(iv) Implementing and reviewing the program periodically

(i) Identifying Potential Losses: The four step is to identity all potential losses that can cause serious financial problems financial losses can result from the following:

- Loss of earned income to the family became of the premature death of the family head.
- Insufficient income and financial assets during retirement.
- Medical bills and the loss of earnings during an extended period of disability.
- Loss of earned income from unemployment.

(ii) Evaluating Potential Losses: The second step is to evaluate the potential losses, it is estimate the frequency and severity of potential losses so that the most appropriate technique can be used to deal with the personal risk. Loss frequency refers to the probable number of losses that may occur during some given time period. Loss severity refers is the probable size of losses that may occur. If these two are not evaluated accurately, then It will be very difficult to adopt the appropriate technique to handle the risk.

(iii) Selecting the Appropriate Technique: The third step is to select the most appropriate technique for handling each potential loss. The major methods for potential losses are:

(a) Avoidance
(b) Risk control
(c) Risk retention
(d) Non-insurance transfers
(e) Insurance

(a) Avoidance: Avoidance is one method for handling a potential loss. It means a certain loss exposure is never acquired or an existing loss exposure is abandoned. For example, one can avoid being mugged in a high crime rate area by staying out of the area. The major advantage of avoidance is that the chance of loss is slightly reduced. However, one can not be able to avoid all losses. For example, a company may not be able to avoid the premature death of a key executive

(b) Risk Control: Risk control refers to the activities that reduce both the frequently and severity of losses. For example, one can reduce the risk of an auto accident by driving within the speed limits, taking a safe driving course, and driving defensively. Risk control also aims at reducing the severity of a loss. For example, weaving a helmet reduces the severity of a head injury is a motor cycle accident. Wearing a seal bell reduces the severity of an injury in a car accident.

(c) ***Retention:*** Retention means that one retains part or all of a loss if it occurs. For example, one can retain the small expenses, say medical expenses like normal check-ups, blood-test and etc. He or she can set aside a certain amount from their income to meet these. Retention can be done if the possible is not serious. Retention can be either active or passive. Active risk retention means that one is aware of the loss exposure and plans to retain all or part of it. Passive retention is the failure to identity a loss exposure, failure to act, no forgetting to out. Retention can be effectively used when not other method is available.

(d) ***Non-insurance Transfers:*** Non-insurance transfers are methods other than insurance by which a pure risk is transferred to a party other than an insurer. For example, periodic (say, half-yearly) medical check-ups for the workers the owner of the plant. This can be done through an agreement between the employer and employees. Non-insurance transfers often cost less than insurance. In Non-insurance transfers, the potential loss may be shifted to someone who is a better position to exercise loss control.

(e) ***Insurance:*** In a personal risk management program, must people rely heavily on insurance as the major method for dealing with risk. Insurance is appropriate for loss exposures that have a low probability of loss but for which the severity of loss is high. Insurance policies to fulfill the needs of the public.

(iv) **Periodic Review:** The last step is to implement and review the programme periodically. At least every two or three years, one should determine all major risks are adequately covered one should also review the program at major events in his/her life such as divorce, birth of a child, purchase of a her life, such as divorce, birth of a child, purchase of a house, change of jobs or death of spouse or family member.

6.6 Factor Affecting Risk

In life insurance, the factors which may affect the risk are usually those factors which are affecting the mortality. They are also called factors affecting longevity of a person. Following are the factors which may affect risk.

1. **Age:** Age of a life to be insured is the most important factor to affect mortality. The age proof is very essential for calculating premium rate. Nowadays, it has been the common practice that age should be admitted at the time of proposal is avoid dispute. Age proof is essential if the policy is term insurance, non-medical policies and immediate annuity. The maximum age limit is fixed is avoid adverse selection. At advance age, the need for insurance is a doubtful proposition, i.e., the chances of moral hazard is higher. The minimum age limit is meant to avoid risk of infant mortality.

2. **Build:** Build refers to physique of the proposed life and includes height, weight, the distribution of weight and chest expansion. There are standards of weight according to maximum weight reveal the indication of certain hidden diseases. Overweight is dangerous in advanced age and underweight is similarly not desirable at younger age, say, below 35 years. Insurers have fixed the minimum weight and maximum weight at a specified height. If the assumed life is not within the standard the proposal may not be accepted or may be accepted at extra premium.

3. **Physical condition:** The physical condition of the age life proposed has a direct bearing on the mortality of the life. Insurers, are, therefore, very particular about the conditions of an applications sight, hearing, heart, lungs, tonsils, teeth, kidneys, nervous system, etc. The experts in the field can assess the longevity or mortality if a person due to impairment of certain organs. The information is confirmed and supplemented by a medical examination. The primary purpose of the medical examination is to detect any malfunctioning of the vital organs of the body.

4. **Personal History:** The personal history of the life propose would reveal the possibility of death to him. The history may be connected with the (i) health record (ii) Past habit (iii) Previous occupation (iv) Insurance history.

   (i) Health Record: The past health record is the most important factor under personal history because it affects the longevity or mortality of a person is a grater extent. It includes any operation of the like proposed. The medical examination may reveal these facts. Particular emphasis in placed on the recent injuries and illness. It has been the practice not is accept the proposal form of the applicant who are suffering from illness.

   (ii) Past Habits: The insurers wants is know the past habit of the life proposed, for drugs or alcohol, became the cune may be only temporary. The post history is usually expected is be repeated. Therefore past habits are very cautiously examined.

   (iii) History of Occupation: If the proponent was employed in hazardous or unhealthy occupation, there is a possibility that he may still retain ill-effects there from or may revert is such occupation. The past hazardous occupations generally affects health slowly and occupational discuses are contacted.

   (iv) Insurance History: The previous amount of insurance may disclose the degree of risk of the applicant. If he was refused insurance, it might be a suspicions factor of his insurability. If it was found that the applicant was already insured for adequate amount this request for more insurance is regarded with suspicious.

5. **Family History:** Like the personal history, family history also requires information of habit, health, occupation and insurance of other family members, particularly of the parents, brothers and sisters. The children's history of health is also required. The family history is considered significant

to know the transmission of certain characteristics by heredity. Heart, lungs, build etc. follow family characteristics.

6. **Occupation:** Occupation is an important factor to affect the risk. The nature of work may be hazardous because he may suffer an accident at any time while as work. If a person is working in a chemical plant, he may contact poison, because chemical effect may be poisonous. The duty or unventilated house, unhealthy or insanitary environments may deteriorate the health of the workers. In certain occupation, the occupational diseases are common.

7. **Residence:** The residence also affects the risk. The risk will be lesser is a good climate area and more in a bad climate although the difference is narrowed down because of better medical and sanitary facilities. The geographical location, atmosphere, political stability, climate construction of house, etc. are important factor which may affect the risk.

8. **Present Habits:** The general mode of living of the proposer effect the risk. Drunkards and non-temperate persons cause increase in mortality. Excessive and careless smoking tends to shorten the life due to development of nicotine poisoning. The introduction affects the health of a person and consequently his mortality. The general mode of living is also considered in habits.

9. **Morales:** It is observed that the departure from the commonly accepted standards of ethical and moral conduct involve extra mortality. Infidelity and departure from the code of sex behaviour are seriously regarded because these may affect the health. Consideration of morals is essential is determine the moral hazard. The moral hazard occurs due to intention of the insured. This hazard is present where the policy is taken not with a view to protect one-self against losses but to obtain gain through crooked means.

10. **Race and Nationality:** The mortality rate differs from race is race and nation is nation. In India, persons of sigh race or caste are expected to like longer than the scheduled castes or tribes. Similarly, countries near to equator have more mortality. The climate and way of life of a country affect the health conditions of the people.

11. **Sex:** Mortality among female sex is, generally, higher than that of male sex because the physical hazard of maternity is present in the former case. The lesser education, conservatism and non-employment of the ladies also affect the mortality. The absence of proper examination of ladies also count more hazards. The chances of moral hazard are also present in female insurance. So, unless woman has financial reasons for insurance, her proposal is not generally conceded.

12. **Economic Status:** It is essential to examine that the family and business circumstances of the proponents are such as to justify the amount of insurance applied for. This investigation also reveals weather the income of the applicant bears a reasonable relationship to the amount of insurance which he proposes to carry. The higher economic status generally provides

a better field for insurance due to various reasons. The chances of death is also lower in higher strata of the society.

13. **Defense Services:** Though there has been much improvement in defence tehnolology, yet flying or gliding, etc., is still considered hazardous one. Sometimes, certain restrictive clauses are imposed for insurance persons engaged in such services. In other words, extra premiums may be required. The war cause is added to avoid the occupation risk in defence, say, navy, air force and military.

14. **Plan of Insurance:** Certain plans involve more responsibility is the insurer at death and so these plans are restricted is only first class lines. Similarly, some plans have lesser risk and, therefore, can be issued without any extra investigation. For example the multi-purpose policy is issued only is first class lines and the pure endowment policy can be issued is any one irrespective of health.

6.7 Measurement of Risk and Mortality

Theory of Probability

Insurance has been-defined as the institution which eliminates risk or which substitutes certainty for uncertainty. The occurrence of events insured against cannot wholly be prevented but the uncertainty of financial loss through such occurrences can be eliminated by distributing the loss over a group. Thus, a man cannot be sure whether or not his house will burn even if he use all the preventive measures known. If the house burns the property is lost and gone forever that much material value has been actually destroyed. But it is not necessary that the owners of houses that they would all contribute to a common fund from which any unfortunate owner who lost his house by fire should be recompensed. Thus, instead of the loss falling on one it can be divided equally among all. This is the essence of insurance and it illustrates the meaning of the statement that insurance is the elimination of uncertainty or the replacement of uncertainty by certainty. The common contribution to the fund above referred to constitutes the certain loss and is measured by the premium; the uncertain loss refers to the uncertainty that a particular house will burn. The same situation exists with respect to life insurance. It is not death itself that can be distributed, i.e., parcelled out among a number of insurers, but is not known in advance upon whom death will fall prematurely, hence all men can contribute to a fund which will be used to satisfy the business and family needs of advance upon whom death will fall prematurely, hence all men can contribute to a fund which will be used to satisfy the business and family needs of those who die early.

These two illustration suggest the that exist for the application of the insurance principle. In whatever field risk is found to exist, there the principle can be applied. The complete working out of a scientific insurance plan necessitates some method of measuring this risk in order to determine the amount of each individuals contribution to the common fund. The correct measurement of risk, therefore, lies at the foundation of any system of insurance. This accomplishment is rendered possible through the application to statistical data, covering the phenomenon in question of certain laws developed in the field of mathematics known as the laws of probability, and it win be necessary to state and explain them before proceeding further.

The Laws of Probability

The science of probabilities furnishes three principles of which practical use is made in life insurance. They may be called respectively (1) the law of certainty, (2) the law of simple probability, and (3) the law of compound probability. Their use makes possible the descriptio of risk in terms of mathematical values, and the statement of the three laws is as follows: (1) certainty may be expressed by unity, or one; (2) simple probability, or the probability or chance that an event will happen or that it will not happen may be expressed by a fraction; and (3) compound probability, or the chance that two mutually independent events will happen is the product of the separate probabilities that the events, taken separately, will happen.

An illustration will serve to make these statements clear. If a box contains twenty marbles and it is known that five of the marbles are black and the remainder white, let us suppose it is desired to know the probability that a marble drawn at random from the box will be black. If any marble has equal chances with any other of being drawn, then there are twenty different draws that might be made and if five of the marbles are black ten it can be said that there are five chances out of twenty of drawing a black marble, or the chances is in the ratio of five to twenty, or is 5/20. This fraction is obtained in the following manner: The denominator equals the total number of marbles in the box; the numerator equals the number that satisfies the condition stated, namely, the quality of being black. In like manner it might be desired to know the chance that the marble will not be clack, and by a like method of reasoning it is found that this probability equals 15/20. From these facts it is possible to formulate a general statement of the method of determining simple probabilities as follows: The denominator will equal he total number of possible trials or chances that thing may happen or may not happen or the total number of instances dealt with - in the example above, total marbles. The numerator will be composed of those instances only which satisfy the conditions imposed - in the same example, black marbles.

In the illustration here used there are marbles of two kinds only, black and white, and any marble withdrawn from the box must be one or other color. The total existing probabilities are therefore the probability of drawing a black marble and the probability of drawing II white one. If certainty is represented by unity, then unity, or the value "one", will represent the fact of drawing any marble. But any marble drawn at random may be either black or white and since the probability of drawing the former is 5/20, and of the latter 15/20, and since certainty must equal the sum of all equals 1, therefore certainty must equal the sum of all separate probability, in this case 5/20 , 15/20 = 1.

This corollary ,that certainty equals the sum of all separate probabilities may be further illustrated by the familiar example of the coin. It is certainty that a coin tossed into the air will come to rest on one side and this fact is represented by the value "one". Now, since it has but two sides, the sum of the separate probabilities that it will alight heads up or tails up must equal one. The probability of falling heads up, determined by the above rule for valuing simple probabilities, is 1/2, since there are two possible sides and one is heads; likewise the probability of falling tails up is 1/2, and the sum of these two fractions equals one.

The probability that both of two mutually independent events will happen is equal to the product of the simple probabilities that the events taken separately will happen. Suppose that two coins are tossed up and it is desired to know the chance that they will both fall heads up. By the statement of the law above it will be 1/2 x 1/ 2 or 1/4 since it is known that the chance is 1/2 that each separate coin will fall heads up. That this is the correct result may easily be demonstrated. Suppose the two coins are a nickel and a dime. Then the different ways in which they may fall are:

Nickel	Dime
Heads up	Heads up
Heads up	Tails up
Tails up	Heads up
Tails up	Tails up

These four combinations comprise the only possible ones that can be made with the two coins and the first combination is the only one of the four that satisfies the stipulated conditions, namely, both coins heads up. Hence there is one chance in four for this combination to appear, or the probability of its occurrence is ¼.

According four law of compound probabilities, as stated herewith, the product of simple probabilities equals the probability that two events will happen at the same time, only when the two events are mutually independent. The happening of the one must have no effect upon the occurrence or non-occurrence of the other, that is, must neither make it necessary for the second to occur nor make it impossible. If the law were valid irrespective of this qualification, such absurd results as the following might be obtained. The chance that the coin will fall heads up is 1/2 and the chance that it will tails up is likewise1/2. Therefore the chance that it will fall both heads up and tails up is 1/2 x 1/2 or ¼. The absurdity results from the fact that the occurrence of the first named event makes it impossible for the second to occur simultaneously.

Forecasting Future Events

The value of these three laws of probability lies in the fact that they can be used to forecast future events. Future events can be foretold in one of two ways: (1) by a priori or deductive reasoning, and (2) from knowledge of what has happened in the past under similar conditions. The validity of a priori reasoning depends on the completeness with which all the causes at work in the determination of any phenomenon are known; and the limitations of the human mind are such that a priori reasoning does not furnish a safe basis upon which to develop a superstructure guaranteeing that degree of certainty which is required in insurance. Reasoning inductively, or on the assumption that what has happened in the past will happen again in the future if the same conditions are present, does not require an analysis of the causes of phenomena in order to predict future events. There lies behind this statement the assumption that all things are governed by law. In the cases here used to illustrate the principles of probability this is the law of pure chance. It is an even chance one with another that any marble may be drawn from the box or that either side of the coin may be "up". Then if in a great number of trials it has been found that the coin falls "heads up" one-half of the time the conclusion follows that this result will follow approximately if the same number of trials is taken again.

This fact has important bearings upon life insurance. From data showing the length of life and ages at death in the past it is possible to predict probabilities of death and of survival in the future. This prediction is based on the assumption that, like the law of chance, there is a law of mortality by which human beings die; that certain causes are in operation which determine that out of a large group of persons at birth a definite number of lives will fail each year until all have died; and that the force of mortality could be measured if only the causes at work were known. But it is not necessary to analyze this law of mortality completely and to know all the operating causes in order to predict the possible rate of mortality in a group of persons. By studying the rate of death among any group and noting all the circumstances that might, according to our best knowledge, affect that rate, it is possible to surround any future group of persons with approximately the same set of circumstances and expect approximately the same rate of death. Thus without complete knowledge of the law of mortality a working basis is found for predicting future rates of death. It is necessary then to have mortality statistics in order to develop a scientific plan of life insurance.

Mortality Rate

Mortality or death rate is the ratio of the number of persons died during a particular to the number of people lived at the beginning of that year. The establishment of any plan of insuring against premature death requires some means of giving mathematical values to the chances of death, and the considerations advanced in the previous paragraphs show that the laws of probability can be used for this purpose as soon as trustworthy data are secured showing the course of past mortality. Mortality tables, as such data are called, are records of past mortality put into such form as can be used in estimating the course of future deaths. Thus, mortality table is to predict future mortality. A large number of persons are selected and they are observed for death and death rates are estimated till all of them are dead.

Sources of Mortality Tables

There are two sources from which the best-known mortality tables in existence today have been obtained: (1) population statistics obtained from census enumerations, and the returns of deaths from registration offices, and (2) the mortality statistics of insured lives. Well-known examples of the former are the English life tables of Drs. Farr, Ogle, and Tatham, successively in charge of the General Registry Office of England and Wales. Dr. Farr's life table, for instance, was based on the registered deaths in England and Wales during the years 1838-54, and on the two census enumerations of population for 1841 and 1851.

Objection to Tables Based on Population Data

For the purposes of measuring the mortality of insured lives, however, it is questionable whether statistics of a general population can be used. Such data, to be Sure, would represent the average mortality of a population group and to that extent would approximate the true law of mortality. But for purposes of insurance this mayor may not be the mortality rate desired. An insurance company wants a measure of the mortality occurring among insured lives, and it is probable that this may differ from that of a specific population group. Insured lives are subject to special influences affecting mortality and these factors must be taken into consideration. The statement has been made that if an insurance company could insure every person who passed II certain corner in a large city until it had a large enough group to guarantee the operation of the law of average, the company could dispense with its medical examination. This is probably true, but the trouble is, when the matter of insurance is left to the choice of the individual, not every one who passed the corner in question would insure; and if this group could be divided into two parts, those who insure and those who do not, the former would show a much higher rate of mortality than the latter. Statistics of insurance companies bear out this statement. Mortality tables based on population statistics formed the first scientific basis for insurance lives, but their approximation to true insurance mortality was not close and they were supplanted by tables based on insured lives as soon as the experience was forthcoming on which to base the latter. The present tables in use by American life-insurance companies and required by most state insurance departments as a basis for the valuation of policy liabilities have been constructed from data of insured lives.

Construction of Mortality Table

The table as given above represents the mortality data in its final form for use in expressing probabilities of death and of survival. It is manifestly impossible for, any insurance company to insure a group of 100,000 persons of exactly the same age and at exactly the same time, and it is equally impossible to keep any such group under observation until all have died. Insurance policies are written at all times of the year and on lives at various ages. It is entirely practicable that a record be kept of all insured lives, .showing at each age the number of persons under observation, and of those observed for one year at least the number who have died. If data are collected, therefore, showing (1) the age at which persons come under observation, (2) the duration of the period of observation, and (3) the number dying during one year, for each age, the materials will be furnished, out of which a mortality table may be constructed. Suppose, for illustration, that statistics have been collected as follows.:

Age	Number Under Observation	Number dying before end of year
10	30,000	210
11	150,000	1200
12, etc.	80,000	720

From these figures death rates may be computed for the respective ages in the following manner:

Age	Rate of death expressed as a Fractions		Rate of Death expressed as Decimal
10	$\frac{810}{30,000}$	=	.007
11	$\frac{1,200}{150,000}$	=	.008
12	$\frac{720}{80,000}$	=	.009

Death rates may be so computed for each separate age to the maximum limit of life, if only the data are collected as required above. If these figures can be considered as representing the yearly probabilities of dying 3 for persons of each given *age,* a mortality table may be constructed from them by assuming a group of say 100,000 persons at the youngest age for which it is desirable to compute the table and then reducing the group by reducing the number *yearly* according to the given figures of the probabilities of death. *The* following simple table will illustrate this method:

1 Age	2 Assume Number Living (Radix)		3 Multiply by Probability of dying		4 Result: Number of Death At Given Age	5 Subtract (4) from (2) Radix At Next Age Equals
10	100,000	x	.007	=	700	99,300
11	99,300	x	.008	=	784	99.506
12	98.506	x	.009	=	887	97,619
13	97,619, etc.					

Since the probability of dying at age 10 is .007, there will occur 700 deaths during the year among the 100,000 starting at age 10, this leaves 99,300 of the group to begin age 11 and this latter number dies at the rate of eight per thousand (.008), making 794 deaths during the year. In this way, the original 100,000 are reduced by deaths year after year until all have died. Thus is the statement true that the mortality table represents "a generation of individuals passing through time". In the mortality table shown on page 132 the two columns denoting yearly probabilities of death and of survival represent the final form of the actual statistics of dying among insured lives. These probabilities were then applied to the assumed population of 100,000 at age 10 in the manner herewith explained, and the *result* was the American Experience table of mortality.

Application of the Theory of Probabilities to the Mortality Table

The statement was made earlier in this chapter that risk in life insurance *is* measured by the application of the laws of probability to the mortality table. Now that these laws are understood and the mortality table has been explained, a few simple illustrations may be used to show this application. Suppose it is desired to insure a managed 35 against death within one year, within two years, or within five years. It *is* necessary to know the probability of death within one, two, or five years from age 35. This probability, according to the laws heretofore explained, will be determined according to the mortality table and will be a fraction of which the denominator equals the number living at age 35 and the numerator will be the number who have died during the one, two, or five years, respectively, following that age. According to the table, 81,822 persons are living at age 35, and 732 die before the end of the year. Hençe, the probability of death in one year is 732/81822. During the two years following the *stated age there are 732* + 737 Deaths, or a total of 1,469. The probability of dying within two years is therefore 1469/85822. Likewise the total number of deaths within five years is 732 + 737 + 743 + 749 +.756 or 3,716, and the probability of dying within five years is thus 3716/81822.

Probabilities of survival can also be expressed by the table. The chance of living one year following age 35 will be a fraction of which the denominator is 81,822 and the numerator will be the number who have lived one year following the specified age. This is the number who are living beginning age 36, or 81,090, and the probability of survival for one year is therefore 81090/81822. These illustrations furnish an opportunity for a proof of the law of certainty. The chance of living one year following age 35 is 81090/81822 and the chance of dying within the same period is 732/81822. The sum of these two fractions equals 81822/81822 or 1, which is certainty, and certainty represents the sum of all separate probabilities in this case two, the probability of death and the probability of *survival.* In like manner many more instructive examples of the application of these laws to the mortality table could be made, but they need not be carried further at this point, for the subject will be fully covered in the chapters on "Net Premiums".

6.8 Risk Premium

The evaluation of the risk premium is based on the mathematical probability of the event happening. The larger the number of lives assured the closer should be the amount of claims to the amount of premiums received.

As in general insurance, life insurance contracts can be arranged on a year to year basis. This system which was tried in the earlier years of modern life assurance business had to be given up for its drawbacks. In the first instance, if the health of the person deteriorates, the insurer may charge a higher rate of premium or may deprive him of the insurance cover next year. On the other hand, a person who is in excellent health may not renew the contract. Even those who want to renew the contract, may have to renew the same with higher premium because of higher age. There would also be *a tendency on the part of the not* so *good lives (under-average lives) to* 20 *in for insurance on a large scale. Such a tendency is called Adverse selection.* The life insurer has to exercise great care in avoiding adverse selection. If this is not checked, the premiums collected may not prove adequate to meet the cost of the claims. Hence, the insurer has to *select* the lives, *assess* the risk on the available data, *classify* it on the basis of degree of under-averageness and *charge suitable extra premium or use some other method to take care of the extra risk involved. This is called 'underwriting'.*

The system of charging increasing premium every year is called assessmentism. The premium that is charged should be adequate to meet the mortality for that age. As the mortality, increases with age, the premium increases with it. It may become prohibitive at higher ages. Hence, an alternative was found by charging a level premium which would be the mathematical equivalent of the single premium required for granting a fixed-term Term insurance.

This can be projected on a Graph.

This level premium tends to be higher than risk premium in the early years of the policy. The burden of heavier premiums in later years is shifted to these earlier years. In these earlier years, premiums received exceed the amount of premiums required in earlier years. This excess is invested in accordance with legislative guidelines to earn interest. Thus, this excess goes on accumulating with interest. *Individually, it is a 'Policy Reserve' which actually represents Policy Liability. Cumulatively it constitutes a 'Life Fund' which gets enhanced by accretion of premiums received and interest earned and gets depleted by claims, commissions, salaries and other expenses.* If the company maintains its *solvency,* the Life Fund steadily goes on increasing. Since it is available in the form of various assets, both should match to a large extent, e.g., LIC's total Life Fund as on 31.3.02 was Rs. 2,27,009 crores, while its assets amounted to Rs. 2,45,331 crores. The two sources of income of any life insurance company are premiums and interest. For LICI, these figures were Rs. 48,963.60 crores and Rs. 22,695.42 crores respectively as on 31.3.02.

The insurers therefore rightly pass on a share of interest earnings to the policyholders by reducing the premium amount. At the same time the policyholder should bear his share of expenses which are necessarily to be incurred for running the life insurance business.

Thus, we start with Risk Premium which is sufficient to cover the mortality for a given age for a period of one year. When adjusted for interest, it becomes *Net Premium.* After loading it with expenses, it becomes *office premium.* Finally the actuary makes provisions for Bonus Loadings in respect of with-profit policies. Provision is also made for inflation, which reduces the value of premiums receivable and the claims payable in future. The final outcome is *Tabular Premium,* which is quoted in company's Tables of Premium Rates.

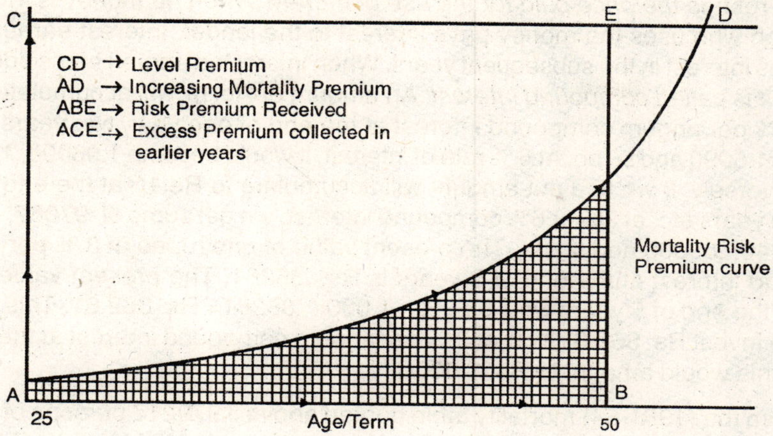

Life insurance contracts are long term contracts. Hence, an actuary has to take into account any possible loss in investments due to fluctuations in interest rates as also loss on some investments. *The higher the interest rate assumed, the lower would be the premium.*

Expenses incurred by the insurer may be classified as follows:-

(1) Expenses connected with selling of new policies, underwriting and issue of new policies such as agents' commission, medical fees, Development staff salaries, New business staff salaries, advertisement and publicity, cost of preparing new policies, stamp duty etc.

(2) Expenses connected with servicing of policies—including cost of servicing claims.

(3) General expenses including valuation expenses.

(4) Expenses connected with investment of funds.

Broadly these are categorised as new business expenses and renewal expenses.

These expensés may vary (a) with the annual premium, e.g., commission, (b) with the number of policies, e.g. policy preparation costs, (c) with the sum assured e.g. medical fees, stamp duty and cost of underwriting decision. The basic premiums are calculated on a yearly basis per thousand sum assured. If the mode of payment is yearly or half-yearly, a small reduction in tabular premium, as a certain percentage of premium, is allowed. This is called mode rebate. If the sum assured is large, incidence of fixed costs which do not vary with the sum assured goes down. Hence, large Sum Assured Rebate is allowed from the Tabular Premium.

It is possible to merge these rebates in the tabular premium itself so that no separate rebates be allowed while calculating the instalment premium, which can be on yearly, half-yearly, quarterly or monthly basis, according to the option of the policyholders.

Interest: *is the price paid for the use of money.* When he money is invested, the person who uses the money pays interest to the lender. Interest earned each year earns interest in the subsequent years. When interested earned earns additional interest, *it is called compound interest.* An amount of Re.1/- will accumulate at the rate of 3% per annum compound interest at the end of one year, two years etc. to 1.03000, 1.6090 and so on. At 6 % rate of interest, it would become 1.06000, 1.12360 etc. Conversely, if we find out amount will accumulate to Re.1/- at the end of one year, two years etc. at 3% or 6% compound interest, we get sums of .97087, .94260 and .94340, .89000 and so on. The present value of one rupee at 3 % per annum compound interest at the end of 5 years is Rs. .86261. The present value of Rs. 1,000 at the end of 5 years would be Rs. 1,000 ´ .86261= Rs. 862.61. This means that if we invest Rs. 862.61 now at 3 % per annum compound interest at the end of 5 years this would amount to Rs. 1,000/-.

From the (1961-64) mortality table quoted above if 979217 persons of age 35 go in for a Temporary Assurance for a period of 10 years and if we expect them to follow the same pattern as displayed by this table, we have to expect 1410 deaths at age 35, 1535 at 36 and so on. If we assume that Rs. 1,000/- would be the sum assured payable on death, the cost of insurance at the end of one, two three... ten years would be 1410/979217 x Rs. 1,000, 1535/979217 x Rs. 1,000, 1679/979217 x Rs. 1,000 3370/979217 x Rs. 1,000. Present value of Re. 1/- to be received at the end of the year at 3% per annum and 6% per annum.

End of the year	@ 3%	@ 6%
1.	.97087	.94340
2.	.94260	.89000
3.	.91514	.83962
4.	.88849	.79209
5.	.86261	.74726
6.	.83748	.70496
7.	.81309	.66506
8.	.78941	.62741
9.	.76642	.59190
10.	.74409	.55839

We assume that the claims would be payable at the end of the year. The present value of each probability of death in case of ten years' assurance will be @ 3% as follows:.

1st year's insurance to provide for death between 35 and 36

$$\frac{1410}{979217} \times 1{,}000 \times .97087 = 1.398$$

2nd year's insurance to provide for death between 36 and 37

$$\frac{1535}{979217} \times 1{,}000 \times .94260 = 1.478$$

3rd year's insurance to provide for death between 37 and 38

$$\frac{1679}{979217} \times 1{,}000 \times .91514 = 1.596$$

4th year's insurance to provide for death between 38 and 39

$$\frac{1842}{797217} \times 1{,}000 \times .88849 = 1.671$$

5th year's insurance to provide for death between 39 and 40

$$\frac{2033}{979217} \times 1{,}000 \times .86261 = 1.791$$

6th year's insurance to provide for death between 40 and 41

$$\frac{2242}{979217} \times 1{,}000 \times 83748 = 1.917$$

7th year's insurance to provide for death between 41 and 42

$$\frac{2479}{979217} \times 1{,}000 \times .81309 = 2.058$$

8th year's insurance to provide for death between 42 and 43

$$\frac{2743}{979217} \times 1{,}000 \times .78941 = 2.211$$

9th year's insurance to provide for death between 43 and 44

$$\frac{3044}{979217} \times 1{,}000 \times .76642 = 2.382$$

10th year's insurance to provide for death between 44 and 45

$$\frac{3370}{979217} \times 1{,}000 \times .74409 = 2.561$$

Total = Rs. 19.036

This is net single premium, that is, total cost of 10 year's Assurance. B. 19.036 is the single premium for 10 years term assurance of Rs.1000.

6.9 Methods of Rating

Insurance rating assesses the cost of the insurance product. Depending upon the type of rating, the price to the buyer may be — *(a)* entirely different from the one paid by another, *(b)* same as that paid by other customers and *(c)* similar to that paid by others, but more or less than the amount for one reason or another. There are basically three recognised rate-making methods:

- Judgement rating
- Class rating
- Merit rating
  - Schedule rating
  - Experience rating
  - Retrospective rating

Judgement Rating

It is used when the risk proposed to be bought is so unusual that little or no statistical information about similar risk is available. Each exposure is individually evaluated, and the rate is determined largely by the underwriter's judgement. Such cases are not unusual to the insurers when the lass exposures are so diverse that a class rate cannot be calculated, or when credible loss statistics are not available. When the judgement rating is used, each premium is unique and is based an the opinion of the person making it. It is widely used in ocean marine insurance and in some lines of inland marine insurance.

Class Rating

Class rates are the mast common rate in insurance business. Insured risks are classified an the basis of one or several important features and all that belong to the same class are subject to the same rate per unit of exposure. The rate charged reflects the claims experience for the class as a whole. It is based an the assumption that future lasses to insured will be determined largely by the same *set* of factors. This type of rating is also termed as manual rating because the various classifications and the respective rates are in the farm of printing manuals.

Life insurance is one of the line where class rates are used, *viz.,* rates based on age, gender, healthiness, smoking and drinking habits etc. Class rating is also used far home owners insurance, automobile insurance, workers compensation and health insurance. The twin considerations in class rating are.

- How many different classifications and rates should there be?
- How many characteristics of the covered risks should class rating take into account?

These two go together because the number of classifications depend upon the number of rating factors that are Considered; the more the factors, the more the classification.

The class rate may be determined by dividing the amount of incurred lasses and lass adjustment expenses by the number of exposure units. Incurred *losses* include all *losses* paid during the accounting Period. plus amounts held as reserves far the future payment of lasses that have already occurred during the same period. Loss adjustment expenses are the expenses incurred by the company in adjusting losses during the same accounting period.

Another technique could be to compare the actual lass ratio with the expected loss ratio., and the rate is adjusted accordingly. The actual *loss ratio* is the ratio of incurred *losses* and *loss* adjustment expenses 10 earned premiums. The expected loss ratio is the percentage of the premiums that is expected to be used to pay losses.

When rates are based on just a few factors, many other characteristics of each exposure are ignored. Number of rating classes is dilemma for the rate-maker. The greater the number of classes, the more the factors that can be taken into account and therefore the more similar risks in any given class will be. On the other hand, increasing the number of classes reduces the number of insured in each one. Law of large number tell that the greater the number of exposures in each class, the more reliable the prediction of future lasses will be. Hence, there are reasons for having so many classes and also for having a few. Increasing the number of classes causes the risks in each class be more nearly alike, but reducing the number of classes causes the rates to be based on a larger body of data and to be more reliable.

Merit Rating

Merit rating is a modification of the class rating. It modifies the class rate of a particular class insured based an individual loss experience. It is based on the assumption that the loss experience of a particular insured will differ substantially from the loss experience of the other insured. In doing so, it reflects the extent to which a specific risk differs from the others in the same class. The various types of merit-rating plans are:

- **Schedule Rating**

Under this plan, each exposure is individually rated. In calculation of schedule rates the first step is to examine the risk (the person or object insured) in order to identify the features that are likely to cause losses or to prevent them. Then the risk is compared with the average or standard risk of its type. Finally deductions are made from the standard rate, for this risk's desirable features and additions are made for its undesirable features, the resultant rate is rate that is tailored made to reflect the characteristics of risk for which it is used. The scheduled rating system (for a building) takes into account the following major factors:

- Occupancy Construction
- Location
- Protection
- Maintenance

The various additions to and subtractions from the basic rate are based upon the judgement of the person who develop the overall scheduled rating system and important feature of this system is that it identifies the factors entering into an insured's rate.

• Experience Rating

This type of rating modifies the class rate on the basis of claim experience of a particular exposure. The actual losses for a period generally of two or three years is .compared with the average risks in the same class. The rate is reduced if the risk has a better record than the average, it is increased if the record is worst than average. Experience rating is used only for large risks, *viz.,* large enough to have many losses each year reflecting a trend. Hence, this type of rating is generally limited to larger firms that generate a sufficiently high volume of premiums and more credible experience.

• Retrospective Rating

Contrary to experience rating retrospective rating modifies the insurance cost on the basis of current experience. This is generally done by making a provision in the policy contract that final rates will be determined *retrospectively.* Generally a range indication maximum and minimum is specified and the final premium is determined after the policy expires and depends upon the amount of losses incurred during the year. If the losses are very small, the insured will pay the minimum premium otherwise if they are very large the insured will be charged the maximum premium. Usually the premium lies between maximum and minimum premium. Retrospective rating increases the insured's incentive to control losses, because the pay-off in premium savings can be substantial. It is generally applied to large liability and workers compensation policies.

6.10 Classification of Risk

The various life risks can not be treated individually, so they are put under a few broad categories based on the degree of each risk. There are two main classes of risk:

(i) Uninsurable risks

(ii) Insurable risks

(1) **Uninsurable Risks:** If the insurance can be purchased at right premium, there should not be any uninsurable risk. Theoretically, after investigating an the factors affecting a risk the life insurance company should be able give

each due consideration and determining the premium charge for the insurance. Practically, however, there are a number of reasons why some persons are not insurable. The premium would be much higher for these persons which will be against the insurance principle because higher premium will stimulate only to those who are at death bed speculation because after payment on a few premium he will be getting it would be unfair to other healthy policyholders. The second reason is that unknown risk cannot be insured to avoid the existing policyholders. So in order to protect existing policyholders, the insurance company must accept those risks against which it can adequate and fair premiums to provide for claims.

(2) **Insurable Risks:** The insurable risks are those which after the selection process can be carried out by an insurer although there can be different terms and conditions for different policyholders. There is a standard or risk, if the risk is not too great (i.e., uninsurable) it can be insured as sub-standard risks even if he does not meet the requirement of a standard risk. The risk of death among sub-standard and super-standard. Every insurer, however, does not use all these classification. Generally distinction between standard and super-standard is not made.

(a) ***Standard Risk:*** The standard risk is related with the normal life where there is no much or no less risk. There are certain criteria on which the risks are judged as normal life. It does not refer to ideal of first class life but it is rather a mix of good and bad lives. This group does not contain only those persons who are free from all impairments nor those persons who are under serious illness. It is the group where majority of the persons can be included and who may be either more or less than the average.

(b) ***Sub-Standard Risk:*** Sub-standard risks are those risks which are higher though insurable than the standard risk. Thus, the sub-standard risks are above the standard risk and below the uninsurable risk, if the life proposed crosses the maximum limit of sub-standard risk, that will be treated as uninsurable. The sub- standard risk is insured after payment of additional premium. This has been discussed in detail in chapter on Treatment of sub-standard risk.

(c) **Super-Standard Risk:** The super-standard risk is present where there is lesser risk than the standard risk. This is also called a preferred risk. An insurer does not prefer to issue preferred risk policies because it increases the premium on other standard risk which may cause reduction in loss of business.

6.11 Method of Risk Classification in Life Insurance

The two methods commonly employed in the classification of risks are:

(a) **Judgement Method:** The underwriters studies all the features of the life to be insured and on the basis of analysis of various factors takes a decision.

Under this method the company depend upon the combined judgement of those in the medical, actuarial, and other areas who are qualified for this work to make underwriting decisions. The judgement method of rating functions effectively when there is only one unfavorable factor to consider whether the decisions to be made is simply whether to accept the proposed insured at standard rates or to reject him or her entirely. However, situations where multiple factors are involved or a proper substandard classification in needed, then this method can not be efficiently applied.

(b) **Numerical Rating:** In this method, a large number of factors, which influence mortality, are taken in account. For various factors, debits (additions) or credits (subtractions) are made to the scores. The numerical ratings vary from company to company 75 to 500. Illustratively, as ratings increases, the quality of risk diminishes. A rating in the range of 75-125 is generally considered as standard and over and above 125 as sub standard. An underwriter has to take into account the nature and combined effects if extra risks e.g. impairments jointly causing additional extra risks. In these cases some additions are made to the arrived rates calculated independently.

In pricing of life insurance products, the main factors used in rating are (a) mortality, (b) expenses, and (c) interest. The first step to rate is to identify the risk class.

6.12 Treatment of Sub-standard Life Insurance Risks

The three broad classifications of sub standard risks are:

(a) **Increasing Extra Risk:** This category reflects the extra mortality risks caused due to impairments with the increase in age. Persons with extra weight are likely to have blood pressure or heart problems, as they grow older.

(b) **Constant Extra Risk:** This group reflects the lives with hazard that remain constant through life. These hazards do not create variations in mortality as such e.g., permanent total disablement-lost of limbs.

(c) **Decreasing Extra Risk:** These lives represent cases where the extra risk decreases with passage of risk since the consideration of proposal. A person who has just been operated for a problem becomes normal over a time period. At the time of proposal the risk was substandard, but with passage of time, it has become a simple risk.

The popular methods of treating sub standard risk are:

(a) **Increase in Premium:** Increase in normal premium (multiple table extra) is the most common method adopted by the insurance companies for treatment of sub-standard risks. Under its method premiums can be treated as follows:

(i) the proposer's age is increased by a few years (e.g. 3-5 years) which results in increase in premium or

(ii) a special mortality table is developed for each sub-standard classification that reflects the experience of each and a set of gross premium is computed for the classification.

(b) Flat Extra Premium: In situation where the extra risk is expected be constant, a flat extra premium may be changed. The policy remains a standard one for all purposes including dividends and non-forfeiture values.

(c) Other Methods: The other methods of refunds are:

(i) Limited death benefit equal to refund of premium if death occurs in the earlier years.

(ii) A lien (contingent debt) may be created an the policy such that upon the assured dies in the lien period, the lien amount shall be deducted from sum payable under the policy.

(iii) A proposal may be declined by the insurer if there is increasing extra risk.

(iv) Restrictive clauses may be imposed as exclusions under the policy.

(v) The insurance cover may be reduced by amount and/or time or the plan may be changed.

(vi) Another option from insurance company is to defer the cover till the extra risk is over.

6.13 Methods of Calculating Economic Risk

Purpose of life insurance as a risk cover, as a savings medium and as an investment tool is easily understood. But the economic purpose of life insurance is often overlooked. Human life as an income-generating asset for his family members is not presented in proper focus. For understanding the security aspect of life insurance, one has to visualize a human life, as one capable of providing a continuous income to his dependents.

It is true no value can be put on human life. In fact, every person has an unlimited insurable interest in his own life. If does not mean that one can take out life insurance for any amount. So this, principle of insurable interest is tempered by two parameters, *viz.,* capacity to pay and need for insurance. Yet these three principles do not give any idea as to how much life insurance one needs.

It was Prof. Hubner who related life insurance to the economic activity of man, through his famous Human Life Value concept. For this purpose, human life as an the economic asset is likened to physical asset. The HLV concept is developed as the economic basis of life insurance. It is to be given the same economic treatment for preservation and capitalization of physical asset. It provides full indemnity if adequate insurance is taken and through savings builds up capital or asset, so that economic value of the human asset which reduces to zero at old age is replaced by life insurance.

Measurement of human life value is possible with the help of compound interest functions. There are five steps in this procedures.

(1) Estimate the individual's average annual earnings from personal efforts over the remaining years of productive life. (E).

(2) Deduct income tax, life insurance premiums and cost of self maintenance (M).

(3) Fix number of years between the individual's present age and expected age of retirement (N).

(4) Select a reasonable rate of interest at which future earnings are to be discounted.

(5) Deduct (20 from (1). Multiply by the present value of Re. 1/- per annum for the period determined as in (3), discount at a given rate in (4)

$$HLV = (E\text{-}M) \times a_N$$

It should be appreciated that economic value of a producer diminishes with passage of time, because the remaining period of productivity becomes shorter. The unrealised earnings go down, as his potential income is converted into actual income, his economic value diminishes.

Let us take an individual aged 30 years with yearly income of Rs. 1,00,000/- with future expected working life span of 30 years. His expenses are as follows:

LI premium	Rs. 10,000
Income Tax	Rs. 7,000
Personal Expenditure	Rs. 18,000
Income devoted to self	Rs. 25,000
Total	Rs. 60,000

Hence expected income for the family for the remaining 30 years = Rs. 40,000 x 30

= Rs. 12,00,000

But the present value of these 30 payments of Rs. 40,000 discounted today at a reasonable rate of interest, say 9%, can be worked out. Present value interest factor for an annuity of Re.1/- for a period of 30 years @ 9% is given by the formula

$$\frac{1-\dfrac{1}{(1+i)^n}}{i}$$

where i = 9 & n = 30. The ready reckoner gives this as 10.274.

Therefore, 40,000 x 10.274 = 4,10,960. So this should be the ideal amount for which he should be insured. Since he is paying LIP of Rs. 10,000, he should already be having life insurance of about Rs. 2,00,000. Hence, he has to take additional insurance of Rs. 2,00,000/-.

One has also to take into account his present assets, their nature and his future plans for acquiring these assets. Thus, Human Life Value approach should be accompanied by a detailed Capital Needs Analysis. Thus the HLV approach provides a scientific basis for selling/marketing life insurance. The present trend in Western countries is to combine this with traditional needs analysis. The needs of the person. Hence, his full purchasing potential may not be exploited. However, 'needs approach' is considered as more practical. These needs are classified as:

(1) Clean up fund (last sickness, burial/funeral expenses, outstanding loans, inheritance costs etc.

(2) Readjustment income — in standard of living etc.

(3) Life income for the spouse.

(4) Special needs of the family.

(5) Retirement needs.

These needs would differ according to the individual status of the person and the stage of the life cycle in which he is at present, i.e., single with dependent parents, recently married and dependent parents, married with children, family member with physical/mental disability, person with heavy mortgage loan etc.

6.14 Summary

Risk is used to describe any situation where there is uncertainty about what outcome will occur. Life of every human being is under risk. Death, disability, sickness are some examples. So there is a need for protection to reduce the sufferings of an individual. That is where life insurance comes. Hazard is the cause of risk. The three types of hazards are physical, occupational and moral. Personal risks are the risks that directly affect an individual. Premature death, insufficient income during retirement, poor health and unemployment are the major personal risks. Personal risk management refers to the identification of pure risk faced by an individual or family and to the selection of the most appropriate technique for treating such risks. Major techniques for handling the potential losses are avoidance, risk control, risk retention, non-insurance transfers and insurance. The factors, which affect personal risk, are age, build, physical condition, personal and family history, occupation, residence, sex and etc.

Measurement of risk is based on the law of probability. The science of probability furnishes three principles: the law of certainty, the law of simple probability and the law of compound probability. Probability is the chance of occurrence of an event. The three laws of probability are used to forecast future events. This concept is used in calculating mortality rate. Mortality or death rate is the ratio of the number of persons died during a particular year to the number of people lived at the beginning of the year.

The evaluation of risk premium is based on the law of probability. Premium when adjusted for interest is called net premium. After loading it with expenses, it becomes office premium. Insurance rating assesses the cost of the insurance product. There are basically three recognized rate making methods: judgement rating, class rating and merit rating. Various life risks are classified as uninsurable and insurable risks. Insurable risks are further classified as standard, sub-standard and super-standard risks.

6.15 Test Yourself

1. Define risk? How does it differ from uncertainty?
2. "Every human being is in need of security. Life insurance is an alternative arrangement for security against any eventuality". Comment.
3. Define Hazard. What are the different types of hazards?
4. Explain the various steps of personal risk management process?
5. What are the major factors affecting personal risk?
6. Explain the theory of probability with suitable examples. How does it play a major role in life insurance?
7. What do you mean by mortality rate? Explain the process of constructing a mortality table.
8. Differentiate net premium and gross premium.
9. What are the major factors to be considered in fixing premium of a life insurance policy?
10. From the following data, find the number of livings at the age 44.

Age x	No. of Livings (l_x)	No. of Dying (d_x)	Mortality Rate (q_x)
40	....	400	0.006
41	....	....	0.007
42	....	....	0.008
43	....	....	0.009

11. What is rate making in life insurance? What are the different methods of rate making?
12. How can a sub-standard risk be treated while rate making?

State whether the following statements are 'True' or 'False'.

1. People express risk in different ways.
2. The indeterminateness of outcome is one of the basic criteria to define a health situation.

3. According to the Dictionary, risk refers to the possibility that something pleasant or dangerous might happen.
4. Uncertainty is often confused with the risk.
5. Uncertainty being a perceptual phenomenon implies different degrees to different person.
6. An individual with training or experience in insurance.
7. Insurance is the single effort to reduce the sufferings of an individual as a result of some inevitable calamities.
8. Loss of property due to external forces also worried the individual human being.
9. Man needs food, shelter and clothing for his life.
10. The greatest risk to which human life is exposed is that of life.
11. Double Accident benefit consists of payment of double the sum assured in the event of a person's death due to accident.
12. Hazard is any factor that subtract to the risk.
13. Sex is occupational hazard.
14. Risk is defined as uncertainty concerning the occurrence of profits.
15. Personal risks are risks that directly affect a people.
16. Premature death is defined as the defined of the household head with unfulfilled financial obligations.
17. Identifying potential losses is a personal risk.
18. Avoidance is a technique to reduce risk.
19. Risk retention is not a technique to reduce risk.
20. Age is the factor affecting risk.
21. Mortality or death rate is the ratio of the number of persons died during a particular to the number of people lived at the beginning of that year.
22. The evaluation of the risk premium is based on the mathematical probability of the event happening.
23. The system of charging increasing premium every month is called assessmentism.
24. Insurance rating assesses the cost of the insurance product.
25. Class rates are the most common rate in insurance business.
26. Merit rating is not a modification of the class rating.
27. Uninsurable risks is a type of classification of risk.
28. Insurable risks is not a type of classification of risk.

29. Purpose of life insurance as a risk cover, as a savings medium and as an investment tool is easily understood.

30. It is true no value can be put on human life.

31. Measurement of human life value is possible with the help of compound interest functions.

32. Human Life Value approach should be accompanied by a detailed Capital Needs Analysis.

Choose the Correct answer from the choice given:

1. Personal risks are risks that directly affect
   (a) Individual (b) Group
   (c) Both are correct (d) Both are wrong

2. Major risk are of
   (a) 3 type (b) 4 type
   (c) 5 type (d) 6 type

3. Personal risk management refers to the identification of
   (a) Pure risk (b) Impure risk
   (c) Both are correct (d) Both are wrong

4. These are the steps of personal risk management
   (a) Identifying Potential Losses
   (b) Evaluating Potential Losses
   (c) Selecting the appropriate technique for handling losses
   (e) All are correct
   (f) All are wrong

5. This/ these Selecting the Appropriate Technique
   (a) Avoidance (b) Risk control
   (c) Risk retention (d) Non-insurance transfers
   (e) All are correct (f) All are wrong

6. In life insurance, the factors which may affect the risk is/ are
   (a) Age (b) Build
   (c) Physical condition (d) All are correct
   (e) All are wrong

7. The science of probabilities furnishes principal
   (a) Three (b) Four
   (c) Five (d) Six

8. The law of certainty is the principal of
   (a) Law of risk (b) Law of uncertainty
   (c) Law of probability
9. Source of mortality are of type
   (a) Two (b) Three
   (c) Four (d) Six
10. The evaluation of the risk premium is based on the
    (a) Mathematical probability
    (b) Scientific probability
    (c) Economic probability
    (e) Financial probability
11. Method of rating is are
    (a) Judgement rating (b) Class rating
    (c) Merit rating (e) All are correct
    (f) All are wrong
12. Location is the part of
    (a) Judement rating (b) Class rating
    (c) Scheduled rating (d) Both are correct
    (e) Both are wrong
13. There is are main classes of
    (a) One (b) Two
    (c) Three (d) Four
14. These are the type of risk
    (a) Uninsurable risks (b) Insurable risks
    (c) Both are correct (d) Both are wrong

Fill in the blanks:

1. Different authors on the subject have defined .... risk.
2. The indeterminateness of outcome is one of the basic criteria to define a risk ....
3. According to the Dictionary, risk refers to the possibility that something unpleasant or dangerous might ....
4. "Risk is a condition in which there is a possibility of an adverse deviation form a desired outcome that is .... or hopped for".

5. The .... of outcome is one of the basic criteria to define a risk situation.
6. According to the Dictionary, risk refers to the possibility that something unpleasant or dangerous might ....
7. The degree of risk refers to the likelihood of occurrence of an ....
8. Uncertainty is often confused with the ....
9. Uncertainty refers to a situation where the outcome is not certain or ....
10. Uncertainty can be perceived as opposite of certainty where you are assure of outcome or what will ....
11. Uncertainty being a perceptual phenomenon implies different degrees to different ....
12. Human beings have been in search of security right from .... days.
13. As human society developed, commerce and business started flourishing and idea of .... was promoted in due course.
14. Kautilya, in his Arthashastra, lays down that the people agree to pay taxes so that they are maintained by those ....
15. Man needs food, shelter and clothing for his ....
16. The greatest risk to which human life is exposed is that of ....
17. Insurance cannot postpone the ....
18. Hazard is any factor that adds to the ....
19. Risk is defined as uncertainty concerning the occurrence of a ....
20. Personal risks are risks that directly affect an ....
21. Age of a life to be insured is the most important factor to affect ....
22. The physical condition of the age life proposed has a direct bearing on the mortality of the ....
23. The personal history of the life propose would reveal the possibility of ....
24. The previous amount of insurance may disclose the degree of risk of the ....
25. Occupation is an important factor to affect the ....
26. The residence also affects the ....
27. The general mode of living of the proposer effect the ....
28. Insurance has been defined as the institution which eliminates risk or which substitutes certainty for ....
29. The science of probabilities furnishes three principles of which practical use is made in ....
30. Three principal of LIC are................, ... , and ....
31. The value of these three laws of probability lies in the fact that they can be used to forecast ....

32. Future events can be foretold in one of ....
33. The evaluation of the risk premium is based on the .... of the event happening.
34. As in general insurance, life insurance contracts can be arranged on a year to ....
35. A person who is in excellent health may not renew the ....
36. The system of charging increasing premium every year is called ....
37. The premium that is charged should be adequate to meet the mortality for that ....
38. The level premium tends to be higher than risk premium in the early years of..............
39. .... is the price paid for the use of money.
40. Insurance rating assesses the cost of the insurance ....
41. There are basically three recognised rate-making methods as ...., ..., and ....
42. Class rates are the mast common rate in...................
43. Merit rating is a modification of the ....
44. Experience rating is used only for..............
45. Contrary to experience rating retrospective rating modifies the insurance cost on the basis of ....
46. The various life risks cannot be treated ....
47. The standard risk is related with the normal life where there is no much or no............
48. There are certain criteria on which the risks are judged as ....
49. Sub-standard risks are those risks which are higher though insurable than the ....
50. The super-standard risk is present where there is lesser risk than the...............
51. Super standard risk is also called as ....
52. In pricing of life insurance products, the main factors used in rating are ...., ... and ....
53. Purpose of life insurance as a ...., as a savings medium and as an..............tool is easily understood.
54. It is true no value can be put on ....
55. Measurement of human life value is possible with the help of .... functions.

CHAPTER 7

ASSIGNMENT OF LIFE POLICIES

Learning Objectives

After studying this chapter, one can understand:

- Meaning and definition of assignment
- Procedure for assignment
- Nomination and procedure for nomination
- Nomination Vs. Assignment
- Surrender and Paid up assurance
- Alteration and Policy related services

7.1 Meaning & Definition

A life insurance policy is freely assignable to another party. Assignment is a means where by the beneficial interest and right, under a policy, gets transferred from 'Assigner' to 'assigneer'. Assigner is the policy holders who transfer the policy and Assigneer is the person who derives the policy from the assigner. Assignment can be made only after acquiring the policy. There are two types of assignments:

7.1.1 Absolute Assignment

Under an absolute assignment all the ownership rights in the policy are transferred to a new owner. For example, a policy owner may wish to donate a life insurance policy to a charity or education institution. The new owner then can exercise the ownership rights of the policy.

7.1.2 Collateral Assignment

Under a collateral assignment, the policy owner assign a life insurance policy as collateral for loan. Here only certain rights are transferred to the creditors to protect its interest, and the policy holder retains the remaining rights. The party to whom the policy is assigned (creditor) can receive the policy amount only to the extent of the loan. The balance amount is paid to the beneficiary of the policy.

7.2 Procedure for Assignment

According to the Insurance Act 1938 under Section (38) provides the following procedures as laid down:

(1) A transfer or assignment of life insurance can be made either by an endorsement on the policy itself or by executing a separate instrument. It must be signed by the assignor or by his duly authorized agent and attested by at least one witness. The endorsement or transfer must specify the facts of assignment.

(2) On valid assignment, a written notice must be given to the insure together with a certified copy of the endorsement of instrument. Only then the assignment or transfer becomes complete and effective on the insure.

(3) The date on which the notice of assignment or transfer is delivered to the insure regulations the priority of all claims between an assignee and a third person. If the policy has been assigned to more than one assignees the priority of the claims of the assignee shall be governed by the order in which the notice to the insure is delivered.

(4) On the receipt of the notice referred to above, the insure shall record the fact of such transfer or assignment together with date thereof, and the name of the person who gave the notice, grant a written acknowledgment of the receipt of such notice on payment of a fee not exceeding one rupee.

(5) From the date of the receipt of the notice the insure shall recognize the transferee or the assignee named in the notice as the only person entitled to the benefits named under the policy and such a person shall be subject to the liabilities and equities to which the transfer or assignor was subject at the time of the transfer or assignment.

(6) Conditional assignment has been held to be valid. Thus, an assignment in favor of a person made with the condition that it shall be operative or that the interest shall pass, to some other person on the happening of specified event during the life time of the person whose life is insured is valid.

7.3 Nomination

Nomination is the process of identifying a persona to receive the policy money in the every of the death of the policy holder. Nomination can be done at the inception of the policy by providing details of the nominee in the proposal form. However, if the nomination is not given at the beginning, the policy holder can give it at a later date by getting it endorsed on the policy bond. Change of nomination can be done by the policy holder any time during this, the policy holder has to give a notice in a prescribed form to the insure and get it endorsed at the back of the policy. Also the nomination can be removed any time by the policy holder with / without giving prior notice to the nominee.

Under nomination, the nominee gets only the right to receive the policy money in the event of the death of the policy holder. If the nominee dies when the policy holder is still surviving, then the nomination would be ineffective. Nomination has no effect, if the policy holder surviving. If nominee dies after the death of the policy holder but before receiving the policy money, then also nomination becomes ineffective and only the legal heirs of the policy holder can claim the policy money. The principle types of nominee (beneficiary designation) are as follows.

7.3.1 Primary and Contingent Beneficiary

A primary beneficiary who is first enticed is receive the policy proceeds on the insured's death. A contingent beneficiary is a nominee who is enticed to receive the claim, if the primary beneficiary dies before the death of the insured. In many families, the husband will name his wife as primary nominee and the children will be named as contingent nominee.

7.3.2 Revocable and Irrevocable Beneficiary

A revocable beneficiary means that the policy holder reserves the right to change the beneficiary without the consent of the beneficiary. Most designation are revocable. In contrast, as irrevocable beneficiary is one that can not be changed without the beneficiary's consent. If the policy holder wishes to change the beneficiary designation, in the former type, the can change when ever designed whereas in the later one the consent of the nominee is must.

7.3.3 Specific and Class Beneficiary

A specific beneficiary means the beneficiary is specifically named and identified. Under a class beneficiary, a specific person

Is not named but is a class beneficiary, a specific person is not named but is a member of a grow designated as beneficiary such as children of the insured. In class beneficiary designation, the insured wishes to divide the policy proceeds equally among members of a particular group.

7.4 Provision for Nomination

According to Sec. 39 of the Insurance Act, the following provisions are made regarding nomination by a policy holder.

(1) The nomination in order to be effectual, by incorporating in the text of the policy or by an endorsement on the policy itself and communicated to the insure who shall register it.

(2) The policy holder is entitled to receive from the insure an acknowledgement of having registered a nomination or a cancellation or change thereof.

(3) When a policy is transferred or assigned, any nomination made in that policy automatically stands cancelled.

(4) Where the policy matures for payment during the life time of the person whose life is insured, or where the nominee dies before the policy matures for payment, the amount is payable to the policy holder or his heirs or legal representatives.

(5) Where the nominee survives the person whose life is insured, the amount shall be payable to the nominee.

7.5 Nomination Vs. Assignment

The distinction between nomination and assignment; will be clear from the comparison below.

NOMINATION	ASSIGNMENT
1. Can be done (a) before issue of the policy by mentioning the nominee's name, age, relationship and address in the proposal from or by a letter giving details or (b) after issue of the policy by an endorsement.	1. Can be done only after issue of the policy by endoresement on policy.
2. Cannot be done by a separate deed.	2. Can be done also by separate deed on stamped paper.
3. The holder of a policy on his own life, i.e. the life assured, alone can make nomination.	3. The absolute owner of the policy may be either proposer or the life assured or the absolute assignee or conditional assignee to the extent of his interest, or the person having requisite authority from such owners, can make assignment.
4. It is effected where Insurance Act 1938 applies, or where similar enactments apply, *viz.*, in Pakistan & Sri Lanka.	4. It can be executed anywhere in the world according to the law of that country, relating on transfer of property.
5. Assured retains full control and can deal with the policy without the consent of the nominee.	5. Assured loses control over the policy. Absolute assignee is the owner of the policy and can deal with it.
6. Need not supported by a consideration.	6. Need out be, but generally is, supported by a consideration.
7. May be witnessed.	7. Must be witnessed, otherwise it will invalidated.

8. Notice is required to safeguard the nominee's interest.	8. Notice is required to enable the assignee to acquire priority over other assignees.
9. Nominee has no right to sue under the policy.	9. Assignee has right to sue under the policy.
10. It can be altered by the life assured during the currency of the policy by cancellation of nomination or by an assignment.	10. It cannot be cancelled by the assignor. The (absolute) assignee has to reassign the policy.
11. Where nominee is a minor, appointment of an appointee by the life assured is required.	11. When assignee is a minor, guardian to be appointed.
12. Appointee can be appointed in the wording of the nomination	12. Guardian cannot be appointed in the wording of the assignment.
13 No vested interest in favor of nominee is created.	13. Assignee acquires interest.
14. Nominee's right is only to collect policy moneys on the death of the assured and when paid by the insure	14. On receipt of the notice, the insure has to recognize the assignee as the person legally entitled to receive the policy moneys.
15. If nominee dies, rights under the revert to the life assured or his legal representatives.	15. If a conditional assignee dies, the policy right under the policy reverts to the life assured, depending upon the terms of assignment. If an absolute assignee dies, the right devolves upon his/her heirs.
16. If the nominee dies after the life assured and before settlement of the claim, the policy moneys would be payable to the heirs of the life assured.	16. If the assignee(absolute or condition) dies after the life assured and before settlement, the policy moneys would be payable to the heirs of the assignee
17. Creditors of the life assured can attach the policy moneys.	17. Creditors cannot attach the policy, unless the assignment is shown to have been made to defraud the creditors

7.6 Surrender of a Policy

Under the section 113 of insurance at 1938, its at least 3 year's premium have been paid, the policy holder can surrender the contract for guaranteed surrender value (GSV) which shall be equal is 30% of the premiums paid excusing first years' premium and all extra premium paid under the policy

However, insurance allow more liberal surrender value, which is a predetermined percentage of paid-up value. For this purpose, surrender value factor (SVF) depends upon number of premium paid and outstanding term of the policy. As premium paid term increase SVF increases.

In case of surrender policy has to be cancelled surrender goes against the interests of the policy holder, since he loses valuable risk cover.

Some type of policies cannot be surrendered:

(1) If the assignee is mirror
(2) If the policy holder or conditional assignee is insane or insolvent, of which notice is received.
(3) If policy holder or assignee is IT defaulter
(4) If court's prohibitory order is received
(5) Annuities
(6) Certain Term assurances.

A policy which has been surrendered can be reinstated within 6 months of surrender, subject to good health and other requirements.

Surrender Value

The term surrender value refers is the amount of money which the insurer agrees to pay in case the life assured decides to surrender his policy before its maturity. It is said that the policy holder wishes to surrender his policy to the insurer and give up his claim in it. Surrender of policy indicates terminals on of the contract of insurance.

The amount of surrender value is determined on the basis of actual premium paid and the number of years the policy has been in force. Surrender value increase with earn payment of premium. Payment is to be made against the full and final discharge of insurer's liability under the contract.

According is life Insurance Corporation of India a policy acquires surrender value only after payment of two or three years premium. Thus, the policy is required to have run for three years before it acquires surrender value. In this regard some Insurance compares guarantee a minimum surrender value of 40 per cent of the total premium paid.

7.7 Paid-up Assurance

Another service is providing the chance to malterens policy paid-up. Under section 113 of Insurance Act 1938, if after at least 3 year's premium and paid, subsequent premium are not paid, the policy will not lapse but concerned in is a paid up assurance. The amount of claim will be available is the life on maturing or on death of earner. Thus the insurer's liability stand reduced.

Once the policy is paid-up, it losses all additional benefits attaching is the policy such as.

(1) double accident and disability benefits
(2) survival benefits under money back plans

(3) Guaranteed and loyalty addition
(4) Term Riders
(5) Critical illness riders.

A paid-up policy is free from further payment of premium but in subject is loan interest and charges of any, already raised on the policy. Since the premium payments have stopped, surrender value will stop growing. Therefore if the insurer finds that the outstanding loan with outstanding interest exceeds the surrender value available under the policy, after adjusting the loan balance, the reaming of the surrender value, if any will be refunded is the policy holder. This is called foreclosure which is a right available is a creditor for foreclosing the loan.

Paid-up Value

If a policy holder discontinues the payment premium after at least two years premiums have been paid and subsequent premium is not paid, the policy does not become void but continues as a paid-up policy. According to Insurance Act, it is defined as the policy paid up for an amount bearing the same proportion is the amount of original sum assured which the number of premiums paid bears is the total number of premiums payable under the policy as a whole,

$$\text{i.e. Paid-up value} = \frac{\text{No. of premium paid}}{\text{No. of premium payable}} \times \text{Sum assured}$$

The elapsed duration is calculated by deduction date of commencement of policy (DOC) from the date of first unpaid premium (FUP)

i.e. Paid-up duration = Date of FUP-DOC

The amount (claim) would be available is the life on maturity or on death whichever is earlier. In case of participating policy, it is assured that bonus or profits will be added to the paid-up value but future gains or profits are not entitled is such policy.

7.8 Difference between Surrender Value and Paid-up Value

(1) Surrender value is the amount which the insurer is prepared is pay before the date of maturity.	(1) Paid-up value in paid tothe policy holder of maturity or on death.
(2) If a policy holder wishes to surrender his policy it means means that the assured does not want to continue the policy.	(2) If a policy holder discontinues the payment of premium, the policy does not become void, but continues as a paid-up policy.
(3) Surrender value represents the present cash value (at the time of surrender) of the policy.	(3) Paid-up value represents the value payable on assureds death or at the maturity of the policy.
(4) Surrender value is calculated on the class of policy and the number of years it has been in force.	(4) Paid-up value is calculated on the basis of number of years premium paid, number of years premium payable andsum assured with accrued profits.

(5) Surrender value increases with each payment of premium.	(5) Paid-up value is always higher than the surrender value since it is not required to be paid immediately after the last premium.

7.9 Alterations

Another service provided by the insurance company is alterations in the terms of the policy. The include very simple alteration little change in mode of payment of premium is more complicated ones like change in plan, change in term of assurance reduction in sum assured, splitting one policy into more policies, concertino the policy from without profit class is with prop class, adding extra benefits like Accident or disability benefits or removal of such benefits, opts in regard is conversion of policies from one class is another class, es. conversion of whole life plan into endowment plan and etc.

Here again each company will have its own procedural rules and regulations as is the permissibility of such alteration and if permitted the pros usually such alterations are not allowed during the first year of the policy and subsequently also if the policy is in a lapsed condition.

Certain atterations are not permissible:

(1) The premium rate gets lower.

(2) In crease in term/premium paying period

(3) Increase in sum assured

(4) With profit is without profit

(5) Reduction in sum assured below the minimum

(6) Paid-up/lapsed policy

(7) Periodical premium is single premium

Alternation can also be classified as:

Compulsory: Such as change of name due to marriage, adoption, correction in policies change in currency.

Automatic: In crease in sum assured, premium if policy condition provide for the same.

Decrease in Premium: Due is automatic removed of extra premium.

Optional: Settlement option.

7.10 Loans in Policies

Some companies may allow policy holder is raise loans against the security of policies. This is not a statutory requirement but may be allowed by the companies in respect of whole life and/ or endowment type of plans. Each company may have its own rules and regulations regarding sanction of policy loan.

Where such loan are sanctioned, the company will have us maintain up to date records of payment, repayments, payment of interest, etc., because policy loans are party of assets of the insurance company and so should be neglected as such in the annual Balance sheet.

Usually such loans are sanctioned on assignment of the policies under section 38 of insurance Act, 1938.

7.11 Duplicate Policy

Yet another service rendered by life insurance companies is issue of duplicate policy bonds" It is not very easy to obtain duplicates of lost policy bonds in the same way duplicate passbook of a savings bank account in a bank is obtained.

7.12 Revival of a Life Policy

When the premium is not paid within the days of grace, the policy lapses, but it may be revived during the lifetime of the assured and when the policy is in force. The grace period is 30 days for all modes of payment, except monthly, for which 15 days of grace period is allowed.

Ordinary Revival Scheme

All the arrears of unpaid premiums with interest along with evidence of good health are required.

Special Revival Scheme

If a policy holder is not in a position to pay all the arrears of premium with interest, this scheme is offered. The date of commencement of policy is shifted to a date prior to the date of revival for which premiums have been received; such period does not go beyond two years prior to original date of commencement. Plan and Term will remain the same, provided new premium ceasing age or new maturity age, does not go beyond the maximum prescribed and/or the plan. Revised premium will be calculated on new age as date of commencement. Under this scheme, arrears of premium become minimal. However, following conditions must be satisfied.

(i) The policy should not have acquired surrender value.

(ii) Application for revival should be made after 6 months but within 3 yrs from the date of lapse. The new date should not go beyond 2 yrs of the date of commencement.

(iii) Such revival should be made only once under the same policy.

Revival by Installment

There are some policy holders who cannot pay the arrears under ordinary revival scheme in one installment and are not entitled to the special revival scheme. The arrears of premium with interest can be paid by installment spread over 2 yrs, to be paid along with normal premium installments. However, arrears of premium should be for more than 1 yrs. Minimum 6 month's premium should be paid at the outset.

Loan-cum Revival Scheme

Under this policy, a loan is granted within the surrender value pressuring that all the premiums have been received. The loan amount is utilized to cover arrears of premiums.

Survival Benefit-cum-Revival Scheme

Revival of Money Back Policies can be done by taking into account of survival benefit the would fall due subject to Revival.

7.13 Change of Address

Change of address of a policy holder assumes great unimportance for the insurance company because any communication is the policy holder will have is be mailed to the correct and latest address many requests are received by the insurance companies from policy holders for noting changes in their addresses and it is the legal and bounden duty of the insurance companies is note the same in their records.

7.14 Transfer of Policy

As a consequence of change of address, sometimes, the policy holder may request transfer of his policy records is another office of the insurance company for further service. This request will have is he attended is by the insurance company. Now a day, since all the branches are inter- connected within networking facilities, requests for transfer are heavily reduced.

7.15 Days of Grace

Insurance company allows certain days after stipulated period of insurance during which the insured can pay the premium to renew or continue the policy. Life Insurance Corporation allows fifteen days of grace from the date to pay monthly premiums and thirty days of grace for the payment of quarterly half yearly and yearly premiums.

A life insurance policy creates a continuing risk and it merely lapses if the premium is not paid. Death of the insured during the days of grace makes the insurance company liable to pay the money due under the policy.

7.16 Summary

Assignment is a means where by the beneficial interest and right, under a policy, gets transferred from one person (Assigner) to another (assignee). There are two types of assignments: absolute assignment and collateral assignment. Nomination is the process of identifying a person to receive the policy money in the event of the death of the policyholder. The nomination can be removed any time by the policyholder with/without giving prior notice to the nominee. Policyholder is the owner of the policy. On the other hand, assignee (Absolute) is the owner of the policy and can deal with it. The policyholder can surrender the contract for guaranteed surrender value. The term surrender value refers is the amount of money which the insurer agrees to pay in case the life assured decides to surrender his policy before its maturity. If a policyholder discontinues the payment of premium, the policy does not become void, but becomes as a paid-up policy. Paid up value is paid to the policyholder/beneficiary on maturity of the policy or on the death of the assured. Other policy related services are alterations, loans, issue of duplicate policy, revival of elapsed policy, change in address and etc.

7.17 Test Yourself

1. Define assignment. What are the different types of assignments?
2. What are the different types of beneficiaries?
3. What are the major provisions for nomination?
4. How does nomination differ from assignment?
5. What do you mean by paid-up value? Explain the method of calculating paid-up value with suitable illustration?
6. Differentiate surrender value and paid-up value.
7. What are different alterations, which are generally allowed in a life insurance policy?
8. Under which conditions, a life insurance policy can be used as a collateral security for obtaining loan?
9. When does a policy become lapsed? What are the different methods of reviving a lapsed policy?
10. Write a short note on the provision of grace period.

State whether the following statements are 'True' or 'False'.

1. A life insurance policy is freely assignable to another person.
2. There is a types of assignments.
3. Under an absolute assignment, all the ownership rights in the policy are transferred to a same owner.

4. The new owner then can exercise the ownership rights of the man.
5. Nomination is the process of identifying a persona to receive the policy money in the every of the death of the women
6. Nomination can be done at the inception of the policy by providing details of the nominee in the proposal examination.
7. A primary beneficiary who is first enticed is receive the policy proceeds on the insured's life.
8. A revocable beneficiary means that the policy holder reserves the right to change the beneficiary without the consent of the beneficiary.
9. Most designation are revocable.
10. A specific beneficiary means the beneficiary is specifically named and undentified.
11. When a policy is transferred or assigned any nomination made in that policy automatically stands cancelled.
12. Where the nominee survives the person whose life is insured, the amount shall be payable to the policyholder.
13. Assignee acquires interest
14. Assignee has right to sue under the policy.
15. The term surrender value refers to the amount of money which the insurer agrees to pay in case the life assured decides to surrender his policy before its maturity.
16. According is Life Insurance Corporation of India a policy acquires surrender value only after payment of two or three years premium.
17. A paid up policy is free from further payment of premium but in subject is loan interest and charges of any, already raised on the life.
18. Another service provided by the insurance company is alterations in the terms of the policy
19. All the arrears of unpaid premiums with interest along with evidence of good health are required.
20. Revised premium will be calculated on new age as date of commencement
21. Under this policy, a loan is granted within the surrender value pressuring that all the premiums have been received.
22. The loan amount is utilized to cover arrears of policy.
23. Insurance company allows certain days after stipulated period of insurance during which the insured can pay the premium to renew or continue the policy.
24. A life insurance policy creates a continuing risk and it merely lapses if the premium is not paid.

Choose the Correct answer from the choice given:

1. A life insurance policy is freely assignable to

   (a) Same party (b) Another party

   (c) Both are correct (d) Both are wrong

2. Assigner is the policy-holders who transfer the policy and Assigneer is the

   (a) Husband (b) Wife

   (c) Child (d) Person

3. Under an absolute assignment all the ownership rights in the policy are transferred to a

   (a) Same owner (b) New owner

   (c) Another person (d) No body

4. Under a collateral assignment, the policy owner assign a life insurance policy as collateral for

   (a) Loan (b) Agreement

   (c) For both (d) None of the above

5. Nomination is the process of identifying a persona to receive the policy money in the every of the death of the

   (a) Policy-holder (b) Policy owner

   (c) Underwriter (d) None of these

6. A primary beneficiary who is first enticed is receive the policy proceeds on the

   (a) Insured's death (b) Insured life

   (c) Insured person (d) Policyholder

7. A revocable beneficiary means that the policy-holder reserves the right to change the beneficiary without the consent of the

   (a) Beneficiary (b) Loss

   (c) Profit (d) Gain

8. A specific beneficiary means the beneficiary is specifically named and

   (a) Identified (b) Unidentified

   (c) Both are correct (d) Both are wrong

9. Another service provided by the insurance company is alterations in the terms of the

   (a) Policy (b) Policy owner

   (c) Policy-holder (d) None of the above

Fill in the blanks.

1. There are .... types of assignments.
2. A life insurance policy is freely assignable to another ....
3. Under an absolute assignment, all the ownership rights in the policy are transferred to a ....
4. The new owner then can exercise the ownership rights of the ....
5. Under a collateral assignment, the policy owner assign a life insurance policy as collateral for ....
6. Conditional assignment has been held to be ....
7. Nomination is the process of identifying a person to receive the policy money in the every of the death of the policy.................
8. Under nomination, the nominee gets only the right to receive the policy money in the event of the death of the ....
9. A primary beneficiary who is first enticed is receive the policy proceeds on the ....
10. A revocable beneficiary means that the policy holder reserves the right to change the beneficiary without the consent of the ....
11. Most designation are ....
12. A specific beneficiary means the beneficiary is specifically named and ....
13. Assignment can be done only after issue of the policy by endorsement on ....
14. Assignee has right to sue under the ....
15. Guardian cannot be appointed in the wording of the ....
16. Assignee acquires ....
17. Nominee has no right to sue under ....
18. Notice is required to safeguard the nominee's ....
19. Creditors of the life assured can attach the policy ....
20. Under the section 113 of insurance at 1938, its at least .... have been paid.
21. As premium paid term increase SVF.......................
22. The amount of surrender value is determined on the basis of ....paid and the number of years the.................. has been in force.
23. Payment is to be made against the full and final discharge of insurer's liability under the ....

24. A policy acquires surrender value only after payment of two or three years ....

25. The amount (claim) would be available is the life on maturity or on death whichever is ....

26. Paid up value in paid to the policy holder of maturity or on.......................

27. If a policy holder is not in a position to pay all the arrears of premium with interest, this scheme is ....

28. Revised premium will be calculated on new age as date of ....

29. The policy should not have acquired surrender ....

30. Insurance company allows certain days after stipulated period of ....during which the insured can pay the premium to renew or continue the ....

31. A life insurance policy creates a continuing risk and it merely lapses if the premium is not ....

Module III

CHAPTER 8

LIFE INSURANCE CLAIMS

8.1 Types of Claims

Settlement of Claims

The life insurance claims can be classified in two categories (*a*) Death claims (*b*) Maturity claims. Settlement procedure of each of these is discussed below:

8.1.1 Death Claims

If the insured dies before the expiry of the term of the policy, it is called as death claim. The death of the life assured has to be intimated in writing to the insurer. It may be done by the nominee, assignee, a relative of the life assured, the employer, agent or development officer. Particulars like policy number, name of the life assured, the date of death, the cause of death and the relationship of the informant to the decreased are to be mentioned. The intimation must satisfy two conditions: (*a*) It must be from a concerned person and (*b*) must establish beyond doubt, the identity of the deceased person as the life assured under the policy.

Sometimes, the office need not wait till the intimation of the claim is received. Obituary columns, the concerned agent or newspaper reports in case of accidents or air crashes may give information and the claim action can be initiated. However, care has to be taken to ensure that identity of the deceased is established.

The facts required to the submitted by the claimant are: (*a*) Date of death (*b*) Reason and Place of Death and (*c*) Full details of policies held by the Life assured should also be submitted. Death claims are categorised as Non-Early Death claims and Early Claims. The procedure for processing these claims is different:

Non-early Death Claims refer to death of the Life assured occurring after 3 years from the date of commencement of policy or Date of last revival/reinstatement. If the policy is in force till death by regular payment of premiums, full sum assured is payable along with bonus (if it is with a profit policy). The requirements for the settlement of the death claim are:

- Policy Document
- Death Certificate from the appropriate authority
- Legal evidence of Title, if the claimant is not an assignee/nominee
- Abridged Claim Form
- Discharge Form duly signed
- Assignment/Reassignment deed, if any
- Age proof, if age is not already admitted

Once these documents are received and if they are found in order, claim is settled and payment is made to the person entitled to.

Early claims refer to the death of life assured occurring within 3 years from commencement of policy. The following forms are to be submitted duly completed:

- Statement from the medical attendants who last treated the deceased Life assured.
- Certificate of treatment issued by the hospital authorities where the deceased was treated last.
- Certificate by the employer if the deceased was an employee.
- Certificate of burial/cremation signed by a person who attended the funeral of the deceased.

Where death takes place due to accident, the death has to be reported to the police and a FIR (First Information Report), police inquest report, and post-mortem report (if conducted only) are to be submitted. Wherever death takes place within 2 years from Date of commencement an enquiry is conducted to determine the genuineness of claim. On the basis of these, the decisions to settle accidental benefits are taken. Under MWPA policy the proceeds of the policy will be paid to the trustees. If there is no trustee, the official trustee will step in. But if the beneficiaries are major and competent to contract, payment can be made directly to them without the intervention of trustees. The assured need not sign the discharge voucher.

- In case of absolute assignment, the payment will be made to the assignee. If the assignment is conditional, payment can be made to the assured himself, after satisfying repayment of loan that may be the reason for assignments.
- If the policy is irretrievable lost, advertisement of the loss of the policy is a necessary precaution. Payment can be made on the basis of an indemnity executed by the policyholder together with a surety of means. It is not necessary to issue a duplicate policy.
- The death claim amount is payable to the nominee or the assignee as the case may be. If the life assured has died without making an assignment or nomination, legal evidence of title (proof of ownership) such as succession certificate or letters of administration or probate of a will where a will exists, would be required.

- The insurer may waive strict evidence of title, if the amount involved is small, there is no other estate left by the deceased and there is no dispute among he survivors about the policy moneys.
- If the intimation claim is received after 3 years from the death, the same is time barred. The claimant has to be informed accordingly. However, if the death had occurred with 3 years of the policy's commencement of revival, simultaneous investigation should be conducted to find out the bonafides of the claim, without the knowledge of the claimant. However, if more than three years have elapsed, since the date of risk, the claimant has to be informed that the claim is barred by limitation. But simultaneously claim forms can be issued without prejudice to see if any ex-gratia payment can be made.
- If the death has occurred within 2 years of the date of the policy (that is the date of FPR) the possibility of suppression of evidence cannot be ruled out. Hence, it is necessary to investigate such cases. The reasons for intimating a claim late may be deliberate attempt to tamper with evidence.
- Death can take place suddenly *e.g.* due to cardiac arrest, downing, burns, air crash, suicide, and murder or at the hand of justice. In case of an air crash, a certificate from airline authorities would be necessary certifying that the assured was a passenger on the plane. In case of ship-accident, a certified extract from the logbook of the ship would be needed. In case of sudden heart failures, doctor's certificate will not be forthcoming.
- In case of defence personnel, a certificate from the commanding officer of the Unit is to be obtained. If a court of enquiry is ordered its findings should be obtained.

8.1.2 Maturity Claims

Maturity claims are payable as per the terms of the policy. These policies are generally endowment polices including money back policies. The amount payable at the time of maturity includes sum assured and bonuses/incentives. The insurer normally sends advance intimations to the insured. The insurer has to satisfy that:

- The life assured is the holder of the policy and his identity is proved.
- The age stands admitted.
- The premiums are all paid.
- The original policy is handed in together with a completed discharge voucher before making payment.

The insurance company is expected to make payment on the maturity date. Post-dated cheques are normally set in advance.

Documents Required

In the case of maturity claims, the insurer will call for the following documents, well before the date of maturity.

- Policy document, if it is not available, it may have been deposited elsewhere as a security for a loan. If policyholder loses the policy, the claim can be settled on the strength of an indemnity bond from the policyholder and a reliable surety of sound financial means. For small amounts, a letter of indeminity may suffice. In case of very small amounts, say Rs. 1,000/- or less, even this can be dispensed with.
- Age proof, if the age is not already admitted.
- Deed of assignment if any.
- Discharge form issued by the office.

If the claim does not determine the policy finally, as in the case of periodical survival payments, the policy document will be returned to the policy holder after due endorsements.

Settlement

Settlement procedure in a maturity claim is simple. After receipt of the completed and stamped discharge voucher from the person entitled to the policy money, along with the policy documents, claim amount will be paid by account payee or crossed and order cheque. In case of survival benefit claims, that is whose sum assured is retuned by instalments, suitable endorsements will be made on the policy document and in policy records, before returning the policy document to the policy holders. If the discharge from is lost in transit, a duplicate discharge form can be issued.

- Where the assured or the person to sign the discharge is known to be mentally deranged, a certificate from a court of law under the Indian Lunacy Act appointing a persons to act as a guardian to manage the properties of the lunatic should be called. If the person has recovered from the mental disorder, a certificate form the Psychiatic Hospital to that effect would be necessary.
- If the assured has been adjudged insolvent by court of law before the policy has matured for payment and if a notice is received from the official assignee of the court along with a certified copy of the court's order declaring assured as insolvent and also on order appointing official assignee as the assignee of the insolvent's estate, the official assignee should be informed about the date of maturity and other details. If the assignee claims the money, the payment has to be made to him under advice to the life assured. If the judicial authority has sold the policy in a court action, the purchaser, who produces certificate of sale, will be entitled to the policy moneys.
- If a prohibitory order of a court of law or a notice from income-tax officer under Section 226 (3) of the Income Tax Act is subsisting, the assured should be asked to have a proper withdrawal order served on the insurer. Otherwise, the insurer will act according to the notice.
- If the life assured is reported to have died before the maturity date, the claim has to be treated as death claim and processed accordingly. But if the assured is reported to have died after the date of maturity but before the

receipt is discharged, the claim is to be treated as a maturity claim and paid to the legal heirs. Death certificate and evidence of title would be necessary.

- Under the Evidence Act, a person who has disappeared is presumed to be dead only if he has not been heard of for seven years. In such cases a decree of presumption of death from a court of law would be needed. The premiums must be paid until presumption of death is made, otherwise, the payment would be made after the court decree is obtained, as per the status of the policy as on the date when the premiums stopped.
- Payments of claim amount to claimants who are non-residents of India are governed by the Foreign Exchange Control Regulations.
- If a policy is financed through HUF funds, the policy belongs to HUF and as such the policy moneys would be payable to the Karta of HUF only.

However, the insurer sometimes provides certain relaxation in settlements of the claims. Legally no claim is acceptable in respect of a lapsed policy or death of the Life assured occurring within 3 years from the date of commencement of the policy. However, some concessions are available and payment of claims are made :

- If the Life assured had paid at least 3 years' premiums and thereafter if premiums have not been paid, the nominees get proportionate paid up value.
- In the event of the death of the Life assured within 3 years and the policy is under the lapsed position, nothing is payable.

If minimum 2 years premiums are paid and if death of Life assured occurs within 3 months from the date of first unpaid premium, then full sum assured along with bonus is payable subject to recovery of the premium already fallen due and the premium that falls during the policy anniversary.

Between 3 to 6 months from fully unpaid premium, only 59% of basic sum assured is payable. No bonus is paid and no arrears of premium are received. If death occurs between 6 months to 1 year, from fully unpaid premium only notional paid up value is given.

Double Accident Benefit is provided as an inject to the life insurance cover. For this purpose an extra premium of Rs. 1/- per Rs. 1000/- S.A. is charged. For claiming the benefits under the Accident Benefit the claimant has to produce the proof to the satisfaction of the corporation that the accident is defined as per the policy conditions. Normally for claiming this benefit documents like FIR, Post-morten Report are insisted upon.

Disability Benefit Claims consist of waiver of future premiums under the policy and extended disability benefit consisting in addition of a monthly benefit payment as per policy conditions. The essential condition for claiming this benefit is that the disability is total and permanent so as to preclude him from earning any wage/ compensation or profit as a result of the accident.

The LIC has also set-up Claims' Review Committees which in cases of repudiation, give opportunity to the claimant to make representation for consideration by the Review committees at the Zonal Office and the Central Office. As a result of such reviews, depending on the merits of each case appropriate sanctions are made.

The Grievance Redressal Machinery has been further expanded with the appointment of Insurance Ombudsman at different centres. At present there are 12 centres operating all over the country. Complaints regarding claims, any dispute regarding premiums, legal construction of the policy in relation to claim and non-issue of insurance document comes under the purview of Ombudsman's consideration.

8.2 Claim Concession

A policy lapses if the premium is not paid. Sometimes, the insurers take a liberal view of the situation and give same treatment as to non-forfeiture and revivals. The practice of LIC is as follows:

(*a*) After at least three full years premiums are paid, the claim will be considered for the full SA, as if the policy had remained in full force, if the death of the life assured occurred within six months from the date of the first unpaid premium.

(*b*) After at least full five years' premiums have been paid, the claim will be considered for the full SA, as if the policy had remained in full force, if the death of the life assured occurred within 12 months from the date of the first unpaid premium.

(*c*) In both cases, the policy monies will be paid after deducting the outstanding premiums with interest and the premiums, falling due in the current year till the next anniversary of the policy.

8.3 Presumption of Death

Under Section 108 of the Indian Evidence Act, 1872, if it is proved that the person has not been heard of for seven years by those who would have naturally heard by him had he been alive, the presumption of law is that he is dead. In case of death by accident while travelling by aeroplane or rail or natural calamities, the body may not be found. Insurers rely on information-supplied carriers, or other organisations in possession of relevant information. If the policyholder is missing for seven years, his heirs can apply to the appropriate civil court and get a court order declaring that the life assured might be presumed to be dead. A claim is payable if the policy is in force or in a paid-up condition, as on the date of the court's order. The exact date and time of death is not a matter of presumption but of active proof. Therefore, in the absence of any such proof, the date of the court's order could be taken as the Date of Death.

The insurer may also sometimes settle the claim on getting an indemnity bond to protect its interest, in case the presumption of death is later found to be wrong. When the insurer takes the responsibility for such action on its own, without the decree from a court, there is a risk that some other claimant to the estate may raise a challenge later. The insurer will not be able to avoid getting involved in the dispute and having to defend its action.

Riders are the additional benefits that may be added to the policy basic features upon payment of additional premium. These benefits allow the insured to enhance the insurance cover, qualitatively and quantitatively. Riders can customise the insurance product best suited to a given insured's needs. The most important rider in life insurance is the *Accident and Disability Rider*, which is now becoming popular especially after the privatisation of Insurance in India.

8.4 Riders

Accident Benefit and Disability Benefit

Accident and Disability benefit is an additional benefit that can be attached to the basic life cover. In this type benefit, typically, an additional amount equal to the Accident Benefit Rider Sum Assured on death is paid arising as a result of accident and for total and permanent disability arising due to accident (within 180 days from the date of accident) an amount equal to the Accident Benefit Rider Sum Assured will be paid over a period of 10 years in monthly instalments. The disability due to accident should be total and such that the Life assured is unable to carry out any work to earn the living. Following disabilities due to accidents are generally covered by the policies:

(*a*) irrevocable loss of the entire sight of both eyes, or

(*b*) amputation of both hands at or above the wrists, or

(*c*) amputation of both feet at or above ankles, or

(*d*) amputation of one hand at or above the wrist and one foot at or above the ankle.

When the claim for disability is paid, the future payment of premiums is waived and the remaining disability instalments have to be paid by the insured.

No benefit will be paid if accidental death or disability arises due to accident in case of:

(*a*) intentional self-injury, attempted suicide insanity or immorality or the Life Assured is under the influence of intoxicating liquor, drug or narcotic

(*b*) engagement in aviation or aeronautics other than that of a passenger in any air craft

(*c*) injuries resulting from riots, civil commotion, rebellion, war, invasion, hunting, mountaineering, steeple chasing or racing of any kind

(*d*) accident resulting from committing any breach of law

(*e*) accident arising from employment in armed forces or military services or police organisation.

The claimant has to provide a proof that–(*a*) the death or injury was outward, violent and visible means (*b*) the death was caused solely and directly and independently of all other causes, from the accident and (*c*) the death occurred within 120 days or such other period as may have been stipulated in the policy.

The maximum limit of sum assured varies among insurers. For, LIC it is Rs. 5 lakhs combined on all policies on a single life.

Free Look Period

In Unit Linked Insurance Plans, the policyholder has the option of cancelling the policy by writing to the Company stating the reasons for cancellation and by returning the original policy document to the Company, within 15 days of the date of receipt of the policy. If the policy is cancelled, the premium have paid is refunded by repurchasing the units at the unit price applicable on the date of cancellation and deducting the proportionate risk premium for the period on cover and the expenses incurred by the Company on medical examination and stamp duty charges.

Major Surgical Assistance Benefit

This rider provides financial support in the event of medical emergencies that require surgery in addition to the basic policy cover. When this rider is claimed for, a part of the sum assured is paid to the policyholder. Most insurers exclude claims arising from pre-existing injuries or illnesses and other predefined specific events and also, expenses on hospitalisation for ailments that do not require surgery are not covered. The premium paid for this rider qualifies for tax deduction under section 80D of the Income Tax Act, 1961. The premium varies in a large range because only some insurers allow the base policy to continue once a claim is made on the rider.

Waiver of Premium Rider

This rider is invoked when the insured person becomes *totally disabled* or loses his source of revenue because of unemployment owing to an injury or sickness. Thereby, the premiums due on the base policy (and other riders, if any) are waived till the person is able-bodied and employed again. Effectively, this rider acts as a "disability insurance" in the life insurance policy. If the premium payment is of a high amount, this rider is of a great benefit. The premium for this rider depends on the premium on the base policy and on other riders. The higher the premium on the basic policy cover and the other riders added, the higher is the premium payable on this rider. The premium paid for this rider qualifies for tax deduction under section 80D of the Income Taxt Act, 1961.

Guaranteed Insurability Option Rider

This rider gives the right to the insured to purchase additional insurance (similar to the basic insurance cover) at different stages, without further medical examination. This rider is useful if there is a need to buy additional insurance to keep pace with changing life circumstances. The insured is not required to give any medical evidence of insurability, even though the health condition deteriorates with age.

8.5 Settlement Options

Upon the maturity of the policy, the beneficiaries have the option either to receive the payment one time or spread over a period of time. This saves them from managing the hassle of large lumpsum settlement. So, the settlement option provides an option to the insured/beneficiary to collect the claim amount in instalments over a period of years, which may be exercised at the commencement or at any time during the currency of a policy.

Different methods for paying out benefits are made available to the insured/ beneficiaries when an individual covered by a life insurance policy dies or survives till maturity. It is also possible to leave the entire settlement with the insurance company and collect interest, retaining the right to withdraw principal funds at any time. Payment schedules are also available based on payment amount or duration. In either case, interest will accrue on the money that remains with the insurance company. There are also ranges of options that pay benefits over the entire life of the beneficiary. The methods of settlement options may be classified as follows:

Lump Sum Payment

The simplest method is a lump sum payment of the value of the policy. The total accumulated value may be taken as a lump sum payment.

Payment of a Specified Amount

Payment will be made periodically at the amount selected by the insured. The payment period cannot exceed the life expectancy of the assured.

Payment for a Specified Period

In this method, payments will be made for the period elected. The period may not be longer than the life expectancy.

Life Annuity

Payments may be converted in annuity till the insured survives. Payments may be guaranteed for a minimum of 10, 15, or 20 years. If the insured dies before receiving payments for the minimum guaranteed period (10, 15, or 20 years), the value of the remaining guaranteed period payments will be paid the beneficiary. Any guaranteed period may be longer than the life expectancy of the assured.

8.6 Valuation, Surplus and Distribution

The conventional form of life policies is "participating policy" with margins of safety built into the valuation elements to allow for protection for adverse events. Premiums are estimated by calculated on the basis of future expectations (probability) and modelling of mortality, interest and administrative expenses.

These estimations are based on assumptions, which may not hold out to be true. If the expected probability confirms to the actual outcome, the premiums are adequate to service claims else the company would be *ruined* or is in the state of financial problems. For a life insurance company, if every thing goes right, surplus or profits maybe be expected to emerge over the life of a portfolio of business. A large proportion of these surpluses is usually distributed to the policyholders as *bonuses or dividends*. These are addition to the guaranteed return allotted annually by a life insurer to holders of with profit (participating) policies. The size of the bonus depends on the insurer's performance. This bonus ensures that the value of the policyholder's insurance cover remains adequate.

However, before deciding about the distribution of surplus, it is logical to first estimate the amount of surplus, which is popularly called as *actuarial valuation*. Insurance Act, 1938 in India requires that actuarial valuations be done every year. Section 13 of the Act deals with Actuarial Reports & Abstract.

***Section 13**: (1) Every insurer carrying on life insurance business shall, in respect of the life insurance business transacted by him in India, and also in the case of an insurer specified in sub clause (a) (ii) or sub clause (b) of clause (9) of section 2 in respect of all life insurance business transacted by him, every year cause an investigation to be made by an actuary into the financial condition of the life insurance business carried on by him, including a valuation of his liabilities in respect thereto and shall cause an abstract of the report of such actuary to be made in accordance with the regulations contained in Part I of the Fourth Schedule and in conformity with the requirements of Part II of that Schedule...*

Section 49: (1) No insurer, being an insurer specified in sub clause (a) (ii) or sub-clause (b) of clause (9) of section 2, who I carries on the business of life insurance or any other class or subclass of insurance business to which Section 13 applies, shall, for the purpose of declaring or paying any dividend to shareholders or any bonus to policy holders or of making any payment in services of any debentures, utilise directly or indirectly any portion of the life insurance fund or of the fund of such other class or sub--class of insurance business, as the case may be, except a surplus shown in the valuation balance sheet in such form as may be specified by the regulations made by the Authority submitted to the Authority as part of the abstract referred to in Section 15 as a result of an actuarial valuation assets and liabilities of the insurer; nor shall he increase such surplus by contributions out of any reserve fund or otherwise unless such contributions have been brought in as revenue account applicable to that class or sub class of insurance business on or before the date of the valuation aforesaid, except when the reserve fund is made up solely of transfers from similar surpluses disclosed by valuations in respect of which returns have been submitted to the Authority under Section 15 of this Act or to the Central Government under Section 11 of the Indian Life Assurance Companies Act, 1912 (6 of 1912):

Provided that payments made out of any such surplus in service of any debentures shall not exceed 50% of such surplus including any payment by way of interest on the debentures, and interest paid on the debentures shall not exceed ten per cent of any such surplus except where the interest paid on the debentures is offset against the interest credited to the fund or funds concerned in deciding the interest basis adopted in the valuation disclosing the aforesaid surplus:

Provided further that the share of any such surplus allocated to or reserved for the shareholders (including any amount for the payment of dividends guaranteed to them, whether by way of first charge or otherwise) shall not exceed such sums as may be specified by the Authority and such share shall in no case exceed 10% of such surplus in case of participating policies and in other cases the whole thereof.

(2) For the purposes of sub section (1) the actual amount of income tax deducted at source during the period following the date as at which the last preceding valuation was made and preceding the date as at which the valuation in question is made may be added to such surplus after deducting an estimated amount for income tax on such surplus, such addition and deduction being shown in an abstract of the report of the actuary referred to in sub-section (1) of section 13.

It therefore follows that any portion of the life insurance fund or of the fund of such other class or sub-class of insurance business cannot be utilised for the payment of bonus to the shareholders/policyholders. Also, the surplus utilisation for servicing debentures cannot exceed 50% and surplus allocation to/reservation for shareholders can, in no case exceed 10% of such surplus in case of participating policies and in other cases the whole thereof.

Section 52 of the act deals with prohibition of business on dividing principle and exempts the life insurers from distributing surpluses based actuarial valuation.

Section 52: (l) No insurer shall after the commencement of this Act begin, or after 3 years from that date continue to carry on, any business upon the dividing principle, that is to say, on the principle that the benefit secured by a policy is not fixed but depends either wholly or party on the results of a distribution of certain sums amongst policies becoming claims within certain time limits, or on the principle that the premiums payable by a policy holder depend wholly or partly on the number of policies becoming claims within certain time limits:

Provided that nothing in this section shall be deemed to prevent an insurer from allocating bonuses to holders of policies of life insurance as a result of a periodical actuarial valuation either as reversionary additions to the sums insured or as immediate cash bonuses or otherwise:

Provided further that an insurer who continues to carry on insurance business on the dividing principle after the commencement of this Act shall withhold from distribution a sum of not less than 40% of the premiums received during each year after the commencement of this Act in which such business is continued so as to make up the amount required for investment under Section 27.

In a actuarial valuation process following are estimated:

(*a*) liabilities which may exist in future - claim and others

(*b*) stream of premiums expected in future

(*c*) the differential of funds available and liability is compared with the actual existing life fund (Life Assurance Fund).

A solvency situation is implied when the funds are greater than liabilities. Accordingly, the surplus is said to have been generated by the insurer, which may be distributed in various styles as discussed above.

If a surplus situation is established for an insurer based on actuarial valuation, the basis of distribution of the surplus has to be decided. This distribution of surplus may be carried out in various ways :

(*a*) One method is to provide for cash payments or reduction of premiums as the surplus arises, or the accumulated value of the cash bonuses may be paid when the policy becomes a claim or expires. By this method, a separate savings account is attached to the policy and the surplus is credited to the account as it emerges.

(*b*) Another way of distributing surplus is through terminal bonuses paid only when the policy expires. By this method, only survivors get a share of the accumulated surplus.

(*c*) The third method, and perhaps the most widely used, is one in which the profit is distributed to the policyholders by means of increasing the insurance benefits. This method provides a gradual increase in the benefits granted under the policy.

LIC method of distribution of surplus to the policyholders is in the form of *bonus additions*. As a logical principle, the method of bonus distribution must be equitable, simple and capable of being understood by the policyholders. Principle of equity implies that policyholders would receive bonuses equivalent to the contribution made by them to the surplus. The bonus may be declared as per thousand *e.g.* Rs. 5.00 per thousand. Therefore, if the Sum assured is Rs. 10,000 the bonus amount is Rs. 50.

There are many complex considerations that influence that decisions on equity in these matters. As an illustration, the variations in the rates of interest over a period of time can be looked at. The actuary takes a conservative view of the future trends in interest rates. This leads to a reserve larger than what is actually required. The policies at that time had been allowed lower rates of bonuses. The additional reserve earns a higher level of interest than what was assumed benefiting the newer policyholders at a time when the interest rates are falling. At higher rates of interest, longer term policies contribute more, including the interest earned on their additional contribution, than the shorter term policies. The contributions between different types of policies, needs careful analysis. The popular bonus systems are:

(a) ***Simple Reversionary Bonus System:*** in this system, the bonus is computed as uniform percentage addition to the basic sum assured and is payable on maturity (death/survival). At the time of payment, only the basic SA is reduced in proportion to the premiums paid and the vested bonus remains intact. Alternatively, the cash value of the bonus additions maybe redeemed to the policyholder or future premiums may be adjusted for bonus payments. If the basic sum assured is Rs. 50,000 and the bonus is Rs. 6.00 per thousand, the benefit would increase by Rs. 3,000.

(b) ***Compound Reversionary Bonus System:*** in this system, the percentage addition is made to the basic sum assured and the vested bonus additions earlier made. If the basic sum assured is Rs. 50,000 and the bonus is Rs. 6.00 per thousand, and the earlier vested bonus is Rs. 5,000, the benefit would increase by Rs. 3,300.

(c) ***Tontine Bonus system:*** under this system, surplus is distributed only for those policyholders who survive a stipulated period.

Based on equity principle, the amount of bonus paid on all policies of same type is uniform. However, it may vary among the different type of policies. Sometimes, the bonus is declared at a uniform rate but made to vest only after a certain period. It is logical to consider only those policies eligible for bonus, which are in force on the valuation date. Where the claims arise in a policy in a given policy year, the bonus is not paid for that year. However, an interim bonus may be paid along with the claims. This ensures the easy claims settlement and the smoothening of the valuation process. As matter of practice, the LIC pays the final additional bonus on policies where the term is equal to or greater than 15 years and which are and which are in full force at the time when claim arises. Some insurers do not pay bonus on money back policies because a proportionate share of sum assured is returned to the policyholders at regular intervals.

The term of the policy is an important consideration for the calculation of bonus The payment of bonus may also differ among the same type of policies, but different terms. The insurers for various plans and terms generally prepare the bonus charts. The reversionary bonus rates of LIC have been increasing steadily in the last 25 years. Following is an illustration of bonus table of HDFC Standard Life for the year ended 31st March 2006.

Reversionary Bonus

Policy Type	*Reversionary Bonus p.a.*
HDFC Endowment Assurance Plan HDFC Money Back Plan HDFC Children's Plan HDFC Savings Assurance Plan	Rs 22.50 per thousand Sum Assured
HDFC Assurance Plan	Rs 32.50 per thousand Sum Assured
HDFC Regular Premium Pension Plan	Rs 22.50 per thousand Sum Assured
HDFC Single Premium Pension Plan	Rs 50.00 per thousand Sum Assured
HDFC Single Premium Whole of Life Plan	Rs 50.00 per thousand Sum Assured and attaching bonuses

Interim Bonus

Policy Type	*Interim Bonus p.a.*
HDFC Endowment Assurance Plan HDFC Money Back Plan HDFC Children's' Plan	Rs 22.50 Per thousand Sum Assured
HDFC Savings Assurance Plan HDFC Assurance Plan	Rs 32.50 Per thousand Sum Assured
HDFC Regular Premium Pension Plan	Rs 22.50 Per thousand Sum Assured
HDFC Single Premium Pension Plan	Rs 50.00 Per thousand Sum Assured
HDFC Single Premium Whole of Life Plan	Rs 50.00 Per thousand Sum Assured and attaching bonuses.

8.7 Key Terms

- Death Claim
- Claim Concession
- Maturity Claim
- Presumption of Death
- Riders
- Accident and Disability
- Free Look Period
- Major Surgical Assistance Benefit
- Waiver of Premium Rider
- Guaranteed Insurability Option Rider
- Settlement Options
- Beneficiary
- Life Annuity
- Distribution
- Surpluses
- Actuarial Valuations
- Bonus Additions
- Reversionary Bonus
- Tontine Bonus

8.8 References

- P.K. Gupta, *Fundamentals of Insurance,* Himalaya Publishing House, Mumbai, 2005.
- S.L. Kane, *Principles of Life Insurance,* Himalaya Publishing House, Mumbai, 2005.
- *Practice of Life Assurance,* ICO2, Insurance Institute of India, Mumbai, 2003.

8.9 Test Yourself

1. Write short notes on:

   (*a*) Claim Concessions

   (*b*) Presumption of Death

2. Briefly explain the procedure of settlement of death and maturity (survival) claims.

3. List the documents required for consideration of a claim.

4. What are riders? Briefly explain the various types of riders in life insurance.

5. Enumerate the provisions of the Insurance Act, 1938 dealing with valuation and distribution of surplus.

6. Write short notes on:

   (*a*) Bonus Systems (*b*) Settlement Options

Choose Correct Answer:

1. What is meant by a claim under an insurance policy

   (a) Any demand made by the policyholder on the insurer

   (b) A demand to fulfill the policyholder's obligations

   (c) A demand to fulfill the insurer's obligations

   (d) All of the above

2. When does a claim arise under an insurance policy

   (a) Whenever the policyholder feels the need for money

   (b) When the insured events happen

   (c) When a premium is not paid

   (d) Whenever any of the three things mentioned above happen.

3. The insurer will not pay a claim unless

   (a) The event insured against, happens

   (b) The policyholder himself makes a demand

   (c) When all the three things mentioned above happen

4. Which one of the following statement is correct

   (a) Life insurance claim classified into four categories.

   (b) Life insurance claim classified into t here categories

   (c) Life insurance claim classified into two categories.

   (d) All are correct statement

5. Which one of the following statement is correct
   (a) A request for loan is considered as a claim
   (b) A request for surrender of policy is considered a claim
   (c) Both the statement are correct
   (d) Both statement are wrong
6. Which one of the following statement is correct
   (a) Death is a claim
   (b) Maturity is a claim
   (c) Both are claim
   (d) None of the above is claim
7. Which of the following statement is correct
   (a) The insurer makes enquiries only in the case of death claim
   (b) The insurer makes enquiries in the case of maturity claims also
   (c) Both the statements above are correct
   (d) Both the statement are wrong
8. Which one of the following statement is correct
   (a) The insurer makes enquiries in the case of all death claims
   (b) The insurer makes enquiries only in the case of early claims.
   (c) Both are correct
   (d) Both are wrong
9. Which one of the following statement is correct
   (a) A death claim within two years of revival is treated as an early claim
   (b) A death claim within two years of revival is treated as an early claim
   (c) Both are correct
   (d) Both are wrong
10. Which one of the following statement is correct
   (a) The death claim is settled in favour of the of the nominee in MWP act cases
   (b) The death claim is settled in favour of the trustee in MWP act cases
   (c) Both are correct
   (d) Both are wrong
11. Before paying a claim, which of the following have to be verified
   (a) Age of the life insured
   (b) Age of the nominee

(c) Age of the assignee, if any

(d) All of the above

12. Before paying a death claim, which of the following have to be verified

 (a) Proof of death of life insured

 (b) Receipts of all premiums paid from commencement

 (c) Entitlement for accident benefits

 (d) All of the above

13. In which of the following cases, is the claimant likely to feel most anxious

 (a) Death claim within two years (b) Surrender cases

 (c) Applications for loans (d) Survival benefit cases

14. In which of the following cases, is the maximum documents asked for

 (a) Death claims (b) Maturity claims

 (c) Survival claims (d) Annuity cases

15. In which of the following cases, will the help of the agent be most useful.

 (a) Death claims (b) Maturity claims

 (c) Survival benefits (d) Annuity cases

State whether the following statements are 'True' or 'False'.

1. The life insurance claims can be classified in three categories.
2. If the insured dies before the expiry of the term of the policy is called as death claim.
3. *Early claims* refer to the death of life assured occurring within 3 years from commencement of policy.
4. The death claim amount is payable to the nominee or the assignee as the case may be.
5. Maturity claims are payable as per the terms of the life.
6. The insurer normally sends advance intimations to the life.
7. The insurance company is expected to make payment on the maturity date
8. Settlement procedure in a maturity claim is hard.
9. If the life assured is reported to have died before the maturity date, the claim has to be treated as death claim and processed accordingly.
10. Under the Evidence Act, a person who has disappeared is presumed to be dead only if he has not been heard of for seven years.
11. If a policy is financed through HUF funds, the policy belongs to HUF and as such the policy moneys would be payable to the Karta of HUF only.
12. Double Accident Benefit is provided as an inject to the life insurance cover.
13. At present, there are 9 centres operating all over the country.

14. A policy lapses if the premium is not paid.
15. The agent will not be able to avoid getting involved in the dispute and having to defend its action.

Fill in the blanks

1. The life insurance claims can be classified in .... categories.
2. If the insured dies before the expiry of the term of the policy, it is called as...............
3. The death of the life assured has to be intimated in writing to the.....................
4. Claim forms can be issued without prejudice to see if any ex-gratia.............. can be made.
5. Maturity claims are payable as per the terms of the ....
6. The amount payable at the time of maturity includes sum assured and...........................
7. The insurer normally sends advance intimations to the.................
8. In the case of maturity claims, the insurer will call for the following documents, well before the date of......................
9. Policy document, if it is not available, it may have been deposited elsewhere as a security for a.................
10. Settlement procedure in a maturity claim is ....
11. If the life assured had paid at least .... premiums and thereafter if premiums have not been paid, the nominees get proportionate paid-up.
12. In the event of the death of the life assured within 3 years and the policy is under the lapsed position, nothing is ....
13. No bonus is paid and no arrears of premium are ....
14. Double Accident Benefit is provided as an inject to the life insurance ....
15. Normally for claiming the benefit documents like ...., ... are insisted upon.
16. A policy lapses if the premium is not ....
17. Sometimes, the insurers take a liberal view of the situation and give same treatment as to .... and ....
18. A claim is payable if the policy is in force or in a paid-up condition, as on the date of the..................
19. The exact date and time of death is not a matter of presumption but of.............
20. The insurer may also sometimes settle the claim on getting an indemnity bond to protect its ....

Module IV

C H A P T E R 9

MARITIME LOSSES AND CLAIMS INSURANCE

Learning Objectives

After studying this chapter, one can understand:

- History of Marine Insurance
- Definition of Marine Insurance
- Marine Insurance Contract
- Insurance Principles Applied to Marine Business
- Types of Marine Insurance
- Marine Cargo Losses and Frauds
- Settlement of Claims

9.1 Introduction

Insurance on the risks of transportation of goods is one of the oldest and most vital forms of insurance. The value of goods shipped by business firms each year cost millions of rupees. These goods are exposed to damage or loss from numerous transportation perils. The goods can be protected by ocean marine and inland marine contracts. Ocean marine insurance provides protection for goods transported over water. All types of ocean going vessels and their cargo can be insured by ocean marine contracts, the legal liability of ship owners and cargo owners can also be insured. Inland marine insurance provides protection for goods shipped on land. It includes insurance on imports and exports, domestic shipments, and means of transportation such as bridges and tunnels. In addition, inland marine insurance can be used to insure fine art, jewellery, fur and other properties.

9.2 History of Marine Insurance

Ocean marine insurance is one of the earliest forms of insurance. Commerce by ship was well-established in the Mediterranean Sea, 2000 years before the birth of Christ. The Babylonians, Phoenicians, Greeks and Romans were great sea traders. Coincident with the development of this trade, insurance transactions emerged as distinct commercial agreements. *Bottomary* was a transaction protecting an owner from financial loss if his ship was destroyed. The bottomary loan was an early forerunner of ocean marine insurance. On the other hand, some elements of the modern insurance transaction were missing. Actuarial science was not practiced, although the Phoenicians were noted mathematicians, so premiums were probably not based on mathematical estimates but on intuition. Today, judgmental estimates remain the basis of marine underwriting. The early sea traders and moneylenders also lacked a highly developed body of law like that providing the environment for the modern insurance transaction.

Respondentia loans were comparable to bottomary loans, the difference being the subject of the loan. Otherwise, the transaction was comparable. A merchant, placing cargo on a ship, would take out a loan using the cargo as collateral. The moneylender, for a premium in addition to the regular interest charged, agreed to forgive the loan if the cargo were lost. Again, modern ocean marine cargo insurance is very similar to the respondentia loan.

Evidences of marine insurance contract are found in Mediterranean voyages the literature of 1400 also indicates the charging of prime for marine insurance policies. The law of Wishky (1300), the Ordinance of Barcelona (1435) and the Guidon de la Mar (1600) provide evidence of marine insurance development in Europe. In 1779, the underinites at Lloyds adopted a uniform marine insurance contract which is a common form of policy in use today.

During the period 1720-1820, the companies like London Association and Royal Exchange Association enjoyed major marine insurance market share.

In 1909, the Marine Insurance (Gambling Policies) Act was adopted and the modest pattern of British regulation was set as it is in substance today.

Major international markets for marine includes U.K., U.S., Europe, Japan, etc. The most dominated UK Marine Insurance market includes players like Lloyds, mutual association and affiliates of non UK based insurance companies.

9.3 Marine Insurance – Definition

A contract of marine insurance is an agreement whereby the insurer undertakes to indemnify the assured in a manner and to the extent thereby agreed, against marine losses, that is, the losses incidental to marine adventure. Marine insurance cover gives financial protection from total loss or partial damage of sea going ships and cargoes. In return for the payment of a premium, the underwriter of a marine risk or 'line' insures the ship owner, ship-charterer or merchant, for part or the whole value of a ship or cargo. Freight charges paid in advance may be insured by the shipowner. Each type of marine insurance requires an assessment of the nature, size are value of the risk and the underwriter calculate his premium according to the quality of the ship or cargo and the destination and route of the voyage at risk. Marine insurance contracts are amongst the least charging and most familiar of all types of risk business. There is a marine adventure when any insurable property is exposed to marine perils.

Marine perils also known as perils of the seas, means the perils consequent on, or incidental to, the navigation of the sea or the perils of the seas, such as fire, war perils, pirates, rovers, thieves, captures, Jettisons, barratry and any other perils which are either of the like, kind or may be designed by the policy. Marine Insurance business means the business of effecting contracts of insurance upon vessels of any description, including cargoes, freights and other interests which may be legally insured minor in relation to such vessels, cargoes and freights, goods, wares, merchandise and property of whatever description insured for any transit by land or water or both, and whether or not including warehouse risks or similar risks in addition or as incidental to such transit and includes any other risks customarily included among the risks insured against in marine insurance policies.

Section 3 of the Marine Insurance Act, 1963 defines a contract of marine insurance as an insurance cover for marine cargo, air cargo and post parcels. Thus, marine insurance is used to cover transportation by any of the following modes of transit singly or jointly:

(a) Sea, air or land.

(b) Inland water voyages.

(c) Rail/road.

(d) Air.

(e) Post.

It provides insurance or protection to goods in 'transit' and also extends to storage of goods provided such storage is incidental to transportation.

9.4 Marine Insurance Contract

Marine insurance contract being a contract should first satisfy the essential elements of a valid contract. In addition it should satisfy the insurance principles as applicable to marine insurance. Further, there are specific provisions given in the Marine Insurance Act, 1973.

The essential elements of a marine insurance contract from the perspective of Indian Contract Act *inter alia* includes:

(a) Offer – in the form of proposal.

(b) Acceptance – issue of a cover note/policy.

(c) *Consideration* – premium payable on the policy

Marine Insurance Contract is an agreement where by the insurance company (insurer) undertakes to indemnify the owner (insured) of a ship or cargo against risks which are incidental to marine adventure. (Section 3 of the Marine Insurance Act, 1963).

The parties to a contract of insurance of follows:

1. The insurance company also known as underwriters who assume the liability when the loss takes place.
2. The insured, *i.e.*, the on who either procures an insurance policy or becomes beneficiary thought the insurance.

9.4.1 Features of Marine Insurance Contract

The basic features of marine policies are as follows:

1. The marine cargo insurance policies are freely assignable as the consignee finally takes the goods pass through various hands before the consignee finally takes their delivery. The assignment of insurance policy is allowed in terms of section 52 and 53 of the Marine Insurance Act 1963. A Marine Insurance Policy can be assigned either before or after the loss.
2. The assignment is done by endorsement and delivery.
3. Insurable interest of the claimant must exist at the time of loss of the cargo.
4. The value of the insurance policy is the sum agreed between the insured and the insurer. Thus, these policies are always on agreed value basis. Since contracts of insurance provide for indemnity the loss suffered by the insured is not just the loss suffered by the insured is not just the loss represented by the value of the goods but also the amount of profit that the parties would have earned from the sale of those goods. That is why the marine insurance policies are taken for a value equal to 110% of the CIF value of the goods, *i.e.*, 10% more than the CIF value to account for the anticipated profits.
5. The contract of marine insurance is a contract of commercial indemnity and not pure indemnity because this insurance provides for indemnity against the loss of profits as well.
6. The duration of the marine insurance policy is based on the institute cargo clause yet it is provided to include the period of transit, the time of discharge of the goods and the time of arrival of the goods. Generally the duration of the policy covers time upto 30 days after arrival of the goods in case of air shipments and 60 days after the arrival of shipments by sea to allow for the transportation of cargo from the final port of discharge to the warehouse of the importer.

9.4.2 Contents of an Insurance Policy

According to section 25 of the Act, a marine insurance policy must specify:

(i) The name insured, or of some person who effects the insurance on behalf of the insured.

(ii) The subject matter insured and the risk insured against losses.

(iii) The voyage or period of time or both, as the case may, covered by the insurance.

(iv) The sum or sums insured.

(v) The name or names of the insurer or insurers.

9.4.3 Procedure for Obtaining Marine Insurance Policy

The following is the procedure for obtaining marine insurance policy:

(a) ***Selecting the Insurance Company:*** General insurance business in India is, the monopoly of General Insurance Corporation ((TIC) of India and its four subsidiaries. However, if an exporter intends to insure with a foreign company, then prior permission of the RBI must be obtained.

(b) ***Deciding the Appropriate Type of Policy:*** There are various types of, marine insurance policies issued by the GIC to suit the requirements of the exporters. The exporter should decide the appropriate type of policy tailing into consideration his requirements.

(c) ***Application to the Insurance Company:*** When the goods are ready for dispatch the exporter' should apply to the insurance company in the' prescribed 'Declaration Form' giving the following details:

- Address of the exporter and importer.
- Description of goods;
- Marks, numbers and kind of packages.
- Value of packages.
- Transportation from the warehouse to its final destination.
- Risk to be covered for insurance.
- Any other information as required:

(d) ***Payment of Premium:*** The insurance premium charges may vary from company to company and country to country. Payment on marine insurance policy can be made in rupees' provided exporter certifies that insurance charges of the shipment in question have to be borne by him.

(e) ***Issue of the Insurance Policy:*** After the completion of all the formalities, the exporter has to produce the Bill of Loading and the name of the ship and the insurance company. The insurance company issues the insurance certificate (in triplicate) as per the declaration given by the exporter. Policy generally contains the following details:

- Name and address of the exporter.
- Type of policy and description of the risks covered.

- Description of the goods insured.
- Amount of sum assured and premium paid.
- Date of issue and the period of policy.
- Special conditions and warranties.
- Special instructions regarding the procedure to be followed in the event of loss.

(f) ***Processing of the Policy:*** The exporter submits the original policy to the bank with his other documents. The second copy of the policy is sent to the importer and the third copy is retained, by the exporter for his own information

9.5 Insurance Principles Applied to Marine Business

The contracts of marine insurance are based on the following principles:

9.5.1 Utmost Good Faith

The insured to bound to disclose all material facts to the insurer before the contract is entered into.

Example

If an equipment is transported and insurance cover was obtained as such implying as is a new one and actually the equipment is one which has been renovated, the insurer may cancel the contract as it was a concealment of fact.

However, if there is certain information, which reduces the exposure, to the insurer or which the insurer is bound to have known or waived *suo moto*, the contract is valid.

If the insurance is affected through a proper or agent, it is the duty of agent/ broker to disclose all material facts. These facts not only include the communicated facts but also (by principal) facts in his knowledge. He must also know every circumstance in ordinary course of business and as communicated by his principal. All representations (material fact/fact/expectations or belief) must be communicated to the insular before obtaining the cover.

9.5.2 Insurable Interest

The insured may not have insurable interest at the time of contract, but he must have a reasonable expectation of acquiring it and it must exist at the time of loss. As per the provisions of the Marine Insurance Act, 1963, every person has an insurable interest who is interested in a maritime adventure". The insurable interest may be:

(a) ***Defeasible:*** which is brought to an end by during the tenure of the voyage by occurrence of an event other than maritime perils. For example–cessation of insurable interest of the seller upon the transfer of title to the buyer.

(*b*) ***Contingent:*** which attaches during the tenure of the voyage on the happening of the contingent event. For example when the goods are sold on FOB terms to the buyer, when the goods are loaded on the vessel, the seller interest terminates, but if the goods are returned by the buyer, the interest again attaches for the seller.

It is essentially required that something must exist feasible which may be exposed to marine perils and there must be some legal or justified relationship which imply a benefit to the holder by its preservation and the insured is affected by its damage/less/detention or occurrence of a liability in connection thereof.

Marine Insurance Act provides that in the event of "lost or not lost" clauses in marine insurance contract, the assured may recover the loss even though at that moment he has not acquired any interest because of ignorance. However, if the insured was aware of loss and the insurer was not informed, the claim may be denied on the grounds of violation of utmost good faith.

Now-a-days, cargo and hull policy forms have disformed with "lost or not lost" clauses. But some ICC clauses provide that if the insured property suffers loss/damage before assured acquires interest, he is protected by the policy condition if any only if risk is transferred to him. In case of PPI (Policy Proof of Interest) policies, the underwriter may dispene with evidence of insurable interest. However, no action is tonable against them if claim is denied. Insurer has insurable interest in respect of risk underwritten which entitles him to get it reinsured.

In case of freight, the cargo owner has insurable interest in freight advanced.

9.5.3 Indemnity

Section 3 of the Act says that indemnity is "in the manner and to the extent thereby agreed". The indemnity depends on the contact. In case of valued policies, the measure of indemnity is the agreed value. However, in case of unvalued policies, unless provided, the indemnity has to be calculated as per the provisions of the Section 18 of the Marine Insurance Act, 1963. Indemnity valuation is difficult because values of cargo keeps on changing and its value increase the more and more it gets closer to destination. Another method of indemnity valuation is:

CIF Value of Goods

+ Allowance (%) for overheads

+ Allowance (%) for profit.

9.5.4 Subrogation

The insurer on the payment of claims for losses which may be partial or total, is subrogated to all the rights and remedies of the assured in respect of the subject matter insured. In case of total loss, insurer is entitled to take over the interest of assured in toto. In case of partial loss, the insurer has not such rights. His rights are limited to the indemnity made. A letter of subrogation is generally taken from the insureds when claims are paid, in situations where the recovery is possible from third parties. If under recovery from third parties, a value greater than insured value is recovered, assured is entitled to proceeds, subject to reimbursement of claim amount due to insurers.

9.5.5 Contribution

When for the same subject matter of marine insurance, there are more than one policy such that sums insured exceed the indemnity allowed by the act, the assured shall be deemed to be cover insured and rateable proportion shall apply to such cases. If the insured has recovered more that indemnity value, the excess amount shall be held in trust by him.

9.5.6 Warranties

Warranties, common to marine insurance contracts are the promises by the insured that something shall be done or shall be done or a certain state of affairs exist or do not exist. The logical reason for imposing warranties by the insurers is to safeguard their interest from hazards and they can avoid liability in case of breach. Warranties may be:

Expressed: appearing in the policy *e.g.* warranties relating to packing, shipping time period, survey/inspection etc. In case of hull insurance express warranties include:

1. *Trading Warranty*: area of operation.
2. *Disbursement Warranty:* employment or use of the vessel for specific trade or traders.
3. *Registration/licencing Warranty*: for the vessels engaged in fishing or sailing activities.

9.5.7 Proximate Cause

This principle implies that the insurer becomes liable to pay for loss if the insured peril or risk is the proximate cause of loss. Thus the insurer would not pay for the loss to the goods if they are stolen because of unworthy packing in case the policy covers the risk theft, pilferage and non delivery. In this case, the proximate cause of loss is the faulty packing which facilitated the goods to be stolen. Since this is not covered under the risks specified in the policy, the insurer would not indemnify the loss.

9.6 Types of Marine Insurance

There are two broad categories of marine insurance: ocean marine insurance and inland marine insurance. Both are here discussed in details.

9.6.1 Ocean Marine Insurance

Ocean marine insurance is one of the forms of transportation insurance. The ocean marine contracts are incredibly complex, reflecting basic marine law, trade customs, and court interpretations of the various policy provisions. Ocean marine insurance can be divided into four basic classes to reflect the various insurable interests:

Hull Insurance covers physical damage to the ship or vessel. It is similar to collision insurance that covers physical damage to a automobile caused by collision. Hull insurance is always written with a deductible. In addition, it contains a collision liability clause that covers the owner's legal liability if the ship collides with another vessel or damages its cargo. However, the running down clause does not cover legal liability on that vessel arising out of injury or death to other persons, damage to piers and docks, and personal injury and death of crew members.

Cargo Insurance covers the shipper of the goods if the goods are damaged or lost. The policy can be written to cover a single shipment. If regular shipments are made, an open-cargo policy can be used that insures the goods automatically when a shipment is made. The shipper is required to report periodically the number of shipments that are made. The open-cargo policy has no expiration date and remains in force until it is cancelled.

Protection and Indemnity (P&I) Insurance is usually written as a separate contract that provides comprehensive liability insurance for property damage or bodily injury to third parties. P&I insurance protects the ship owner for damage caused by the ship to piers, docks and harbour installations, damage to the ship's cargo, illness or injury to the passengers or crew, and fines and penalties.

Freight Insurance indemnifies the ship owner for the loss of earnings if the goods are damaged or lost and are not delivered.

Ocean marine insurance has certain fundamental concepts:

Covered Perils: An ocean marine policy provides broad coverage for certain specified perils, including perils of the sea, such as damage or loss from bad weather, high waves, collision, sinking, and stranding. Other covered perils include loss from fire, enemies, pirates, thieves, jettison (throwing goods overboard to save the ship), barratry (fraud by the master or crew at the expense of the ship or cargo owners), and similar perils. Ocean marine insurance can also be written on an "all-risks" basis. All unexpected and fortuitous losses are covered except those losses specifically excluded. Common exclusions are losses due to delay, war, inherent vice (tendency of certain types of property to decompose), and strikes, riots, or civil commotion.

Particular Average: In marine insurance, the word average refers to a partial loss. A particular average is a loss that falls entirely on a particular interest, as contrasted with a general average, a loss that falls on all parties to the voyage. Under the free of particular average clause (FPA), partial losses are not covered unless the loss is caused by certain perils, such as stranding, sinking, burning or collision of the vessel. The FPA clause can be written with franchise deductible, where the franchise amount is stated as a percentage of the insured property. Thus, an FPA clause of 3% means that a covered loss under 3% falls entirely on the insured; if the loss is 3% or more, the insurer pays the loss in full.

General Average: A general average is a loss incurred for the common good and consequently is shared by all parties to the venture. Each party must pay its share of the loss based on the proportion that its interest bears to the total value in the venture. Four conditions must be satisfied to have a general average loss:

- *Necessary:* the sacrifice is necessary to protect all interests in the venture-ship, cargo, and freight.
- *Voluntary:* the sacrifice must be voluntary.
- *Successful:* the effort must be successful. At least part of the value must be saved.
- *Free from Fault:* any party that claims a general average contribution from other interests in the voyage must be free from fault with respect to the risk that threatens the venture.

Sue and Labour: Under this, the insured is required to do everything possible to save and preserve the goods in case of loss. The insured who fails to do this has violated a policy condition, hence loses the rights of recovery.

Abandonment: In ocean marine insurance, two types of total losses are recognized: actual and constructive. Actual total loss occurs when the property is completely destroyed. Constructive total loss occurs when, even though the ship or other subject matter of insurance is not totally destroyed, it would cost more to restore it than it is worth. The ship may be abandoned to the insurer and the insured collects the full amount of the policy. The salvage then belongs to the insurer, who is usually in a better position to dispose of it than the insured because the insurer deals with salvage companies all over the world and is experienced in such matters.

Warehouse to Warehouse: Under the terms of the warehouse to warehouse clause, such protection as is afforded under the insuring agreement extends from the time the goods leave the warehouse of the shipper, even if it is located far inland, until they reach the warehouse of the consignee.

Coinsurance: Although an ocean marine policy does not contain a specific coinsurance clause, losses are settled as if there is a 100 per cent coinsurance clause. An ocean marine policy is a valued contract, by which the face amount is paid if a total loss occurs. If the insurance carried does not equal the full value of the goods at the time of loss, the insured must share in the loss.

Warranties: There are two types of warranties in marine insurance: express and implied. Express warranties are written into the contract and become a condition of the coverage relating to potential causes of an insured event. And can be of the type free of capture and seizure warranty (FC&S), strike, riot and civil commotion (SR&CC), delay warranty and trading warranty. Implied warranties are not written into the policy but become a part of it by custom. Breach of warranty in marine insurance voids the coverage, even if the breach is immaterial to the risk. It can be of types of seaworthiness, deviation and legality.

9.6.2 Inland Marine Insurance

Inland marine insurance grew out of ocean marine insurance. Ocean marine insurance first covered property from the point of embarkation to the place where the goods landed. As commerce and trade developed, the goods had to be shipped over land as well. Inland marine insurance developed in the 1920s to cover property being transported over land, means of transportation such as bridges and tunnels, and property of a mobile nature.

Commercial property that can be insured by inland marine contracts can be conveniently classified into five categories:

- *Domestic Goods in Transit.*
- *Property Held by Bailees:* bailees are legally liable for damage to customer's property only if they or their employees are negligent.
- *Mobile Equipment and Property:* Inland marine property floaters can be used to cover property that is frequently moved from one location to another.
- *Property of Certain Dealers:* Certain "block" policies are used to insure dealers. Most policies provide coverage on an "all-risks" basis.
- *Means of Transportation and Communication:* This refers to property at a fixed location that is used in transportation or communication.

For purposes of regulation, inland marine contracts are classified into two categories; *filed forms* and *non-filed forms.* With filed forms, the policy forms and rates are filed with the state insurance department. Filed forms are typically used in situations where there are a large number of potential insurers and the loss exposures are reasonably homogenous. In contrast, non-filed forms refer to policy forms and rates that are not filed with the state insurance department. Non-filed forms are used in situations where the insured has specialized or unique needs, the number of potential insureds is relatively small, and the loss exposures are diverse.

9.7 Marine Cargo Losses and Frauds

The various causes of marine losses are: (*a*) Theft Pilferage and non-delivery, (*b*) Handling and Stowage damage, (*c*) Loss from water damage and (*d*) Marine perils. However, maritime frauds are very common. These are categorised as follows:

(*a*) Scuttling of ships–deliberate sinking of ships.

(*b*) Documentary Frauds–the manipulation of shipping frauds, use of forge documents.

(*c*) Chartering of vessels–fraudulent chartering companies.

(*d*) Cargo thefts–deviation of ships from standard routes, "paper shipping companies".

Marine losses under the marine policy are defined in the Marine Insurance Act, 1963. These may be of following types:

1.	Total Loss	–	Actual or Constructive
2.	Partial Loss	–	(a) Particular Average
			(b) General Average
3.	Expenses	–	(a) Sue and Labour Charges
			(b) Particular Charges
			(c) Salvage Charges

4. Extra charges which include fees of surveys, sale of property etc.

Actual Total Loss

Section 57(1) of the Marine Insurance Act, 1963 defines actual total loss as the loss where the subject-matter insured is destroyed, or so damaged as to cease to be a thing of the kind insured, or where the assured is irretrievably deprived thereof.

Section 58 of the Act provides that if no news has been received after the lapse of a reasonable period, it is presumed to be an actual total loss on account of a marine peril.

Constructive Total Loss

Section 60 (1) defines a constructive total loss as the loss when the subject-matter is reasonably abandoned because either:

(a) actual total loss appears unavoidable, or

(b) to prevent actual total loss requires expenditure exceeding the saved value.

Section 60(2) in addition, provides that there is a constructive total loss when the insured is deprived of the subject-matter and,

(a) it is unlikely that he can recover it, or

(b) the cost of recovery would exceed its value when recovered.

Therefore, a constructive total loss would occur if the cost of repairing the damage would exceed the value of the ship when repaired.

The cost of repairs is ascertained on the basis of estimates prepared by the insurers' surveyors and those representing the shipowners.

Section 60(2) (iii) provides that there is constructive total loss of goods where the cost of repairing the damage and forwarding the goods to their destination would exceed their value on arrival. The latter cost would include such charges as landing, drying, and warehousing, reshipping and onward carriage to the port of destination.

Section 61 of the Act states "where there is a constructive total loss the assured may either treat the loss as a partial loss, or abandon the subject-matter insured to the insurer and treat the loss as if it were an actual total loss."

Section 56 of the Act provides that any loss other than a total loss is a partial loss.

Section 64(1) defines a particular average loss as the partial loss of the subject matter insured, caused by a peril insured against, and which is not a general average loss.

Particular average, therefore implies a fortuitous partial loss caused by a an insured peril. Examples of particular average include damage to the ship by stranding, running a ground, collision or damage to the cargo by fire, seawater etc.

General average loss defined in Section 66(1) of the Act as "a loss caused by or directly consequential on a general average act. It includes a general average expenditure as well as a general average sacrifice."

Section 66(2) provides that "There is a general average act where any extraordinary sacrifice or expenditure is voluntarily and reasonably made or incurred in time of peril for the purpose of preserving the property imperilled in the common adventure."

Particular Charges

Section 64(2) of Marine Insurance Act, 1963 defines particular charges as expenses incurred by or on behalf of the assured for the safety or preservation of the subject-matter insured. They are expenses other than general average and salvage charges.

Sue and Labour Clause

This clauses enforces common law duty of the assured and his agents to act at all times, though uninsured, and to take such measures as may be reasonable for the purpose of averting or minimising loss or damage which is covered by the insurance.

Examples of the sue and labour charges are:

(i) Hides damaged by sea-water; reconditioning expenses at an intermediate port to prevent aggravation of damage are sue and labour charges.

(ii) Due to a maritime casualty a ship puts into a port of refuge for repairs which would take some weeks. The cost of extra fodder fed to the live cattle insured against 'All Risks' during the period of repairs is sue and labour charge.

(iii) The additional cost of forwarding cargo from a port of refuge to earn the freight payable on delivery at destination is recoverable, if, in the absence of such cost, a claim could result for a total loss on freight.

Extra Charge

Survey fees are payable only if the loss is payable under the policy.

Salvage Charges

Section 65 of Marine Insurance Act defines salvage charges as the charges that are recoverable under maritime law by a salvor independently of marine contract.

Average Adjusters

Average adjuster adjust the general average losses. He has specialised knowledge and the/also the parties reputation for strict impartiality which ensure that his findings are acceptable to all concerned. The adjuster's fees are allowed in general average calculation.

Apart from various measures taken by the concerned parties, following should be taken into care to reduce the frequency of frauds:

(a) Vessels approved by GIC (entered in IRS) should be used.

(b) Exercise of reasonable care and diligence wile dealing with unknown parties or parties new in the business.

(c) Payments should be affected by confirmed IRLC.

(d) The agents involved in the whole process should be reliable.

(e) Reputed charterer should be hired.

9.8 Settlement of Claims

Marine insurance claims are of two broad types–marine hull and marine cargo. Both are dealt separately in the following sections.

9.8.1 Marine Hull

9.8.1.1 Types of Marine Hull Claims

Marine Hulls are divided into three groups, *viz.:*

(a) Oceangoing vessels and other vessels rated exclusively by the Tariff Advisory Committee.

(b) Vessels insured under Builder's Risk Policies, Ship Repairer's Liability Policies, Ship Breaking Policies and the Charterer's Liability Policies.

(c) All the vessels and/or operations of which rates have been provided in Marine Hull Manual under specific Tariffs or otherwise and all other vessels/ operations not covered by (*a*) and (*b*) above.

The types of hull claims are:

- Total Loss/Constructive Total Loss;
- Particular Average/Particular Charges *i.e.,* Partial Losses/Expenses;

- Salvage and Salvage Charges–either Salvage Awards or Salvage under contract;
- General Average;
- Collision Liability;
- Liability and Non-liability Claims (such as wreck removal) falling under the P & L section for the policy where such cover is granted;
- Sue & Labour charges;
- Personal Accident Claims for crew covered under Sailing/Fishing vessels Tariffs.

Following claims are generally considered for reference to professional Average Adjusters:

(1) All claims falling under Category 1.1 "A" unless the claim involved is straightforward and also for a nominal amount.

(2) (*a*) GA or GA/PA claims on vessels under Category 1.1 "C".

(*b*) Collision Liability claims requiring cross Liability adjustment in respect of risk falling under Category 1.1 "B" and "C".

9.8.1.2 Procedures of Claims Settlement

Following considerations are important while deciding on *Ocean going vessels*:

(a) nature and quantum of claims likely to arise under this category;

(b) likelihood of occurrence of loss in distant foreign waters;

(c) involvement of laws and practices of foreign jurisdictions, and

(d) involvement of foreign professional and/or firms like surveyors, repair yards, adjusters, solicitors, arbitrator, courts, etc.

The current system of processing these claims in accordance with the international practices and these practices are likely to continue except in so far as the provisions of the Indian Statutes are concerned.

Sundry Hulls (including Sailing vessels, Fishing vessels, Inland vessels etc.).

Following procedure is generally adopted for claim settlement:

- A Licensed Surveyor is appointed in all cases of Partial Losses/Expenses. Also licensed Surveyor are appointed in case of TL/CTL only where the vessel or its wreck, of reasonable value is available for inspection or making reasonable attempt to salvage.
- On receipt of loss intimation a letter is written "on *without prejudice basis* to the insured advising about the appointment of Surveyor and/or investigator requesting the insured to render full co-operation to the Surveyor/Investigator appointed and to return the claim form duly completed and signed.

- Notice of Abandonment of the vessel/wreck in writing is a prerequisite for a constructive Total Loss Claim. Practically speaking, insurers decline *prima facie* acceptance of the Notice of Abandonment. However, insurer's refusal to accept abandonment does not legally prejudice the insured's claim for a CTL once the Notice of Abandonment has been issued by the insured and received by the insurer. Notwithstanding this the insurer generally refuse acceptance of abandonment of the wreck till the probable liabilities attaching to the wreck (Port and other dues, statutory requirement of wreck removal in case of vessel sunk in navigate channel; etc.) are reasonably estimated as considered.
- Total loss claim is settled on the basis of the statements and documents, as also the investigator/s Surveyor's report as the case may be if the circumstances are found to be reasonably acceptable. As per the Marine Insurance Act, following acceptance of a claim for total loss of a vessel, the insurers become entitled to the wreck or the proceeds thereof, if any. However, before enforcing such entitlement, the insurers ascertain whether or not any liability, statutory or otherwise, is reasonably likely to attach to such wreck or proceeds thereof.
- Since Marine Hull Policy is issued for a composite sum insured, representing the aggregate values of Hull and Machinery and showing Hull or Machinery values separately in the policy being prohibited, no claim for total or Constructive Total Loss is considered for settlement on the basis of and on account of either Hull or Machinery value alone.
- In case of partial loss, surveyors are duty bound to achieve assessment net of salvage, if any because it is difficult and very often not economical for the underwriters to get involved in salvage take-over and disposal. However, where this is not possible, arrangements are made to take over the salvage from the insured before the settlement of the claim and disposed accordingly.
- Claims occurring in foreign waters are generally dealt with in the same manner as in the case of Ocean-going vessels.

Documents Required

The documents required for the settlement of Sundry Hull claims are:

(1) A final survey Report *inter alia* incorporating the following :

   (a) Name of the registered owner of the vessel.

   (b) Identity of the vessel including registration details. License particulars including validity thereof wherever applicable.

   (c) The details of loss suffered.

   (d) The Surveyor's observation on the alleged circumstances of the loss.

   (e) The reasonable probability of the alleged circumstances giving rise to the losses noticed and/or claimed.

(f) Quantification of repairs/replacement cost, Salvage, Sue and labour etc. Where applicable.

(g) Cause of loss as per the Perils Clause of the Policy and the deposit to be collected by the steamer.

In lieu of cash deposit, steamer companies often accept unlimited guarantee of the Insurance Company covering the goods.

Documents for General Average Claims

1. Original Policy or certificate of insurance duly endorsed.
2. Bill of Lading (signed copy)
3. Invoice (original or signed copy)
4. A copy of Notice declaring General Average by the Shipowner/Agent.
5. General Average Deposit Receipt (GADR) on the original Lloyds form duly endorsed.

(GADR indicates the name of the steamer, details of the casualty, the Bill of Lading no., the provisional net arrived value of the goods, description of the goods, the name of the GA Adjusters, the amount of the deposit by the consignees etc.)

General Average Guarantee and Counter Guarantee

As an alternative to cash deposit, ship owners are willing to accept a Guarantee from a bank or if the goods are insured from the insurers. Insurers grant this Guarantee on the behalf of the insured in terms of which they agree to pay the General Average Contribution. In such cases, a Counter Guarantee is obtained from the insured. The Counter Guarantee is required because the General Average adjustment may be based on a contributory value of the cargo which may be higher than its insured value.

Letter of Transfer

This letter is signed by the consignees whereby they:

(i) surrender their rights in respect of the deposit paid to ship owners by the insurers;

(ii) agree to transfer the deposit amount to the credit of the insurers;

(iii) authorize the insurers to receive from the ship owners the difference between the amount of general average as adjusted and the amount of the deposit;

(iv) undertake to refund to the insurers any sum deducted by the ship owners from the deposit which may not be recoverable under the insurance policy; and

(v) undertake to repay to the insurers, if the contributory value exceeds the insured value the proportion of general average applying to such value.

If it is reported that the General Average Act has included sacrifice of cargo, then the consignee clear the damaged cargo only after the General Average Survey is conducted by the ship's Surveyors.

9.8.2 Consignments by Rail/Road

In the case of sea/air/multi-modal transport/postal claims, the insured has to furnish evidence of: (1) insurance, (2) transit, (3) value and (4) loss. The following documents are required to be submitted to insurers in support of claims under rail/road transit policies:

General Documents

1. Original policy or certificate of insurance duly endorsed.
2. Invoice (original or copy)/packing list/weight specification.
3. Independent Surveyor's Report, if any.
4. Letter of Subrogation (if recovery is possible).

Other Documents Depending on the Nature of Claim

1. Original Railway Receipt (Non-delivery cases)
2. Copy of the Railway Receipt (damage claim)
3. Original Consignment Note (Non-delivery cases–Road transit claims)
4. A copy of the Consignment Note (Damage claim–Road transit claims)
5. 'Non-delivery' or 'Partial delivery' certificate from the Railways/Road Transport Operators.
6. Open Delivery/Assessment Delivery Certificate (Rail/Road)
7. Certified copy of the Remarks in the Railway Delivery Book (Damage claims).
8. Certified copy of the remarks in the delivery Challan (Road Transit Claims).
9. Copy of (*a*) Notice of claim lodged on the carriers (Rail/Road) (*b*) Acknowledgement (*c*) Subsequent correspondence with the carriers.
10. Special Power of Attorney (Rail Transit Claims).
11. Letter of Authority (Rail Transit Claims).

9.8.3 Marine Cargo

Documents generally required for settlement of various types of cargo claims are as under:

General

(a) Original insurance policy/declaration under the open policy duly endorsed by the insured. A letter of indemnity may be furnished if the original is lost.

(b) Original or a signed copy of sale invoice along with packing list wherever is available.

(c) Signed copy of Bill of Lading (in case of sea voyage)/Air Consignment Note (for air cargo/MTD/CTD (For multi-modal transport)/postal receipt for sending by post.

(d) Triplicate or exchange control copy of Bill of entry (to facilitate verification of the date of filing to ascertain whether there has been any delay and also to check duty payment details).

(e) In case of General Average. G.A. Guarantee and Counter Guarantee of original Cash Deposit Receipt with the Letter of Transfer as the case may be. Reference be made to the separate para on G.A.

(f) Letter of Subrogation duly stamped and executed (only where recovery from carriers/other third parties is possible).

(g) Special Power of Attorney (wherever recovery from Railway/other carriers is involved. In other cases as required).

9.9 Summary

Ocean marine insurance is one of the earliest forms of insurance. A contract of marine insurance is an agreement whereby the insurer undertakes to indemnify the assured in a manner and to the extent thereby agreed, against marine losses, that is, the losses incidental to marine adventure. Marine insurance is used to cover transportation by any of the following modes of transit singly or jointly: Sea, air or land, Inland water voyages, Rail/road, Air and Post. Steps in the procedure for obtaining marine insurance policy are selecting the insurance company, deciding the appropriate type of policy, application to the insurance company, payment of premium, issue of the insurance policy and processing of the policy. Insurance principles applied to marine business are Utmost Good Faith, Insurable Interest, Indemnity, Subrogation, Contribution, Warranties, and Proximate Cause. There are two broad categories of marine insurance: ocean marine insurance and inland marine insurance. Ocean marine insurance can be further divided into four basic classes such as Hull Insurance, Cargo Insurance, Protection and Indemnity (P&I) Insurance, and Freight Insurance. Inland marine contracts can be conveniently classified into five categories: Domestic Goods in Transit, Property Held by Bailees, Mobile Equipment and Property, Property of Certain Dealers and Means of Transportation and Communication.

The various causes of marine losses are Theft Pilferage and non-delivery, Handling and Stowage damage, Loss from water damage and Marine perils. However, maritime frauds are very common. These are categorised such as Scuttling of ships, Documentary Frauds, Chartering of vessels, and Cargo thefts. Marine losses are categorized as Total Loss, Partial Loss, Expenses, and Extra charges. Marine insurance claims are of two broad types–marine hull and marine cargo. Marine Hulls are further divided into three groups, *viz.*, oceangoing vessels and other vessels rated exclusively by the Tariff Advisory Committee, Vessels insured under Builder's Risk Policies, and all the vessels and/or operations of which rates have been provided in Marine Hull Manual under specific Tariffs. In the case of sea/air/multi-modal transport/postal claims, the insured has to furnish evidence of insurance, transit, value and loss.

9.10 Test Yourself

1. Define Marine Insurance. Briefly explain the history of marine insurance business.
2. What are the main features of a marine insurance contract?
3. Explain the procedure for obtaining marine insurance policy?
4. What do you mean by the principle of utmost good faith? Explain how this principle is applicable to marine insurance?
5. How is the principle of contribution applied to marine insurance claims? Illustrate with suitable example.
6. Explain the various causes of marine losses?
7. Briefly explain the different types of marine insurance losses?
8. What do you mean by marine frauds? What are the steps would you suggest to reduce the frequency of frauds?
9. How will you classify marine insurance claims?
10. Explain the procedure of claim settlement in marine insurance.
11. Classify marine insurance.

State whether the following statements are 'True' or 'False.'

1. Insurance on the risks of transportation of goods is one of the oldest and most vital forms of insurance.
2. The value of goods shipped by business firms each year vital forms of life.
3. inland marine insurance can be used to insure fine art, jewellery, fur and other lives.
4. Ocean marine insurance is one of the earliest forms of Aeroplane insurance.
5. Respondentia loans were comparable to bottomary loans, the difference being the subject of the matter.
6. Marine insurance contract being a contract should first satisfy the essential elements of a valid agreement.
7. Insurable interest of the claimant must exist at the time of loss of the cargo
8. The assignment is done by endorsement and delivery.

9. Risk to be covered for insurance.
10. The insurance premium charges may vary from company to company and country to state.
11. The insurance company issues the insurance certificate (in triplicate) as per the declaration given by the exporter.
12. The insured to bound to disclose all material facts to the insurer before the contract is entered into Utmost Good Faith.
13. Marine Insurance Act provides that in the event of "lost or not gain" clauses in marine insurance contract.
14. Now-a-days, cargo and hull policy forms have disformed with "lost or not lost" ....
15. Proximate cause principle implies that the insurer becomes liable to pay for loss if the insured peril or risk is the proximate cause of loss.
16. There are two broad categories of marine insurance: ocean marine insurance and hull marine insurance.
17. Ocean marine insurance is one of the forms of life insurance.
18. Hull Insurance covers physical damage to the ship or outer part.
19. Cargo Insurance covers the shipper of the goods if the goods are damaged or lost.
20. Covered Perils is the fundamental concept of freight insurance.
21. Covered peril is the fundamental concept of ocean marine insurance.
22. In marine insurance, the word average refers to a partial gain.
23. A general average is a loss incurred for the common good and consequently is shared by all parties to the venture.
24. In ocean marine insurance, two types of total losses are recognized: formal and informal.
25. There are four types of warranties in marine insurance.
26. Types in marine insurance are express and approved.
27. The types in marine insurance are express and applied.
28. The types in the marine insurance are express and implied.
29. Express warranties are written into the contract and become a condition of the coverage relating to potential causes of an insured event.
30. Inland marine insurance grew out of ocean marine insurance.
31. The various causes of marine losses are: Theft Pilferage and non-delivery, Handling and Stowage damage, Loss from water damage and measurement.

32. Extra charge is Survey fees are payable only if the loss is payable under the policy.

33. Marine insurance claims are of two broad types–marine hull and marine inland.

34. Marine Hulls are divided into four groups.

35. Notice of Abandonment of the vessel/wreck in writing is a prerequisite for a constructive Total loss Claim.

36. As an alternative to cash deposit, ship owners are willing to accept a Guarantee from a bank or if the goods are insured from the insurers.

37. In the case of sea/air/multi-modal transport/postal claims, the insured has to furnish evidence of: insurance, transit, value and loss.

38. Documents generally required for settlement of various types of cargo claims.

39. Ocean marine insurance is one of the earliest forms of insurance.

Choose the Correct answer from the choice given:

1. Insurance on the risks of transportation of goods is one of the oldest and most vital forms of

   (a) Insurance (b) General insurance

   (c) Life insurance (d) All are correct

2. The goods are exposed to damage or loss from numerous transportation

   (a) Perils (b) Hazards

   (c) Both are correct (d) Both are wrong

3. Ocean marine insurance provides protection for goods transported over

   (a) Earth (b) Water

   (c) River (d) None of the above

4. Ocean marine insurance is one of the earliest forms of

   (a) Life insurance (b) Non-life insurance

   (c) General insurance (d) Insurance

5. The bottomary loan was an early forerunner of ocean marine

   (a) Insurance (b) Life insurance

   (c) Non-life insurance (d) All are wrong

6. Actuarial science was not practiced, although the Phoenicians were noted

   (a) Mathematician (b) Physician

   (c) Economist (d) Chemist

7. Respondentia loans were comparable to bottomary loans, the difference being the subject of the

(a) Loan (b) Gain

(c) Loss (d) All are correct

8. During the period 1720-1820, the companies like London Association and Royal Exchange Association enjoyed major marine insurance

(a) Market share (b) Exchange market

(c) Both are correct (d) None of the above is correct

9. Marine insurance cover gives financial protection from total loss or partial damage of sea going ships and

(a) Ships (b) Cargo

(c) Ships and cargo (d) Neither ship nor cargo

10. Sea, air or land these are the modes of

(a) Marine insurance (b) General insurance

(c) Life insurance (d) Non of the above

11. Marine insurance contract being a contract should first satisfy the essential essential element of a

(a) Void contract (b) Valid contract

(c) Both are correct (d) Both are wrong

12. Offer and acceptance is the essential part of the

(a) Contact (b) Agreement

(c) Both are correct (d) Both are wrong

13. Part of the essential contract is are

(a) Offer (b) Acceptance

(c) Consideration (d) All are correct

(e) All are wrong

14. The assignment is done by endorsement and delivery

(a) In marine insurance contract

(b) In general life insurance

(c) In life insurance

(d) All are wrong

15. The indemnity depends on the

(a) Contract (b) Agreement

(c) Consideration (d) Offer

16. There are two broad categories of marine insurance: ocean marine insurance and
    (a) Inland marine insurance
    (b) Hull insurance
    (c) Both are correct
    (d) Non of the above is correct
17. Hull Insurance covers physical damage to the ship or
    (a) Vessel (b) Ships
    (c) Both are correct (d) Both are wrong
18. In ocean marine insurance, two types of total losses are recognized
    (a) Actual
    (b) Constructive
    (c) Actual and constructive
    (d) None of the above
19. There are two types of warranties in marine insurance
    (a) Express
    (b) Implied
    (c) Express and implied
    (d) All are correct
20. The causes of marine losses are
    (a) Theft Pilferage and non-delivery
    (b) Handling and Storage damage
    (c) Loss from water damage
    (d) Marine perils
    (e) All are correct
21. Survey fees are payable only if the loss is payable under
    (a) The policy (b) The policyholder
    (c) Policy owner (d) Policy agent
22. Marine insurance claims are of two broad types–marine hull and marine
    (a) Cargo (b) Claim
    (c) Policy (d) Marine

Fill in the blanks with appropriate word.

1. Insurance on the risks of transportation of goods is one of the oldest and most vital form of ....
2. The value of goods shipped by business firms each year cost millions of.................
3. The value of goods shipped by business firms each year cost millions of transportation ....
4. The goods can be protected by ocean marine and inland marine ....
5. All types of ocean going vessels and their cargo can be insured by ocean..................., the legal liability of ship owners and cargo owners can also be.......................
6. The legal liability of ship owners and cargo owners can also be ....
7. Evidences of marine insurance contract are found in Mediterranean voyages he literature of .... also indicates the charging of prime for .... policies.
8. .... the Marine Insurance (Gambling Policies) Act was adopted and the modest pattern of .... regulation was set as it is in substance today.
9. The most dominated UK Marine Insurance market includes players like .... mutual association and affiliates of non UK based.....................
10. Section 3 of the Marine Insurance Act,............ defines a contract of marine insurance as an insurance cover for marine cargo, air cargo and ....
11. Marine insurance contract being a contract should first satisfy the essential elements of a...............
12. The insurance company also known as .... who assume the liability when the loss takes place.
13. A Marine Insurance Policy can be assigned either before or after the ....
14. The assignment is done by endorsement and ....
15. General insurance business in India is, the monopoly of General Insurance..............
16. The insurance premium charges may vary from company to company and................. to ....
17. The exporter submits the original policy to the bank with his other ....
18. The second copy of the policy is sent to the importer and the third copy is retained, by the exporter for his own ....

19. The insured to bound to disclose all material facts to the .... before the contract is entered into.

20. Marine Insurance Act provides that in the event of .... clauses in marine insurance contract.

21. The indemnity depends on the ....

22. Proximate cause principle implies that the insurer becomes liable to pay for loss if the insured .... or .... is the proximate cause of ....

23. There are .... broad categories of marine insurance.

24. Ocean marine insurance is one of the forms of ....

25. Hull Insurance covers physical damage to the .... or ....

26. Cargo Insurance covers the shipper of the goods if the goods are ....or ....

27. In marine insurance, the word average refers to a partial ....

28. A general average is a .... incurred for the common good and consequently is shared by all parties to the ....

29. In ocean marine insurance, ... types of total losses are recognized.

30. There are .... types of warranties in marine insurance.

31. This principle implies that the insurer becomes liable to pay for loss if the insured peril or risk is the .... cause of loss.

32. Inland marine insurance grew out of ocean marine ....

33. Section 56 of the Act provides that any loss other than a total loss is a ....

34. Section 65 of Marine Insurance Act defines salvage charges as the charges that are recoverable under maritime law by a salvor independently of ....

35. Marine insurance claims are of two broad types–marine .... and marine ....

36. Notice of Abandonment of the vessel/wreck in writing is a prerequisite for a constructive ....

Module V

CHAPTER 10

FIRE INSURANCE

Learning Objectives

After studying this chapter, one can understand:

- Fire Insurance Contracts
- Fire Insurance Proposals
- Fire Insurance Coverages
- Special Fire Coverages

10.1 Fire Insurance Contracts

Section 2(6A) of Insurance Act, 1938 defines "Fire insurance business" as "the business of effecting, otherwise than incidentally, to some other class of insurance business, contracts of insurance against loss by incidental to fire or other occurrence customarily included among the risks insured against in fire insurance policies."

The contract of fire insurance is similar to other contracts and comes into being when a person seeking insurance protection enters into a contract with the insurer to indemnify him against the loss of property by or incidental to fire and or lighting, explosion etc. There is no statutory enactment for regulation of fire business in India akin to Marine insurance which is governed by the Indian Marine Insurance Act, 1963.

10.1.1 Features of a Fire Insurance Contract

(a) ***It is personal in nature:*** It does not ensure the safety of the insured property. Its purpose is to see that the insured does not suffer loss by reason of his interest in the insured property. So it is personal in nature in the sense that it involves the payment of money if the loss occurs.

(b) ***Cause of fire is immaterial:*** The insurer irrespective of the cause of fire will reimburse the loss due to fire. The doctrine of cause proxima applied unless there is a suspicion of fraud or willful act or otherwise falling outside the scope of the contract.

(c) ***Indivisibility:*** The fire insurance contract covers the fire losses in whole and generally indivisible unless specifically provided by the contract.

10.1.2 Application of Insurance Principles to Fire Insurance

Insurable Interest

Ownership is a conclusive evidence of an insurable interest. Where the property is charged or mortgaged to a financier as security, the financier acquires insurable interest. The insurable interest in fire insurance must exist at the time of cover, continue throughout its currency and should exist at the time of loss. In case the subject matter of insurance is transferred, the policy does not transfer automatically, it must be agreed by the insurer and endorsed on the policy document.

Indemnity

The indemnity for loss or damage suffered is the reinstatement or the market value. In case of property, market value or the reinstatement value is used. However, stocks are valued on the basis of market value. The sum insured should always represent the true value of the property.

Utmost Good Faith

The insured is bound to disclose all material facts to the insurer, which have a bearing on the contract. If the subject matter of insurance is materially altered, the insured should give notice the insurer immediately. The guiding principle states that the insured should assume as if uninsured all times and accordingly is bound to take care of the insured property always.

Subrogation and Contribution

The insurers are entitled to subrogation rights when they have indemnified the losses to the insured and can proceed to recover the losses from third parties. In case the property has been insured from more than one insurer, the rateable proportion shall apply in the event of claims.

10.2 Fire Insurance Proposals

Acceptance of fire insurance proposals is governed by regulations of Tariff Advisory Committee All India Fire Tariff. A fire insurance proposal generally requires the following information.

Proposer's Details

- Name and address including phone, fax no. and e-mail address.
- Business and its nature of the proposer.
- Paid-up capital of the proposer's enterprise.
- Names of various parties having insurable interest.
- Location of risk to be covered and insurance period.
- Whether the fire insurance was declined by other insurers or accepted subject to special conditions in respect of given proposal.
- Claims experience.

Coverage

- Inclusion of Flood, Cyclone, type of perils and inclusion/deletion of Riot, Strike, Malicious damage, Terrorism.
- Coverage of Plinth and foundation to be covered along with the building.
- Whether Add-on covers required.

Details of Property

- Type of property – commercial/residential.
- If shop whether hazardous goods (as per list) are stored; if so, whether the stock value exceeds 5% of the total stock value.
- If warehouse/godown (not located in a manufacturing unit), details of the goods stored.
- If industrial/manufacturing unit details of goods manufactured and capacity utilisation.
- Utilities
- Height of building.
- Age of building
- Fire Protection devices
- Construction material details.

Declaration is normally required as to the authentication of information furnished.

Risk Inspection Report

Risk Inspection Report is generally prepared to arrive at a correct risk assessment and rate the proposal. The risk inspection generally covers the following:

- Generic Information
- Lighting, Heating and Power

- Process of Manufacturing/Provision
- Exposure Details
- Fire Protection Mechanism
- Management and Supervision of Proposed Risk
- Moral Hazards
- Sum Insured and PML – Adequacy and Efficiency
- Claims Experience
- Risk Improvement Measures
- Conclusion and Comments.

Section 64 VB of the Insurance Act requires that no risk can be assumed unless and until the full premium is received in advance.

Warranties

Class of Construction

"Warranted that the buildings are not of Kachcha construction consisting of walls and/or roofs of wooden planks/thatched leaves and/or grass/hay of any kind/ bamboo/plastic cloth/asphalt cloth/canvas/tarpaulin and the like."

Fire Warranty

"Warranted that Fire Extinguishing Appliances in respect of which discount is given shall conform to the Tariff Advisory Committee regulations and shall be maintained in efficient working condition at all times and an annual maintenance contract with an external agency shall be in force at all times throughout the currency of this policy."

Apart from warranties which are not in printed form the other ones are types in policy. Special clauses, extensions, etc. (if applicable) are also attached and referred to in the Schedule.

10.3 Fire Insurance Coverages

10.3.1 Standard Fire Policy

The fire insurance policy has been nomenclatured Section II of the All India Fire Tariff as Standard Fire and Special Perils Policy. The standard risks covered, add-on covers, exclusions, conditions as prescribed by the tariff are described as follows:

Standard Risks

Fire

Destruction or damage to the property insured by its own fermentation, natural heating or spontaneous combustion or its undergoing any heating or drying process cannot be treated as damage due to fire. For *e.g.*, paints or chemicals in a factory undergoing heat treatment and consequently damaged by fire is not covered. Further, bring of property insured by order of any Public Authority is excluded from the scope of cover.

Lightning

Lightning may result in fire damage or other types of damage, such as a roof broken by a falling chimney struck by lightning or cracks in a building due to a lightning strike. Both fire and other types of damages caused by lightning are covered by the policy.

Explosion/Implosion

Explosion is defined as a sudden, violent burst with a loud report. An explosion is caused inside a vessel when the pressure within the vessel exceeds the atmospheric pressure acting externally on its surface. An explosion may cause fire damage or concussion damage. An implosion means bursting inward or collapses. This takes place when the external pressure exceeds the internal pressure. This policy, however, does not cover destruction or damage caused to the boilers (other than domestic boilers), economisers or other vessels in which steam is generated and machinery or apparatus subject to centrifugal force by its own explosion/implosion. These risks can be covered in a Boiler and Pressure Plant Insurance Policy, which is specially designed to handle these risks.

Aircraft Damage

The loss or damage to the property (by fire or otherwise) directly caused by aircraft and other aerial devices and/or articles dropped there from is covered. However, destruction or damage resulting from pressure waves caused by aircraft travelling at supersonic speed is excluded from the scope of the policy.

Riot, Strike, Malicious and Terrorism Damage

The act of any person taking part along with others in any disturbance of public peace (other than war, invasion, mutiny, civil commotion etc.) is construed to be a riot, strike or a terrorist activity. Any loss or physical damage to the property insured directly caused by such activity or by the action of any lawful authorities in suppressing such disturbance or minimising its consequences is covered. Further the wilful act of any striker or locked out worker, in connection with a strike or a lock out, or the action of any lawful authority in suppressing such act, resulting in visible physical damage by external means, is also covered. Malicious act would mean an act with malicious intent but excluding omission of any kind by any person, resulting in visible physical damage to the insured property, whether or not the act is committed in the course of disturbance of public peace or not. Burglary, housebreaking, theft or larceny does not constitute a malicious act for the purpose of this cover. Total or partial cessation of work or the retarding or interruption or cessation of any process or operations; or, permanent dispossession resulting from confiscation, commandeering, requisition or destruction by order of the Government or any lawfully constituted authority; or permanent or temporary dispossession of any building or plant or unit or machinery resulting from the unlawful occupation by any person of the same or prevention of access to the same, are not covered.

Storm, Cyclone, Typhoon, Tempest, Hurricane, Tornado, Flood and Inundation

Storm, Cyclone, Typhoon, Tempest, Tornado and Hurricane are all various types of violent natural disturbances that are accompanied by thunder or strong winds or heavy rainfall. Flood or Inundation occurs when the water rises to an abnormal level. Flood or inundation should not only be understood in the common sense of the terms, *i.e.,* flood in river or lakes, but also accumulation of water due to choked drains would be deemed to be flood.

Impact Damage

Impact by any Rail/Road vehicle or animal by direct contact with the insured property is covered. However, such vehicles or animals should not belong to or owned by the insured or any occupier of the premises or their employees while acting in the course of their employment.

Subsidence and Landslide Including Rockslide

Destruction or damage caused by Subsidence of part of the site on which the property stands or Landslide/Rockslide is covered. While Subsidence means sinking of land or building to a lower level, Landslide means sliding down of land usually on a hill. However, normal cracking, settlement or bedding down of new structures; settlement or movement of made up ground; coastal or river erosion; defective design or workmanship or use of defective materials; and demolition, construction, structural alterations or repair of any property or ground-works or excavations, are not covered.

Bursting and/or Overflowing of Water Tanks, Apparatus and Pipes

Loss or damage to property by water or otherwise on account of bursting or accidental overflowing of water tanks, apparatus and pipes is covered.

Missile Testing Operations

Destruction or damage due to impact or otherwise from trajectory/projectiles in connection with missile testing operations by the Insured or anyone else, is covered.

Leakage from Automatic Sprinkler Installations

Damage caused by water accidentally discharged or leaked out from automatic sprinkler installations in the insured's premises is covered. However, such destruction or damage caused by repairs or alterations to the buildings or premises; repairs removal or extension of the sprinkler installation; and defects in construction known to the insured, are not covered.

Bush Fire

This covers damage caused by burning, whether accidental or otherwise, of bush and jungles and the clearing of lands by fire, but excluding destruction or damage caused by Forest Fire.

The policy may be extended to cover earthquake, fire and shock; deterioration of stock in the cold storages following power failure as a result of insured peril, additional expenditure involved in removal of debris, architect, consulting engineers' fee over and above the amount covered by the policy, forest fire, spontaneous combustion and impact damage due to own vehicles. In case of a partial loss, Insurance Company shall effect payment for repairs and replacement. In case of policy with reinstatement value clause, cost of reinstatement will be paid on completion of reinstatement subject to overall limit of the sum insured. Insurance company may at its option, also repair or replace the affected property instead of paying for the cost of restoration.

Exclusions

This policy does not cover:

1. 5 per cent of each and every claim resulting from lighting/storm/tempest/flood/inundation/subsidence and landslide including rockslide covered under the policy.
2. Loss destruction or damage caused by war, invasion, act of foreign enemy hostilities or war-like operations (whether war is declared or not), civil war, mutiny, civil commotion assuming the proportions of or amounting to a popular rising, military rising, rebellion, revolution, insurrection or military or usurped power.
3. Loss, destruction or damage directly or indirectly caused to the property insured by:
   - Ionising radiations or contamination by radioactivity from any nuclear fuel or from any nuclear waste from the combustion of nuclear fuel.
   - The radioactive toxic, explosives or other hazardous properties of any explosive nuclear assembly or nuclear component thereof.
4. Loss, destruction or damage caused to the insured property by pollution or contamination excluding:

- Pollution or contamination which itself results from a peril hereby insured against.
- Any peril hereby insured against which itself results from pollution or contamination.

5. Loss, destruction or damage directly to solution or unset precious stones curios, works of art for an amount exceeding Rs. 10,000, manuscripts plans, drawings, securities, obligations or documents of any kind stamps, coins or paper money, cheques, books of accounts or other business books, computer systems, records, explosives unless otherwise expressly stated in the policy.
6. Loss, destruction or damage to the stocks in cold storage premises caused by change of temperature.
7. Loss, destruction or damage to any electrical and/or electronic machine, apparatus, fixture or fitting (excluding fans and electrical wiring in dwellings) arising from or occasioned by over-running, excessive pressure, short circuiting, arcing, self-heating, or leakage of electricity, from whatever cause (lightning included).
8. Expenses necessarily incurred on: (*i*) Architect's surveyor's and consulting engineer's fees and (*ii*) Debris removal by the insured following a loss, destruction or damage to the property insured by an insured peril in excess of 3 per cent and 1 per cent of the claim amount, respectively.
9. Loss of earnings, loss by delay, loss of market or other consequential or indirect loss or damage or any kind or description whatsoever.

The clauses covered above are subject to the normal general conditions of the insurance company.

Add-on Covers

The insurers can issue the standard fire policy as per the New Fire Tariff along with added benefits at the option of the policyholders by charging additional premium. These added benefits or add-on covers are as follows:

- Architect's, surveyor's and consulting engineer's fees (in excess of 3 per cent claim amount).
- Debris removal (in excess of 1 per cent of claim amount).
- Deterioration of stocks in cold storage premises due to power failure following damage due to an insured peril.
- Forest fire.
- Impact damage due to insured's own vehicles, forklifts and the like and articles dropped therefrom.
- Spontaneous combustion.

- Omission to insure additions, alterations or extensions.
- Earthquake (fire and shock) as per minimum rates and excess applicable as specified in the Tariff.

In respect of the above add-on covers. The insurance company will compulsorily deduct 5 per cent of each claim before paying the claim proceeds to the insured.

The standard policies exclude certain perils from the scope of cover. The main reasons for the exclusions are:

(i) To restrict the cover to normal coverage required by the typical or average insured. Personal Accident Policy which provides for the agreed benefits to be paid under certain specified Contingencies, does not cover medical expenses, which can be included on payment of an additional premium. Similarly, Workmen Compensation Policy indemnifies the insured against his liability at law to his direct employees, and provides for the Insureds legal liability to employees of sub-contractor to be included by payment of premium at a tariff rate on the wages payable to workmen of sub-contractor. Similarly, policy can be extended to cover medical expenses, and the diseases specified in Part III of the Schedule C on payment of an additional premium.

(ii) To exclude loss which are of an extraordinary or catastrophic nature, e.g., the earthquake peril for locations involving storage of materials, and industrial/ manufacturing risks. In view of concentration of material, property involving huge sum insured, perils of earthquake, and/or flood etc. Could cause losses which might assume proportion of a catastrophe. While for residences, offices, shops and for Tiny Sector, etc., these perils (of earthquake and flood, etc.) are offered as in-built perils, as for these risks, perils of earthquake and flood may not cause catastrophic losses.

(iii) To precisely define and clarify the scope of cover. For example, to prevent disputes in the event of a loss which is akin to fire but is not within the meaning of the policy, spontaneous combustion is excluded under fire policy.

(iv) To exclude risks which may be accepted after obtaining more underwriting information or arranging inspection, *e.g.,* flood risk in fire insurance, pollution cover under public liability policy, and cover for exports under Products Liability Policy.

(v) To exclude losses which are convertible under other policies. This eliminates duplication of coverage. For example, the general public liability policy excludes liability arising out of the use of Motor Vehicle, because a Motor Third Party Policy is available. Similarly, Plate Glass Policy does not cover loss of or damage by fire, which can be covered separately under a Fire Insurance Policy.

(vi) To exclude risks which cause losses of high degree of frequency, e.g. the risks of larceny under Burglary (Business Premises) Policy, and shortages, which are discovered at periodic stock taking.

(vii) To exclude loss which are caused intentionally, *e.g.*, suicide under personal accident policies.

(viii) To exclude losses, which are inevitable, *e.g.*, wear and tear and depreciation under motor policies and 'inherent vice' under marine cargo policies.

(ix) To exclude losses which are commercially uninsurable, *e.g.*, war and nuclear risks.

(x) The standard policies may also exclude certain classes of property from the coverage. For example, the fire policy excludes certain classes of property, *e.g.*, documents, coins, paper money, books of account, unless expressly stated in the policy. The intention is to ascertain the existence of such property and, if necessary to include certain classes of property in the coverage subject to special terms and conditions. Similarly curios, works of art, paintings can be covered after obtaining valuation report, from the Director of Museum and stamps collection can be covered on production of valuation certificate from Philatelic Society.

10.3.2 Standard Policy Coverages

The tariff Advisory Committee has prescribed three types of fire coverages, *viz.*, Policy A, Policy B and Policy C.

Policy A

Fire Policy A covers the following perils – (*i*) fire, (*ii*) lightning, (*iii*) explosion/implosion, (*iv*) impact damage, (*v*) aircraft damage, (*vi*) riot, strike and malicious and terrorist damage, (*vii*) storm, cyclone, tempest, hurricane, tornado, flood and inundation, (*viii*) earthquake, (*ix*) subsidence and landslide (including rockslide).

Only Policy A can be issued to cover artisans workshops, bio-gas plants, village and cottage industries, tiny sector or small scale industries.

Policy B

Fire Policy B covers the perils – (*i*) fire, (*ii*) lightning, (*iii*) explosion/implosion, (*iv*) impact damage (*v*) aircraft damage, (*vi*) riot, strike and malicious and terrorist damage. (The cover is similar to Policy C).

The tariff permits exclusion of riot, strike and malicious and terrorist damage perils, with specified reduction in the premium rate under the policy.

Policy C

Fire Policy (Policy 'C') is issued to cover industrial/manufacturing risks and storage risk and covers – (*i*) fire, (*ii*) lightning (*iii*) explosion/implosion, (*iv*) impact damage, (*v*) riot, strike and malicious and terrorist damage.

The riot, strike and malicious and terrorist damage perils can be excluded on specific request with an agreed reduction in the premium rate.

The fire policy C may be extended to cover special perils on payment of extra premium. These special perils are:

(a) Spontaneous combustion

(b) Earthquake (shock and fire)

(c) Storm tempest, flood and inundation

(d) Subsidence and landslide

(e) Accident Leakage or contamination of oil

(f) Spoilage of stock/machinery due to interruption of process of manufacture by insured perils

(g) Deterioration of stocks due to power failure following damage to premises of Public Power Stations

(h) Bursting/overflowing of water tanks, apparatus and pipes

(i) Sprinkler leakage

(j) Bush or forest fire

(k) Subterranean fire

(l) Missile testing operations cover.

Fire Policy A and B (Simple Risks): Fire Policy A and B are issued in respect of dwellings, offices, hotels and shops, educational institutions, etc.

10.4 Special Coverages

Apart from standard coverages, fire, policy may also be issued to meet the specific requirements of clients. Some of these are:

(a) Reinstatement Value Polices

(b) Stock Policies

(c) Consequential Loss Policies.

10.4.1 Reinstatement Value Policies

In this policy, attaching the Reinstatement Value Clause of the fire policy modifies the basis of settlement of claims. Under the latter policy, losses are settled on the basis of market value of the property on the date of fire. This value, which takes into account depreciation, wear and tear, etc. will not be found adequate by the insured who desires to replace the property by a new one of the same kind, type of capacity. *This policy is issued in respect of building, plant, machinery, furniture & fixtures, fittings etc.*

Under the policy, the insurers pay, not the depreciated value (*i.e.*, market value) but *the cost of replacement of the damaged property by new property of the same kind.* The advantages are obvious – during inflationary periods the new reinstatement value is far higher than the depreciated value. The sum insured is required to reflect the new replacement value and not the market value as under the normal fire policy. The reinstatement value clause of the policy places liability on the insured to complete the reinstatement work within 12 months of the loss/damage. Else, the claim will be settled on the basis of normal indemnity (market value). Also of the cost of reinstatement > Sum Insured, the rateable proportion applies.

10.4.2 Policies for Stocks

There are three types of policies for stocks.

Floater Policies

Stocks at various locations can be covered under one sum insured by floater policies, since these policies take care of frequent changes in sum insured at various locations.

These policies may be issued to cover stocks in one amount situated in a more than one specified building situated (1) within the limits of one city/town/village, (2) more than one city/village/town but upto 50 locations, (3) for more than 50 locations in various cities/towns/villages. The Floating policies are not issued in respect of immovable property nor are they issued to Transport Contractors and Cleaning and Forwarding Agents.

Floating policies for risks situated within the limits of one city/town/village may be issued by charging 25% loading over and above the highest rate applicable to any one risk. 50% loading over and above the highest rate applicable to any one risk is charged under Policies covering upto 50 locations in more than one city town/village.

The maximum sum insured at any one location should not be more than 10% of the total sum insured. It is essential that the insured should have a good internal audit and accounting procedure under which total amount of risk and locations can, if required, be established. The condition of average is applied to the limit of sum insured at each location, and also to the total sum insured under the policy.

A policy issued to cover in one amount, more than 50 locations in various cities/towns/villages is subject to the undernoted regulations:

Total sum insured in respect of all locations should not be less than Rs. 3 crores.

The maximum sum insured at any one location should not be more than 10% of the total sum insured.

The address of the locations should be declared to the company, at the inception, and changes advised as and when they occur. However, when locations cannot be identified or change is very frequent, the requirement of specifying address of locations is relaxed, but the number of unspecified locations should not exceed 10% the total number of locations, or 20 locations whichever is lower.

The insured should have a good internal audit and accounting procedure to establish total amount at risk and locations at a particular time.

The pro-rata conditions of average is applied to the limit of sum insured at each location and also to the total sum insured under the policy.

Declaration Policies

Declaration policies are useful to businesses, which face frequent fluctuations in stock quantity or value. Insurance companies can issue these policies subject to the following conditions.

- The minimum sum insured is Rs. 1 crore.
- Monthly declarations based on the average of the highest value at risk on each day or highest value on any day of the month are to be submitted by the insured to the insurer.
- Reduction in sum insured is not allowed under the policy.
- The insured cannot claim refund of premium on adjustment based on the declarations in excess of 50 per cent of the total premiums.
- The basis of value for declaration shall be the market value prior to the loss or as otherwise agreed to between the insurance company and the insured.

Exclusions

Declaration policies cannot be issued in respect of insurance required for a short period stocks undergoing process and stocks at railway sidings. Also, these policies are not sanctioned to (a) Transport contractors and Forwarding and clearing agents, (b) in respect of stock-in-process, and (c) insurances for short period.

Advantages

(1) The premium is limited to the actual amount of risk irrespective of the sum insured.

(2) The liability of the insurer is concurrent under the policy.

(3) Provision for adjustment of premium is an incentive to the insured to effect cover for the maximum amount.

Example

Assume that the sum insured is Rs. 1,00,00,000 and the rate per mille is Re. 1.20. The insured is liable to pay a provisional premium of Rs. 12,000. Now, if the aggregate of monthly declarations comes out to be Rs. 13,20,00,000. The average monthly declaration value will be Rs. 1,10,00,000 (Rs. 13,20,00,000/12). Accordingly, the premium on the policy will be Rs. 13,200 (Rs. 1,10,00,000 × 1.20). The additional premium to be borne by the insured will be Rs. 1,200.

Floater Declaration Policies

These policies combine the features of the floater and declaration policies. All rules relating to Floater Policies and Declaration Policies shall apply here except:

- The minimum premium retention of the insurance company shall be 80 per cent of the annual premium.
- Minimum sum insured is Rs. 2 crore.

10.4.3 Consequential Loss Policies

Coverage and Suitability

This policy is suitable for business establishments and corporate for whom business interruption would mean heavy monetary loss in view of huge fixed costs. Fire consequential loss policy provides cover for expenses and increased cost of working as a result of business interruption following a loss covered by the fire policy. Insurance cover can be taken for the maximum period of the anticipated interruption in the event of loss. In addition, the supplier's and the customer's premises on which the business is dependent, cost of auditors fee (required to submit the monetary claim) can also be insured.

Because of the business interruption following a loss, there may be a reduction in turnover and this may affect the anticipated gross profit. Fixed costs are to be incurred immaterial of the production activity. Consequential loss policy covers reduction in gross profit due to business interruption. The additional expenditure necessarily incurred for avoiding or reducing the fall in turnover during the interruption period is covered under this policy. Also, there are overhead expenses of running the business such as salaries, wages, taxes, interest etc. which continue to be incurred inspite of the interruption of the production.

Premium

Premium chargeable depends on the type of industry/business, the anticipated gross profit, indemnity period chosen and additional covers required. Refund of premium (not exceeding 50%) can be claimed based on the actual gross profit figures as per the audited balance sheet after the expiry of the policy.

Basic fire policy to cover the assets at the business premises is a prerequisite. For claiming benefits under this policy, the *loss* should first be admitted under the fire policy. Amount of gross profit required to be insured, the indemnity period, details of the business premises to be covered and additional covers required shall be provided in the proposal form.

Advantage

In case of major fire loss, the business operations get interrupted resulting in reduced turnover and eventually in loss of profits. It is a well known fact that fixed or standing charges have to be incurred immaterial whether there has been any production or not. All these are not covered by the normal fire policy. It is here that the consequential loss policy comes into force. Thus, for overall protection to the business and its profitability, consequential policy is necessary in addition to the fire insurance policy.

10.5 Summary

Fire insurance contracts of insurance against loss by incidental to fire or other occurrence customarily included among the risks insured. Insurance Principles Applied to Fire Insurance are Insurable Interest, Indemnity, Utmost Good Faith, Subrogation and Contribution. A fire insurance proposal generally requires the information such as Proposer's Details, Coverage, Details of Property, Risk Inspection Report. The standard risks covered under a Standard Fire Policy are Fire, Lightning, Explosion/Implosion, Aircraft Damage, Riot, Strike, Malicious and Terrorism Damage, Storm, Cyclone, Typhoon, Tempest, Hurricane, Tornado, Flood and Inundation, Subsidence and Landslide Including Rockslide, Bursting and/or Overflowing of Water Tanks, Apparatus and Pipes, and etc. The tariff Advisory Committee has prescribed three types of fire coverages, *viz.,* Policy A, Policy B and Policy C. Apart from standard coverages, fire, policy may also be issued to meet the specific requirements of clients. Some of these are Reinstatement Value Polices, Stock Policies and Consequential Loss Policies.

10.6 Test Yourself

1. Define fire insurance. What are the basic features of a fire insurance contract?
2. Write short notes on:
   (*a*) Fire Extinguishing Appliance Discount
   (*b*) Dual Basis of Wages Insurance
   (*c*) Debris Removal Clause.
3. Distinguish between:
   (*a*) Standard Fire Policy and Reinstatement Value Policy
   (b) Floater and Declaration Policies
   (*c*) Originating Factors vs. Contributory Factors.
4. Explain the major principles applicable to fire insurance?
5. Why does fire insurance policies contain exclusion clause? What are the exclusions attached with a fire policy?
6. Briefly explain the different types of policies for stocks.

Choose correct alternative of the following:

1. Which section define fire insurance
   (a) Section 2 (6A) (b) Section 3 (3B)
   (c) Section 4 (2A) (d) Section 5 (4B)

2. Fire insurance business defined through the act of

(a) 1936 (b) 1937

(c) 1938 (d) 1939

3. The contract of fire insurance is

(a) Similar to other contract

(b) Different to other contract

(c) Neither similar nor different

(d) All are wrong assumptions

4. Marine insurance act is/was

(a) 1963 (b) 1964

(c) 1965 (d) 1966

5. Ownership is a conclusive evidence of an

(a) Insurable interest (b) Insurable prize

(c) Insurable cost (d) Insurance

6. The indemnity for loss or damage suffered is the reinstatement or

(a) Human value (b) Valuable life

(c) Market value (d) Time value

7. The sum insured should always represent the true value of the

(a) Property (b) Priority

(c) Punctuality (d) Power

8. The insured is bound to disclose all material facts to the insurer, which have a bearing on the

(a) Agreement (b) Contract

(c) Offer (d) Acceptance

9. The indemnity for loss or damage suffered is the reinstatement or

(a) Market value (b) Vessel value

(c) Cover value (d) Value of the property

10. Stocks are valued on the basis of

(a) Cost value (b) Price value

(c) Face value (d) Book value

(e) Market value

11. Acceptance of fire insurance proposals is governed by regulations of Tariff Advisory Committee

(a) All India Fire Tariff

(b) All India association of fire

(c) All India Marine Tariff

(d) All are correct

12. Apart from warranties which are not in printed form the other ones are types in

(a) Policy (b) Policyholder

(c) Policy agent (d) Performa

13. Lightning may result in fire damage or other types of

(a) Profit (b) Loss

(c) Gain (d) Damage

(e) None of the above

14. Both fire and other types of damages caused by lightning are covered

(a) By the Insurance (b) By the policy

(c) By the agency (d) All are correct

(e) All are wrong

15. Explosion is defined as a

(a) Sudden (b) Violent burst

(c) With a loud report (d) All of these

(e) None of these

16. Impact by any Rail/Road vehicle or animal by direct contact with the insured property is

(a) Covered (b) Insurance

(c) Policy (d) Life

17. Loss or damage to property by water or otherwise on account of bursting or accidental overflowing of water tanks, apparatus and

(a) Pipes are covered

(b) Cover of vessel is covered

(c) Rust is covered

(d) All of these

(e) Non of the above

18. Bush fire covers damage caused by
    (a) Firing (b) Burning
    (c) Bursting (d) None of the above
19. Loss, destruction or damage to the stocks in cold storage premises caused by change of
    (a) Priority (b) Value
    (c) Time (d) Temperature
20. Earthquake (fire and shock) as per minimum rates and excess applicable as specified in the
    (a) Tariff (b) Rules
    (c) Low (d) None of the above
21. To exclude loss which are caused
    (a) Internationally (b) Intentionally
    (c) Intention (d) Internal
    (e) None of the above
22. To exclude losses which are commercially
    (a) Insurable (b) Uninsurable
    (c) Both are correct (d) None of the above is correct
23. The tariff Advisory Committee has prescribed types of fire coverage
    (a) Two (b) Three
    (c) Four (d) Five
24. Tariff advisory committee has prescribed
    (a) Policy A (b) Policy B
    (c) Policy c (d) None of the above
25. Stocks at various locations can be covered under one sum insured by floater
    (a) Policies (b) Life insurance
    (c) General insurance (d) None of the above
26. The maximum sum insured at any one location should not be more than
    (a) 5% (b) 105
    (c) 15% (d) 20%
    (e) All are wrong

27. Reduction in sum insured is not allowed under the

    (a) Policy (b) Insurance

    (c) Both are correct (d) Both are wrong

28. Provision for adjustment of premium is an incentive to the insured to effect cover for the maximum

    (a) Money (b) Time

    (c) Value (d) Amount

29. The minimum premium retention of the insurance company shall be 80 percent of the

    (a) Annual premium (b) Half yearly premium

    (c) Monthly mode (d) None of the above

30. Premium chargeable depends on the type of industry/business, the anticipated

    (a) Gross loss (b) Gross profit

    (c) Both are correct (d) None of the above is correct

State whether the following statements are 'True' or 'False'.

1. Section 2(6A) of Insurance Act, 1938 defines.
2. There is no statutory enactment for regulation of fire business in India akin to Marine insurance which is governed by the Indian Marine Insurance Act, 1966.
3. Feature of a fire insurance does not ensure the safety of the insured property
4. The insurer irrespective of the cause of fire will reimburse the loss due to loan.
5. Ownership is a conclusive evidence of an insurable loss.
6. The sum insured should always represent the true value of the property.
7. The insured is bound to disclose all material facts to the insurer, which have a bearing on the agreement.
8. The insurers are entitled to subrogation rights when they have indemnified the losses to the insured and can proceed to recover the losses from second parties.
9. Acceptance of fire insurance proposals is governed by regulations of Tariff Advisory Committee All India Fire Tariff.
10. Risk Inspection Report is generally prepared to arrive at a correct risk assessment and rate the proposal.

11. Both fire and other types of damages caused by lightning are covered by the life.
12. Explosion is defined as a sudden, violent burst with a loud report.
13. An explosion may cause fire damage or concussion profit.
14. These risks can be covered in a Boiler and Pressure Plant Insurance Policy, which is specially designed to handle these risks.
15. Impact by any Rail/Road vehicle or animal by direct contact with the insured property is covered.
16. Destruction or damage caused by Subsidence of part of the site on which the property stands or Landslide/Rockslide is covered.
17. Gain or profit to property by water or otherwise on account of bursting or accidental overflowing of water tanks, apparatus and pipes is covered.
18. Destruction or damage due to impact or otherwise from trajectory/projectiles in connection with missile testing operations by the Insured or anyone else, is covered.
19. Damage caused by water accidentally discharged or leaked out from automatic sprinkler installations in the insured's premises is covered.
20. Loss, destruction or damage to the stocks in cold storage premises caused by change of temperature.
21. The insurers can issue the standard fire policy as per the New Fire Tariff along with added benefits at the option of the policyholders by charging additional rights
22. To precisely define and clarify the scope of cover.
23. To exclude risks which may be accepted after obtaining more underwriting information or arranging inspection.
24. To exclude loss which are caused intentionally, *e.g.*, suicide under personal Accidental life.
25. To exclude losses, which are inevitable.
26. To exclude losses which are commercially business.
27. War and nuclear risk are the example of commercial insurance.
28. The standard policies may also exclude certain classes of property from the coverage.
29. The riot, strike and malicious and terrorist damage perils can be excluded on specific request with an agreed reduction in the premium rate.
30. The fire policy C may be extended to cover special perils on payment of extra life.

31. Apart from standard coverages, fire, policy may also be issued to meet the specific requirement of policy.

32. Total sum insured in respect of all locations should not be less than Rs. 3 crores.

33. The maximum sum insured at any one location should not be more than 10% of the total sum assured.

34. The insured should have a good internal audit and accounting procedure to establish total amount at risk and locations at a particular time.

35. Consequential loss policy covers reduction in gross profit due to business interruption.

36. Premium chargeable depends on the type of industry/business, the anticipated gross profit, indemnity period chosen and additional covers required.

37. In case of major fire loss, the business operations get interrupted resulting in reduced turnover and eventually in loss.

Fill in the blanks

1. Section 2(6A) of Insurance Act, ... defines .... as "the business of effecting, otherwise than incidentally, to some other class of insurance business, contracts of insurance against loss by incidental to fire or other occurrence customarily included among the risks insured against in ....

2. There is no statutory enactment for regulation of .... in India akin to Marine insurance which is governed by the Indian Marine Insurance.............

3. The insurer irrespective of the cause of fire will reimburse the loss due to ....

4. Ownership is a conclusive evidence of an insurable ....

5. The indemnity for loss or damage suffered is the reinstatement or the market............

6. Stocks are valued on the basis of ....

7. The insurers are entitled to subrogation rights when they have .... losses to the insured and can proceed to recover the losses from...............

8. Acceptance of fire insurance proposals is governed by regulations of Tariff Advisory Committee All India ....

9. Risk Inspection Report is generally prepared to arrive at a correct risk assessment and rate the ....

10. The fire insurance policy has been nomenclatured Section II of the All India Fire .... and ....

11. To restrict the cover to normal coverage required by the typical or average ....

12. To precisely define and clarify the scope of ....

13. To exclude losses which are convertible under other ....

14. To exclude risks which cause losses of high degree of ....

15. To exclude losses, which are ....

16. To exclude losses which are commercially ....

17. The standard policies may also exclude certain classes of property from the...............

18. Only Policy A can be issued to cover artisans workshops, bio-gas plants, village and cottage industries, ... or ....

19. Fire Policy (Policy 'C') is issued to cover industrial/manufacturing risks and .... And ....

20. The riot, strike and malicious and terrorist damage perils can be excluded on specific request with an agreed reduction in the...................

21. Apart from standard coverages, fire, policy may also be issued to meet the specific requirements of ....

22. In this policy, attaching the Reinstatement Value Clause of the fire policy modifies the basis of settlement of ....

23. There are .... types of policies for stocks.

24. Stocks at various locations can be covered under one sum insured by floater .... since these policies take care of frequent changes in sum insured at various ....

25. The maximum sum insured at any one location should not be more than .... of the total sum ....

26. A policy issued to cover in one amount, more than .... in various cities/ towns/villages is subject to the undernoted ....

27. Total sum insured in respect of all locations should not be less than ....

28. The maximum sum insured at any one location should not be more than .... of the total ....

29. The insured should have a good internal audit and accounting procedure to establish total amount at .... and .... at a particular time.

30. Declaration policies are useful to businesses, which face frequent fluctuations in stock .... or ....

31. Because of the business interruption following a loss, there may be a reduction in turnover and this may affect the anticipated ....

32. Basic fire policy to cover the assets at the business premises is a ....

33. In case of major fire loss, the business operations get interrupted resulting in reduced turnover and eventually in ....

34. All these are not covered by the normal ....

35. It is here that the consequential loss policy comes into ....

CHAPTER 11

REINSURANCE

Learning Objectives

After studying this chapter, one can understand:

- Fire Reinsurance – An Illustration
- Introduction to Reinsurance
- Role of the Reinsurers
- Techniques of Reinsurance
- Nature of Reinsurance Risks
- Reinsurance in Indian Perspective
- Fire Reinsurance – An Illustration

Reinsurance of fire business in India is primarily headed by GIC in accordance with the IRDA guidelines (Annexure 11a). The obligatory session (20% quota share) is compulsorily needed to GIC and rest is dealt by treaties. The quota cession is retained in India itself to protect drainage of foreign exchange. The treaties take into account the sum insured and probable maximum loss. This requires classification of risk as illustrated below :

Non-risk Booked Risks: Smaller risks having sum insured less than Rs. 5 crores, which are not normally entered into the risk register maintained for the purpose-retention is 100% in India and reinsurance is affected using excess of loss cover.

Booked Risks: Medium Risks – Sum insured > Rs. 5 crores and PML < Rs. 26 crores.

The risks are entered in the register and are termed as Risk Booked. The underwriting of medium sized risks is as under :

Obligatory	20.00%
Net Account	45.00%
Market fire pool	30.00%

Cos. Fire surplus treaty	0.5.00%
Total	**100.00%**

The Indian market retention for Medium Size Risks is 95%.

Listed Risks : All risks having a PML greater than Rs. 26 crores are classified as listed risks.

11.2 Introduction to Reinsurance

Reinsurance Defined

Reinsurance is a transaction in which one insurer agrees, for a premium, to indemnify another insurer against all or part of the loss that insurer may sustain under its policy or policies of insurance. The company purchasing reinsurance is known as the ceding insurer; the company selling reinsurance is known as the assuming insurer, or, more simply, the reinsurer. Reinsurance can also be described as the "insurance of insurance companies".

Reinsurance provides reimbursement to the ceding insurer for losses covered by the reinsurance agreement. It enhances the fundamental objective of insurance — to spread the risk so that no single entity finds itself saddled with a financial burden beyond its ability to pay. Reinsurance can be acquired either directly from a reinsurer or through a broker or reinsurance intermediary.

Objectives of Reinsurance

Insurers purchase reinsurance for essentially four reasons: (1) to limit liability on specific risks; (2) to stabilise loss experience; (3) to protect against catastrophes; and (4) to increase capacity. Different types of reinsurance contracts are available in the market commensurate with the ceding company's goals.

Limiting Liability

By providing a mechanism in which companies limit loss exposure to levels commensurate with net assets, reinsurance allows insurance companies to offer coverage limits considerably higher than they could otherwise provide. This function of reinsurance is crucial because it allows all companies, large and small, to offer coverage limits to meet their policyholders' needs. In this manner, reinsurance provides an avenue for small-to-medium size companies to compete with industry giants. In calculating an appropriate level of reinsurance, a company takes into account the amount of its available surplus and determines its retention based on the amount of loss it can absorb financially. Surplus, sometimes referred to as policyholders' surplus, is the amount by which the assets of an insurer exceed its liabilities.

A company's retention may range from a few lakh rupees to thousands of crores. The reinsurer indemnifies the loss exposure above the retention, up to the

[1] Fire and Consequential Loss, Insurance Institute of India, Mumbai, 2004.

policy limits of the reinsurance contract. Reinsurance helps to stabilise loss experience on individual risks, as well as on accumulated losses under many policies occurring during a specified period.

Stabilisation

Insurers often seek to reduce the wide swings in profit and loss margins inherent to the insurance business. These fluctuations result, in part, from the unique nature of insurance, which involves pricing a product whose actual cost will not be known until sometime in the future. Through reinsurance, insurers can reduce these fluctuations in loss experience, thus stabilising the company's overall operating results.

Catastrophe Protection

Reinsurance provides protection against catastrophic loss in much the same way it helps stabilise an insurer's loss experience. Insurers use reinsurance to protect against catastrophes in two ways. The first is to protect against catastrophic loss resulting from a single event, such as the total fire loss of a large manufacturing plant. However, insurers also seek reinsurance to protect against the aggregation of many smaller claims, which could result from a single event affecting many policyholders simultaneously, such as an earthquake or a major hurricane. Financially, the insurer is able to pay losses individually, but when the losses are aggregated, the total may be more than the insurer wishes to retain.

Through the careful use of reinsurance, the disruptive effects catastrophes have on an insurer's loss experience can be reduced dramatically. The decisions a company makes when purchasing catastrophe coverage (e.g., size of retention and coverage limits) are unique to each individual company and vary widely depending on the type and size of the company purchasing the reinsurance and the risk to be reinsured.

Increased Capacity

Capacity measures the rupee amount of risk an insurer can assume based on its surplus and the nature of the business written. When an insurance company issues a policy, the expenses associated with issuing that policy — taxes, agent commissions, administrative expenses — are charged immediately against the company's income, resulting in a decrease in surplus, while the premium collected must be set aside in an unearned premium reserve to be recognised as income over a period of time. While this accounting procedure allows for strong solvency regulation, it ultimately leads to decreased capacity because the more business an insurance company writes, the more expenses that must be paid from surplus, thus reducing the company's ability to write additional business.

Companies experiencing rapid expansion are particularly susceptible to the timing problem between expenses (which must be debited immediately) and income (which must be credited over time) generated by new business. By reinsuring a portion of the business it writes, an insurance company reduces the problem of decreased surplus. Through reinsurance, the company shares a portion of its underwriting expenses with its reinsurer and reduces the drain on surplus.

Reinsurance also permits the ceding company to expand capacity by permitting the ceding company to take credit for reinsurance on the annual accounting statement it files with state regulators.

If the reinsurer satisfies certain regulatory requirements intended to assure the security of the reinsurance arrangement, the ceding company may count as asset reinsurance payments owed to it on claims it has paid, thus expanding its surplus. The ceding company can also reduce liabilities and loss reserves attributable to the business ceded to the reinsurer.

In addition, the ceding company often receives a ceding commission from the reinsurer as reimbursement for expenses, such as agent commissions and overhead, associated with acquiring the business being reinsured. The ceding commission is added directly to the ceding company's surplus, thus increasing it further.

Another type of reinsurance transaction, which may affect surplus, is known as *loss portfolio transfer*. In such an arrangement, one insurer cedes to another insurer its reserves for incurred but unpaid losses and loss adjustment expenses. Typically, these reserves are associated with a particular class or line of business, such as medical malpractices. The ceding insurer transfers cash to the assuming insurer equal to the assuming insurer's estimate of the present value of these liabilities, plus an amount the reinsurer may require to carry the additional risks involved in the transfer.

In addition, reinsurers often provide insurers with a variety of other services. Some reinsurers provide guidance to insurers in underwriting, claims reserving and handling investments and even general management. These services are particularly important to smaller companies or companies interested in entering new lines of insurance.

In any discussion of reinsurance, limitations of the business must be considered along with the advantages. First and foremost, reinsurance does not change the inherent nature of a risk being insured. Thus, it does not make a bad risk insurable or an exposure more predictable or desirable. While it may limit an insurance company's exposure to a risk, the total risk exposure is not altered through the use of reinsurance.

11.3 Role of the Reinsurers

Reinsurance is governed by the same principles as for insurance. But instead of covering property or casualty risks directly, the reinsurer insures insurance companies. Reinsurance spans the diversity of situations specific to each type of insurance and is consequently more complex and much broader in range, since it covers the whole world. An insurance company issues contracts called *policies*. The insurance company is the direct or primary insurer of an individual or a business. The policy is written in its name, making it liable for all claims arising under the policy. The insured deals exclusively with the insurance company. But the insurance company spreads its risks arising under the policy by transferring all or part of those risks to one or more reinsurance companies.

In the event of a claim, the insurance company must pay to the insured the full amount of compensation due under the policy. It is then up to the insurance company to recoup the sums corresponding to the risk transferred from its reinsurers. At the beginning of each year, the insurance company takes out contracts with one or more reinsurance companies to cover it for policies issued to its customers for the year in question. Reinsurers in turn usually cede a share of the risk they accept to other reinsurers known as retrocessionnaires; this system is roughly equivalent to bank syndicates. To put it differently as discussed in section 30.1, the reinsurer performs three essential services, together with a number of additional services.

First, reinsurance enables direct writing companies to even out their results when major, exceptional, losses occur: a hurricane or an earthquake for instance can seriously affect the accounts of an insurance company. Reinsurance considerably reduces this type of potential imbalance.

Second, insurance companies use reinsurance to increase the maximum amount they are able to cover as primary insurer for any given potential loss or loss category; in other words, their available capacity is increased. As a result, insurance companies can write more risks, or larger risks, without becoming over-extended.

Third, reinsurance also provides insurers with the large amounts of cash needed in the event of a major loss, enabling them to manage their assets safely and profitably.

In addition to the above services the reinsurance companies also provide the following advisory services to their ceding companies:

Formulating the Reinsurance Program

The types of reinsurance cover selected can considerably influence the profitability and solvency of an insurance company.

Support Services

This range from training of technical and administrative personnel to practical assistance in organisation, accounting and data processing, risk inspection and co-operation in claims settlement.

Specialised Services

In certain highly specialised areas such as major public works' projects or death term life insurance policies written on substandard patients, reinsurers are more familiar with the relevant statistic and rates applicable, and they have the permanent capacity available to cover cedants' exposures.

Capital Base

In most of the developing/developed countries laws have been enacted on the minimum ratio of capital to retained premiums needed to transact business. This ratio is referred to as the solvency margin. It means that a dynamic but narrow capital base insurance company must rely heavily on reinsurance in order to grow; reinsurance can in some instances play a more direct role in financing insurance companies. In life insurance, for example, considerable outlays are required to build up marketing outlets and other facilities needed when new types of policies are first issued. Reinsurers are often called on as partners to help finance this type of investment; in turn they are entitled to share in the return on the investment.

Reinsurers are often a source of hard currency for ceding companies in weak currency countries. Many developing nations reinsure imported equipment and machinery in order to secure the hard currency needed for repairs or replacements in the event of damage or destruction.

11.4 Techniques of Reinsurance

The two main types of reinsurance agreements are *proportional* and *excess of loss.*

A reinsurance contract written on a proportional basis simply prorates all premium, losses and expenses between the insurer and the reinsurer on a pre-arranged basis. The proportional approach is used extensively in property reinsurance. Excess of loss contracts require the primary insurer to keep all losses up to a predetermined retention and the reinsurer to reimburse the company for any losses above that retention, up to the limits of the reinsurance contract. In simplest terms, retention is analogous to the deductible a policyholder may have on a personal insurance policy, such as an automobile or homeowner's policy. These are detailed in section 30.33.

The reinsurance coverages can be broadly classified into two — *treaties* and *facultatives.*

11.4.1 Reinsurance Treaties

Reinsurance treaties are a form of comprehensive coverage bought by ceding companies, either directly or through a reinsurance broker, to protect all or a share of their portfolios for a given class of business. All policies covering risks insured under a treaty are automatically reinsured; in other words the reinsurer cannot decline a risk coming under the treaty. Treaties may be either proportional or non-proportional.[2]

Non-proportional Treaty

In this type of treaty, reinsurance cover begins once the amount of the claim exceeds a predetermined amount. Let us imagine a reinsurance treaty for Rs. 400 crores in excess of Rs. 100 crores; this is what reinsurers call a Rs. 500 crores cover with a deductible of Rs. 100 crores. If a loss occurs and its total cost is less than the Rs. 100 crores, only the primary insurer is concerned. If, however, the cost of the claim is in excess of the Rs. 100 crores, the direct-writing company pays its share equal to Rs. 100 crores and the reinsurance company the remainder, up to Rs. 400 crores. The reinsurance premium for this type of business is computed on the basis of the amounts insured under each individual policy the treaty covers, referred to as *portfolio exposure*, and other factors such as previous loss statistics.

Proportional Treaty

In this type of treaty, the reinsurer and ceding company share the premium and losses proportionally. If an insurance company for example takes out a proportional cover for 40% of its portfolio and if the claims amount to a total of Rs. 100 crores, the insurer pays 60%, or Rs. 60 crores and the reinsurer the remaining 40%, or Rs. 40 crores. The reinsurer will have received 40% of the original premium the ceding company charged its insureds, and will pay a percentage of the premiums representing a fraction of the ceding company's expenses incurred in acquiring and managing the business. This is known as the *commission* or acquisition expense.

In most cases, reinsurance companies only accept a share of a treaty. Each year, insurance companies provide their reinsurers with information on intended policies concerning maximum exposures, estimated premium income, classes of business, marketing strategies etc. Before the start of the year, they finalise treaty conditions with the lead reinsurer exclusions, commissions, and so forth. They then invite other reinsurers to accept a share in their treaties, depending on the program announced and terms negotiated.

11.4.2 Facultatives

Facultative insurance is an optional case by case method that is used when the ceding company receives application for insurance that exceeds its retention limit. Facultative treaties are inter company agreements for optional or voluntary reinsurance transactions. Facultative covers are written on an individual risk basis when a primary company insures risks for amounts in excess of its treaty capacity or risks not covered by its treaties. The lead reinsurer assesses each risk individually and, in consultation with the insurance company, sets the rates and terms of the primary cover. Facultatives serve essentially to cover major industrial and civil engineering risks and, for much smaller amounts, insurers' exposure to liability claims. The reinsurer retains the right to accept or reject any business offered by the insurance company.

11.4.3 Reinsurance Arrangements

Quota Share Reinsurance

In this type of arrangement, the reinsurer receives a quota share of both the exposures and the premiums *less* agreed costs incurred by the ceding company in writing the business.

Pro-rata Reinsurance

It states that the reinsurer will assume all risk upto some specific policy and will cede a portion of the risk above the retention limit.

Excess-of-loss Reinsurance

It specifies the extent of reinsurance in terms of losses rather than in terms of liability. Under such a treaty, the ceding company would pay all claims upto a specified amount per event or per period. Any losses over the agreed amount would be paid in full or part as agreed by the reinsurer. This is different from quota and pro-rata arrangements in the sense that agreement does not refer to any specific policy but covers all of the insurer's business. This type of arrangement is in the nature of catastrophe coverage.

Loss Ratio Reinsurance

It provides for reimbursement by the reinsurer when a specific loss ratio is exceeded. The loss ratio is generally the ratio of losses incurred to premiums earned. The loss ratio is generally fixed in such a fashion that it is over the normal one and, at such a level that the insurer could not bear without sustaining severe damages to its financial condition. Therefore, this arrangement is also a kind of catastrophe coverage.

11.5 Nature of Reinsurance Risks

As stated previously, the two major types of reinsurance are proportional and excess of loss. Because the ceding insurer and the reinsurer automatically share all premiums and losses covered by the contract on a pre-agreed prorated basis, there are no characteristics uniquely attributable to the risk associated with proportional reinsurance.

On the other hand, a great deal of uncertainty characterises the risk associated with excess of loss reinsurance. This uncertainty stems from the fact that the level of risk is dependent on the nature of the reinsurance undertaking. In addition to the actual risk being underwritten, reinsurers must take into account the overall stability of the ceding insurer and the layer of coverage on which the reinsurer is being asked to participate.

Reinsurance, particularly excess of loss reinsurance, is characterised by relatively low and unstable claims frequency and very high but also unstable loss severity. Due in part to this unique nature of the reinsurance business, reinsurers may absorb a disproportionate share of total losses. The lines of insurance in which liability is slowest to manifest itself or develop — the "long tail" lines — create the worst problems for reinsurers. By the end of this century, only a small portion of the ultimate liability on reinsurance contracts issued today covering general liability exposures will be known to reinsurers. Into the first decade of the twenty-first century, a significant portion of the ultimate payout on losses will still be unknown to reinsurers. These losses will be adjudicated in the social, legal and economic environments prevailing in the future, but the premiums to pay those losses must be collected now.

Insurance loss costs are determined by a combination of frequency (how many claims per unit), severity (average cost of each claim) and the total number of units insured. Generally, the higher the number of similar units insured, the more reliable the data. This is particularly true in automobile property damage liability insurance. There are many automobiles insured and year to year the frequency of claims is relatively stable.

Evaluating insurance risk depends on the law of large numbers, which is often not applicable to reinsurance. Relevant and credible loss data are often unavailable. Therefore, in contrast to an insurance underwriter, a reinsurance underwriter depends much more on professional judgement and experience to evaluate the nature of an exposure.

General liability insurance contracts traditionally provide coverage for losses occurring during the policy term, regardless of when the loss is reported. This type of contract, called an occurrence policy, leaves the insurer exposed to claims, which may be filed many years after the policy expires. Certain exposures, such an environmental liability, are particularly susceptible to this latency factor commonly referred to as the long tail.

Reporting delays create serious problems for all insurers, but marked differences exist in reinsurer loss development patterns. The retention feature of excess of loss reinsurance is the primary basis for these differences. Many claims are not initially valued at ultimate cost. Because the ceding insurer's reserve is within the retention established in the reinsurance contract, the ceding insurer may not report such claims to its reinsurer. However, when the claim is ultimately paid, it may exceed the retention. It is only at this point, usually after considerable time has passed, that the reinsurer is notified. Reinsurers are trying to mitigate this problem by requiring all serious injuries to be reported, regardless of the insurer's reserve, and by conducting on-site visits to examine claims files to better determine the likelihood of losses under the reinsurance contract.

"Reinsurance is used heavily in commercial lines, which have demonstrated considerable instability over the past several years in frequency and severity of losses and often have long tails. All insurers and reinsurers set aside loss reserves for claims, which have been incurred but not, reported (IBNR). As claims are reported to the company, these reserves are reduced."

Companies use a variety of methods to establish IBNR reserves. Because IBNR is such a major component of reinsurers' reserves, much effort is taken in determining and making these calculations. Despite the use of sophisticated professional techniques, these reserves, representing future loss payments, are extremely sensitive to changes in social, legal and economic environments. Thus, they represent a "best guess estimate" of future loss payments.

If IBNR reserves represent only a small portion of a company's total loss reserves, the impact of these unknown claims on total losses reported on past policies is likely to be small. If, however, IBNR reserves represent a large portion of a company's reserves, the impact on total losses reported on past policies may be significant. Reinsurers, particularly those participating in casualty and workers' compensation lines, fit into this latter category.

The impact of inflation on insurers' claims liability typically results from increases in the cost of living, increases in the number of claims paid and increase in large jury verdicts, which raise settlement costs. Insurers and reinsurers have been hit by all three, but the impact has been more pronounced on reinsurers, because their losses develop much more slowly and may not be capped to a retention limit.

If losses are paid within a relatively short period following the issuance of an insurance policy, inflation has little effect on claims payments. However, in many instances the reinsurer may not become aware for years, sometimes decades, of a loss it will ultimately pay. For this reason, inflation's impact on reinsurers may be dramatic.

During the last decade, retention levels were reached and exceeded with unexpected frequency in nearly all lines of insurance.

11.5.1 The Reinsurance Contract

Based on its business needs, an insurer negotiates with a reinsurer, directly or through a broker, to determine the terms, conditions and costs of a reinsurance contract. Under a reinsurance contract, an insurer is indemnified for losses occurring on its insurance policies and covered by the reinsurance contract. There are no standard reinsurance contracts although two basic types, treaty and facultative, are used and adapted to meet individual insurers' requirements.

Underwriting treaty reinsurance differs greatly from that of facultative reinsurance. Reinsurance treaties automatically cover all risks written by the insured that fall within their terms unless they specifically exclude exposures. While treaty reinsurance does not require review of individual risks by the reinsurer, it demands a careful review of the underwriting philosophy, practice and historical experience of the ceding insurer, as well as a thoughtful evaluation of the company's attitude toward claims management and engineering control and management's general background, expertise and planned objectives.

Facultative reinsurance contracts cover individual underlying policies and are written on an individual basis. Stated simply, facultative reinsurance covers a specific risk. Both facultative and treaty contracts may be written on a proportional or an excess of loss basis, or a combination of both.

A facultative agreement covers a specific risk of the ceding insurer. A reinsurer and ceding insurer agree on facultative terms and conditions in each individual contract. In contrast, a reinsurance treaty is a broad agreement covering some portion of a particular class or classes of business (e.g., an insurer's entire workers' compensation or property book of business). Historically, treaties remain in force for long periods of time and are renewed on a fairly automatic basis unless either party wishes to negotiate a change in terms.

Facultative reinsurance agreements often cover catastrophic or unusual risk exposures. Prior to the 1950's, U.S. insurers made relatively little use of facultative reinsurance and Lloyd's of London was virtually the sole source of facultative coverages. U.S. reinsurers began to compete with Lloyd's for facultative business in the 1950's and today facultative reinsurance plays a major role in the U.S. reinsurance market.

Facultative reinsurance requires substantial personnel and technical resources for underwriting individual risks. Often, facultative business presents significant potential for loss, thus a reinsurer must have the necessary staff knowledge to underwrite each exposure accurately.

Facultative reinsurance contracts are also used to supplement treaty arrangements when treaties contain specific exclusions, such as exposures involving long haul trucking or munitions manufacturing. Insurers may fill coverage voids created by reinsurance treaty exclusions by negotiating a separate facultative reinsurance contract for a particular policy or group of policies.

Certain classes of risks anticipated to develop significant losses may adversely affect an insurer's treaty experience. Although not excluded from a treaty, these risks may be placed facultatively. For example, a primary insurer that may not ordinarily provide commercial automobile coverage might agree, as a service to its insured, to write such a policy as an accommodation. The company may then seek facultative reinsurance to protect its loss experience under treaty agreements. The reinsurer providing an insurer's treaty coverage may not necessarily provide its facultative reinsurance.

Reinsurers also purchase their own reinsurance protection, called *retrocessions*, in the same forms and for the same reasons as ceding insurers. By protecting reinsurers from catastrophic losses, as well as an accumulation of smaller losses, retrocessions stabilise reinsurer results, thus serving the same risk-spreading objectives as the initial reinsurance transaction.

Reinsurance relationships range from the simple to the complex. An insurer may enter into a single reinsurance treaty to cover certain loss exposures or may purchase numerous treaties until the desired level of reinsurance protection is achieved. This process, known as layering, uses two or more reinsurance agreements to obtain desired level of coverage. At the time a claim comes due, the reinsurers respond in a predetermined sequence, as necessary, to cover the loss. Layering of reinsurance coverage is no different in principle than the layering of excess and umbrella coverage by a policyholder, or the purchase of specific risk coverage through a rider on an insurance policy. It is simply a means of securing the type and amount of insurance or reinsurance protection desired by a purchaser.

Certain fundamental principles underlie all reinsurance contracts, regardless of how simple or complex the reinsurance transaction. First, the only parties to a reinsurance contract are a reinsured company and its reinsurer. All contractual rights and obligations run only between these two companies. Second, the proceeds collectible under the reinsurance contract are an asset of the ceding company. Finally, as a contract of indemnification, the reinsurance is payable only after the reinsured company has paid losses due under its own insurance or reinsurance agreements, unless there is an insolvency clause, which allows the receiver of an insolvent insurer to collect on reinsurance contracts.

11.6 Reinsurance in Indian Perspective

11.6.1 Reinsurance Exposure of GIC in a Fire Portfolio

After the nationalisation of insurance business, the GIC was made responsible for reinsurance protection. 20% of the small risks and medium risks in a fire portfolio are currently ceded to GIC. 25% of the listed risks are also ceded subject to a maximum of Rs. 50 crores, In market place, 30% of each risk is ceded to pool and retroceded back which is fully retained by the companies, subject to a monetary limit of Rs. 750 crores Probable Maximum Loss (PML). The net retention of GIC is Rs. 125 crores (maximum) and Rs. 15 crores (Absolute).

11.6.2 Regulation of Reinsurance Business

The apex insurance regulatory body IRDA has issued two sets of separate regulations for general insurance and life insurance business (Annexure 11(A)).

Example

PML	Rs. 1000 crores
Obligatory Cession (20%)	Rs. 200 crores
Ist Surplus Treaty (10%)	Rs. 100 crores
IInd Surplus Treaty (10%)	Rs. 100 crores
Facultative Insurance	Rs. 100 crores
Total Underwritten Rest	Rs. 1000 crores

ANNEXURE 11(A)

INSURANCE REGULATORY AND DEVELOPMENT AUTHORITY
(General Insurance — Reinsurance) Regulations, 2000

New Delhi, the 14th July, 2000

In exercise of the powers conferred by Section 114A of the Insurance Act, 1938(4 of 1938), the Authority in consultation with the Insurance Advisory Committee hereby makes the following regulations, namely:

CHAPTER I : PRELIMINARY

1. Short Title and Commencement

These regulations may be called the Insurance Regulatory and Development Authority (Reinsurance) Regulations, 2000 and are issued in pursuance of Section 114 of the Act.

They shall come into force from the date of its publication in the *Official Gazette.*

These regulations apply to all general insurers transacting direct insurance business.

2. Definitions

'The Act' means the Insurance Act, 1938 (4 of 1938).

'The Authority' means the Insurance Regulatory and Development Authority constituted under sub-section (1) of Section 3 of the Insurance Regulatory and Development Authority Act, 1999.

'Cession' means the unit of insurance passed to a reinsurer by the insurer, which has issued a policy to the original insured. A cession accordingly may be the whole or a portion of a single risk, defined policies or defined sections of business, as agreed in the reinsurance contract.

'Facultative' means the reinsurance of part of or all of a single policy in which cession is negotiated separately. The reinsurer and the insurer has the option of accepting or declining each individual submission.

'Indian re-insurer' means an insurer who carries on exclusively reinsurance business and is approved in this behalf by the Central Government.

'Pool' means any underwriting operation of insurance or reinsurance in which the participants assume a predetermined and fixed interest in all business written subject to agreed scope of business and limits.

'Retrocession' means the transaction whereby a reinsurer cedes to another Insurer all or part of the reinsurance it has previously assumed.

'Retention' means the amount, which an insurer assumes, for its own account. In pro rata contracts, the retention may be a percentage of the policy limit. In excess of loss contracts, the retention is an amount of loss.

'Treaty' means a reinsurance agreement between an insurer and a reinsurer, usually for one year or longer, which specifies the limits of liabilities and terms of reinsurance in respect of a portfolio of business.

Words and expressions used and not defined in these regulations but defined in the Insurance Act, 1938 or the General Insurance Business Nationalisation Act, 1972 or Insurance Regulatory and Development Authority Act, 1999 rules made under this Act shall have the meanings respectively assigned to them in those Acts or the rules as the case may be.

CHAPTER II

3. Procedure to be Followed for Reinsurance Arrangements

The Reinsurance Programme shall continue to be guided by the following objectives to:

(*a*) maximise retention within the country;

(*b*) develop adequate capacity;

(*c*) secure the best possible protection for the reinsurance costs incurred;

(*d*) simplify the administration of business.

Every insurer shall maintain the maximum possible retention commensurate with its financial strength and volume of business. The Authority may require an insurer to justify its retention policy and may give such directions as considered necessary in order to ensure that the Indian insurer is not merely fronting for a foreign insurer.

Every insurer shall cede such percentage of the sum assured on each policy for different classes of insurance written in India to the Indian reinsurer as may be specified by the Authority in accordance with the provisions of Part IVA of the Insurance Act, 1938.

The reinsurance programme of every insurer shall commence from the beginning of every financial year and every insurer shall submit to the Authority, his reinsurance programmes for the forthcoming year, 45 days before the commencement of the financial year;

Within 30 days of the commencement of the financial year, every insurer shall file with the Authority a photocopy of every reinsurance treaty slip and excess of loss covernote in respect of that year together with the list of reinsurers and their shares in the reinsurance arrangement;

The Authority may call for further information or explanations in respect of the reinsurance programme of an insurer and may issue such direction, as it considers necessary;

Insurers shall place their reinsurance business outside India with only those reinsurers who have over a period of the past five years counting from the year preceding for which the business has to be placed, enjoyed a rating of at least BBB (with Standard & Poor) or equivalent rating of any other international rating agency. Placements with other reinsurers shall require the approval of the Authority. Insurers may also place reinsurances with Lloyd's syndicates taking care to limit placements with individual syndicates to such shares as are commensurate with the capacity of the syndicate.

The Indian Reinsurer shall organise domestic pools for reinsurance surpluses in fire, marine hull and other classes in consultation with all insurers on basis, limits and terms which are fair to all insurers and assist in maintaining the retention of business within India as close to the level achieved for the year 1999-2000 as possible. The arrangements so made shall be submitted to the Authority within three months of these regulations coming into force for approval.

Surplus over and above the domestic reinsurance arrangements class-wise can be placed by the insurer independently with any of the reinsurers complying with sub-regulation (7) subject to a limit of 10% of the total reinsurance premium ceded outside India being placed with any one reinsurer. Where it is necessary in respect of specialised insurance to cede a share exceeding such limit to any particular reinsurer, the insurer may seek the specific approval of the Authority giving reasons for such cession.

Every insurer shall offer an opportunity to other Indian insurers including the Indian Reinsurer to participate in its facultative and treaty surpluses before placement of such cessions outside India.

The Indian Reinsurer shall retrocede at least 50% of the obligatory cessions received by it to the ceding insurers after protecting the portfolio by suitable excess of loss covers. Such retrocession shall be at original terms plus an over-riding commission to the Indian Reinsurer not exceeding 2.5%. The retrocession to each ceding insurer shall be in proportion to its cessions to the Indian Reinsurer.

Every insurer shall be required to submit to the Authority statistics relating to its reinsurance transactions in such forms as the Authority may specify, together with its annual accounts.

4. Inward Reinsurance Business

Every insurer wanting to write inward reinsurance business shall have a well-defined underwriting policy for underwriting inward reinsurance business. The insurer shall ensure that decisions on acceptance of reinsurance business are made by persons with necessary knowledge and experience. The insurer shall file with the Authority a note on its underwriting policy stating the classes of business, geographical scope, underwriting limits and profit objective. The insurer shall also file any changes to the note as and when a change in underwriting policy is made.

5. Outstanding Loss Provisioning

Every insurer shall make outstanding claims provisions for every reinsurance arrangement accepted on the basis of loss information advices received from Brokers/Cedants and where such advices are not received, on an actuarial estimation basis.

In addition, every insurer shall make an appropriate provision for incurred but not reported (IBNR) claims on its reinsurance accepted portfolio on actuarial estimation basis.

INSURANCE REGULATORY AND DEVELOPMENT AUTHORITY (Life Insurance – Reinsurance) Regulations, 2000

New Delhi, the 22nd December, 2000

In exercise of the powers conferred by Section 114A of the Insurance Act, 1938, read with Sections 14 and 26 of the Insurance Regulatory and Development Authority Act, 1999, the Authority, in consultation with the Insurance Advisory Committee hereby makes the following regulations, namely:

1. Short Title and Commencement

(1) These regulations may be called the Insurance Regulatory and Development Authority (Life Insurance - Reinsurance) Regulations, 2000.

(2) They shall come into force on the date of their notification in the *Official Gazette.*

2. Definitions

In these regulations, unless the context otherwise requires:

(*a*) *'Act'* means the Insurance Act 1938 (4 of 1938);

(*b*) *'Authority'* means the Insurance Regulatory and Development Authority established under sub-section (1) of Section 3 of the Insurance Regulatory and Development Authority Act 1999 (41 of 1999);

(*c*) *'Retention'* means the amount of risk which an insurer assumes for his own account.

(*d*) Words and expressions used and not defined in these regulations but defined in the Insurance Act, 1938 (4 of 1938) or Insurance Regulatory and Development Authority Act, 1999 (41 of 1999), shall have the meanings respectively assigned to them in those Acts as the case may be.

3. Procedure to be Followed for Reinsurance Arrangements

Every life insurer shall draw up a programme of reinsurance in respect of lives covered by him.

The profile of such a programme, duly certified by the Appointed Actuary, which shall include the name(s) of the reinsurer(s) with whom the insurer proposes to place business, shall be filed with the Authority, at least forty five days before the commencement of each financial year, by the insurer.

Provided that the Authority may, if it considers necessary, elicit from the insurer any additional information, from time to time, and the insurer shall furnish the same to the Authority forthwith.

The Authority shall scrutinise such a programme of reinsurance as referred to in sub-regulation (2), and may suggest changes, if it consider necessary, and the insurer shall incorporate such changes forthwith in his programme.

Every insurer shall retain the maximum premium earned in India commensurate with his financial strength and volume of business.

The reinsurer, chosen by the insurer, shall enjoy a credit rating of a minimum of BBB of Standard and Poor or equivalent rating of any international rating agency.

Provided that placement of business by the insurer with any other reinsurer shall be with the prior approval of the Authority.

Provided further that no programme of reinsurance shall be on original premium basis unless the Authority approves such programme.

Provided further that no life insurer shall have reinsurance treaty arrangement with its promoter company or its associate/group company, except on terms which are commercially competitive in the market and with the prior approval of the Authority, which shall be final and binding.

Every insurer shall submit to the Authority statistics relating to its reinsurance transactions in such forms as it may specify, together with its annual accounts.

4. Inward Reinsurance Business

Every insurer who wants to write inward reinsurance business shall adopt a well-defined underwriting policy for underwriting inward reinsurance business.

An insurer shall ensure that decisions on acceptance of reinsurance business are made by persons with adequate knowledge and experience, preferably in consultation with the insurer's appointed actuary.

An insurer shall file with the Authority, at least forty five days before the commencement of each financial year, a note on its underwriting policy indicating the classes of business, geographical scope, underwriting limits and profit objective.

An insurer shall also file any changes to the note referred to in sub-regulation (3) as and when a change in underwriting policy is made.

11.7 Key Terms

- Reinsurance
- Surplus
- Treaty
- Reinsurance Arrangements
- Facultatives
- Risk Register
- Obligatory Cessions

11.8 Suggested Readings

- Irving Pfeffer and David, R., Klock, *Perspectives on Insurance,* Prentice Hall, Englewood Ciffs, 1974.
- *Fire and Consequential Loss Insurance,* Insurance Institute of India, Mumbai, 2004.
- www.globalreinsurance.com.
- www.reinsurance.org
- www.re-world.com

11.9 Test Yourself

1. Define Reinsurance. Briefly explain the various objectives of reinsurance.
2. "Reinsurance is a well-thought well-structured expense for insurance company? Explain.
3. Distinguish between Facultatives and Treaties.
4. Give an example of how fire exposure worth Rs. 5,000 crores would be reinsurance using various arrangement.

Choose correct alternative of the following:

1. Reinsurance can also be described as the "insurance of insurance

   (a) Companies (b) Product

   (c) Man (d) All are correct

   (e) None of the above is correct

2. Reinsurance provides reimbursement to the ceding insurer for losses covered by the reinsurance

(a) Contract (b) Agreement

(c) Both are correct (d) Both are wrong

3. Insurers purchase reinsurance for essentially

(a) Two reasons (b) Three reasons

(c) Four reasons (d) Five reasons

4. Insurers purchase reinsurance for essentially reasons

(a) To limit liability on specific risks

(b) To protect against catastrophes

(c) To increase capacity

(d) All are correct

(e) All are wrong

5. A company's retention may range from a few

(a) Rupees lakh to thousands of crore

(b) Rupees thousand to lakh

(c) Rupees lakh to crore

(d) All are correct

(e) None of the above is correct

6. Insurers often seek to reduce the wide swings in profit and loss margins inherent to the insurance

(a) Company (b) Interest

(c) Business (d) All are correct

(e) All are wrong

7. Financially the insurer is able to pay losses

(a) Individually (b) Grouped

(c) Both are correct (d) Both are wrong

8. Capacity measures the rupee amount of risk an insurer can assume based on its surplus and the nature of the business

(a) Written (b) Verbal

(c) Non-verbal (d) All of the above

9. Another type of reinsurance transaction, which may affect surplus, is known as
   (a) Profit portfolio transfer
   (b) Average portfolio
   (c) Loss portfolio transfer
   (d) All are wrong
   (e) All are correct
10. Reinsurers often provide insurers with a variety of other
   (a) Property (b) Insurance
   (c) Life (d) Services
   (e) Marketing
11. In any discussion of reinsurance, limitations of the business must be considered along with the
   (a) Profit (b) Life
   (c) Average (d) Advantage
12. Reinsurance is governed by the same principles as for
   (a) Insurance (b) Non insurance
   (c) General insurance (d) None of the above
13. An insurance company issues contracts called
   (a) Policies (b) Product
   (c) Both are correct (d) Both are wrong
14. The insured deals exclusively with the insurance
   (a) Companies (b) Factory
   (c) Industry (d) None of the above
15. The types of reinsurance cover selected can considerably influence the
   (a) Profitability
   (b) Solvency
   (c) Both profit and solvency
   (d) Neither profit nor solvency
16. Reinsurers are often a source of hard currency for ceding companies in
   (a) Weak currency
   (b) Strong currency
   (c) Semi strong currency
   (d) All are correct

17. The two main types of reinsurance agreements are
    (a) Proportional and anti-proportional
    (b) Excess loss and excess profit
    (c) Proportional and excess of loss
    (d) All are wrong
    (e) All are correct
18. The reinsurance coverages can be broadly classified into two
    (a) Treaties and believe
    (b) Facultative and truth
    (c) Treaties and facultative
    (d) None of the above
19. In this type of treaty, the reinsurer and ceding company share the premium and
    (a) Losses proportionally
    (b) Profit proportionally
    (c) Both are correct
    (d) Both are wrong
20. In most cases, reinsurance companies only accept a share of a
    (a) Treaty (b) Trust
    (c) Faith (d) All are correct
21. It provides for reimbursement by the reinsurer when a specific loss ratio is
    (a) Increase (b) Decrease
    (c) Exceed (d) Enhance
22. On the other hand, a great deal of uncertainty characterises the risk associated with excess of
    (a) Loss
    (b) Profit
    (c) Loss and profit both
    (d) Neither loss nor profit
23. "Reinsurance is used heavily in
    (a) Business lines
    (b) Commercial lines

(c) Non commercial lines

(d) All are wrong

24. Companies use a variety of methods to establish

(a) IBNR reserves (b) FOREX reserves

(c) Both are correct (d) Both are wrong

25. Underwriting treaty reinsurance differs greatly from that of

(a) Facultative reinsurance

(b) General reinsurance

(c) Both are correct

(d) Both are wrong

26. Reinsurance treaties automatically cover all risks written by the insured that fall within their terms unless they specifically exclude

(a) Proposer (b) Prospectus

(c) Exposure (d) Extensive

(e) None of the above

27. Facultative reinsurance contracts cover individual underlying policies and are written on an

(a) Individual basis (b) External basis

(c) Absolute basis (d) None of the above

(e) All are correct

28. A facultative agreement covers a specific risk of the ceding

(a) Insurer (b) Insurance

(c) Policy (d) None of the above

29. A reinsurer and ceding insurer agree on facultative terms and conditions in each individual

(a) Agreement (b) Consideration

(c) Offer (d) Contract

30. Facultative reinsurance agreements often cover catastrophic or unusual risk

(a) Exposures (b) Proposer

(c) Priority (d) None of the above

31. Reinsurance relationships range from the simple to the

(a) Complex (b) Mixed

(c) Unique (d) All are correct

32. After the nationalisation of insurance business, the GIC was made responsible for reinsurance

    (a) Life (b) General

    (c) Protection (d) Saving

State whether the following statements are 'True' or 'False'.

1. The obligatory session (20% quota share) is compulsorily needed to GIC and rest is dealt by treaties.
2. he risks are entered in the register and are termed as Risk Booked.
3. Reinsurance provides reimbursement to the ceding insurer for losses covered by the reinsurance acceptance.
4. Insurers purchase reinsurance for essentially six reasons.
5. Insurers often seek to reduce the wide swings in profit and loss margins inherent to the insurance corporation.
6. Reinsurance provides protection against catastrophic loss in much the same way it helps stabilise an insurer's loss experience. Insurers use reinsurance to protect against catastrophes in two ways.
7. The insurer is able to pay losses individually, but when the losses are aggregated, the total may be more than the man wishes to retain.
8. Through the careful use of reinsurance, the disruptive effects catastrophes have on an insurer's loss experience can be increase dramatically.
9. Capacity measures the rupee amount of risk an insurer can assume based on its surplus and the nature of the written bibliography
10. Through reinsurance, the company shares a portion of its underwriting expenses with its reinsurer and reduces the drain on surplus..
11. Another type of reinsurance transaction, which may affect surplus, is known as *loss portfolio transfer.*
12. The services are important particularly important to smaller companies or companies interested in entering new lines of reinsurance.
13. In any discussion of reinsurance, limitations of the business must be considered along with the disadvantage.
14. Reinsurance is governed by the same principles as for reinsurance.
15. An insurance company issues contracts called *product.*
16. The insurance company is the direct or primary insurer of an individual or a business.
17. The policy is written in its name, making it liable for all claims arising under the insurance.

18. The insured deals exclusively with the insurance company.
19. The insurance company must pay to the insured the full amount of compensation due under the policy.
20. Reinsurers in turn usually cede a share of the risk they accept to other reinsurers known as retrocessionnaires.
21. The types of reinsurance cover selected can considerably influence the profitability and solvency of an insurance company.
22. The ratio is referred to as the solvency margin.
23. The two main types of reinsurance agreements are *proportional* and *excess of profit.*
24. The reinsurance coverages can be broadly classified into three technique of reinsurance.
25. Three type classification of reinsurance coverage are treaties, facultatives and savings.
26. Reinsurance treaties are a form of comprehensive coverage bought by ceding companies.
27. In non-proportional treaty, reinsurance cover begins once the amount of the claim exceeds a predetermined amount.
28. In this type of treaty, the reinsurer and ceding company share the premium and losses proportionally.
29. In most cases, reinsurance companies only accept a share of a treaty.
30. Facultative insurance is an optional case by case method that is used when the ceding company receives application for insurance that exceeds its retention limit.
31. Facultative treaties are inter company agreements for optional or voluntary reinsurance transactions.
32. It states that the reinsurer will assume all risk upto some specific policy and will cede a portion of the risk above the detention limit.
33. It specifies the extent of reinsurance in terms of losses rather than in terms of liability.
34. Loss ratio reinsurance provides for reimbursement by the reinsurer when a specific loss ratio is decrease.
35. The loss ratio is generally the ratio of losses incurred to premiums earned.
36. The two major types of reinsurance are proportional and excess of profit.
37. On the other hand, a great deal of uncertainty characterises the risk associated with excess of loss reinsurance.
38. The uncertainty stems from the fact that the level of risk is dependent on the nature of the reinsurance undertaking.

39. Evaluating insurance risk depends on the law of large numbers which is often not applicable in insurance.
40. Relevant and credible loss data are often unavailable.
41. General liability insurance contracts traditionally provide coverage for losses occurring during the policy term, regardless of when the loss is reported.such type of contract are known as occurance psychology.
42. Reporting delays create serious problems for all insurers, but marked closeness exist in reinsurer profit development patterns.
43. The retention feature of excess of gain reinsurance is the primary basis for these differences..
44. Many claims are not initially valued at ultimate cost.
45. Usually after considerable time has passed, that the reinsurer is notified.
46. "Reinsurance is used heavily in commercial lines, which have constructed considerable instability over the past several years in frequency and severity of gain and often have long tails.
47. All insurers and reinsurers set aside loss reserves for claims, which have been incurred but not, reported (IBNR).
48. Companies use a variety of methods to establish IBNR reserves.
49. IBNR is such a major component of reinsurers' reserves, much effort is taken in determining and making these calculations.
50. During the last decade, retention levels were reached and exceeded with unexpected frequency in nearly all lines of reinsurance.
51. Facultative reinsurance contracts cover individual underlying policies and are written on an individual basis.
52. A facultative agreement covers a specific risk of the ceding policy.
53. A reinsurer and ceding insurer agree on facultative terms and conditions in each individual contract.
54. Facultative reinsurance agreements often cover catastrophic or unusual saving exposure.
55. Facultative reinsurance requires substantial personnel and technical resources for underwriting group profit.
56. Certain classes of risks anticipated to develop significant losses may adversely affect an insurer's treaty experience.
57. Although not excluded from a treaty, these risks may be placed facultatively.
58. The company may then seek facultative reinsurance to protect its loss experience under treaty contract.

59. The reinsurer providing an insurer's treaty coverage may not necessarily provide itsfacultative reinsurance.

60. Reinsurers also purchase their own reinsurance protection, called *retrocessions.*

61. Reinsurance relationships range from the simple to the complex.

62. Certain fundamental principles underlie all reinsurance contracts, regardless of how simple or complex the reinsurance transaction.

63. First, the only parties to a reinsurance contract are a reinsured company and its reinsurer.

64. The proceeds collectible under the reinsurance contract are an liability of the ceding company.

65. 'The Authority' means the Insurance Regulatory and Development Authority constituted under sub-section (1) of Section 3 of the Insurance Regulatory and Development Authority Act, 1999.

66. *'Cession'* means the unit of insurance passed to a reinsurer by the insurer, which has issued a policy to the duplicate insured.

67. *'Facultative'* means the reinsurance of part of or all of a single policy in which cession is negotiated separately.

Fill in the blanks:

1. Reinsurance of fire business in India is primarily headed by........... in accordance with the ....
2. The obligatory session (20% quota share) is compulsorily needed to .... and rest is dealt by ....
3. The quota cession is retained in India itself to protect drainage of ....
4. The treaties take into account the sum insured and probable ....
5. Reinsurance is a transaction in which one insurer , for a premium, to .... , for a premium, to Indemnify another insurer against all or part of the loss that insurer may .... under its policy or policies of ....
6. The company purchasing reinsurance is known as the ....
7. The company selling reinsurance is known as the ....
8. Reinsurance can also be described as the insurance of the ....
9. Reinsurance provides reimbursement to the ceding insurer for losses covered by the reinsurance ....
10. Insurers purchase reinsurance for essentially ....reasons.
11. Insurers often seek to reduce the wide swings in .... and .... Margins inherent to the ....

12. Reinsurance provides protection against catastrophic loss in much the same way it helps stabilise an insurer's ....
13. The insurer is able to pay .... individually, but when the are aggregated, the total may be more than the insurer wishes to ....
14. Capacity measures the rupee amount of risk an insurer can assume based on its .... and .... of the business written.
15. Through reinsurance, the company shares a portion of its .... expenses with its reinsurer and reduces the drain on ....
16. The ceding company often receives a ceding .... from the reinsurer as reimbursement for ....
17. The ceding commission is added directly to the ceding company's ...., thus increasing it further.
18. Another type of reinsurance transaction, which may affect surplus, is known as ....
19. one insurer cedes to another insurer its reserves for incurred but unpaid .... and .... adjustment expenses.
20. Reinsurers often provide insurers with a variety of other ....
21. Services are particularly important to smaller companies or companies interested in entering new lines of ....
22. Reinsurance does not change the inherent nature of a risk being ....
23. Reinsurance is governed by the same principles as for ....
24. An insurance company issues contracts called ....
25. The insurance company is the direct or primary insurer of an .... or a ....
26. The insured deals exclusively with the insurance ....
27. The insurance company must pay to the insured the full amount of compensation due under the ....
28. It is then up to the insurance company to recoup the sums corresponding to the risk transferred from its ....
29. Reinsurers in turn usually cede a share of the risk they accept to other reinsurer known as ....
30. Reinsurance considerably reduces this type of potential ....
31. The types of reinsurance cover selected can considerably influence the .... and .... of an insurance company.
32. Reinsurers are often a source of hard currency for ceding companies in weak ....

33. The two main types of reinsurance agreements are .... and .... of loss.

34. A reinsurance contract written on a proportional basis simply prorates all .... , ... and expenses between the insurer and the reinsurance on a prearranged ....

35. The proportional approach is used extensively in property ....

36. The reinsurance coverages can be broadly classified into ....

37. Treaties may be either proportional or ....

38. In this type of treaty, reinsurance cover begins once the amount of the claim exceeds a predetermined ....

39. In most cases, reinsurance companies only accept a share of a ....

40. Facultative insurance is an optional case by case method that is used when the .... receives application for insurance that exceeds its .... limit.

41. Facultative treaties are inter company agreements for .... or .... reinsurance transactions.

42. The reinsurer retains the right to accept or reject any business offered by the ....

43. It states that the reinsurer will assume all risk upto some specific policy and will cede a portion of the risk above the ....

44. It specifies the extent of reinsurance in terms of losses rather than in terms of ....

45. Any losses over the agreed amount would be paid in full or part as agreed by the ....

46. Loss ratio reinsurance provides for reimbursement by the reinsurer when a specific loss ratio is ....

47. The two major types of reinsurance are proportional and ....

48. A great deal of uncertainty characterises the risk associated ....

49. The two major types of reinsurance are proportional and ....

50. A great deal of uncertainty characterises the risk associated with excess of loss ....

51. General liability insurance contracts traditionally provide coverage for .... occurring during the ...., regardless of when the loss is ....

52. Reporting delays create serious problems for all insurers, but marked differences exist in reinsurer loss development ....

53. The retention feature of excess of loss .... is the primary basis for these ....

54. As claims are reported to the company, these reserves are ....

55. Companies use a variety of methods to establish ....

56. The impact of inflation on insurers' claims liability typically results from .... in the cost of living, in the number of claims paid and increase in large jury verdicts, which raise settlement ....

57. During the last decade, retention levels were reached and .... with unexpected frequency in nearly all lines of ....

58. There are no standard reinsurance contracts although basic .... types, treaty and facultative, are used and adapted to meet individual.................... requirements.

59. Underwriting treaty reinsurance differs greatly from that of facultative ....

60. .... reinsurance contracts cover individual underlying policies and are written on an individual ....

61. A facultative agreement covers a specific risk of the .... insurer.

62. A reinsurer and ceding insurer agree on facultative terms and conditions in each .... contract.

63. Facultative reinsurance agreements often cover or .... risk exposures.

64. Facultative reinsurance requires substantial personnel and .... for underwriting individual.......................

65. Certain classes of risks anticipated to develop significant losses may adversely affect an insurer's treaty ....

66. Although not excluded from a treaty, these .... may be placed ....

67. Reinsurers also purchase their own reinsurance protection, called ....in the same forms and for the same reasons as ....

68. Reinsurance relationships range from the .... to the ....

69. Certain fundamental principles underlie all reinsurance .... , regardless of how simple or complex the reinsurance ....

70. .... means the unit of insurance passed to a reinsurer by the .... , which has issued a policy to the ....

CHAPTER 12

HEALTH INSURANCE

Learning Objectives

After reading this chapter, you will be able to understand:

- Basics
- Current Scenario
- Health Insurance Scheme
- Imperative for Health Insurance in India

12.1 Basics

Health insurance is a safeguard against rising medical costs. A health insurance policy is a contract between an insurer and an individual or group, in which the insurer agrees to provide specified health insurance at an agreed-upon price (the premium). Depending upon the policy, premium may be payable either in a lumpsum or in installments. Health insurance usually provides either direct payment or reimbursement for expenses associated with illnesses and injuries. The cost and range of protection provided by health insurance depends on the insurance provider and the policy purchased. There are many health concerns including the following which accentuate the demand for health insurance:

(a) Environmental pollution is causing serious health problems to humans.

(b) The fast spreading AIDS, poisonous gases, various wastes including nuclear waste generated by the people are seriously endangering the life on earth.

(c) A person may face serious monetary problems for the medical treatment and hospitalisations during life.

Now-a-days, most companies give the benefit of health insurance to its employees.

12.2 Current Scenario

Healthcare, with global revenue of over Rs.2.75 trillion is the largest industry in the world. The nation of India with a population of 1000 million experiences a vast inequity that exists in the healthcare industry with barely 3 per cent of the population covered by some form of health insurance, either social or private. During the last 50 years, India has made considerable progress in improving its health status. Death rate has reduced from 40 to 9 per thousand, infant mortality rate reduced from 161 to 71 per thousand live births and life expectancy increased from 31 to 63 years. However, many challenges remain and these are: life expectancy 4 years below world average, high incidence of communicable diseases, increasing incidence of non-communicable diseases, neglect of women's health, considerable regional variation and threat from environment degradation. At any given point of time 40 to 50 million of population are on medication for major sickness. About 200 million days are lost annually. The annual rate (range) of out-patient: rural 30-152/1000, urban 9-81/1000 and for hospitalisation: rural 16-76/1000, urban 5-38/1000.

In India, presently the health insurance exists primarily in the form of Mediclaim policy offered to the individual or to any group, association or corporate bodies. Although, total expenditure on health in India is nearly 6 per cent of the entire GDP, the government spending is less than 25 per cent against the average spending of 30-40 per cent in other developing countries. Penetration of Mediclaim is currently done by state-owned insurance companies, covering only about 2.5 million people i.e. less than 0.50 per cent of the country's population.

The primary health care system in India is managed mainly by the shallow structure of government health-care facilities and other public-health care systems in a traditional model of health funding and provision. But, it is unable to justify the demand for health security for 200 million Indian health insurable population mainly due to service costs being out of the reach of many people, absence of good and effective number of physicians, low rate of education programs, less number of hospitals, poor medical equipment and over all, the poor budget of government towards the health program.

12.3 Health Insurance Schemes

Based on ownership the existing health insurance schemes can be broadly divided into the following categories:-

(a) Government or State-based Systems (including CGHS and ESIS)

(b) Market-based Systems (Private and Voluntary)

(c) Employer provided Insurance Systems

(d) Member Organization (NGO or Cooperative)-based Systems

12.3.1 Government/State Based Systems

The best documented and largest system of health care delivery in India is the diverse network of hospitals, primary health Centres, community health centres, dispensaries and speciality facilities financed and managed by the Central and State local Governments. These facilities are officially available to the entire population either free or for nominal charges. Along with some other networks of village health workers, maternal and child health programmes and speciality disease prevention programmes these public facilities carry out a central role in India's primary health care system. Studies have shown that these facilities are mostly underfunded, understaffed and short of drugs and essential supplies and that they sometimes suffer from low morale and inadequate motivation.

The health facilities made available to the public are managed and operated under the authority of central and state agencies. The state governments mostly own and manage the public sector delivery system and have to bear the costs of operation. But the Central Government plays a major role in the planning, financing and transfer of resources that determine new investment in health facilities and specialised programmes. Much of the funding for health facilities originates from the Union Ministry of Health and Family Welfare and is channelled to the state governments, which retain considerable authority for the spending decisions. Virtually all decisions are made by the central and state governments – including the staffing and supply decisions, with little autonomy for the providers of health care at the lower levels. Over the years, the Central Government has been the main source of funds for the primary health care facilities, whereas the states bear the major responsibility of recurrent costs, especially the costs of running hospitals. This system has added to the overall inefficiency of public health facilities.

12.3.1.1 Central Government Health Scheme

The Central Government Health Scheme (CGHS) was introduced in 1954 as a contributory health scheme to provide comprehensive medical care to the central government employees and their families. It was basically designed to replace the cumbersome and expensive system of reimbursements (Ministry of Health and Family Welfare, *Annual Report 1993-94*). Separate dispensaries are maintained for the exclusive use of the central government employees covered by the scheme. Over the years, the coverage has grown substantially with provision for the non-allopathic system of medicines as well as for allopathic. In addition, the CGHS reimburses patients for part of their out of pocket costs on treatment at the government hospitals and some other facilities.

The list of beneficiaries includes all categories of current as well as former government employees, members of parliament and so on. Since the large central bureaucracy in India definitely belongs to the middle-income and high-income categories, they are likely to make above-average use of health services. The CGHS has been in the recent past, widely criticised from the point of view of quality and accessibility.

12.3.1.2 Employees State Insurance Scheme

Established in 1948, the Employees State Insurance Scheme (ESIS) is an insurance system which provides both the cash and the medical benefits. It is managed by the Employees State Insurance Corporation (ESIC), a wholly government-owned enterprise. It was conceived as a compulsory social security benefit for workers in the formal sector. The original legislation creating the scheme allowed it to cover only factories which have been 'using power' and employing 10 or more workers.

However, since 1989 the scheme has been expanded, and it now includes all such factories which are 'not using power' and employing 20 or more persons. Mines and plantations are explicitly excluded from coverage under the ESIS Act.

12.3.2 Market Based Systems

GIC Mediclaim Coverages

The GIC holds a major share in the market-based health insurance segment. It introduced the standard " Mediclaim" health insurance scheme in 1986, and became operational in 1987. This product was later on modified in 1997 to allow for premium differentials for various age groups meant for both individuals and groups. As on date, the GIC and its subsidiaries offer the following products:

Mediclaim or Hospitalization Benefit Insurance Policy

Suitability

Anyone in the age group of 5 to 80 years can take the policy. Children in the age group below the age of 5 years can also be covered from the age of 3 months onwards provided one or both of the parents are covered concurrently. Higher limits are permitted if the policy is in renewal for the preceding three years. Suitable for persons of any nationality but treatment should be availed of within the country and the claim is paid in Indian currency.

Salient Features

- Provides cover, which takes care of medical expenses following hospitalization from sudden illness or accident.
- Cover extends to pre-hospitalisation and post-hospitalisation for periods of 30 days and 60 days respectively.
- Domiciliary hospitalisation is also covered.

Benefits

- Reimbursement of medical expenses.
- Discount in insurance premium is allowed on family package, cumulative bonus and health check. In case of family package cover, a single member can avail of the entire policy limits.

- Pre-existing diseases not covered.
- The premium paid by a cheque upto a maximum of Rs. 10,000 is totally exempt from income tax.

Domiciliary Hospitalisation

The term means that a patient can be treated at home when he is not in a fit condition to be moved to the hospital or where there is no accommodation in the specialist hospital provided,

1. The treatment was for a period not less than 3 days.
2. The sub-limits of sum insured towards domiciliary hospitalisation are furnished in the sum insured and premium schedules.

Exclusions

- The facility is not available if any illness is contracted within 30 days from the commencement of risk except in case of an accident.
- Any pre-existing diseases.
- Treatment for cataracts, benign prostatic hypertrophy, hydrocele, congenital internal diseases, fistula in anus, piles, sinusitis and related disorders for 1st year of policy.
- All the expenses incurred in respect of any treatment relating to pregnancy or childbirth.
- AIDS or conditions of similar kind.
- Directly or indirectly connected with war or nuclear waste.

Requirements

A completed proposal form. If the prosper is a 'Diabetic', a separate questionnaire completed by the family physician.

Bhavishya Arogya Insurance Policy

Suitability

Bhavishya Arogya is a life term policy where medical benefits are made available after retirement of the insured. Therefore, by paying premiums during the earning period, one can make a provision for medical benefits after retirement. Persons in the age group of 25 to 55 years are eligible for this policy.

Salient Features

- The policy provides hospitalization benefits for lifetime after retirement age of the insured.

- Premiums can be paid in equated annual installments up to the age of retirement.
- Premiums can also be remitted in lumpsum on one time basis. Discount is offered for one time payment.

Benefits

The policy comes into force after retirement and provides for hospitalization and domiciliary hospitalization benefits, following an accident or sickness.

A sub-limit of Rs. 20,000 for any one accident or illness is fixed.

Other Conditions

- The minimum sum to be insured is Rs. 50,000 and can be increased in multiples of Rs. 10,000 as a unit, thereafter.
- For every Rs. 10,000 increase of sum insured, the premium is loaded by 20%.
- Maximum sum insured is Rs. 2 lakh.
- After commencement of the risk (i.e after retirement) cumulative bonus @ 5% for every successive claim free year is added upto a maximum of 50%.
- In case of death of insured before retirement, refund of premium will be at a pre-determined scale and is payable to the nominee/assignee.
- In the event of voluntary cancellation of the policy, the refunds will be 75% of the set scales applicable for death claims, provided there is no claim under the policy.

Requirements

- A completed proposal form.
- Proof of age is necessary as the payments of premiums depends on the age.

LIC Coverages

The Life Insurance Corporation of India introduced a special insurance programme in 1993 which covered medical expenses for only four dreaded diseases. It was withdrawn and introduced subsequently in 1995. At present the modified versions are available in the form of two products viz. Jeevan Asha and Asha Deep. A brief of these plans is as follows:

Jeevan Asha

Features:

- Open ended scheme.
- Covers many surgical procedures.

- Fixed benefit for surgical treatment can be availed twice (subject to conditions).
- Exclusive Double/Triple accident benefit.
- Option to switch over from existing Jeevan Asha plan.

Suitable for:

The Jeevan Asha II plan is apt for people who whose family history tends to show a hereditary lineage of maladies and afflictions that have required major or minor surgery from time to time.

Special Features:

Under the Jeevan Asha plan, the major surgical procedures covered for are:

- Nervous system (non-malignant causes).
- Respiratory system.
- Cardiovascular system.
- Haemic and lymphatic system.
- Endocrine system.
- Ocular system.
- Muskoskeletal system.

Benefits

Survival Benefits:

- 2% of the sum assured paid every second year. Option to get lumpsum benefit for any health emergency at a later date.
- Payment of full Sum assured + Guaranteed addition @ Rs.70/- per thousand sum Assured + Loyalty addition. (Subject to deduction of Survival & Surgical benefits paid earlier).

Plan Parameters:

	Minimum	Maximum
Entry Age (years)	18	50
Sum Assured (Rs.)	50,000	5,00,000
Term (years)	15	25

Mode of Payment: Maximum Maturity Age

Policy loan available: Monthly, Quarterly, Half-Yearly, Yearly,

65 years No

Salary Saving Scheme.

Asha Deep

Features:

Cover the risk of four major ailments namely, Cancer (malignant), Paralytic stroke resulting in permanent disability, Renal failure of both kidneys or Coronary artery diseases where by-pass surgery has been done.

Suitable for:

The Asha Deep II (with profits) policy is best suited for people if they anticipate or have a family history of serious diseases like Cancer, Paralysis, Renal failure and Coronary disease.

Special Features:

During the term of the policy, if the life assured is afflicted by any of the major ailments listed above and the same is established as per rules (in case of Coronary artery disease, the life assured must have undergone the by-pass surgery), the policyholder will be eligible for the following benefits, provided, the policy is in force for the full sum assured.

Immediate payment of 50% of the sum assured.

Waiver of premiums falling due from the policy anniversary immediately following the date on which the conditions for the eligibility to the benefits are established.

Payment of an amount equal to 10% of the sum assured, every year commencing from the policy anniversary falling on or after the date of affliction and ending with the policy anniversary preceding the date of maturity or the date of death of the life assured, whichever is earlier.

Payment of balance 50% of the sum assured and vested bonuses on the date of maturity or on death of life assured, whichever is earlier. The bonuses will be calculated on the full sum assured even though 50% of the sum assured would have been paid earlier.

A lien for a period of one year will be imposed on all policies under this plan. That is, if the life assured is afflicted by any of the four ailments mentioned above and its onset falls within a period of one year from the date of issue of first premium receipt, then the policyholder will not be eligible for additional benefits mentioned under sub-section (a) above.

If the life assured does not get afflicted by any of the diseases mentioned above, the full sum assured and vested bonuses will be paid on the date of maturity or on death of the life assured, whichever is earlier.

Diseases Covered:

Brief description of major ailments covered under this plan with relevant definition (medical terms referred herein will bear meaning as given in the Butterworth's Medical Dictionary).

Cancer (Malignant):

It is the presence of uncontrolled growth and spread of malignant cells. The definition 'cancer' includes leukaemia, lymphomas and Hodgkin's disease.

Exclusions:

This excludes non-invasive carcinoma(s) *in-situ,* localised non-invasive tumour(s) revealing early malignant changes and tumour(s) in presence of HIV infection or AIDS; any skin cancer excepting malignant melanoma(s) are also to be included.

Paralytic Stroke:

(Cerebro-vascular accidents): Death of a portion of the brain due to vascular causes such as Haemorrhage (cerebral), Thrombosis (cerebral), Embolism (cerebral) causing total permanent disability of two or more limbs persisting for 3 months after the illness.

Exclusions:

Transient/Ischaemic attacks.

Stroke-like syndromes resulting from Head injury.

Intracranial space occupying lesions like abscess, traumatic haemorrhage and tumour.

Tuberculous meningitis, pyogen meningitis and meningococcal meningitis.

Renal Failure:

It is the renal failure stage due to chronic irreversible failure of both the kidneys. It must be well documented. The life assured must produce evidence of undergoing regular haemodialysis and other relevant laboratory investigations and doctor's certification.

Coronary artery disease where the by-pass surgery has been actually done:

The use of surgery on the advice of a consultant cardiologist to correct narrowing or blockage of one or more coronary arteries.

Exclusions:

Non-surgical techniques such as the use of either balloon or laser via a catheter introducer through the arterial system are excluded.

Nature of evidence required to establish eligibility for benefits under this plan will be as stipulated by the corporation.

Benefits

Survival Benefits:

Sum Assured and vested Bonus on maturity.

Death Benefits:

Natural: If the life assured is not afflicted by any of the specified ailments, the legal heirs get the full Sum assured + Accrued bonus.

Accidental: Accidental benefits available to the life assured whether afflicted or not afflicted by any of the specified ailments —

Plan Parameters:

	Minimum	Maximum
Entry Age (years)	18	50
Sum Assured (Rs.)	50,000	5,00,000
Term (years)	15	25
Mode of Payment: Maximum Maturity Age		
Policy Loan Available: Monthly, Quarterly, Half-Yearly, Yearly,		
65 years	Yes	

Salary Saving Scheme: Health Polices offered by private players.

Bajaj Allianz and Royal Sundaram have also ventured into the health insurance business last year. Bajaj Allianz is presently offering three products titled (a) Health Guard, (b) Critical Illness and (c) Hospital Cash Daily Allowance Policy. Royal Sundaram is offering Health Shield. The details of these policies are given below:

Hospital Cash Daily Allowance Policy – Bajaj Allianz

Suitability

- Policy provides for the cash benefits in the event of insured person(s) being hospitalised due to sickness or accident. It provides cash for each and every completed day of hospitalisation. It can be taken by anyone in the age group of 3 months to 60 years.

Salient Features

- The Company pays a daily allowance for every day of hospitalisation. The daily allowance can to be Rs. 500/- Rs. 1000/- or Rs. 2000/- per day, at the option of the insured.
- The policy pays for a maximum of 30/60 days of hospitalisation per policy period, irrespective of number of confinements to hospital/nursing home per

policy period. Number of days of hospitalisation shall be selected by the insured.

- A day for this purpose may be a period of 12 hours reckoned from the time of hospitalisation but must include 0300 hours.
- Dependant spouse and children can also be covered under the policy. The benefits payable to the dependants shall be linked to that of insured as above regardless of the fact whether they are employed or not. Further discounts are given if spouse and children are insured.
- There is no limit on the number of children to be covered. The minimum age for the children is 3 months with maximum being 21 years.
- Premium paid upto Rs. 15,000 per annum is eligible for tax benefit under Section 80 D of IT Act.
- In case of ICU admission double the scheduled amount will be paid (maximum of 7 days).
- There is no need to submit medical bills. Only a discharge certificate is sufficient for admitting the claim.
- Annual premium table (Indicative):

Coverage Per day	Proposer Age	Premium (Rs.) for 30 day cover	Premium (Rs.) for 60 day cover
Rs. 500	Upto 25 years	200	240
	Above 25 upto 40 years	220	270
	Above 40 upto 50 years	350	480
	Above 50 upto 55 years	390	520
	Above 55 upto 60 years	470	620
Rs. 1,000	Upto 25 years	280	450
	Above 25 upto 40 years	320	520
	Above 40 upto 50 years	550	1,020
	Above 50 upto 55 years	600	1,120
	Above 55 upto 60 years	740	1,320
Rs. 2,000	Upto 25 years	520	880
	Above 25 upto 40 years	600	1,020
	Above 40 upto 50 years	1,160	2,020
	Above 50 upto 55 years	1,260	2,200
	Above 55 upto 60 years	1,560	2,600

Service tax 5%; Family discount 5%.

Benefits

The policy pays a daily allowance for every day of hospitalisation. The daily allowance depends on the amount selected by the insured. Number of days of hospitalisation is limited to 30/60 days per policy period, as selected by the insured.

Exclusions

1. Pre-existing disease.
2. Treatment not carried out by a qualified Medical Practitioner.
3. Cosmetic and plastic surgery, unless resulting from an accident.
4. Officially recognised epidemics.
5. Suture of skin.
6. Any expense of hospitalisation incurred during the first 30 days of insurance.
7. Dental treatment or surgery of any kind unless due to accident requiring hospitalisation.
8. Procedures concerned with sterilisation or infertility.
9. Treatment arising from or traceable to pregnancy, childbirth including caesarian section.
10. Voluntary medical termination of pregnancy during first 12 weeks from the date of conception.
11. Drunken driving.
12. Sexual diseases.
13. AIDS and related problems.
14. War and nuclear perils.
15. Naval or military or Airforce operations requiring the use of arms.
16. Natural perils like avalanche, earthquake, volcanic eruption or any kind of natural hazard.
17. Epilepsy, fits of any kind.
18. Any sanatoriums, spa or rest cures or long term care or hospitalisation undertaken as a preventive measure.
19. Racing of any kind.
20. Sexual dysfunction, trans-sexual surgery and related services.
21. Physiotherapy.
22. Weight reduction, improvement/enhancement therapy.
23. Connected with aircraft or watercraft or similar craft other than as a fare paying passenger.
24. Consequential loss or legal liability or any kind.

Health Guard – Bajaj Allianz

Suitability

Policy provides for the cash benefits in the event of insured person(s) being hospitalised due to sickness or accident. It also offers you cashless benefit and medical reimbursement for hospitalisation expenses.

Salient Features

- Policy provides for the cash benefits in the event of insured person(s) being hospitalised due to sickness or accident.
- Cashless facility: With Health Guard, the member has access to the cashless facility at various hospitals across India (*Subject to exclusions and conditions).*
- The member can opt for hospitals besides the empanelled ones, in which case the expenses incurred by him shall be reimbursed within 14 working days from submission of all the documents.
- Pre and post-hospitalisation expenses: Covers relevant medical expenses incurred 60 days prior to and 90 days after hospitalisation.
- Cumulative bonus of 5% to your sum assured for every claim free year.
- Family discount of 5% is available.
- Waiver of pre-existing diseases: Pre-existing diseases are normally excluded at the time of taking the policy, however, from 5th year onwards it is covered if the policy is continuously renewed for 4 years with the company and the insured has declared such ailment while taking the policy for the first time.

Benefits

- Policy provides financial assistance in case of hospitalisation following an accident or sickness.
- Policy holder can avail cashless hospitalisation facility in the Networked Hospitals.
- Premiums paid under the policy are eligible for tax rebate under Section 80-D of the Income Tax Act 1961.
- Health check up for maximum amount of Rs. 1,000 at the end of continuous four claims free year.
- Covers ambulance charges in an emergency subject to limit to Rs. 1,000.

Premium Table

Indicative Premium Table: All the premiums are per annum

Age (Yrs.) Sum insured (Rs.)	*3m-25yrs.*	*26-40*	*41-50*	*51-55*	*56-60*	*61-65*	*66-70*	*71-75*
1,00,000	1,023	1,481	2,176	2,436	3,216	3,298	3,373	3,451
2,00,000	1,554	2,587	3,978	4,479	5,964	6,110	6,255	6,585
3,00,000	2,095	3,492	5,552	6,342	8,490	8,697	8,904	9,571
4,00,000	4,544	4,938	7,542	8,951	9,174	10,665	10,919	
5,00,000	5,355	5,820	9,161	10,911	11,184	13,040	13,350	

Other Conditions

- Age from 5-75 years.
- Age at entry: not more than 55 years.
- Children below 5 years can be insured if the parents are concurrently insured with Bajaj Allianz.

Exclusions

The policy is not paid in case of:

- All diseases/injuries existing at the time of proposing this insurance.
- Any disease contracted during the first 30 days of commencement of the policy.
- Certain disease such as hernia, cataract, piles, sinusitis shall be covered after a waiting period of 2 years.
- Non allopathic medicine.
- Congenital diseases.
- All expenses arising from AIDS and related diseases.
- Cosmetic, aesthetic or related treatment.
- Use of intoxicating drugs, alcohol.
- Network Hospitals.

Critical Illness — Bajaj Allianz

Suitability

The policy can be availed by any one in the age group of 6 to 59 for a sum assured between Rs. 50,000 and Rs. 50,00,000.

Salient Features

- Policy provides financial assistance in the event of life insured contracting to any of the covered critical illness.
- The policy covers first heart attack, by-pass surgery (coronary artery), stroke, cancer, kidney failure, major organ transplantation, multiple sclerosis, aorta graft surgery, primary pulmonary arterial hypertension, and paralysis.
- Unlike in most medical insurance polices where settlement is on reimbursement basis, benefits under this plan are paid in advance.
- Expenses like donor expenses in a transplant surgery can be paid out of the amount received under this cover both in India and abroad.
- Claims procedure is simple and all the insured needs to do is submit the claim form along with certificate from the specialist confirming occurrence of the critical illness.
- Premiums paid are exempt under Section 80D of Income Tax Act.

Benefits

The benefit amount is payable as soon as the life insured contracts to any of the covered illness and survives 30 days after the diagnosis.

Premium Table		
Indicative Premium Table — All the Premiums are Per Annum.		
Insured	*35 years*	*45 years*
1,00,000	300	800
2,00,000	600	1,600
5,00,000	1,500	4,000

Recommendations

Statistics have shown a rise in the incidence of life threatening diseases. Advancement of technology and rapid progress made in medical sciences has helped us cure such life threatening diseases. However, financial strain to both the affected person and his/her family is extremely painful. Hence, this policy which provides financial support in such event is recommended.

Exclusions

- Any critical illness for which care, treatment or advice was recommended or which was first manifested or contracted before the start of the policy period, or for which a claim has or could have been made under any earlier policy.
- Any critical illness diagnosed within the first 90 days.
- Death within 30 days following the diagnosis of the critical illness.

- Presence of HIV/AIDS infection.
- Treatment arising from or traceable to pregnancy or childbirth, including caesarian section. Birth defects.
- Occupational diseases.
- War, invasion, act of foreign enemy, terrorism, hostilities (whether war be declared or not), civil war, rebellion and/or revolution.
- Naval or military operations of the armed forces or air force and participation in operations requiring the use of arms or which are ordered by military authorities for combating terrorists, rebels and the like. Any natural peril.
- Consequential losses of any kind, be they by way of loss of profit, loss of opportunity, loss of gain, business interruption.

Health Shield — Royal Sundaram

Suitability

The policy covers hospitalisation expenses following sickness or accident and can be availed by any one in the age group of 90 days to 75 years.

Salient Features

- This is a medical insurance policy providing financial assistance in case of hospitalisation following any sickness or accident.
- Single policy can be issued to cover spouse, dependent children and dependent parents. Family discount of 10% can be availed of, if three persons or more are insured.
- Cumulative bonus: Sum insured is increased by 5% for every claim free year without any increase in premium. However, cumulative bonus is subject to a maximum of 50%.
- Premium paid under the policy, subject to a maximum of Rs. 10,000, is eligible for income tax exemption under Section 80 D of IT Act 1961.
- Policyholder can avail cashless hospitalisation facilities in certain networked hospitals provided pre-admission authorisation has been obtained from the insure/insurer's TPA.
- Policyholder can have online access to family's medical history, illnesses and information on hospitals using unique user id and password on www.royalsundaram.com.

Benefits

- The policy pays for all in-patient hospitalization expenses in case of accidents/illnesses covered under the policy up to the amount of the sum insured, provided hospitalisation is for a minimum period of 48 hours.

- Certain cases which does not require 48 hours hospitalization are also covered such as kidney stone removal, tonsillectomy, eye surgery, D&C and cataract. Cataract is covered only from the second year of insurance.
- Pre-hospitalisation and post hospitalisation expenses for 30 days and 60 days respectively are payable.
- Expenses on maternity are covered after 9 months of inception of cover.

Requirements

- Completed proposal form.

Recommendations

With the corporatisation of hospitals, cost of medical treatment is on the rise, at times making the treatment inaccessible to a common man. This policy enables the policyholder to avail of the best of the treatment without any financial constraints (Subject to sum assured limit).

12.3.3 Employee-Managed Systems

"Employer-managed health facilities", and the "reimbursement of health expenses by employers" are the other means of health insurance in India. Generally, the public sector undertakings and big industrial houses have their own dispensary and hospitals and provide medicines, etc, across the counter, usually within the company premises/township. These include defence services also. Also, educational institutions, particularly universities also provide medical services to their employees.

In addition, there are various medical reimbursement plans offered by employers for private medical expenses in the private sector including commercial banks and autonomous institutions. Also, in some organisations we may find a self-insurance system known as medical benefit or medical allowance scheme. Under this scheme, employees incurring medical expenses are required to submit their claims to their employers for reimbursement, and reimbursements are not linked to their individual contribution. Such coverages generally vary according to the employee's salary or designation. Overall, the performance of these systems in India have been satisfactory.

12.3.4 NGO Systems

Health facilities are also provided by voluntary and charitable or Non-government organisations(NGOs). Some of the important NGOs are Child In Need Institute (CINI), Self-employed Women's Association (SEWA), Streehitkarni and Parivar Seva Sanstha. The health care facilities offered by these organisations are a part of their main objectives. Though, these are not exactly health insurance programmes, yet they have potential to generate awareness and associate themselves with the major health insurers.

12.4 Imperatives for Health Insurance in India

Health insurance in India need an immediate attention in the following areas:

- Focus on public spending on primary and health care services
- Reformation of ESIS and CGHS
- Withdrawal of public services on "ability to pay basis"
- Restructuring of premiums
- Increase in visibility and awareness
- Discourage specific exclusions for disease in health care policies
- Encouragement of health insurance for those specially vulnerable.

12.5 Key Terms

- Heath insurance
- Medical Reimbursement
- Mediclaim
- Health insurance systems
- CGHS
- CSIS
- NGO sponsored systems

12.6 Test Yourself

1. Define Health Insurance. Briefly trace the history of health insurance in India.
2. List the various health insurance systems in India. What is the opinion as to the performance of these systems?
3. Evaluate the medicare plans of LIC and GIC. Do you think that life insurance products can provide an umbrella cover which includes health insurance?
4. Write short notes on:
   (a) Mediclaim policy of GIC
   (b) Healthcare issues in India.

Choose correct alternative of the following:

1. Health insurance is a safeguard against rising
   (1) Medical cost (2) Medical claim
   (3) Medical insurance (4) Health plan
2. A health insurance policy is a contract between an insurer and an individual or
   (a) Policyholder (b) Policy owner
   (c) Group (d) Particular

3. Depending upon the policy, premium may be payable either in a lumpsum or in
   (a) Monthly (b) Yearly
   (c) Installments (d) Half yearly
4. Environmental pollution is causing serious health problems to
   (a) Human beings (b) Humans
   (c) Animals (d) None of the above
5. A person may face serious monetary problems for the for the medical treatment and hospitalisations during.
   (a) Life (b) Policy
   (c) Both are correct (d) Both are wrong
6. Now-a-days, most companies give the benefit of health insurance to its
   (a) Employees (b) People
   (c) Working class (d) None of the above
7. Healthcare, with global revenue of over Rs.2.75 trillion is the largest industry in
   (a) State (b) Government
   (c) Union (d) Capital
   (e) None of the above
8. Based on ownership the existing health insurance schemes can be broadly divided into the following categories
   (a) Government or State-based Systems (including CGHS and ESIS)
   (b) Market-based Systems (Private and Voluntary)
   (c) Employer provided Insurance Systems
   (d) Member Organization (NGO or Cooperative)-based Systems
   (e) All are correct
   (f) All are wrong
9. The health facilities made available to the public are managed and operated under the authority of central and
   (a) Capital agencies (b) Insurance agencies
   (c) State agencies (d) None of the above
10. Own and manage the public sector delivery system and have to bear the costs of
   (a) Operation (b) Performance
   (c) Both are correct (d) None of the above is correct

11. The list of beneficiaries includes all categories of current as well as former government

(a) Employees (b) Worker

(c) Both are correct (d) None of the above is correct

12. Holds a major share in the market-based health insurance segment.

(a) The LIC (b) The GIC

(c) Both are correct (d) Both are wrong

13. GIC introduced the standard "Mediclaim" health insurance scheme in 1986, and became operational in

(a) 1986 (b) 1987

(c) 1988 (d) 1989

14. Anyone in the age group of 5 to 80 years can take the

(a) Policy (b) Premium

(c) Amount (d) Sum assured

15. The treatment was for a period not less than

(a) 3 days (b) 3 weeks

(c) 3 months (d) 3 years

16. The sub-limits of sum insured towards domiciliary hospitalisation are furnished in the sum insured and premium

(a) Policy term (b) Nominee

(c) Installment (d) Schedules

17. All the expenses incurred in respect of any treatment relating to pregnancy or

(a) Child birth (b) Delivery period

(c) Both are correct (d) Both are wrong

18. Bhavishya Arogya is a life term policy where medical benefits are made available after retirement of the

(a) Life (b) Wife

(c) Insured (d) Insurance

19. A lien for a period of one year will be imposed on all policies under this

(a) Policy (b) Plan

(c) Project (d) All are correct

20. Cancer is the presence of uncontrolled growth and spread of malignant
    (a) Cells (b) Body
    (c) Both are correct (d) Both are wrong

21. definition 'cancer' includes leukaemia, lymphomas and Hodgkin's
    (a) Patient (b) Disease
    (c) Both are correct (d) Both are wrong

22. The renal failure stage due to chronic irreversible failure of both the
    (a) Longs (b) Legs
    (c) Eyes (d) Kidneys

23. Non-surgical techniques such as the use of either balloon or laser via a catheter introducer through the arterial system are
    (a) Included (b) Excluded
    (c) Both are correct (d) Both are wrong

24. Nature of evidence required to establish eligibility for benefits under this plan will be as stipulated by the
    (a) Business (b) Organization
    (c) Policy (d) Corporation

25. Sum Assured and vested Bonus on maturity these are
    (a) Survival benefits (b) Death benefits
    (c) Both are correct (d) Both are wrong

26. Policy provides for the cash benefits in the event of insured person(s) being hospitalised due to sickness or
    (a) Health problem (b) Injured
    (c) Accident (d) All are correct

27. There is no limit on the number of children to be covered. The minimum age for the children is 3 months with maximum being
    (a) 21 years (b) 22 years
    (c) 23 years (d) 24 years

28. In case of ICU admission double the scheduled amount will be paid
    (a) Maximum 6 days (b) Maximum 7 days
    (c) Maximum 8 days (d) Maximum 9 days

29. The policy pays a daily allowance for every day of
    (a) Medical (b) Health problem
    (c) Hospitalization (d) All are correct

30. Premiums paid are exempt under Section
    (a) 80 A (b) 80 B
    (c) 80C (d) 80D
31. Health facilities are also provided by voluntary and charitable or
    (a) Non government organisations
    (b) Government organization
    (c) Both are correct
    (d) Both are wrong

State whether the following statements are 'True' or 'False'.

1. Health insurance is a safeguard against rising medical claim.
2. A health insurance policy is a contract between an insurer and an individual or group.
3. Depending upon the policy, premium may be payable either in a lumpsum or in installments.
4. Health insurance usually provides either direct payment or reimbursement for expenses associated with illnesses and injuries.
5. Healthcare, with global revenue of over Rs.2.00 billion is the largest industry in the world.
6. Government facilities are officially available to the entire population either free or for nominal charges.
7. The health policies made available to the public are managed and operated under the authority of central and state government.
8. It was basically designed to replace the cumbersome and expensive system of reimbursements (Ministry of Health and Family Welfare, *Annual Report 1993-94*).
9. Established in 1948, the Employees State Insurance Scheme (ESIS) is an insurance system which provides both the saving and the medical certificates.
10. The GIC holds a major share in the market-based health insurance segment.
11. Anyone in the age group of 5 to 80 years can take the policy.
12. Suitable for persons of any nationality but treatment should be availed of within the country and the claim is paid in Indian currency.
13. Bhavishya Arogya is a life term policy where medical benefits are made available after retirement of the insured.
14. The policy provides hospitalization benefits for lifetime after retirement age of the insured.

15. The policy comes into force after retirement and provides for hospitalization and domiciliary hospitalization benefits,

16. The Life Insurance Corporation of India introduced a special insurance programme in 1993 which covered medical expenses for only four dreaded diseases.

17. The Jeevan Asha II plan is apt for people who whose family history tends to show a hereditary lineage of maladies and afflictions that have required minor surgery from long time.

18. A lien for a period of one year will be imposed on all policies under the plan.

19. Cancer is the presence of uncontrolled growth and spread of malignant cells.

20. Definition 'cancer' includes leukaemia, lymphomas and Hodgkin's disease.

21. Non-surgical techniques such as the use of either balloon or laser via a catheter introducer through the arterial system are excluded.

22. Nature of evidence required to establish eligibility for benefits under this plan will be as stipulated by the business.

23. The policy pays a daily allowance for every day of purchasing.

24. Policy provides for the cash benefits in the event of insured person(s) being hospitalised due to sickness or accident.

25. Health facilities are also provided by voluntary and charitable or Non-government organizations (NGOs).

26. The health care facilities offered by these organisations are a part of their main objectives.

Fill in the blanks:

1. Health insurance is a safeguard against rising ....

2. A health insurance policy is a contract between an insurer and an .... or group, in which the.................. agrees to provide specified health insurance at an agreed-upon price (the premium).

3. Depending upon the policy, premium may be payable either in a .... or in ....

4. Health insurance usually provides either direct payment or .... for expenses associated with illnesses and ....

5. The cost and range of protection provided by............. depends on the insurance provider and the ....

6. Environmental pollution is causing serious health problems to ....

7. A person may face serious monetary problems for the .... and............ during life.

8. Now-a-days, most .... give the benefit of............... to its employees.

9. Healthcare, with global revenue of over Rs. .... is the largest industry in the ....

10. The health facilities made available to the public are managed and operated under the authority of .... and .... Agencies.

11. The state governments mostly own and manage the public sector delivery system and have to bear the cost of.....................

12. The list of beneficiaries includes all categories of current as well as former ....members of parliament and so on.

13. Established in .... the Employees State Insurance Scheme (ESIS) is an .... system which provides both the .... and the................

14. The GIC holds a major share in the market-based health insurance ....

15. .... introduced the standard "Mediclaim" health insurance scheme in 1986, and became operational in ....

16. Anyone in the age group of .... to .... years can take the ....

17. The treatment was for a period not less than............

18. The sub-limits of sum insured towards domiciliary hospitalisation are furnished in the sum insured and premium ....

19. The facility is not available if any illness is contracted within .... from the commencement of risk except in case of an ....

20. All the expenses incurred in respect of any treatment relating to pregnancy or.....................

21. Bhavishya Arogya is a life term policy where medical .... are made available after retirement of the ....

22. The policy comes into force after retirement and provides for hospitalization and domiciliary hospitalization..................

23. The Life Insurance Corporation of India introduced a special insurance programme in 1993 which covered medical expenses for only four dreaded.................

24. The Jeevan Asha II plan is apt for people who whose family history tends to show a hereditary lineage of maladies and afflictions that have required................ or .... minor surgery from time to time.

25. Waiver of premiums falling due from the policy anniversary immediately following the date on which the conditions for the eligibility to the benefits are ....

26. A lien for a period of one year will be imposed on all policies under this ....

27. Cancer is the presence of uncontrolled growth and spread of malignant ....

28. Definition 'cancer' includes leukaemia, lymphomas and Hodgkin's ....

29. The renal failure stage due to chronic irreversible failure of both the ....

30. The life assured must produce evidence of undergoing regular haemodialysis and other relevant laboratory investigations and .... certifications.

31. If the life assured is not afflicted by any of the specified ailments, the legal heirs get the full sum assured and ....

32. There is no limit on the number of children to be .... The minimum age for the children is .... with maximum being ....

33. There is no need to submit medical .... Only a discharge certificate is sufficient for admitting the ....

34. The daily allowance depends on the amount selected by the ....

35. The policy can be availed by any one in the age group of 6 to 59 for a sum assured between Rs. 50,000 and ....

36. Policy provides financial assistance in the event of life insured contracting to any of the covered critical ....

37. Unlike in most medical insurance polices where settlement is on reimbursement basis, benefits under this plan are paid in................

38. Statistics have shown a rise in the incidence of life threatening ....

39. Health facilities are also provided by .... or .... or ....

40. The healthcare facilities offered by these organisations are a part of their main ....

CHAPTER 13

MOTOR MISCELLANEOUS INSURANCE

Motor Insurance originated in U.K. where the first motor insurance policy was introduced into England in 1894 to cover third party liabilities. And in 1899 the policy was extended to cover the accidental damage similar to what is known as comprehensive policy. In India the Motor Vehicles Act was passed in 1939 and in 1946 the third party insurance was introduced compulsorily.

The need for compulsory motor insurance is obvious. There has been a phenomenal rise in the motor accidents in the last 4-5 years. Much of these are attributable to a sudden spurt in the number of vehicles. Every vehicle before being driven on roads has to be compulsorily insured. The automobile insurance policy represents a combined coverage of the vehicles including accessories, loss or damage to his property or life and the third party coverage.

13.1 Overview of the Losses due to Automobile Ownership and Usage

The major sources of loss exposure arising from the automobile accidents are [1]

- Legal liability for harm caused to others as a result of negligence
- Bodily injury
- Property damages and or theft of vehicles

Risk managers realise that insurance should be considered within the context of all available risk management tools. There are several ways to lower losses from automobile accidents:

(1) reduce the frequency and severity of accidents, (2) restrict payments, and (3) redistribute expenses and losses.[2]

Loss Control and Prevention

The loss to the automobile insurance service providers is mainly in the form of claims arising from accidents. Accidents can be minimised by providing better infrastructure in terms of roads, limit on speed and other sophisticated traffic control measures. Also, automobile manufacturers must be encouraged to continuously pursue enhancement of the safety measures in the vehicles.

Globally speaking, there has been a demand for smaller, light-weight vehicles, which has resulted in increased severity of accidents and consequential losses.

Restriction on Claims

Putting restrictions on the insured's claims in the sense the fraudulent claims can be easily detected and effectively reduce the cost to the insurers. Another way is to incentivise the good clients by way of attractive rates and discounts.

Redistribution of Losses and Expenses

The auto liability claims, which frequently arise from driver's negligence, can be tackled through redistributions. In such a mechanism, first the guilty party is to be determined and then the guilty party pays to the suffered party the amount of loss. Such processes are generally channelled through the judicial system.

Automobile Coverages[3]

The coverage for automobiles differs in countries. However, in most of the developed countries following types of coverage are available :

Automobile Liability Insurance

Automobile Liability Insurance protects the insured against the loss arising from legal liability when his or her automobile injures someone or damages another's property.

Medical Payments Coverage

Automobile Medical Payments coverage reimburses the insured and members of the insider's family for medical expenses that result from automobile accidents. The protection also applies to other occupants of the insured's automobile.

---

1 Harrington & Neihaus, *Risk Management and Insurance*, McGraw–Hill, 1999, p. 533.

2 J.S. Triechmann, S.G. Gistavson and R.E. Hoyt, *Risk Management and Insurance*, South-Western College Publishing, 2001, pp. 270-272.

3 Vaughan and Vaughan, *Essentials of Risk and Insurance Management and Insurance*, John Wiley and Sons. Inc., 2001, pp. 435-436.

Physical Damages Insurance

Automobile Physical Damage Coverage insures against the loss of the policyholder's own automobile. The coverage is written under the two insuring agreements (also called as Comprehensive coverage) and Collusion–which indemnifies for collusion losses. Physical damage coverage applies to the insured auto regardless of the default. If the other driver is at fault, the insured that carry collusion coverage has the option of proceeding against the other driver or collecting under his or under policy coverage. In India, the GIC offers two types of policy coverage. Form A policy cover is legally compulsory under the Motor Vehicles Act, while Form B policy is optional, known as comprehensive cover. Both of these are discussed in section 14.3 of this chapter.

13.2 Need for Automobile Insurance[4]

In Indian conditions, the vehicles are subject to many hazards like potholes, open manholes, puddles, untarred roads, traffic management system, poor pedestrian management, absence of footpaths for pedestrians, jaywalkers, increasing number of accidents etc. which accentuate the need for automobile insurance. Some of these hazards are discussed below :

Footpaths

As footpaths are encroached by hawkers, pedestrians have a tough time dodging between vehicles to reach the other end of the road. Large potholes and manholes are a common sight and during the monsoon the situation can get only worse causing untold damage to your vehicle.

Drunken Driving

Drunken driving is another very common feature. Be it a car, a two-wheeler, or even a truck, drunken driving is one of the major reasons for increase in accidents. Though drunken driving is a punishable offence the penalty has hardly proved to be a deterrent.

Reckless Driving

Besides, rash driving by youngsters is another of the dangerous realities that you should consider. Majority of the youngsters drive recklessly caring little for the law, causing serious accidents resulting in loss of life or limb.

Theft

Cases of stolen cars are on the rise. Experts in stealing cars are well aware of the loopholes that can be exploited and accordingly have also been successful in manipulating with the chasis number of vehicles in order that they are not traced.

[4] www. Insuremagic.com/Auto Insurancebasics–Need for Automobile Insurance.htm

Fire

Other than these there is also a danger of fire or theft of vehicle. Therefore, vehicle insurance under such unsafe conditions is a must not only to cover risks towards the owner and the vehicle but also to cover the financial liability that may arise from an accident in which the other party is injured. The cost of repairs that you would have to pay to the other party in case of an accident may be exorbitant. Besides if the accident involves hospitalisation too, the expenses can go through the roof. It would be a great burden if all these costs are borne by the individual. The insurance company can indemnify against such losses and the financial liability arising thereof.

Should Auto Insurance be made Compulsory?

If the auto insurance is not made compulsory, there is a strong possibility that some may not buy these voluntarily. This is because most of them think that the cost of accidents or losses will fall on others or they underestimate the risk of loss. "Economic arguments for compulsory insurance laws in these people to consider more of the costs of their actions when deciding whether to drive, what kind of car to buy, how safely to drive, and so on."[5]

The economic rationale for insurance may be that it affects people's decision to drive. Some people are likely to forgive driving if the insurance is made compulsory since it acts as a financial disincentive. Another could be that it encourages people to drive safely, which may reduce cost of risk. Those who criticise compulsory auto insurance plead that it results in lowering the disposable income or it results in a shift of income from lower group to the higher group. Also, the success of the compulsory law depends on its enforcement and way it is perceived by the insureds. In India, most of the insurance companies are facing huge losses due to false/heavy claims, the insurance being used for dubious advantages.

13.3 Types of Motor Insurance Policies

The All India Motor Tariff governs motor insurance business in India. According to the Tariff, all classes of vehicles use two types of Policy Forms. They are Form A and Form B. Form A, or what is commonly known as Act Policy, covers Act Liability, which is a compulsory requirement of the Motor Vehicles Act. No vehicle can be used without this minimum insurance cover. Use without such insurance is a penal offence. The following liabilities can be covered in this policy :

- Unlimited liability towards Third Party bodily injury;
- Liability towards Third Party Property Damage to the extent of Rs. 6000/- only;
- Unlimited liability towards bodily injury of passengers of the vehicle;

[5] Harrington & Neihaus, *op. cit.,* pp. 553-554.

- Liability towards employees of the owner of the vehicle while travelling in or using it, against bodily injury, to the extent required under the Workmen's Compensation Act.

Form B, or what is commonly known as Comprehensive Policy, is an optional cover, which takes care of the following additional losses and liabilities :

- Loss or damage to the vehicle and its accessories and extra fittings, protection and removal costs, and towing disabled vehicles (only for commercial vehicles).
- Liability towards Third Party Property Damage, in excess of Rs. 6000/-.
- Liability towards employees under Common Law and Fatal Accidents Act, over and above the liability under Workmen's Compensation Act.
- Personal Accident Benefits for the owner, passengers and employees.

The above losses or liabilities can be separately covered in conjunction with the liabilities covered under the Act Policy, by taking a Comprehensive Policy paying an additional premium.

13.3.1 Form A Policy

As per the provisions of Motor Vehicles Act, all the vehicles plying in the Territorial Limits of India must possess an ACT POLICY at all times. The violation is punishable with fine etc., as per Motor Vehicle Act (as prevalent at the time of detection). As described earlier, this policy covers:

(1) Third Party Property Damage/Bodily Injury (Fatal or Non-fatal) when Insured vehicle is used in a public place,

(2) Insured's legal liability, as per Motor Vehicle Act, arising out of accident caused by or arising out of the use of the vehicle anywhere in India, and

(3) Such liability as above in respect of injury (fatal or non-fatal) to any third party and damage to any third parties' property.

The owners of the vehicle having insurable interest in it undertake this policy. The period of the cover is generally a period of 12 months from the date of inception. However, Short period covers are also available at higher rates. Subject to limit of liability laid down in the Motor Vehicle Act, the policy pays the insured's legal liability for death/disability for third party, loss or damage to third party property. Also, the liability for claimant's cost is also met (Maximum Rs. 6,000/-) unless additional premium for opting unlimited cover is paid. In addition, all costs and expenses incurred with insurer's written consent are paid.

In case of death of the Insured/Person entitled to compensation for a liability incurred under this policy, his legal heirs will be indemnified as in the case of the Insured, subject to the limitations of use of the vehicle provided that the Driver was holding a valid and effective driving license.

Third Party (A person other than Insured and the Insurer) who is injured/dies due to an accident with the Insured Vehicle, the amount of compensation adjudged by the Motor Accident Claims Tribunal is made good by the insurers and is payable to the legal heir of the deceased or the injured. The amount of compensation is unlimited/has no preset limit.

All costs and expenses are incurred by the insured with Insurer's written consent. The compensation payable to Third Party for damage to its property (movable or fixed) is restricted to Rs. 6000/- {Rupees Six Thousand Only}, irrespective of the amount adjudged by the Motor Accident Claims Tribunal/Court. This compensation limit can be increased to Unlimited by paying of an additional Premium at the time of taking insurance. All costs and expenses incurred by Insured with Insurer's written consent.

Claims arising out of and in the course of employment of a person in the employment of the Insured are compensated to the extent of Rs. 20,000 when an Employee (other than paid driver) is in the driving seat.

When vehicle is used outside the geographical area, when used contrary to limitation as to use, driven by a person other than the driver as stated in the clauses mentioned in the policy of insurance.

13.3.2 Form B Policy[6]

Form B is an optional cover, which offers some specific advantages. Although the Act Policy Form A is identical for different classes of vehicles, the comprehensive policy cover differs for various classes of vehicles. For private cars and motorcycles, there are two Sections in the Comprehensive Policy. Additionally, Section III is provided for commercial vehicles.

Section I

It concerns loss or damage to the vehicle and covers the risks like :

- Fire, Explosion, Self-ignition and Lightning
- Burglary, Housebreaking and Theft
- Riot, Strike, Malicious and Terrorism Damage
- Earthquake
- Flood, Typhoon, Hurricane, Storm, Tempest, Inundation, Cyclone, Hailstorm
- Accidental External Means
- Transit by road, rail, inland waterway, lift, elevator or air.

For motorcycles and commercial vehicles, the risk of frost damage is also covered. From the above coverage, for all classes of vehicles, the risks of riot, strike, malicious and terrorism damage, earthquake and flood and storm; can be opted out

[6] www. Insuremagic.com/Auto Insurancebasics—Risk covered by a Comprehensive Policy.htm.

of with a consequent discount in premium. In addition to these, cover is also available for 'Protection and Removal Costs' and 'Authorisation of Repairs'. If a motor vehicle is disabled as a result of loss or damage due to the perils mentioned above, the insurance company bears the reasonable cost of protection and removal to the nearest repairer and the cost of redelivery to the owner/insured subject to a maximum limit, in respect of any one accident. The limits for various class of vehicles are as follows:

Motor Cycles/Scooters :	Rs.	300
Private Car & Taxis	Rs.	1,500
Other Commercial Vehicles	Rs.	2,500

The owner/insured is also allowed to authorise repair expenses upto Rs. 500 per accident.

Section II

It covers the liabilities towards third parties, *i.e.,* liabilities of bodily injuries and property damage.

Section III

It is applicable to commercial vehicles. It covers the vehicle while it is being used for the purpose of Towing Disabled Vehicles. This section covers Third Party Liabilities that the insured vehicle or the one being towed for reward/remuneration. Further, the insurance company is also not liable for damages to the towed vehicle or any property being conveyed thereby.

Benefits of Comprehensive Policy Cover — An Illustration

Mr. Tom has an Act Only policy covering his private car. He employs a paid driver. While driving the vehicle, after dropping Mr. Tom at his office, the vehicle collides with a truck and the driver dies on the spot. Being an old car, Mr. Tom had nothing much to lose and that is why he had not taken a Comprehensive Policy. However, the family of the driver lost their breadwinner.

As an employer, Mr. Tom is liable to compensate for the driver, since he was driving the vehicle in course of employment. The Motor Vehicles Act, 1988 makes it compulsory to insure liabilities under Workmen's Compensation Act.

Accordingly, the legal heir of the deceased driver filed an application to the Labour Commissioner and an Award of Rs. 1,50,000 was passed against the employer. Mr. Tom, equipped with an Act Policy, approached the insurance company, who in turn satisfied the Award. The legal heir of the driver received the compensation from the Labour Court soon after and everyone was happy.

The liability for compensation as per the Workmen's Compensation Act, depends on the wages of the employee and his age, and represents mainly the loss of earnings. However, other losses representing mental pain and agony for the family, loss of consortium, future expenses on dependents and loss of prospective earnings are not accommodated in this compensation.

The legal heir of the driver, in the instant case then approached the Motor Accident Claims Tribunal, demanding a compensation of Rs. 1,00,000 towards these losses. The Tribunal passed an award of Rs. 50,000, found reasonable as per provisions of Common Law and Fatal Accidents Act. Mr. Tom had an Act Policy, which did not cover this liability, and he was saddled with the responsibility of satisfying the Court Order. You can imagine the financial burden he had to bear. Had he taken a Comprehensive Policy, covering his driver by payment of a small premium, he would not have to face this difficulty. The insurance company would have paid this additional amount of compensation too. It is, therefore, always beneficial and advisable to take a comprehensive policy covering these liabilities.

Exclusions to the Comprehensive Insurance Cover

This insurance does not cover loss or damage caused due to:

(*a*) Driver being under intoxication

(*b*) Vehicle being driven by a person not holding an effective, valid licence.

It also does not cover:

(*a*) Damage to tyres (unless the vehicle is also damaged).

(*b*) Wear and tear, mechanical breakdown.

Calculation of Premiums

In the case of Comprehensive Insurance Cover, for the purpose of premium, vehicles are categorized as follows :

Private Car

This is used for personal purposes. The premium is computed on the following basis:

- Geographical area of use and cubic capacity
- Value of the vehicle.

Accessories are to be specified separately under electrical and non-electrical items.

Two-wheeler

It is used for personal purposes only. Premium is calculated on cubic capacity and value of vehicle. Accessories are to be specified. Theft of accessories is not covered, unless the vehicle is stolen at the same time.

Commercial Vehicle

This is a vehicle used for hire and is classified as follows :

Goods-carrying commercial vehicle : In this case premium is calculated on carrying capacity–gross vehicle weight and value of the vehicle. Accessories extra, as specified.

Passenger-carrying commercial vehicle : In this case premium is calculated on carrying capacity of the vehicle–number of passengers and value of the vehicle. Accessories extra, as specified.

13.3.3 Auto Policy in United States

The personal auto policy, famous in the U.S. includes four main types of coverage:[7]

(*a*) "third party" liability coverage for liability to third parties harmed by negligence of an insured person;

(*b*) "first party" medical payments coverage for the insured, or in states with no-fault or related laws, personal injury protection coverage for the insured's medical expenses and loss of income;

(*c*) uninsured and under insured motorists coverage for losses caused to an insured by drivers without liability insurance and drivers with comparatively low liability insurance limits; and

(*d*) coverage for physical damage to or theft of insured autos.

The auto liability coverage in the personal auto policy provides broad coverage for liability for bodily injury and property damage to other parties arising out of the use of an automobile by an insured person. As is customary with the liability insurance, the insurer also agrees to defend the insured and bear the defence costs and is responsible for negotiating and setting the claims.

Personal auto liability coverage may be sold with a "single limit" that specifies the maximum amount that the insurer will pay for all damages from a single accident.

Under the first-party auto medical payments coverage, the auto owner can receive payment for medical expenses arising out of an accident. Coverage is for the medical expenses for the named insured and family members hurt in any auto and other persons that are hurt while occupying a covered auto. Coverage limits under such policies are comparatively low.

In U.S. with no-fault or related laws, the personal auto policy includes personal injury protection coverage for the named insured, family members, and parties hurt while occupying a covered auto instead of medical payment coverage.[8]

13.4 Factors Considered for Premium Rating

Automobile insurance pricing has always been a matter of controversies to the consumers, service providers and the regulators. Auto claims have increased significantly in India since last 10 years. Auto insurance rates charged to different customers reflect differences in the discounted expected costs of providing coverage. In order to classify different persons into homogeneous groups with respect to expected claim costs, insurers generally use rate classification system that include (1) driver

[7] Harrington & Neihaus, *Risk Management and Insurance,* McGraw-Hill, 1999, p. 534.

[8] *Ibid.*, p. 537.

classes that reflect the characteristics of individual insureds, and (2) territorial rating to reflect expected differences in claim costs for people that live in different geographical areas (holding individual characteristics constant). Of course, physical damage rates also depend upon the value and type of vehicle. Liability insurance rates sometimes also depend on the type of vehicle, given evidence that certain vehicles are more likely to be involved in at-fault accidents. The major factors considered in establishing driver classes and the use of territorial rating factors are :[9]

Driver Classes

The parameters are Age, Gender, and Marital Status, Use of automobile, driving education and driving record. The insureds in younger age group, the males, the married ones and new and inexperienced drivers have on average high accidental claims. The loading on the premium increases by the numbers and amount of accident claims.

Territorial Rating

Large cities have higher average claim costs followed by suburban areas, smaller cities, and small towns or rural areas. In India, the geographical areas have been classified into Group A and Group B.

Motor/Automobile Insurance business in India is governed by the All India Motor Tariff, which lays down the premium rates, terms and conditions. The main factors taken into consideration for rating in India are vehicle classifications on several parameters, the geographical area of operations and experiences.

Vehicle Classification

Vehicles are generally classified on the basis of its technical specifications, its value or use.

Technical Specifications ("The Type")

The typology of a vehicle is more or less based on its cubic capacity or gross vehicle weight and its carrying capacity. Heavier vehicles are more exposed to accidents since the resultant damages they incur are more. Similarly, vehicles with higher carrying capacity expose more passengers to risk. Therefore heavier vehicles attract higher premium rate. In private cars, taxis and motorcycles, the factor is the cubic capacity. The more the cubic capacity, the higher the premium rate. Whereas in goods-carrying commercial vehicles and passenger-carrying commercial vehicles, the criteria are gross vehicle weight and passenger carrying capacity respectively.

The Value of the Vehicle

The premium rate is applied on the value of the vehicle to arrive at the premium payable. It is the owner/insured who has to select a correct value of the vehicle and

---

[9] *Ibid.*, p. 545.

declare the same for insurance. This value is known as the Insured's Estimated Value (IEV) in motor insurance and represents the sum insured.

Normally, this value is arrived at by considering the age of the vehicle and its present purchase price. A Maruti 800 was purchased in 1998 for Rs. 1,80,000. Considering the conventional 10% depreciation each year and the present purchase price of a similar vehicle at Rs. 2,00,000/. The IEV for year 2000 is Rs. 1,80,000 less 20% of Rs. 2,00,000 = Rs. 40,000.00

IEV = Rs. 1,40,000.00

However, this is not sufficient for deriving the correct IEV of the vehicle in terms of motor insurance. In motor insurance, the basis for payment of claims is the market value of the vehicle at the place and time of loss. This market value may be understood as, the price that the vehicle would fetch in the second-hand market. For certain vehicles, there is a good demand in the second-hand market. Maruti is one of them. The 1998 model mentioned above may fetch a price of say, Rs. 1,50,000. In such situations, the correct IEV for the Maruti of 1998 model should be Rs. 1,50,000.

Now take the case of a Premier Padmini car of 1998 model. The purchase price in 1998 was say, Rs. 1,80,000 . The depreciated value in year 2000 works out to Rs. 1,40,000. But, the second-hand value would be at most Rs. 30,000, since it has virtually no demand in the market.

In this case, the correct IEV should be Rs. 30,000 only. It is not worthwhile to insure your vehicle at a higher value since that will increase the premium payable but, in case of total loss, only the market value would be payable.

In motor insurance, the IEV is the limit of liability per accident and not for the entire period of insurance. In cases of partial loss or losses, which may be made good by repairs, there is no limit to the number of accidents in any period of insurance. Suppose the Premier Padmini car, as described above, claims for two accidents in the year 2000, the first for an amount of Rs. 20,000 and the second for Rs. 15,000 under its insurance policy with IEV of Rs. 30,000 . Both these claims can be recovered from the insurance company, since their respective values are within the limit of IEV, irrespective of the fact that the insured in this process recovers more amount during the period of insurance than he was insured for.

However, if the vehicle is totally lost or damaged and cannot be repaired, the insured would be paid the market value or IEV, whichever is less. It is very important to select a correct IEV for insurance. There is a tendency of motor vehicle owners to declare a lower value for insurance to reduce the premium expenditure. Although, insurance companies check the IEV for its sufficiency before accepting the insurance, this is not a correct practice as the insured is exposed to a greater loss in case the vehicle is totally lost or damaged.

The Use of the Vehicle

Risk exposure varies in relation to the use the vehicle is put to. Private cars are lesser exposed than taxis, as the latter is used extensively for maximum revenue.

Taxi's therefore attract a higher premium rate. Similarly, goods carrying vehicles, which are used as private carriers and transport, only their owners' goods attract a lower premium, than those used as public carriers for transporting goods for hire.

The Geographical Area of Operation

The area of operation of a vehicle also has a direct bearing on the premium rate. This is so because, certain areas of operation are more congested with high densities of population and road traffic than others and poses higher exposure to accidents. For this purpose, the tariff differentiates two zones in India, i.e., Zone A and Zone B, for private cars and taxis. Zone A represents the Chennai region and Mumbai region (excluding Mumbai city) and Zone B represents the Kolkata region, Delhi region and Mumbai city. In Zone B, the densities of population and road traffic are more and hence attract a higher premium rate.

Such differential rating does not apply to commercial vehicles such as trucks and buses, as these vehicles normally travel throughout India for their operation. However, a discount is allowed on the premium for commercial vehicles used as contract carriage, school buses, public and private buses used for carrying passengers/workers and operate within a radius of 50 kilometres from the city limits.

Details of States under Zone A & Zone B

	Zone A	*Zone B*
Andhra Pradesh	Andaman & Nicobar Islands	Mumbai City
Goa, Daman, Diu	Arunachal Pradesh	Nagaland
Gujarat	Assam	Orissa
Karnataka	Bihar	Punjab
Kerala	Delhi	Rajasthan
Madhya Pradesh	Haryana	Sikkim
Maharashtra	Himachal Pradesh	Tripura
(Excluding Mumbai City)	Lakshadweep Islands	Uttar Pradesh
Pondicherry	Manipur	West Bengal
Tamil Nadu	Mizoram	

The Claims Experience

Unfavourable claims experience is obviously a bad risk. The tariff has adopted a system called the "No Claim discount", to give discounts for good claims experience and a loading for bad experience. The claim experience of expiring year's policy is the basis for allowing discount or charging a loading.

13.5 Motor Insurance Claims

13.5.1 Own Damage Claims

Documents

Following Documents generally required for settlement of motor claims. However depending on the merits of the case, a particular document may not be necessary or an alternate document could be used to serve the purpose of the Insurer.

(*a*) *Claim form* required to be completed.

(*b*) ***Registration Certificate***: the details usually verified from the RC can instead be obtained from purchase details of the vehicle if the circumstances so warrant.

(*c*) ***Driving License***: as per policy condition the driver is required to hold an effective driving license both in terms of the period validity and the class of vehicle that is being driven at the time of the accident. The MV Act provides for a grace period of 30 days after expiry of a license during which period the license may be accepted as effective, provided the holder has not been qualified from holding a license. For loss sustained by parked vehicles, driving license may not be relevant.

(*d*) ***Load Challan/Trip Sheet:*** to verify that the load carried was within the permissible limits and the trip sheet giving details of number of passengers carried in the vehicle.

(*e*) ***Fitness Certificate***: the fitness certificate indicates the roadworthiness of a commercial vehicle.

(*f*) ***Report to Police***: a copy of the FIR and Panchanama is required wherever third parties are involved in an accident.

(*g*) ***Survey Report:*** surveyor ascertains the damage, assess the quantum of payable claim, verify vehicular documents and confirm that the loss/damage being claimed for is in conformity with the narration of the accident. Wherever replacement of parts is allowed surveyors physically verify serial numbers as appearing on major parts, which carry such numbers.

Procedure

- In order to proceed for claim, the insured immediately informs the insurer.
- The policy documents are verified to ensure that the policy is force and the loss is entered in the claims register and the claim form is issue to the insured to be completed and returned.
- The insurer, immediately on receipt of intimation of loss, either in writing or over telephone, a surveyor is appointed based on the estimate of repairs. The surveyors are supplied with the copy of the claim form, copy of policy and the repairer's estimate.

- In case of major accidents, the insured would be asked to arrange for photographs of the vehicle at the spot of the accident, showing all the external damages and the number plate of the vehicle. The photo expenses are to be reimbursed upto Rs. 500. Alternatively, the insured may inform the nearest office of the insurer to arrange for such photographs.
- The survey report is examined and settlement is done based on surveyor's recommendations.
- If reinspection after repair is considered necessary it may be conducted by the same surveyor who has assessed the loss.
- Conventionally, the payment is made to the repairer directly.
- If for any reason, to be specified, the driving license cannot be produced, the claim may be considered only on non-standard basis. However for settlement of such claims the authority should be vested only with the Managers and above in the RO. Where the driving license is not endorsed for tourist taxis, since, different practices prevail in different states, it is necessary to check the local practice. The claim is to be treated as standard or non-standard on the basis of the practice prevailing in the state where the accident occurs and this will be decided by a Manager and above in the RO.
- The repairers are bound to keep aside the value of salvage and if the salvage is desired to be retained, the value is deducted from the claim bill.

Partial Loss Claims

A. Submission of bills/cash can be dispensed with for claims upto Rs. 50,000 in respect of private cars and two wheelers only, subject to

(*a*) The survey report correctly indicating the cost of parts allowed for replacement

(*b*) Claims being settled on the basis of a report of reinspection after repairs by the surveyor certifying that the repairs and replacements have been carried out as per assessment. For other classes of vehicles bills/cash memos have to be obtained and verified.

B. If surveyor confirms replacement of the engine and chassis if allowed for replacement and indicates the new numbers, claims may be settled whilst simultaneously advising the insured that

(*a*) As per the provision of the Motor Vehicles Act, the new numbers have to be incorporated in the RC book.

(*b*) Insurance company be informed about the incorporation of the new numbers in the RC book for endorsing on the policy document to facilitate settlement of future claims.

(*a*) Where the vehicle is totally damaged or when the net cost of repairs is almost close to the market value of the IEV the claim could be considered to be a total loss. Such total loss claims should be encouraged on net of salvage basis i.e., salvage being retained by the insured and an appropriate amount towards salvage value as determined by the surveyor in consultation with the company be deducted from the total loss amount.

(*b*) However, if the insured to retain the salvage, arrangements should be made for the safe custody of the damaged vehicle to prevent further loss or damage. The RTO should be informed by Registered AD post. An inventory on the major parts should be taken before taking possession of the vehicle. Immediate steps thereafter should also be taken for its disposal as per company's guidelines for disposal of salvage.

13.5.2 Theft Claims

1. ***Partial Loss due to Theft***: Theft of parts/accessories from a vehicle should be reported to the police immediately by the insured. If parts are found missing or changed after recovery of stolen vehicle this be recorded in panchanama/recovery memo. Final police investigation report will also be required. However, if the competent authority is satisfied about the genuineness of the loss, final investigation report may be waived provided the insured sends a registered AD letter to the SP/ACP requesting that the insurer should be informed of any recovery.

2. ***Total Loss due to Theft***: Unless claims settling authority is fully satisfied, investigation of the theft to be arranged by an investigator who may be appointed with specific terms of reference.

3. The following documents should be collected from the insured in addition to a certified copy of the FIR, for considering "on account" payment of the admissible claim after expiry of 90 days from the date of loss.

   (*a*) Surrender of the Registration Book and the Tax Book to the insurer duly transferred in the name of the insurers. The RTO is to be informed about the theft of the vehicle and this should be entered in Tax Book so that further tax will not accrue.

   (*b*) Letter of indemnity and subrogation.

   (*c*) Ignition keys of the vehicle.

   (*d*) Certificate of insurance and the original insurance policy, if not stolen with the vehicle.

   (*e*) Specially worded discharge voucher.

4. The balance payment may be released on receipt of the Final Police Investigation Report or on expiry of a suitable waiting period from the date of the "on account" payment, after obtaining the discharge voucher in full and final settlement of the claim.

5. The Police and the Registration authorities and the NCRB should be notified in writing about disposal of the claim on "total loss" basis following theft of the

vehicle. They should be requested to advise the company if the vehicle is recovered subsequently. Immediately after receipt of advise from the Police regarding recovery of the vehicle, necessary steps for taking possession of the vehicle from the Police custody should be taken and, if necessary, an advocate should be appointed for filing recovery application in the court.

6. Municipal Authorities, where applicable and the RTO should be advised by registered Letter with Acknowledgement. Due to record 'non use' of the vehicle on account of theft and about the cancellation of the Insurance Certificate.

7. If the vehicle is recovered subsequently, the insured will have the option to repay the claim amount already paid and retain the recovered vehicle. If the vehicle is found damaged, the insured will be indemnified against loss of damage. The insured should be advised to obtain recovery memo from the Police and to get the vehicle surveyed at the Police Station before taking delivery, as mentioned under partial loss theft claims.

8. In cases of criminal breach of trust each case should be dealt with an individual basis depending upon facts of each case and subject to legal opinion.

13.5.3 Third Party Bodily Injury Claims: Fatal and Non-fatal

1. ***Intimation of Claim***: Intimation about an accident resulting into third party claim is received through various sources :

   (*a*) Insured directly or by mention in passing whilst lodging own damage claim

   (*b*) Claimant

   (*c*) MACT/Courts by notice

   (*d*) Through accident report from police in Form 54 prescribed under Central Motor Vehicles Rules, 1989.

2. ***Investigation***: Investigation about the accident to collect the relevant data to quantify reasonable and just compensation as per the specified formats in respect of all third party claims is mandatory. The companies should ensure that this investigation helps the insurance company in finalizing out of court settlement at the earliest.

3. ***Appointment of Advocate:*** On receipt of notice from the MACT a competent advocate from the panel may be appointed if necessary. The following relevant documents and information should be given to him/her immediately to enable him/her to draft written statement (w/s) on behalf of the Company and ensure that the proper defense is taken where necessary and no frivolous statements are made.

4. ***Policy Copy***: Duly certified true copy of the complete policy with the relevant clauses and endorsements as actually attached with the original issued covering the vehicle at the material time of accident.

5. ***Driving Licence:*** In case it has been observed that driver was not duly licensed the necessary information should be given to the advocate. Though under Section 149(2) of the MV Act, 1988, Insurance Company has no liability if the driver is not duly licensed, the onus to prove that the driver was not holding a license rests on insurance company and this obligation is required to be discharged fully to the satisfaction of the court.

6. ***Compliance Policy Conditions***: If a breach of a specific policy condition has been observed it should be brought to the notice of the Advocate to enable proper defense if possible.

7. (*a*) Written statement on behalf of the insurance company incorporating all defenses available as enumerated under Section 149 of MV Act should be promptly filed.

   (*b*) Wherever necessary when there is collusion between the insured and the claimants or when the insured fails to defend the claim, the company's advocate must be instructed to obtain the MACT's permission under Section 170 of the MV Act to Defend the claim on merits.

8. ***Payment of No Fault Liability Claims***: If liability under affected policy is established after taking into consideration the foregoing defenses, company should take immediate steps to deposit No Faulty Liability amount as per Section 140 of the MV Act, 1988.

9. ***Payment of Fault Liability Claims***: Companies may initiate action to settle such claims either through

   (*a*) Jald Rahat Yojna

   (*b*) Lok Adalats

   (*c*) Direct negotiation with the claimant through DICC & RICC.

10. ***Jald Rahat Yojna:*** Section 152 of MV Act, 1988 authorizes insurance company to settle motor third party non-fatal bodily injury claims where claimant is an adult without claimants taking recourse to MACTs. Industry has already launched the Scheme since 1991.

Guidelines for Placing Claims in Lok Adalats

- Maximum participation and disposal of large number of claims in Lok Adalats sessions should be ensured.
- Companies should place the claims normally falling within the following parameters before lok adalat:

  (*a*) where occurrence of the accident is within the policy period.

  (*b*) where estimated liability is not expected to be exceeding Rs. 5,00,000 per application for compensation.

  (*c*) where no substantial point of law is involved.

(*d*) where no defences are available under Section 149 of the MV Act, 1988, such as driver not holding effective driving license and breach of policy condition relating to limitations as to use.

(*e*) where policy record shows that the driver was holding effective driving license.

(*f*) where despite concerted efforts on the part of the insurance companies. They are not in a position to prove conclusively to the satisfaction of the court that a person drove the vehicle not duly licensed.

(*g*) since there is a provision of automatic transfer of insurance in pursuance of Section 157 of MV Act, 1988 the companies cannot take defense of non-transfer of insurance of the vehicle on their books.

(*h*) where more than one vehicle insured with different insurance companies is involved in an accident resulting into a third party claim, companies should agree for settlement on 50-50 basis to apportion the liability between them.

- Companies should not accept conditional settlement such as subject to verification of certain documents, production of documents etc.
- On having reached the agreement for compromise settlement concerned MACT issues a Consent Order specifying *inter alia* the period during which the agreed amount should be deposited. On receipt of such order, companies must deposit the amount as agreed to with the MACT within 30 days from the date of award as per schedule.
- In the event of lok adalat for pending appeals before High Courts is organized, such claims where quantum of compensation is in dispute may be considered.
- Appeals which are filed to decide a point of law should not be considered for placing before lok adalat.
- Applications for compensation filed by the paid employees may also be placed before lok adalat, whether wider legal liability is covered or not.

13.6 Burglary Insurance

Burglary insurance covers indemnity against losses or damage due to burglary and is available to commercial establishments, factories, private premises, godowns etc. The various types of burglary covers available are:

(1) Burglary (Business Premises Policy)

(2) Burglary (Private Residences) Policy

(3) Burglary All Risks Policy

(4) Money-in-transit insurance

(5) Baggage Insurance Policy

The basic burglary insurance policy covers

1. Property contained in a business premises, stocks owned, held in trust/ commission and for which one is responsible.
2. Premises itself against damage (which one has to make good).
3. Cash, valuables, securities kept in a locked safe or cash box in locked steel cupboard can be specifically covered.

The cover can be obtained by any individual whose [illegible] of burglary; one which is liable for goods in trust/commission; one who is liable to make good damage to premises. The burglary cover provides indemnity in respect of property lost/damaged by burglary/house breaking and damage to premises caused by burglars during burglary or attempts at burglary. The cover can be extended to include riot and terrorism. The claim under the policy is restricted to actual loss/ damage to the insured property caused by burglary/house breaking, subject to the limit of sum insured. If sum insured is not adequate, policy pays only proportionate loss. Policy does not pay for loss/damage

4. To goods in trust/commission, jewellery, curios, title deeds, business books–unless specifically insured
5. Due to shop lifting, acts involving insured/his family members/employee
6. Recoverable under Fire/Plate glass insurance policy
7. Due to war perils, Riot & Strike, Acts of God, Nuclear perils
8. By abstraction from a safe using a key or duplicate key, unless it is obtained by violence or threat

The following documents are required while processing such claims under the policy:

(*i*) Duly completed claim form.

(*ii*) Final investigation report from the police.

(*iii*) Survey report.

(*iv*) Photographs.

In case of small losses the dealing office arranges for settlement of claim on the basis of completed claim form, First Information Report registered with the police provided the office is satisfied about the genuineness of the claim. It is considered preferable to appoint an investigator with surveyor's license and knowledge of accounts as assessment of losses involves checking books of accounts. Waiver of Final Investigation Report of the police is sometimes considered at the discretion of the Competent Authority so long as the investigator cum surveyor's report does not raise any doubt regarding the cause and quantum of loss. Subrogation/indemnity letter from the Insured is a must.

13.7 Money Insurance

1. "Money" carried by authorised messengers of the insured while in transit from the time it is taken out till received at the destination—points of origin and destination being specified before-hand.
2. Undisbursed money retained in a burglar-resistant and safe against burglary-risks.
3. Cash carried by, insured/proprietor/partner/director and also one firm carrying the cash of another firm in the same premises is also insurable.
4. Cash retained overnight by the employees in their residences in locked steel cupboard when on collection duty, up to 48 hours from the time of collection.

   Any industrial, manufacturing or business concern who periodically draw large sums of money for their day-to day transactions, payment of salaries, one time payments like arrears of pay, bonus etc.

   Loss by robbery, theft, hold-up or any fortuitous cause when the cash is in transit. When cash is retained over-night, it is covered only against burglary, house-breaking and theft risks.

   Money or money's worth actually lost, up to the "limit per carrying" specified in the policy.
5. Shortage due to error or omission.
6. Riot, strike, terrorism, war and Nuclear group of perils.
7. Money entrusted to any person other than the insured or an authorised employee (except due to the employee's fraud or dishonesty discovered within 48 hrs).
8. Legal liability. consequential loss, theft from an unsecured vehicle.
9. Money entrusted to a carrier.
10. Loss due to any act in which the insured is involved as principal or accessory.

13.8 Jewellers' Block Insurance

The policy contains four separate sections covering separate possessions.

Section I

This section covers loss or damage to property at business premises or other specified premises where property is deposited by fire, theft, riot, strike etc.

Section II

This section covers property carried/conveyed outside the specified premises for the business purpose by any cause other than the specified exclusions under the policy.

Section III

This section covers loss or damage to property whilst in transit with in India by

1. Insured Post
2. Air Freight

Section IV

This section covers loss or damage to office furniture, fixtures in the premises covered and safes at specified residence by fire and allied perils, house breaking, theft, riot, strike.

The risks are classified as 3 classes :

Class I–Having 24 hours watchman for the premises employed by the insured in all listed premises.

Class II–Common watchman for the building or night watchman employed.

Class III–All others.

Rating

Section I

Sum Insured	*Ratio for*		
	Class I	*Class II*	*Class III*
Upto Rs. 25 lakhs	0.25%	0.35%	0.50%
Upto Rs. 50 lakhs for over Rs. 25 lakhs	0.20%	0.30%	0.45%
Above Rs. 50 lakhs and upto Rs. 75 lakhs for the sum over Rs. 50 lakhs	0.175%	0.275%	0.425%
Over Rs. 75 lakhs (on the sum excess of Rs. 75 lakhs)	0.15%	0.25% 0.40%	

Section II

On the first part of the aggregate of the individual limits under Section II upto 50% of Section I Sum Insured 0.30%

On the next 25% of Section I Sum Insured 0.40%

On the next 25% of Section I Sum Insured 0.50%

Section III

1% on the aggregate Sum Insured under this section.

Section IV

0.10% on the Sum Insured

Discounts may be allowed in the premium rate for the following:

1. Physical features discount- In case the shop has additional security arrangements, like close circuit TV, electronic alarms, *etc.,* then a discount of 5% for each additional feature restricted to a maximum of 10% may be allowed subject to an inspection report of premises by an officer of the company being kept along with the Underwriting papers.

2. Good claims experience discount may be allowed when

   1. Policy is in force for a minimum period of three consecutive years

   2. If average claims experience is less than 50% for the last three years, 5% discount may be allowed

   3. Less than 30%,10% discount may be allowed

Exclusions

4. Loss or damage during cleaning, repairing, restoring
5. Property missing at stock taking
6. Articles in public exhibition
7. Depreciation, wear, tear etc.
8. Window display after close of business hours
9. Earth quake, Flood, cyclone etc.

13.9 Baggage Insurance

Baggage cover is available to the people who travel frequently. The cover provides indemnity in respect of Loss or damage to accompanied baggage by accident or mishappenings or from vehicle (car) provided that it has total locking system. Rate of premium is 0.75% of the Sum Insured. The exclusions are:

1. Cover is for accompanied baggage only. Unaccompanied baggage to be covered under transit policy
2. Loss within the municipal limits of the place where the insured resides permanently is not covered
3. Loss or damage to securities and other negotiable instruments is not covered
4. Loose articles such as walking sticks umbrellas fans, sun shades or deck chairs are not covered
5. Loss of or damage to valuables like jewellery and ornaments or precious stones etc. are excluded

13.10 Personal Accident Insurance

Personal accident cover provides indemnity to the insured in respect of any bodily injury resulting solely and directly from accident caused by violent and visible means, as agreed in the policy. Any individual or group of individuals (through employer, association, and institution etc.) aged between 12 and 70. Subject to medical examination at 70, a person can be covered up to 80. When an accidental injury being the sole and direct cause results (during the period of insurance) in:

Event	***Claims Paid***
Death	100% of Sum Insured
Permanent Total Disablement	100% of Sum Insured
Loss of two limbs/Two eyes or one limb and one eye	100% of Sum Insured
Loss of one limb or one eye	50% of Sum Insured
Permanent Partial Disablement	Varying% of Sum Insured as per policy
Temporary Total Disablement	1% of Capital Sum Insured per week, Subject to a maximum of Rs. 3,000 per week, for a maximum period of 100 weeks

On payment of extra premium, medical expenses incurred up to 25% of claim or 10% of Sum Insured can be covered. Policy also pays for education fund for dependant children (2) of deceased insured and expenses of carriage of dead body of insured from accident site (as per details in policy)

Attractive cumulative bonus at the time of renewal, by way of increasing the Sum Insured by 5% for each completed claim free year of insurance (maximum of 50% CSI) without collecting extra premium as per policy.

Classification of Risks

Group I

Doctors, Accountants, Lawyers, Architects, Consulting Engineers, Teachers, Bankers, Persons engaged in administration functions, persons primarily engaged in occupation of similar hazards.

Group II

Builders, Contractors and Engineers in superintending functions only, Veterniary Doctors, Paid drivers of motor cars and light motor vehicles and persons engaged in occupation of similar hazards and not engaged in manual labour. All persons engaged in manual labour (Except those falling under Group III), Cash Carrying Employees, Garage and Motor Mechanics, Machine Operators, Drivers of trucks or lorries and other heavy vehicles, Professional Athletes, and sportsman, Woodworking Machinists and persons engaged in occupation of similar hazards.

Group III

Persons working in underground mines, explosives, magazines, workers involved in electrical installation with high tension supply, Circus Personnel, Persons engaged in activities like racing on wheels or horseback, big game hunting, mountaineering, winter sports, skiing, ice hockey, ballooning, hang gliding, river rafting, polo and persons engaged in occupations/activities of similar hazard.

Exclusions

1. Compensation under more than one clause for same period of disability not exceeding capital sum insured
2. Any payment after admission of a claim for 50%/100% of Capital Sum Insured
3. Any claim in the same period of insurance exceeding the Capital Sum Insured
4. Suicide, attempt there at, VD, criminal breach of law, accidental death/injury under influence of liquor/drugs
5. Pregnancy related claim
6. War and nuclear perils

13.11 Banker's Indemnity Insurance

This policy is provided to Banks, NBFC's and other institutions who deal with operations involving money. The policy covers risks associated with :

1. *Premises*–By fire, riot & strike, burglary or house breaking or hold up resulting in loss to money/securities at the premises.
2. *Transit*–Lost, stolen, mislaid, misappropriated or made away either due to negligence or fraud of employees of the insured whilst in transit.
3. *Forgery*–Loss by bogus, fictitious or forged or raised cheque/drafts/FDRs or forged endorsements.
4. *Dishonesty*–Loss to money and/or operations by dishonesty.
5. *Hypothecated Goods*–By fraud and/or dishonesty or criminal act of the insured's employees.
6. *Registered Postal Sendings*–Loss by robbery, theft or by other courses to the parcels insured with the post office.
7. *Appraisers*–Infidelity or criminal acts by appraisers on the approved list.
8. *Janata Agents*–Infidelity or criminal acts by Janata Agents/chhoti Bachat Yojana Agents/Pygmy Collectors.

The indemnity provided under this policy in respect of direct losses shall not exceed the sums insured set against each cover. Excess is applicable except for fire and burglary claims. By charging appropriate premium, the sum insured under the policy is maintained constant so as to have full cover even after a claim. The insured is required to lodge a complaint with the police and take all practical steps to recover the property lost/apprehend the guilty person/take departmental action in the event of a loss. All material evidence should be made available to the insurers. The major requirements for obtaining this cover are:

1. All jewellery/ornaments shall be valued and recorded in the register of the bank at the time of pledging.
2. The insured is required to exercise reasonable care to safeguard the property insured.
3. Installation of alarm systems and security arrangements are mandatory.
4. Escort with fire arms is required during transit of cash upto Rs. 10 lakhs and two guards where value exceeds Rs. 10 lakhs.

13.12 Aviation Insurance

Aircraft Comprehensive Insurance Policy

The Policy covers (*a*) Loss of damage to the aircraft. (*b*) Legal liability to the third party and passengers. (*c*) Legal liability for freight, mail etc. carried. (*d*) Personal accident risk to the pilots, crew and ground staff. (*e*) Loss of professional licence of pilots and other crew members.

Air Line Insurance (Hull and Liability)

The hull policy covers loss and accidental damage (including emergency landings) to air and ground risks; the liability policy covers the airline against legal action from third parties or customers in respect of death, injury or physical damage to property. Most airlines have 'manuscript' wordings devised by the brokers, insurers and purchasers to reflect individual needs, circumstances and preferences. Hull claims are quickly determined and settled. Liability losses are usually complex, as accidents often result from a combination of factors. Often liability will be split with other parties, such as airports and, particularly, manufacturers.

Airline Insurance (Hull War)

These policies provide cover to airlines for loss of, or damage to, their property (aircraft and spares). The risks covered are excluded from hull all risks policies, and arise from war or war related activities including:

- War, invasion, hostilities, civil war, rebellion, attempted coups etc.
- Strikes, riots, civil commotion or labour disturbances
- Sabotage
- Hijacking (attempted or actual) or seizure of control (including pilot suicide)
- Acts of political or terrorist purposes
- Confiscation, naturalisation, detention etc. for the use of any government or public authority.

Product Liability

Product liability covers an insured's legal liability to third parties for injury and loss or damage arising out of the defective design or manufacture of an aircraft product. It encompasses all types of aircraft products, for example airframes, engines, seats and minor components.

General Aviation

General aviation is the insurance of "all aircraft other than commercial and military aircraft, and commercial aircraft capable of carrying less than 40 passengers". Different insurers use different definitions. Often planes that can carry between 40 and 60 passengers may be included in either this book or the airline book, depending on the insurer's reinsurance program.

Miscellaneous Covers

There are a number of other types of aviation cover available. Long term policies (of up to 3 years) are common for each of these types of covers.

Aviation Insurance can be purchased in two ways : (1) from a "direct writing" company where the insured contacts the company direct; or (2) through an independent insurance agent who represents several companies. The Indian aviation insurance business is worth around $20 million. In India, the major chunk of this business is owned by GIC. However hardly 2 per cent of the same is retained by it since the premium is large, various complexities are involved and as the risk is huge and it will have to be reinsured. On a global basis, the loss ratio in general aviation insurance has exceeded 1.1 to as much as 1.25 or more for the last several years. The key reasons that the insurance companies have been losing money in aviation business are:

1. The cost of repairs is increasing fastly
2. The number of insured accidents is up
3. The value of the aircraft is soaring

To keep insurance costs under control in the current difficult environment, aircraft and aviation business owners have to think on the following aspects:

- Self-insurance
- Matching equipment to needs
- Optimise maintenance cots
- Promote revenues
- Promote personal aviation
- Focus on safety

13.13 Other Urban Non-Traditional Insurance

Besides the major insurance categories discussed earlier, theh following covers are also available:

- Horse Insurance
- Cycle Risk Shaw Insurance
- Pedal Cycles Insurance
- Plate Glass Insurance
- Household Appliances Insurance
- Shopkeepers' Policy (Composite)
- Carriers Legal Liability
- LPG Dealers
- Office Umbrella
- Special Contigency
- Electronic Equipment Policy
- Gun Insurance
- Baggage Insurance

13.14 Key Terms

- Bodily Injury
- Legal Liability
- Act only Policy
- Aviation Insurance
- Burglary Insurance
- Personal Accident Insurance
- Comprehensive Policy
- Maturity Claim
- Premium Rating
- Baggaged Insurance
- Capital Accident Insurance
- Permanent Total Disablement

13.15 Suggested Readings

- Harrington & Niehaus, *Risk Management and Insurance,* McGraw-Hill, 1999.
- J.C. Trieschmann, S.G. Gistavson and R.E. Hoyt, *Risk Management and Insurance,* South-Western College Publishing, 2001.
- Vaughan and Vaughan, *Essentials of Risk Management and Insurance,* John Wiley and Sons Inc., 2001.
- *Insurance Law Manual,* Taxmann, 2001.
- *Motor Insurance,* IC 72, Insurance Institute of India, Mumbai, 2003.

- Engineering Insurance, IC 77, Insurance Institute of India, Mumbai, 1999.
- Miscellaneous Insurance, IC 78, Insurance Institute of India, Mumbai, 1991.
- Barry D. Smith *et. al.*, Property and Liability Insurance Principles, Insurance Institute of America, 1994.

13.16 Test Yourself

1. Is automobile insurance compulsory in India? What types of insurance covers are available for automobiles?
2. Write short notes on:
   (*a*) No claim discount.
   (*b*) Factors considered for premium rating.
   (*c*) Insured Declared Value
3. Briefly explain the various documents required for settlement of own damage and third party documents.
4. Explain the major point of differences between the procedure for settlement of third party claims and own damage claims.
1. "Aviation insurance is a high risk business." Do you agree? Substantiate your answer with suitable arguments.
2. Briefly explain the procedure for loss settlement in burglary insurance.
3. Write short notes on:
   (*a*) Classification of risks in Jweller's Block Insurance.
   (*b*) Table of Benefits in Personal Accident Insurance.
   (*c*) Banker's Indemnity Insurance.

Choose correct alternative of the following:

1. Motor Insurance originated in
   (a) India (b) China
   (c) U.S.A. (d) United Kingdom
   (e) None of the above
2. The first motor insurance policy was introduced into
   (a) U.S.A. (b) Brazil
   (c) U.K (d) England
   (e) None of the above

3. The first motor insurance policy was introduced into in the year

(a) 1890 (b) 1891

(c) 1892 (d) 1893 (e) 1894

4. In India the Motor Vehicles Act was passed in

(a) 1936 (b) 1937

(c) 1938 (d) 1939

(e) None of the above

5. The third party insurance was introduced compulsorily in

(a) 1943 (b) 1944

(c) 1945 (d) 1946 (e) 1947

6. The need for compulsory motor insurance is

(a) Obvious (b) Unobvious

(c) Both are correct (d) Both are wrong

7. Every vehicle before being driven on roads has to be compulsorily

(a) Insured

(b) Secured

(c) Neither secured nor insured

(d) Either secured and insured

8. Risk managers realise that insurance should be considered within the context of all available

(a) Risk transfer tool

(b) Risk strategic tool

(c) Risk management tools

(d) Leadership management tools

(e) None of the above

9. The loss to the automobile insurance service providers is mainly in the form of claims arising from

(a) Accident (b) Health problems

(c) Both are correct (d) Both are wrong

10. The auto liability claims, which frequently arise from driver's negligence, can be tackled through

(a) Distributions (b) Redistributions

(c) Both are correct (d) Both are wrong

11. The coverage for automobiles differs in

(a) Countries (b) States

(c) Union (d) Companies

(e) None of the above

12. Automobile Physical Damage Coverage insures against the loss of the policyholder's own

(a) Residence (b) Office

(c) On the way (d) Automobile

13. Drunken driving is another very common

(a) Feature (b) Part

(c) Both are correct (d) Both are wrong

14. Cases of stolen cars are on the

(a) Fall (b) Down

(c) Rise (d) None of the above

15. There is also a danger of fire or theft of

(a) Clothes (b) Mobiles

(c) Gold (d) Silver

(e) Vehicles

16. The economic rationale for insurance may be that it affects people's decision

(a) To derive (b) To ride

(c) To stand (d) None of the above

17. As per the provisions of Motor Vehicles Act, all the vehicles plying in the Territorial Limits of India must possess an ACT POLICY at

(a) All times (b) Some times

(c) Never (d) All times

18. The owners of the vehicle having insurable interest in it undertake this

(a) Price (b) Policy

(c) Both are correct (d) Both are wrong

19. All costs and expenses are incurred by the insured with Insurer's written

(a) Letter (b) Consent

(c) Document (d) None of the above

20. Form B is an optional cover, which offers some specific
(a) Disadvantage (b) Loss
(c) Agreement (d) Advantage

21. "Third party" liability coverage for liability to third parties harmed by negligence of an insured
(a) House (b) Property
(c) Person (d) None of the above

22. Vehicles are generally classified on the basis of its technical specifications, its value
(a) Profit (b) Loss
(c) Use (d) None of the above

23. The typology of a vehicle is more or less based on its cubic capacity or gross vehicle weight and its carrying
(a) Priority (b) Popularity
(c) Capacity (d) None of the above

24. The premium rate is applied on the value of the vehicle to arrive at the premium
(a) Insurable (b) Adjustable
(c) Examinable (d) Payable

25. IEV stands for
(a) Insured's Estimated Value
(b) Insurance estimation value
(c) Indian examination verification
(d) All are correct
(e) All are wrong

26. In motor insurance, the IEV is the limit of liability per accident and not for the entire period of
(a) Injured (b) Insurance
(c) Patient (d) Accident

27. Private cars are lesser exposed than taxis, as the latter is used extensively for maximum
(a) Policy (b) Product
(c) Revenue (d) None of the above

28. The area of operation of a vehicle also has a direct bearing on the premium
    (a) Price (b) Cost
    (c) Interest (d) Rate
29. Unfavourable claims experience is obviously a bad
    (a) Life (b) Policy
    (c) Risk (d) All are correct
30. Following Documents generally required for settlement of motor
    (a) Settlements (b) Claims
    (c) Insurance (d) All are correct
31. Theft of parts/accessories from a vehicle should be reported to the police immediately by the
    (a) Generation (b) Insured
    (c) Both are correct (d) Both are wrong
32. Undisbursed money retained in a burglar-resistant and safe against burglary
    (a) Loss (b) Profit
    (c) Risk (d) Insurance
    (e) None of the above
33. Baggage cover is available to the people who travel
    (a) Risk (b) Frequently
    (c) Popularity (d) Priority
34. policy is provided to Banks, NBFC's and other institutions who deal with operations involving
    (a) Life (b) Property
    (c) Assets (d) Money
35. The hull policy covers loss and accidental damage (including emergency landings) to air and ground
    (a) Non-risk (b) Risk free
    (c) Risk (d) With risk

State whether the following statements are 'True' or 'False'.

1. Motor Insurance originated in England .
2. The first motor insurance policy was introduced into England in 1894 to cover third party liabilities.
3. In India the Motor Vehicles Act was passed in 1939 and in 1946 the third party insurance was introduced compulsorily.

4. The need for compulsory motor insurance is compulsory.

5. The automobile insurance policy represents a combined coverage of the vehicles including accessories, loss or damage to his property or life and the third party insurance.

6. The major sources of loss exposure arising from the automobile accidents are Legal liability for harm caused to others as a result of negligence, Bodily injury, Property damages and or theft of vehicles.

7. Risk managers realise that insurance should be considered within the context of all available strategic management tools.

8. The loss to the automobile insurance service providers is mainly in the form of claims arising from insurance.

9. The coverage for automobiles differs in state.

10. Automobile Medical Payments coverage reimburses the insured and members of the insider's family for medical expenses that result from automobile insurance.

11. Automobile Physical Damage Coverage insures against the loss of the policyholder's own life.

12. Drunken driving is another very common feature.

13. Cases of stolen cars are on the low.

14. Other than these there is also a danger of fire or theft of money.

15. The economic rationale for insurance may be that it affects people's decision to ride.

16. The owners of the vehicle having insurable interest in it undertake this policy

17. The period of the cover is generally a period of 12 months from the date of inception.

18. All costs and expenses are incurred by the insured with Insurer's written consent.

19. Form B is an optional cover, which offers some specific disadvantages.

20. For motorcycles and commercial vehicles, the risk of frost damage is alsouncovered.

21. Section 3rd is applicable to commercial vehicles.

22. The personal auto policy, famous in the U.S. includes four main types of coverage.

23. The parameters are Age, Gender, and Marital Status, Use of automobile, driving education and driving record.

24. The typology of a vehicle is more or less based on its cubic capacity or gross vehicle weight and its carrying capacity.

25. The premium rate is applied on the value of the vehicle to arrive at the premium insurable.

26. Risk exposure varies in relation to the use the vehicle is put to

27. Private cars are lesser exposed than taxis, as the latter is used extensively for minimum revenue.

28. The area of operation of a vehicle also has a direct bearing on the price rate.

29. Unfavourable claims experience is obviously a bad risk.

30. Burglary insurance covers indemnity against losses or damage due to burglary and is available to commercial establishments, factories, private premises, godowns etc.

31. The cover can be obtained by any individual whose property is exposed to risk of price.

32. Baggage cover is available to the people who travel frequently

33. The indemnity provided under this policy in respect of direct losses shall not exceed the sums insured set against each cover.

34. Excess is applicable except for fire and burglary claims.

35. Aviation Insurance can be purchased in two ways.

Fill in the blanks:

1. Motor Insurance originated in .... where the first motor insurance policy was introduced into .... in 1894 to cover third party liabilities.

2. In 1899 the policy was extended to cover the accidental .... similar to what is known as comprehensive ....

3. In India the .... Act was passed in .... And in .... the third party insurance was introduced compulsorily.

4. The need for compulsory motor .... is obvious.

5. The major sources of loss exposure arising from the automobile ....

6. Risk managers realise that insurance should be considered within the context of all available ....

7. The loss to the automobile insurance service providers is mainly in the form of claims arising from ....

8. The coverage for automobiles ....

9. Automobile Liability Insurance protects the insured against the loss .... from legal liability when his or her automobile injures someone or damages another's ....

10. The protection also applies to other occupants of the insured's ....

11. Automobile Physical Damage Coverage insures against the loss of the .... own automobile.

12. The coverage is written under the .... insuring agreements and Collusion–which indemnifies for collusion ....

13. As footpaths are encroached by hawkers, pedestrians have a tough time dodging between .... to reach the other end of the ....

14. Besides, rash driving by youngsters is another of the .... realities that you should ....

15. Cases of stolen cars are on the ....

16. Other than these there is also a danger of fire or theft of ....

17. If the auto insurance is not made compulsory, there is a strong possibility that some may not buy these ....

18. The .... rationale for insurance may be that it affects people's decision to................

19. The All India Motor Tariff governs motor insurance business in ....

20. According to the Tariff, all classes of vehicles use .... types of Policy ....

21. The owners of the vehicle having .... interest in it undertake this ....

22. The period of the cover is generally a period of .... from the date of ....

23. All costs and expenses are incurred by the insured with Insurer's written ....

24. Form B is an optional cover, which .... some specific ....

25. Personal auto liability coverage may be sold with a .... that specifies the maximum amount that the insurer will pay for all .... from a ....

26. Under the first-party auto medical payments .... the auto owner can receive payment for .... expenses arising out of an ....

27. Automobile insurance pricing has always been a matter of controversies to the .... service providers and the ....

28. Auto claims have increased significantly in .... since last ....

29. The parameters are Age, Gender, and Marital Status, Use of automobile, ... education and driving ....

30. The typology of a vehicle is more or less based on its cubic capacity or gross .... weight and its carrying ....

31. ....vehicles are more exposed to accidents since the resultant damages they incur are ....

32. The premium rate is applied on the value of the .... to arrive at the premium ....

33. In motor insurance, the basis for payment of claims is the .... of the vehicle at the place and time of ....

34. In motor insurance, the .... is the limit of liability per accident and not for the entire period of ....

35. Private cars are lesser exposed than taxis, as the latter is used .... for maximum ....

36. The area of operation of a vehicle also has a direct bearing on the .... rate.

37. Unfavourable claims experience is obviously a bad ....

38. Maximum participation and disposal of large number of claims in .... sessions should be ensured.

39. Burglary insurance covers indemnity against losses or damage due to .... and is available to commercial establishments, factories, private premises, ... etc.

40. The policy contains four separate sections covering separate ....

41. Baggage cover is available to the .... who travel ....

42. Banker's indemnity insurance policy is provided to Banks, NBFC's and other institutions who deal with .... Involving ....

43. Airline insurance policies provide cover to airlines for loss of, or .... to, their ....